The New Nations
in International
Law and Diplomacy

The New Nations in International Law and Diplomacy

THE YEARBOOK OF WORLD POLITY: VOLUME III

Edited by William V. O'Brien

Published for
THE INSTITUTE OF WORLD POLITY
Georgetown University, Washington, D.C.

by
FREDERICK A. PRAEGER, *Publishers*
New York · Washington

BOOKS THAT MATTER

Published in the United States of America in 1965
by Frederick A. Praeger, Inc., Publishers
111 Fourth Avenue, New York 3, N.Y.

All rights reserved

© 1965 by Frederick A. Praeger, Inc.

Library of Congress Catalog Card Number: 65-13962

Printed in the United States of America

INSTITUTE OF WORLD POLITY

Chairman
PROFESSOR WILLIAM V. O'BRIEN

Research Staff
MR. JEAN-ROBERT LEGUEY-FEILLEUX, *Director of Research*
MR. ULF H. GOEBEL, *Research Assistant*

Secretaries
MISS DANUTE M. PARAMSKAS
MISS MICHAEL ANN HUGHES

Research Associates

SHERMAN L. COHN, ESQ.
U.S. Department of Justice

DR. JAMES F. DUGGAN
U.S. National Labor Relations Board

Advisory Council

REV. ROBERT BOSC, S.J.
Professor of the Sociology and Ethics of International Relations, Institut d'Etudes Sociales, Facultés Catholiques, Paris, France

PROFESSOR ROMAN DEBICKI
Georgetown University

JAMES FAWCETT, ESQ.
Fellow, All Souls College, Oxford University

PROFESSOR WALTHER W. HUG
University of Zurich

PROFESSOR HEINRICH KRONSTEIN
Georgetown University Law Center, Frankfort University

PROFESSOR MYRES S. MCDOUGAL
Sterling Professor of Law, Yale University Law School

REV. BRIAN A. MCGRATH, S.J.
Academic Vice-President, Georgetown University

DEAN WILLIAM E. MORAN, JR.
School of Foreign Service, Georgetown University

PROFESSOR D. P. O'CONNELL
University of Adelaide

COLONEL WILLIAM A. ROBERTS
Senior Partner, Roberts & McInnis, Washington, D.C.

PROFESSOR HEINRICH A. ROMMEN
Georgetown University

PROFESSOR ROBERT W. TUCKER
The Johns Hopkins University

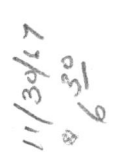

THE INSTITUTE OF WORLD POLITY

The Institute of World Polity is devoted to the study of international law, organization, and politics from both an empirical and philosophical standpoint. It was founded by Father Edmund A. Walsh, Professor Ernst H. Feilchenfeld, and Professor Joseph P. Chamberlain in April, 1945. Their work has been continued by the present chairman, Professor William V. O'Brien, and several research assistants under the direction of Professor Jean-Robert Leguey-Feilleux. Thus far, the studies of the Institute have been devoted to the problems of mitigating and controlling international conflict and of developing a coherent theory concerning the use of force on behalf of international justice and order. This volume is the first to deal with another perennial problem, that of reconciling the distinctively Western character of international law with the evolution of a pluralistic world society in which non-Western cultures play an increasingly important role.

The Institute is located in the Edmund A. Walsh School of Foreign Service, Georgetown University, Washington, D.C. Primary financial support for its research and publications programs is provided by Georgetown University. In addition to the Institute's regular projects, both the Institute as a whole and its staff members as individuals engage in projects on a contractual or grant basis with government and private organizations.

The *Yearbook* of the Institute of World Polity is not published at regular intervals. It appears whenever it is believed that a number of worthwhile studies on a particular subject have been produced by the Institute's staff or by other scholars. A fourth volume in the series, dealing with the problem of intervention in international law and relations, is presently in preparation. A monograph series, of which the first work will be a comprehensive study of the international law of guerrilla warfare by Jean-Robert Leguey-Feilleux, will be instituted in the near future.

Currently, a study of the law of limited international conflict is being conducted for the United States Department of Defense.

The purpose of this project is twofold: first, to analyze the legal implications of existing and future forms of international conflict short of total war between the major powers; and, second, to recommend the adoption of legal principles to guide United States policy so that, even in the most bitter conflicts, the long-term interests of the West will be served and the basic values for which the Free World stands will be respected.

In addition to these projects, the Institute of World Polity has devoted considerable attention to problems of international ethics. Realization of the limitations of contemporary positive international law has brought to light the need for a revival of interest in the neglected discipline of international ethics. Where the positive law has failed and new law is needed, re-examination of ethical principles is an indispensable prerequisite to the formulation of new legal principles and rules. Yet much of the relevant doctrine in the Western ethical tradition is couched in such broad terms as to be of little guidance in solving the normative problems of the contemporary world. In cooperation with a number of organizations and individual scholars, the Institute is working on the problems of translating the great concepts of our ethical tradition into more specific goals for international law and organization. To this end, the Institute has organized or participated in a number of interdenominational conferences dealing with current problems of ethics and foreign policy. Among the organizations with which it has cooperated are the Catholic Association for International Peace, the Council on Religion and International Affairs, and the Jewish Theological Seminary of America.

> WILLIAM V. O'BRIEN
> *Chairman*
> *Institute of World Polity*

Georgetown University
Washington, D.C.
August, 1964

PREFACE

The editor wishes to express his appreciation to the United States Department of State for its cooperation in locating public statements with regard to U.S. recognition policy. He thanks the librarians of both the Georgetown University Library and the Library of Congress for their assistance. Part of the preparation for this volume was done while the editor was Visiting Research Professor at the Max-Planck-Institut für Ausländisches Öffentliches Recht und Völkerrecht in Heidelberg, Germany. The editor is grateful for the use of the facilities of the Institut, and for the counsel of Professor Hermann Mosler and the members of the Institut.

Valuable editorial assistance was rendered by Sherman L. Cohn of the United States Department of Justice. Miss Danute M. Paramskas, Secretary of the Institute of World Polity, typed the manuscript and contributed substantially to its final editing. Her successor, Miss Michael Ann Hughes, worked on the galley and page proofs.

William E. Moran, Jr., Dean of the Edmund A. Walsh School of Foreign Service, Professor Victor Ferkiss of Georgetown University, and Dr. William Lewis, Intelligence Research Specialist, Office of Research and Analysis for Africa, United States Department of State, and Lecturer in British and African History, Georgetown University, supplied valuable information and insight with respect to the characteristics and problems of the developing new nations. Mr. Denys P. Myers, now retired from the Department of State, provided an invaluable critique of "United States Recognition Policy Toward the New Nations." The editor wishes especially to thank the Reverend Brian A. McGrath, S.J., Academic Vice-President of Georgetown University, for his advice and assistance in continuing the work of the Institute of World Polity.

For permission to reproduce copyrighted material, the editor is grateful to the following publishers:

To the American Society of International Law for the quotation from Denys P. Myers, "Contemporary Practice of the United States

Relating to International Law," 55 *American Journal of International Law* (1961), 103.

To Cambridge University Press for the quotation from Hersch Lauterpacht, *Recognition in International Law* (1948), p. 95.

To the Carnegie Endowment for International Peace for the quotations from Agnese Nelms Lockwood, "Libya—Building a Desert Economy," DXII, 312; and from A. A. Castagno, Jr., "Somalia," DXXII, 347, in *International Conciliation*.

To Chatto & Windus, Ltd., for the quotation from Peter Calvocoressi, *World Order and New States* (1962), p. 39.

To Little, Brown and Company for the quotation from Max F. Millikan and Donald L. M. Blackmer (eds.), *The Emerging Nations: Their Growth and United States Policy* (1961), pp. 132–33; and from Charles Cheney Hyde, *International Law Chiefly as Interpreted and Applied by the United States* (1945), I, 153.

To Longmans, Green and Company for the quotations from H. Lauterpacht, *Private Law Sources and Analogies of International Law* (1927), pp. 123–24; and from L. Oppenheim, *International Law: A Treatise*, ed. H. Lauterpacht (8th ed., 1955), I, 541, and 927, n. 2.

To Oxford University Press for the quotations from J. L. Brierly, *The Law of Nations: An Introduction to the International Law of Peace*, ed. Sir Humphrey Waldock (1963), pp. 19–20; from Brian Crozier, *The Morning After* (1963), pp. 16–17 and 285; from A. D. McNair, *The Law of Treaties* (1938), p. 232, and "So-Called Servitudes," 6 *British Yearbook of International Law* (1925) CXXVI, 122–23; and from D. P. O'Connell, "State Succession and the Effect upon Treaties of Entry into a Composite Relationship," 40 B.Y.I.L. (1963).

To Frederick A. Praeger, Inc., for the quotations from F. A. Váli, *Servitudes of International Law* (2d ed., 1958), pp. 42, 59–60, and 324; from Guy Benveniste and William E. Moran, Jr., *Handbook of African Economic Development* (1962), pp. 20, 21; from James S. Coleman, "The Character and Viability of African Political Systems," in Walter Goldschmidt (ed.), *The United States and Africa* (rev. ed., 1963), p. 46; and from Elliot J. Berg, "The Character and Prospects of African Economies," in *ibid.*, pp. 130–31.

To Stevens and Sons, Ltd., for the quotations from Ti-Chiang Chen, *The International Law of Recognition*, ed. L. C. Green (1951), p. 197.

To the University of Chicago Press for the quotation from H. D. Reid, *International Servitudes in Law and Practice* (1932), pp. 25, 209.

W.V.O'B.

CONTENTS

PREFACE, by William V. O'Brien — ix
INTRODUCTION, by William V. O'Brien — 3
1. INDEPENDENCE AND PROBLEMS OF STATE SUCCESSION
   by D. P. O'Connell — 7
   Succession to Treaties / Succession to Governmental Contracts / Succession to Delictual Claims / Succession to the Legal System / The Problem of *Inter Se* Relations in the Commonwealth / Conclusions
2. MILITARY SERVITUDES AND THE NEW NATIONS
   by Albert J. Esgain — 42
   The Doctrine of International Servitudes / History and Development of the Private-Law Servitude / The Doctrine of Military Servitudes of International Law / Significant Aspects of the Problem of International Servitudes / The Practice of States / Is There a Necessity for a Concept of Military Servitudes in International Law? / Conclusions
3. UNITED STATES RECOGNITION POLICY TOWARD THE NEW NATIONS
   by William V. O'Brien and Ulf H. Goebel — 98
   The Function of Recognition and the Criteria for Recognition of New States / The Objects and Types of Recognition / The Modes of Recognition / The Methods of Recognition / The Record of U.S. Recognition Practice Toward the New Nations, 1943–64 / Conclusions
4. THE NEW STATES AND THE UNITED NATIONS
   by J. E. S. Fawcett — 229
NOTES — 253
ABBREVIATIONS USED IN THE NOTES — 315
NOTES ON THE CONTRIBUTORS — 317
INDEX — 319

The New Nations in International Law and Diplomacy

INTRODUCTION

The admission of nearly sixty new nations into the international juridical order since World War II has given rise to much speculation as to its consequences for traditional international law, organization, and diplomacy. The world's international institutions are known to be almost exclusively the product of Western civilization. Even when non-Western nations such as Turkey and Japan were admitted into the Western international system of international law, the character of the institutions, of international juristic logic, and of legal-diplomatic processes all remained overwhelmingly Western. Nor did the appearance of Communist Russia decisively alter the near monopoly of Western thought and institutions in international law, relations, and diplomacy. During the interwar period the Soviet Union was treated as an exception to the rule, and not always as a very important exception.

This was all to change after World War II, when Communist nations proliferated and the age of the bipolar blocs began. It seemed unlikely that any substantial body of truly universal law could subsist in the face of the fundamental rift between the East, meaning the Communist world, and the West, meaning all non-Communist states. On the other hand, it was at first taken for granted that all states that were not under Communist domination were therefore "free," therefore part of the "West." Reasoning from such assumptions, Secretary of State John Foster Dulles was able to arrive at his condemnation of "neutralism."

Yet within five or six years after the commencement of the Dulles era, the so-called Third World had sprung into existence. The vast majority of the new nations were underdeveloped and anti-colonial. Some were vague and unconcerned about the dangers of Communism, and others nurtured the hope that Communism might supply solutions to their problems or, at least, that Communists might give them assistance under better terms than the Western powers. It was widely predicted that the new nations would sweep aside the traditional principles, institutions, and habits of mind of international law, organization, and diplomacy. First, it was pointed out, everything connected with colonialism would presumably be hated or at least suspect. Second, the emerging nations represented non-Western cultural, philosophical, and religious systems. They would certainly challenge institutions, principles, and habits of mind grounded in Western civilization.

Since the days of the Roman Empire, Western civilization has believed its concepts of law and order to be universally valid and self-evident to all men of good will. The philosophical and religious concepts of Greece and Rome and, later, of Christendom, were believed to be applicable to all nations. Thus modern international law grew out of the natural law traditions of Aristotle, St. Thomas, Victoria, and Suarez on the one hand, and those of Grotius, Pufendorf, and Vattel on the other. Moreover, many of the detailed, concrete rules of international law grew out of the use of analogies from Roman law, or from Western legal systems based on Roman law. Thus our traditional international law comes not only from concepts and principles expounded by the natural law theories and by Roman law, but also from the "juristic logic" (as Professor O'Connell puts it) that was developed by the Scholastics, by the classical international law writers, and by the legal scholars and practitioners who worked in the Roman law tradition.

Brierly, in what may be the most influential book on international law of our century, has well expressed the decisive influence of the Roman law tradition on the formative period of modern international law. He tells us:

> The position of Roman law in Europe in the sixteenth century has an important bearing on the beginnings of international law. There were some countries, such as Germany, in which a "reception" of Roman law had taken place; that is to say, it had driven out the local customary law and had been accepted as the binding law of the land. In other countries the process had not gone so far as this; but even in these the principles of Roman law were held in great respect and were appealed to whenever no rules of local law excluded them. Everywhere in fact Roman law was regarded as the *ratio scripta*, written reason; and a medieval writer, seeking to expound the law of nature, had only to look about him to see actually operative in the world a system of law which was the common heritage of every country, revered everywhere as the supreme triumph of human reason. Moreover, this law had a further claim to respect from its close association with the Canon Law of the Church.
>
> Thus Roman law reduced the difficulty of finding the contents of natural law almost to vanishing-point; and in fact the founders of in-

Introduction 5

ternational law turned unhesitatingly to Roman law for the rules of their system wherever the relations between ruling princes seemed to them to be analogous to those of private persons. Thus, for example, rights over territory, when governments were almost everywhere monarchical and the territorial notions of feudalism were still powerful, bore an obvious resemblance to the rights of a private individual over property, with the result that the international rules relating to territory are still in essentials the Roman rules of property. It is not difficult, therefore, to see how the belief in an ideal system of law inherently and universally binding on the one hand, and the existence of a cosmopolitan system of law everywhere revered on the other, should have led to the founding of international law on the law of nature. We have to inquire further, however, whether this foundation is valid for us today.*

The question that confronts us, obviously, is whether the product of natural law and Roman law, modern international law, will in its substance and its legal logic recommend itself to non-Western nations as *ratio scripta*, written reason. Despite the tendency of scholars specializing in studies of the new nations to answer in the negative, it is worthwhile to ponder the question in the light of what evidence we have.

This *Yearbook* approaches the problem primarily from the viewpoint of the older nations. The scholars in some of the more advanced new nations may be engaging in building their own schools of thought about international law and their own historical records summarizing and analyzing the actual practice of the new nations. It seems fair to say, however, that comprehensive, distinctly non-Western approaches to international law are not particularly evident as yet. Professor Röling may well be right when he says that new nations take defiant attitudes toward traditional law, e.g., on questions of succession, property rights, nationalization, and the like, not because they have different philosophical or jurisprudential concepts, but simply because they are new, poor, and against the *status quo*.

Nevertheless, as O'Connell asserts, the new nations are born into a world of law, and one of the first tasks in asserting their impact on traditional international law is to observe how they have been greeted in that world of law. Professor O'Connell, in "Independence and Problems of State Succession," surveys that part of

---

* J. L. Brierly, *The Law of Nations: An Introduction to the International Law of Peace*, ed. Sir Humphrey Waldock (6th ed.; New York: Oxford University Press, 1963), pp. 19–20.

the world of law inherited by the new nations that deals with the perennially difficult problem of state succession. Albert J. Esgain, in "Military Servitudes and the New Nations," gives us a classic example of the lingering death of a Roman law concept, that of servitude, in contemporary international law and, ironically, of its invocation against new-nation successor states. Mr. Esgain's treatment of the subject goes far beyond the new-nation aspect, but it was thought appropriate to publish it in its entirety in this volume because of the depth and usefulness of his scholarship. In "United States Recognition Policy Toward the New Nations," Ulf H. Goebel and the present writer recount how the eruption of the new nations into international society has affected the difficult problem of balancing flexibility with order in the recognition process. Finally, James E. S. Fawcett, in "The New States and the United Nations," which he writes from the vantage point of his experience as a former legal adviser to the International Monetary Fund, analyzes the impact of the new nations on the organization and political processes of the United Nations.

W. V. O'B.

1. INDEPENDENCE AND PROBLEMS OF STATE SUCCESSION

BY D. P. O'CONNELL

The sudden appearance in the international community in recent years of a large number of new states has focused attention on the law governing the legal effects of change of sovereignty.[1] There are, however, new dimensions to the problem that call for examination. The "law of state succession," as the relevant body of rules is traditionally called, is the product of the nineteenth century and of two radically different political situations: The first of these was the boundary adjustments that occurred in Europe at regular intervals as a result of the Napoleonic Wars, the Independence of Greece, the Unification of Italy, the Bismarck Wars, and the dismemberment of the Ottoman Empire in the Balkans; the second was the extension of European political authority in Africa and Asia. In the first situation, there was every reason for the successor states to minimize the impact of the change of sovereignty on the economy and social structure of the affected territory, whereas, in the second, it was more usual for a European Power to be confronted with an inheritance of misgovernment. When, as was so often the case with Great Britain, the extension of sovereignty was made reluctantly and under pressure from merchants and missionaries, or to preserve the balance of power, the impulse toward disengagement from the results of administrative chaos or skullduggery was strong. Hence there developed two streams of attitude, in part complementary, in part antithetical, the one favoring an orderly transmission of rights and duties from the predecessor to the successor state, the other disfavoring the settlement of the predecessor's liabilities for misuse of the faculties of government.

Authors who reflected the one or the other attitude tended to be dogmatic in their enunciation of the rules of law, selecting the evidence as it suited them, and finding plenty of it. Hence the Continental writers, influenced by the comprehensive treaty provisions for transmitting rights and obligations in Europe, tended toward a general thesis of universal succession, which they supported by importing the Roman law institution of the *hereditas jacens*,[2] whereas the English writers, much more conscious of the British Government's reluctance to dip into the British taxpayer's pocket to pay off creditors of sundry bankrupt regimes in the new colonial world, tended toward a negative view of the responsibilities of the successor state for the liabilities of the predecessor.[3] American writers found themselves midway between the two.[4] Considerations identical to those motivating the English authors led the Americans to abhor the idea of the United States salvaging the credits of investors in Cuba or the Philippines, yet the property guarantees in the United States Constitution gave a sacrosanctity to legal interests in the vast territories of France and Mexico that the United States acquired during the nineteenth century that could not but influence the solution of the problem in non-American territories. Hence the American writers developed a thesis of the "burdens with the benefits,"[5] making succession dependent upon proof that the territory (and more specifically the "people" in their democratic context) had benefited from the investment.

A conscious state practice reflecting one or the other theory cannot be said to have crystallized much before the end of the nineteenth century, and it is not surprising that the views of authors were utilized according to national advantage. This explains why it is that in almost the only instances that are relevant to the present process of succession, namely, the independence of the United States and the Spanish American Colonies and of Greece (the later Balkan changes were really aspects of multilateral dispute settlements), offer remarkably little guidance. The problems of state succession at that time were not appreciated or were ignored. Except in the case of treaties, few actual issues calling for settlement arose. (We will return to this point when the analogy between a grant of independence to colonial territories and other forms of change of sovereignty is examined in detail.)

The textbook treatment of state succession has been excessively dogmatic, but, even worse, it has been juristically unreflective. Too little attention has been paid to the intricacies of legal reasoning that an appreciation of concrete problems ordinarily involves, and the subject has as a result been monolithic in structure and insufficiently analytical in treatment. A "new look" at it is called for, and a new breakdown in the process of examination is necessary if the peculiar problems of the contemporary breakup of colonial empires are to be handled in a juristically satisfying way. This does not mean that there is either no law at all to be found in the books, or that it is outdated and inapplicable. On the contrary, the reflections of the authors on past state practices—such as they are—are most valuable, and a law of state succession there most certainly is. Indeed, one might almost say that there is a law of state succession despite the authors, for once a problem arises and is solved, we have law willy-nilly, and when it is solved uniformly on a large number of occasions, we have a law that defies the efforts of the writers to negate it. Rather, the point of the criticism is that the law that was apposite for the solution of the problems of the nineteenth century is not necessarily cogent for those of the present, and new qualifications must be introduced, and new exceptions urged, if these are to be grappled with satisfactorily. In particular, it must be recognized that the key to the solution is most often not to be found in some abstract and generalized formula of state succession so much as in detailed and technical construction of a treaty, contract, or other document. What is called for is a judicial approach to concrete issues, rather than a lofty enunciation or repudiation of abstract formulas.

This also calls for a caveat on superfluous theorizing. The nineteenth-century authors betray to a marked degree the influence of the schools of legal philosophy. The Hegelians found the *hereditas jacens* notion entirely consistent with their views on personality, and the concept of a devolution of sovereignty was to them only an aspect of the whole question of the absorption of the individual will into the total will. The Austinians, who made law entirely dependent upon the decree of an identifiable superior and his faculty of enforcement, found it difficult to conceive of fetters upon sovereignty deriving from the acts of will of a predecessor, and were in consequence driven into a negative position on the whole question of the survival of institutions created by the predecessor's law.[6] Legal philosophy is far from irrelevant in the appreciation of any problem, but the law of state succession has been its particularly chosen battleground, and, so long as the issues between the disputants are recognized to be dead, so much will the outcome of the conflict appear irrelevant. In the mid-twentieth century we speak a great deal of a sociological approach to law, and though sociology unguided by philosophy is apt to lead us into a legal miasma, it must be recognized that the problems of colonial independence raise social questions that are novel, important, and urgent. The law must provide for a cogent solution, and in many respects the nineteenth-century doctrine of state succession is notably lacking in cogency for mid-twentieth-century purposes.

Another aspect of the traditional theory of succession that must be called into question in approaching the independence of excolonial territories is the distinction between succession of states and succession of governments. The distinction is really between transfers of territory from one state to another, or the total extinction of one state in another, and change of government by revolution. Proponents in the nineteenth century of the traditional theory were clearly not contemplating any distinction between secessionary revolution and merely unconstitutional change of administration. Indeed, it was only the negative theorists of state succession who adverted to the distinction at all,[7] for the universal-succession theorists, who were in the majority until the end of the century, allowed for continuity in both the case of conveyance of territory and change of dynasty or constitution. Clearly the rigid separation of secessionary revolution from nonsecessionary revolution is artificial, and is insufficient to support a structure of legal principle.

Take, for instance, the case of leased military bases. These are politically significant, and the pressure to repudiate them is considerable when a new regime appears with different ideological and political alignments from that of its predecessor. If the new regime is in fact the government of a newly independent excolony, the tendency will be great to regard the lease as an instance of that sort of "personal" treaty that cannot survive a succession of states. On the other hand, if it is no more than a new government of an old state, the argument will be that it cannot dispossess itself of the state's pre-existing commitments. Yet what are the realities of the situation? The United States has openly admitted that its base leases in the West Indies will lapse upon West Indian independence and require renegotiation, because, it was said, a new state cannot be burdened with the military commitments of the old.[8] But not even Castro's Cuba has, at least with any conviction, asserted that in virtue of the revolution in that country the Guantanamo Naval Base Agreement has lapsed.[9] Yet the social, political, and ideological change in Cuba has been far more violent than it has in the West Indies, and though in form it is a change not affecting "personality," it is in fact a change more fundamental than a change of personality.

To say that Katanga was an instance of change of government rather than of change of sovereignty is a judgment of Solomon.

Independence and Problems of State Succession

Whether the Katanga government succeeded the government of Belgium directly or whether it succeeded it indirectly, by breaking away from the Congo, is disputable; whether its continued willingness to associate with the Congo, but on a basis of autonomy, negated its personality as a secessionary is even more disputable. But again, what are the realities? The case of Katanga was hardly distinguishable from that of Israel except in the degree of successful self-assertion, for Israel, like Venus, arose full-fledged, when Britain departed from Palestine, in territory claimed by the Arabs. Looked at from the Egyptian side, Israel is only a pretender to independence, its pretense being constantly, and not ineffectually, challenged by the Arab League. The only factors distinguishing the case of Israel from that of Katanga—and they are factors of degree —are Israel's recognition by a great many states, thus securing for her some guarantee of permanent survival, and the blessing of the United Nations. In contrast, not only did Katanga fail to secure recognition, but her "secession" occurred within the context of a United Nations endeavor to make the Congo as a whole viable. To treat the one instance as a case of change of sovereignty and the other as a succession of governments, and to base distinctions in the substantive treatment of rights and wrongs upon the difference, is to render the whole issue intolerably artificial.

The concept of "personality," with its Hegelian overtones, seems to have misled the theorists. Modern jurisprudence has assisted us in recognizing that the word "personality" does not stand for something, is not descriptive of anything, and cannot be substituted for by a synonym; it is not, in fact, a reflection of some prototype sitting on a cloud somewhere, but merely a shorthand expression indicating the faculties of legal action.[10] Some writers, notably Scelle, have suggested that the whole thesis of sovereignty, with which personality is entangled, be discarded, and the idea of governmental competence substituted for it. There is often, even in a case of state succession, no transfer of the plenitude of legal competence, but only of specific faculties. For example, the United Arab Republic left Syria and Egypt alone competent in the monetary field.[11] When the faculties of government are thus partitioned, the line between a succession of states and a succession of governments wears pretty thin.

The point is important in an analysis of the situation in Africa, for there political entities become independent, tend to coalesce for a time, and then fragment.[12] A series of changes occurs, with restricted conveyance of the faculties of government, and a nice judgment is required to distinguish a change of government from a change in sovereigns. "Personality" is a concept of misleading relevance in this situation. The universal-succession theorists, in urging a complete devolution of the rights and obligations of the predecessor state upon the successor state, were closer to the mark for this reason than they have been given credit for. Where they failed was in their dogmatic solution of all problems by reference to a unique rubric, whereas concrete problems can only be solved after an exact appreciation of the factors involved. We shall see as we proceed that the empirical and pragmatic approach, provided it is "informed" by an adequate philosophy, is the only practical one, and it leads us down a path midway between the universal-succession theorists and the negative-succession theorists, and prompts an assimilation of the problems of change of sovereigns and of change of governments.

At this point it is necessary to point out that a new state is born into a world of law. Indeed it is a state, inasmuch as the term is meaningful to a lawyer, only because of a law that lays down the conditions for and the attributes of statehood. There is a tendency to argue that the international law we know is a product of European politics and Western philosophy, and is an emanation of the Age of Reason and nineteenth-century statecraft, and that as such it has little cogency for the new states of African or Asian culture.[13] The argument, of course, disposes altogether of a law of state succession. However, it is unacceptable for the very explanation that the Age of Reason offered, namely, the social contract. In asserting the faculties of statehood, the new state is accepting the structure and the system of Western international law, and it may not, without offending all juristic doctrine, pick and choose the acceptable institutions, if only because its next-door neighbor, also a new state, will claim a like privilege. But neighbors may not, without self-canceling consequences, both pick and choose to advantage. Suppose States A and B made a treaty providing for the spraying against tsetse flies along a certain frontier area in Africa between Colonies X and Y. Colonies X and Y then become independent. X insists on performance of the treaty, and Y denies that it is a successor to it. Here we have a case of two excolonies disputing an issue of succession, both of them responding to political motivation. A political solution is impossible, and a juristic one is called for. Either the treaty devolves or it does not, and in either case the proposition is one of law. The point is that next week the parties

Independence and Problems of State Succession 13

cannot reverse their positions with respect to an extradition treaty without offending juristic logic. They may have their cake, or they may eat it, not both. An objective, analytical treatment of succession problems of new states is thus not only necessary if we are to preserve juristic integrity, but ultimately serves the interests of the new states themselves. When "political realities" are urged in opposition to legal doctrine, they must be viewed by the lawyer with very much of a fishy eye, though of course they cannot be totally ignored.

I. Succession to Treaties

It became abundantly clear after the experience of the nineteenth-century territorial reconstructions that the proposition of the universal-succession theorists that the treaties of the predecessor state devolve upon the successor state *in toto* was unrealistic, yet the conclusion of the negative theorists that no treaties at all devolve appeared to be an overstatement of the case.[14] Clearly some treaties did devolve as a matter of practice, and equally clearly the great majority did not. The explanation then advanced was suggested by the thesis of "personality." Treaties "personal" to the predecessor state were alleged not to devolve; treaties of a "dispositive" character, that is, treaties in the nature of territorial conveyances or easements, were alleged to do so. A number of features of the distinction call for comment. The first is that the idea of "personal" treaties appears to derive from the implications of personal rule in the Age of Enlightenment, when treaties were contracts of brother monarchs and suffered the ordinary legal fate of contracts upon the expiry of the contracting party. This heritage from the eighteenth century conformed very well with the implications to be drawn from the Hegelian thesis of state personality in the nineteenth century. Another feature is that the distinction was supported principally upon practice in two quite peculiar instances of state succession. The first is total annexation where the contracting state, Hanover, completely disappeared. Clearly it was impossible to urge on Prussia her obligation to execute all Hanoverian treaties, if only because this might involve conflict with her own treaty commitments, and dilemmas are juristically abhorrent. The second instance is partial secession where part of a country, Alsace-Lorraine, was ceded. In this case it is equally clear that there can be no devolution of treaties: France remains unaffected in her treaty performance, save in the exceptional instance where this performance is affected by loss of territory. The other contracting party could hardly expect Germany to fulfill France's treaty obligations in matters of tariffs or extradition.

The important thing about both of these types of situations was that the treaties concerned were mostly unrelated to the actual territory affected. The case of colonial secession at present, however, is radically different inasmuch as the overseas territories were more than mere administrative districts, since they had their own governments, and the mother country's treaties were applied to them specifically. The case is not one of multiplying the signatories to a treaty that does not distinguish between metropolitan and nonmetropolitan territories, as it was in the nineteenth century, but of continuing the application of treaties specifically localized in the nonmetropolitan territories by act of the political superior.

The significance of the distinction between "personal" and "dispositive" treaties is perhaps that in the one case the treaties are nonlocalized, whereas in the other they *are* localized, thus the terms appear to be insufficiently antithetical: A treaty may be "personal" and yet localized; conversely, a treaty that is localized is not necessarily an instance of "servitude," "casement," or restricted conveyance. Inasmuch as the authors sought to treat the terms "servitude" and "dispositive" as synonyms, they perhaps misled the practitioner into assuming that the only category of treaty to survive a change of sovereignty was that called "servitude," and, conversely, that the only category called "servitude" was that which devolved in fact upon successor states. This made the succession of treaties dependent upon the cogency of an analogy drawn from Roman law, whereas perhaps it should have been made dependent upon the actual localization of the treaty.[15]

A further preliminary point must be made, and that is that the rubric of nonsuccession to personal treaties and succession to dispositive treaties took no account of the specific questions raised by particular treaties. Analysis of the instances where succession did not occur discloses that the question was mainly one of treaty interpretation or of the operation of the *rebus sic stantibus* doctrine. The essential basis of the treaty vanishes if the contracting party is annexed; a treaty with elaborate machinery for performance by the predecessor state is not, as a pure matter of construction, susceptible of performance by its successor. One does not need a law of state succession at all in order to arrive at the conclusion that most treaties do not devolve upon successor states, for this, clearly, is a conclusion yielded by the ordinary law of treaties that looks to the

Independence and Problems of State Succession

effective fulfillment of the parties' intentions—intentions ordinarily frustrated by a change of sovereignty.

The question is obviously quite different when the treaty is deliberately applied to an autonomous territory, or when it upon construction contemplates the independent execution by a non-metropolitan administration. Here again the ordinary law of treaties would yield a sufficiently persuasive conclusion, albeit it involves an actual succession to treaty rights and obligations. The perspective from the point of view of succession rather than from that of treaty interpretation discloses a structure that is excessively monolithic.

The contemporary law is left, because of the misleading direction given to it in the nineteenth century, to grapple with new problems inhibited by an unsatisfying structure of analysis. Practice is decidedly groping toward an actual succession in many instances, but inconsistencies and anomalies manifest themselves because jurisprudence has proved unable to locate a satisfactory foundation for it other than that afforded by the doctrine of "dispositive" obligations. Except in the case of Israel, in respect of whom the question has not arisen, every new country is regarded by the Secretariat of the International Labor Organization as having succeeded to the Labor Conventions of its predecessor. Dr. Jenks, who has inspired and guided this practice, would explain it as an illustration of succession to "lawmaking" treaties, and would in consequence rationalize the process as one of devolution of nonpersonal treaties.[16] Doctrinally there are difficulties with this thesis, for it is not clear what is meant by a "lawmaking" treaty. If the reference is to treaties that declare or stimulate customary law, then the instance is not one of succession to treaties at all, because the new states would be bound in any event by the rule. If it is to multilateral treaties generally, then the reference to "lawmaking" character is no more than a euphemism, for the process of laying down rules legislatively and comprehensively for a large number of signatories is distinct from the making of contracts between individual states. But the treaty is still a contract and still excludes nonsignatories, so that it is difficult to see why the number of parties and the comprehensiveness of the arrangement should of themselves fundamentally affect the problem of succession.

So far as membership of international organizations is concerned, there are very few occasions when a new state has been permitted to claim a seat in virtue of the participation in the relevant convention of an old state. The International Monetary Fund and the

International Bank for Reconstruction and Development, for example, have resisted the contention that successor states can become members by virtue of succession.[17] They have permitted this only in the case of the United Arab Republic, where there were peculiar reasons for it. Egypt and Syria were already members, had quota and borrowing rights, and, after federation, each retained its own central-banking system and control of monetary policy. There was, then, real continuity at the financial level, and it was only at the political level that the new federal government had to be substituted for the former regimes. The instance is by no means typical of state succession. So far as the former colonies are concerned, they have had to make formal application for membership.[18] Where debts to the Bank had been contracted on their behalf by the mother state, the loan agreements had been guaranteed by that state, though amortization was to be effected by the colonial administration out of colonial resources. The loan agreement with Kenya is an example. The result has been to leave the mother countries liable in the event of default of their offspring. No doubt there is here a succession vis-à vis the mother country under the ordinary rules relating to devolution of debt, but there is none vis-à-vis the creditor, at least in current Bank policy.

Upon reflection it becomes clear that the most obvious cases of nonsuccession to treaties would be those concerning membership of international organizations, for membership involves all manner of political rights and commitments, and it is by no means certain that a given successor state would be either competent or willing to participate in such arrangements. The United Nations Charter, with its stated commitments, is the most obvious example, and no new state that did not already enjoy membership by virtue of its effectively independent status has been permitted to claim membership by virtue of its parent's membership. Membership of the specialized agencies and other organizations is no different.

The most obvious "lawmaking" treaties are, therefore, those that most obviously do not devolve on successor states. Yet it cannot be said with confidence that there is not a category of multilateral conventions that does devolve. A quick survey of the *Status of Multilateral Conventions* of the United Nations[19] discloses that several new states have in fact claimed to be parties to a number of conventions by virtue of their parents' signature. The claims are by no means consistent—Morocco, for example, claims the Road Traffic Convention whereas Tunisia does not.[20] One fact does emerge, however, and that is a willingness on the part of new states to succeed to conventions with a humanitarian aim. Perhaps Dr. Jenks may not be far off the mark in arguing for succession to "lawmaking" treaties in the light of this practice, but this means that the treaties in question are lawmaking in the sense of supplementing customary international law, or in exercising an influence upon its development.[21] In groping toward a succession, states may, in fact, be stimulating the transformation of these conventions, or at least the principles they enshrine, from the domain of contract into the domain of law. In any event, conventions such as those relating to narcotics and slavery do not involve the ordinary incidence of membership in international organizations, as is the case with the World Food Organization.

At this point an example of indirect succession to membership must be discussed as an overture to an analysis of the selective succession indicated by a treaty construction. This is the continued associate membership in the European Economic Community of the former colonies of France and Belgium. The Treaty of Rome provided for the association of listed overseas territories, and an Applicatory Convention specified the process for the first five years.[22] Continued association was achieved by general agreement in 1963.[23] This is not, strictly speaking, a case of succession because it does not illustrate a transmission of treaty rights and obligations, but it is an illustration of continuity throughout the process of political fracture, and hence is a typical instance of that sort of succession that is already contemplated by the treaty itself. What is significant is that before independence the overseas territories were associated by virtue of the rights of their parents. Now they would seem to be associated by virtue of their own rights.

It now becomes a little clearer that the pragmatic approach of examining each treaty will yield a diversified conclusion, favoring succession in some instances, disfavoring it in others. Only a residue of cases can be solved with reference to a general touchstone of succession, and here the "dispositive" notion, or the "lawmaking" thesis, may serve, with the qualifications later to be suggested. At this stage it is necessary to examine how the pragmatic approach is actually implemented. First, the policy of the new state will be examined, and then the attitude of the Secretary General of the United Nations as the depositary will be examined.

It is not surprising to find remarkable discrepancies in the policies of the new states. Even Australia and New Zealand, which may be taken to illustrate the most complete, normal, and orderly devolution of treaties, are not in agreement upon all of the treaties of Great Britain that they have inherited. How, then, could it be expected that the more recently independent states would find themselves in total agreement? By way of preliminary observations, it is desirable to explain how the older British Dominions became parties, by devolution, to a large number of Imperial treaties. At one time it was thought that this was so because they shared a common Crown, which remained the nominal contracting party. Until the early 1930's, indeed, this theory would have explained the devolution of Head of State treaties, including the majority of nineteenth-century ones, but, in the 1930's, the doctrine that the Dominions could claim, by virtue of the Crown's personal signature and ratification, the benefits of Head of State treaties *inter se* broke down, and this explanation wore thin.[24] (The Warsaw Convention on Air Carriage is an example: It was legislatively applied *inter se*.) In any event, the explanation was irrelevant in the case of intergovernmental treaties, of which there are many that Australia, New Zealand, and Canada claimed to have inherited.

Although the newly independent ex-Crown colonies have not passed through the slow process of evolution of the older members of the Commonwealth, the tendency has been for them to continue the treaty relationships contracted territorially for them by the United Kingdom. The practice is for the Commonwealth Relations Office to prepare a list of treaties that were applied to the colony before independence and to secure a devolution by instrumental means. In the earlier cases the instrument was statutory; its binding effect upon the successor state could only be by virtue of proof that the law of state succession permits succession of such public-law legislation. In the later cases an agreement was entered into between the United Kingdom and the newly independent states.[25] These agreements, however, are models of evasive draftsmanship, and almost any point of view may be sustained by reference to them. Far from securing a general treaty devolution, as appears at first glance, these agreements may prove restrictive of it when read with the actual treaties.

It has been generally assumed that the devolution agreements constitute assignments to the new states of the United Kingdom's rights and obligations. This assumption is only justified if the theory is accepted that new states begin their lives uncommitted by their predecessor's acts. If, under the ordinary operation of law, treaties of the United Kingdom would continue to affect the emancipated territories, then the agreements would be confirmatory, intended only as acknowledgments *ex abundanti cautela*, and would not constitute assignments at all. In such a case, the problem of securing assent to the assignment on the part of other contractors would not arise. The attitude of the United Kingdom Government is that the new states, like the former Dominions, continue to be affected by the majority of relevant British treaties, and that the devolution agreements are a useful diplomatic method of declaring the affirmative attitudes of both the United Kingdom and the new states. They are not intended to commit other parties, for this would not in any event be possible, but they are intended to notify such other parties that the successor state's policy is generally favorable to the maintenance of treaty relationships. This permits the other parties to presume an affirmative practice on the part of the successor state with respect to specific treaties, and diplomatic action may be based on this presumption. But, since serious questions of interpretation arise in the case of most treaties that could give occasion for exempting them from the general presumption, no irrevocable commitment is made by any state. Perhaps the ambiguity in the terms of the devolution agreements is deliberate, and designed to afford escape when politically justified.

Although, in the absence of specific confirmation, there must always remain doubt that a new state is in fact reciprocating treaty advantages, the benefit of the doubt is usually accorded if that state is a party to a devolution agreement, and withheld if it is not. The United Nations Secretary General, for example, takes the existence of such an agreement into account in determining his attitude toward the question of a new state's participation in the regime of conventions administered by him. Also, the United States automatically lists against new states that are parties to devolution agreements all relevant Anglo-American treaties. There is no doubt, therefore, that these agreements, whatever the lawyers may make of them, contribute to a stabilizing of diplomatic relations at a time when stability is a political desideratum. The alternative course of conduct, pursued by Tanganyika, Uganda, and Zanzibar, of issuing a declaration that treaty relationships will be maintained for a limited period while the new states make up their minds which treaties they wish to continue indefinitely, is diplomatically inconvenient. Foreign Offices, confronted with the prospect that given treaties will be regarded as terminated by the new state on expiry of the due date, have been placed in a quandary with respect to interim reciprocity. Inevitably they have sought in advance from the new state an affirmative attitude toward each treaty, and this has led to an excessive volume of correspondence.

Not surprisingly, Foreign Offices have preferred the line of least resistance, which the existence of a devolution agreement allows them to take.

Five possible attitudes toward continuity of treaties might be taken by successor states. They might deny continuity, or succession, altogether with respect to the treaties of their predecessor (an attitude taken by Algeria, Israel, and, with inconsistencies, Upper Volta); they might, in the absence of a devolution agreement, declare their continued application of such treaties (Congo-Brazzaville, Malagasy Republic, Congo-Leopoldville); they might enter into devolution agreements and base positive action upon them (most of the former British countries); they might take a reserved attitude (Tanganyika, Uganda, Zanzibar); or they might, without any commitment to principle, in fact continue to apply treaties (most of the former French countries). It is evident from the practice that the "clean slate" theory, or the theory that a new state begins its life unencumbered by treaties, has very few adherents among the new states themselves.

There is a very good reason for the new state's reluctance to take a general and affirmative attitude, and it is that the actual operation of a treaty in a colonial territory is not in itself sufficient to make for inheritance. Many treaties upon construction would be excluded, and treaty interpretation is a notoriously hazardous endeavor. Time and reflection will be necessary before decisions can be taken, even if political factors can be eliminated. Two examples of the problems suggested by the empirical approach may be taken. The first is the expression "High Contracting Party" in the Warsaw Convention, which has been held by the House of Lords to mean actual signatories.[26] Whether the new state is to be regarded as a signatory is obviously a matter for debate, so that even if a complete devolution is secured it by no means follows that this Convention is included in it. A converse problem is suggested by the Counterfeiting Convention, which is a closed convention that is restricted to states that participated in it. The United Kingdom did not ratify the Convention until some years after some of her territories gained independence, but before others of them did so. Does this mean that some of the territories may accede to the Convention, or succeed to it, and that others may neither accede nor succeed? Every treaty must be examined in this manner, and, in many treaties, there will be found room for debate, upon interpretation, as to the suitability of the treaty for devolution.

This consideration is much less relevant in the case of bilateral treaties than it is in the case of multilateral treaties. For example, extradition treaties are normally straightforward documents; this is true by and large of commercial treaties also. But in both of these types of treaties there are factors militating strongly against succession. In extradition treaties, new countries of differing ideological persuasion may not want to surrender persons *inter se* when there is no basis for agreeing on the criminal nature of the act, save in respect of municipal law, and when there is no confidence in each other's judicial process. True, the ordinary law of extradition with its principles of specialty and nonrendition of political offenders may offer sufficient safeguards, but nonetheless the political overtones of extradition cannot be ignored. Similarly, commercial treaties are matters of economic, social, and political context, and when the context radically changes with a transfer of sovereignty the continued operation of such treaties would be artificial.

On the other hand, it is highly arguable that such problems can be disposed of without importing theories of succession or nonsuccession. The *rebus sic stantibus* doctrine has been mentioned. More specifically, and practically, almost all treaties of this sort have denunciation clauses, and even when they have not, at least in the case of commercial treaties, denunciation on reasonable notice is argued for by authorities as important as, for example, Lord McNair.[27] In other words, international law has quite adequate and effective machinery for permitting new states to divest themselves of most inconvenient bilateral treaties within a short time after independence. Why, then, resort to succession ideas unless the "personality" thesis is really the dominant factor? If this thesis turns out to be no more than irrelevant ideological superstructure, we are pressed toward the conclusion that succession rather than nonsuccession should be the rule. The actual successions that have occurred, and that seem to be so perplexing when viewed in the light of the "personality" thesis, appear thus to be instances rather than exceptions, and the nonsuccessions are to be explained as dictated by interpretation of the actual treaties concerned. The proposition that there is no succession to personal treaties would thus seem to be unqualifiedly valid only in the case of total annexation, and, indeed, the historical precedents stem mainly from such instances.

Before pursuing this inquiry to a conclusion, however, it is necessary to turn to the practice of the United Nations Secretariat when confronted by the problem of showing or not showing a new state as a party to a treaty.[28] The practice is not greatly significant inasmuch as the Secretariat follows the dictates of the new states, rather than making its own appreciation. The Secretary General sends to each new state a list of multilateral treaties of which he is the depository, and to which the parent state was a party, and asks the new state to declare its attitude. The Secretary General's own attitude depends upon whether the treaty contained a territorial-application clause and was in fact applied to the colonies. Although he has decided that the Convention on the Privileges and Immunities of the United Nations applied in all colonies, this has not prevented Morocco from regarding the Convention as not being among those to which she has succeeded.[29] Where there was no territorial-application clause, or the treaty was not in fact applied, the Secretary General assumes that the new state is not, in fact, a successor.[30]

What is the point of this application at all, if the determinitive factor is the attitude of the new state? There is indeed very little point in the exercise save that when the treaty was territorially applied, the Secretariat goes through the motions of ascertaining the views of the new states when inviting them to become parties to amending protocols, or requiring them to accede, whereas otherwise it assumes that an accession will be necessary, and leaves the initiative to the new state. The entire practice appears to be procedural rather than substantive, but it has the effect of requiring the new state to declare its attitude with respect to a specific convention, and thus keeps up the pace, which otherwise might lag.

At this point it is useful to make a digression and discuss the extraordinarily complex and muddled state of multilateral conventions, and the overwhelming difficulty of ascertaining the parties involved. The United Nations' *Status of Multilateral Conventions* is a valuable though inconclusive guide, since many eligible members have not declared their attitudes.[31] In the case of other conventions, the problem assumes the dimension of a nightmare. To find out the parties to the Warsaw Convention on Air Carriage, for instance, one must ask the Polish Government; to find out the parties to the Brussels Convention on Collisions at Sea, one must approach the Belgians. If the approach is made by a private litigant who seeks to establish that his contract of carriage is affected by the Convention, it is most likely he will be met by a blank refusal. If the approach is made by a government, a list will be forthcoming, but it will contain only names of those states that have deposited some kind of document, and since most new states will not have done this, the list is by no means complete. It is not surprising that few new states have made any effort to tidy up their treaty lists. Furthermore, those that have, such as Australia, New Zealand, or Southern Rhodesia, will most likely not be shown at all on the depository's list because they will not have deposited any document but merely shown themselves as parties on their own lists. Other parties may not agree, and therefore the lists are no more than prima facie evidence of partnership in the relevant treaties.

In the case of the British Commonwealth, an attempt has been made to introduce some order into the system by drawing up the lists earlier mentioned. In the case of France, on the other hand, the whole problem has been left to chance.[32] When one reflects upon the permutations and combinations involved in treaties with and without territorial-application clauses, treaties accepted by some ex-British territories and by some ex-French, rejected by others, and to which yet others are uncommitted, one sees that the chances of one ex-British colony and one ex-French being united by a *vinculum juris* are restricted.

In returning to the main question of whether there is any jurisprudential basis to the successions that have actually occurred, it is desirable to reiterate that there is very little historical precedent for secession, and that almost all precedent is to be discovered in instances of annexation and cession. We have made the point that not much significance is to be attributed to the cases of the independence of the United States and of Latin America, since an adequate explanation is afforded with respect to most of the affected treaties by construction of the treaties themselves, and since none of the treaties had, presumably, been specially contracted for the territories. They were "personal" in the most complete sense of the term. The independence of various European states in 1919 is the nearest modern instance, but again it is perhaps not typical for the reason that these were not autonomous provinces to which treaties had been specifically applied, but were carved haphazardly out of existing political entities on an ethnological and not administrative basis.

What, then, is peculiar about the process of independence in the contemporary world so far as treaties are concerned? Surely it is that each colony that has become independent was an autonomous region with its own administration and budget, and, up to a point, with discretion in internal policy-making. Treaties of the parent states were not, at least in more recent times, extended to nonmetropolitan territories without specific act and the prior consent of the contracting parties. In a sense they were local treaties. But do they, because they are local, fall into the category of dispositive treaties? Only, it may be answered, if that category can be disengaged from the notion of servitude or easement and extended to become synonymous with the territorial application of treaties, irrespective of whether they are "personal" in the traditional sense of the word, or constitute restraints on sovereignty. And this answer is possible if practice indicates a pressure toward an actual succession in instances not ordinarily regarded as servitudes.

That there is some such pressure is beyond dispute. What inhibits the drawing of inferences therefrom is the baffling inconsistency of the practice, which suggests that the new states are more inclined to pick and choose than to act in response to the dictates of theory. Perhaps, if the emphasis is to be placed anywhere, it should be placed on the instances of succession rather than on those of nonsuccession, for the affirmation rather than the denial probably most accurately reflects the sociological need and advantage. That the negative instances are of questionable significance may be established by discussing the specific cases of Tunisia and Morocco, both of which were protected territories, with France acting merely as an instrument in making treaties. Theoretically, these countries should remain bound by treaties contracted on their behalf just as they are held by the International Court to have remained bound by their own treaties contracted before the French extended protection,[33] and just as India has remained bound by British treaties specially signed "for India" between 1919 and 1947.[34] Yet Tunisia and Morocco have picked and chosen as freely as if they were novel apparitions, like Dahomey and Chad; furthermore, they have not been consistent between themselves in their choices; or scrupulous to distinguish between treaties specially applied to their territories and treaties in which they might have participated as French territories. For example, Morocco does not regard herself as having succeeded to the Convention on the Privileges and Immunities of the United Nations, which the Secretary General had decided applied in all colonial territories;[35] on the other hand, Malaya, also a protectorate, regards herself as bound by it.[36]

One might, then, dismiss the negative instances in the cases of the protectorates as politically and not juristically motivated, and in answer to the objector who will protest that the protectorates were in reality no more than species of colonies, and hence should be allowed to shake off the impediment of imperial commitments once they are unleashed; it might be pointed out that the rulers of

Independence and Problems of State Succession 25

the Malay States, when they imagined their sovereign immunity was being undermined in the English courts, indignantly asserted their sovereign status under protection.[37] They cannot with much conviction now argue that there has been a change of sovereignty so vitally affecting their personality as to cancel the application of all imperial treaties. In actual fact, Malaya has acted no differently from Tunisia and Morocco or from her comembers in the British Commonwealth, and offers a practice no less perplexing to the jurisprudence of the subject.

This analysis has been exploratory and designed to measure the light and shadow thrown on the traditional theory by modern practice and a consideration of modern needs and problems. It is now necessary to approach a conclusion. One could adhere to the traditional doctrine and argue that all "personal" treaties lapse, yet this fails to justify the instances where succession is alleged to occur. Are such instances to be explained away on political grounds alone? It is believed not, since at least the common denominator of humanitarian interest has been detected, and in any event a political explanation is utterly unsatisfying because it fails to establish any *vinculum juris* between the successor state and the other parties to the treaty, which is surely the whole object of the exercise. One must, then, either regard the instances of succession as unilateral acts with no effect on third parties, or as juristically significant of the continuation of contractual links with those parties; if the latter solution is accepted the problem of finding a legal rationalization is back in our lap.

It now becomes evident that we must take the juridical bull by the horns and propose that succession should be the rule and nonsuccession the exception, in cases of independence of nonmetropolitan territories. The arguments favoring it are the localization of treaties by specific act; the autonomous administrative character of the territories that makes for legal continuity upon independence; the dubious validity of the whole thesis of "personal" and "dispositive" treaties as applied to secession; and the virtual irrelevance of the distinction, save in form, between state succession and government succession. Add to these the important consideration that succession to treaties was argued for by the great majority of jurists until well into the nineteenth century. The argument against succession is that new states cannot be expected to tolerate the surviving encumbrances of imperial government, but, apart from the fact that we have already rejected the cogency of a political solution that offends juristic logic, the argument is much weakened by the fact that in most instances burdensome treaties can be got rid of quite conveniently by the ordinary processes of treaty law.

There is, however, one final and important point to be made, and that is that not all independence movements involve a straight transfer of authority from an imperial government to colonial territories. We have witnessed the process of federation of newly independent states and the dissolution of the federation. This is likely to continue. To make treaty operation dependent upon the hazards of political flux of this sort is to add to the confusion of the problem. The important factor to be emphasized is continuity, not chaos.

II. Succession to Governmental Contracts

The negative theorists denied that there could be any transmission of rights and obligations under governmental contracts upon a change in sovereignty. The universal-succession theorists contended that there was such a transmission. It has been assumed that the latter were patently wrong in their opinion, but juristically, and not taking practice into account, there was no doubt that their thesis was cogent, for subrogation in contractual rights and obligations is a doctrine well understood by municipal lawyers, and obviously apposite for the solution of problems of state succession. When we turn to the practice, we discover that such a subrogation is not admitted, though it has occurred, but also that a complete repudiation of all liability under the contract on the part of the successor state is rare and to be explained on grounds of exception. The middle-of-the-way solution seems to have been to admit that, upon a change of sovereignty, one of the parties to the contract has disappeared from the place of the performance, that the contract as such lapses from "frustration," but that the benefit to the private contractor under the contract insofar as it has been performed must be satisfied under the doctrine of unjust enrichment.[38] This is a solution suggested by the comparable problem under both English law and the civil law. The result is that the government is released under the contract, but must pay the contractor whatever is due to him at the date of change of sovereignty if the benefits of his work accrue to the territory affected. If the contract is totally executory, the matter is at an end altogether.

The middle-of-the-way solution has merits when the case is one of annexation, but the considerations explored in the case of treaties also operate with respect to the fate of governmental contracts in cases of independence of colonial territories. Indeed, the element of autonomy is perhaps even more significant in the case of contracts than in that of treaties, for normally, though there is a change of sovereignty, there is a continuity of administration. Government departments such as Boards of Works continue to function without interruption—not even, in many instances, changing their staffs. Surely it is artificial in the extreme to contend that the contracts of such departments lapse merely because the ultimate political authority has altered; the artificiality is emphasized if the comparison between succession of states and succession of governments is borne in mind. Nor, as a matter of practice, are such contracts discontinued. There is very little material collected on the treatment accorded contractors by the new governments, but one may take a fairly accurate guess that the discontinuance thought of has not even crossed the minds of either governmental officials or the contractors themselves in 999 cases out of 1,000. From the point of view of accepted theory, this has to be explained as a "novation" of the contract, yet is this not arguing from the exceptional, indeed the rare, instead of from the normal and the frequent, and is not the supposed principle, from the point of view of jurisprudence, severely suspect in the result?

The important factor in the attitude of states toward the question of the survival of governmental contracts has been a reluctance to be saddled with contracts that could be described as survivals of imperialist exploitation, and consequently as abhorrent to the policies of the new government. The "practice" of the United States with respect to concessionary contracts of Spain in Cuba and the Philippines was much motivated by that consideration, and in turn has motivated subsequent practice. It must be conceded that there is great and valid pressure favoring the abstract right of the successor state to scrutinize contracts to decide which of them conforms with its own economic, social, and political policies, but it must be remembered that the right was asserted at a time when it was generally thought that international law protected contracts to the date of their full performance, so that if the successor state became a party to the contract, it would have to see it through to the bitter end or incur responsibility for wrongful repudiation. If modern international law does not protect contracts for their duration, then the sting is taken out of the objection to a doctrine of succession, for, just as in the case of treaties, the successor state may utilize ordinary legal techniques for disengaging itself from inconvenient contracts.

Clearly, then, the central point for investigation is the extent to which international law protects contractual performance, for if it does not, then the doctrine of nonsubrogation in the case of a successor state is, from a practical point of view, irrelevant, whereas if it does, then such a doctrine would place a successor state in a more advantageous position than its predecessor was in. In actual fact, the problem of contractual performance in international law is immensely complex, and the solution depends mainly upon the subtleties of municipal law. Briefly, the position, without throwing the picture into too high relief, may be stated as follows: International law protects only rights acquired under the proper law of the contract. If specific performance is not a feature of the proper law, then international law does not enjoin it; if it was, then it does enjoin it. If municipal law is altered by the contracting state so as to modify the rights of the contractholder, this will engage the interest of international law only if this modification fundamentally alters the acquired right to the holder's disadvantage. The problem is very much more complex if the governing law is international law or the general principles of law, but since this is rare it may be ignored for our purposes.

From a practical point of view, it may be said with some assurance that the extent to which governmental contracts in former colonial territories are exposed to the protection of international law is slight. This is, at least, the case with the British territories, for English law does not normally insist upon specific performance, but merely requires damages to be paid that are extremely restrictive in character. What international law does protect is the resort to local remedies to sue for breach of contract. Since the damages likely to be awarded are hardly greater than the compensation that would be payable in any event by the successor state under the traditional doctrine of nonsubrogation, the effort to argue a case for nonsuccession seems scarcely worthwhile, and only raises legal conundrums in the very great majority of cases where the contracts are continued. The chances of a successor state being "stuck with" an inconvenient concessionary contract are very slight indeed when one reflects that, even in cases where no change of sovereignty was involved, governmental repudiation of a contract has not been followed by an award of specific performance of *restitutio in integrum* by tribunals empowered to deal with the case, but by an award of *damnum emergens* and *lucrum cessans*. This means that at most a repudiating state may have to pay a forfeiting contractholder his loss of expected profits. The question is whether it is better to accept this possibility with good grace and preserve an orderly continuity in the remaining 999 contracts, or seek to escape altogether from the payment of more than the capital investment in the one inconvenient case and thereby place in legal jeopardy the other 999 cases.

It is unrealistic to assume that in every case it is the private contractholder who is seeking to enforce rights against the successor state and the latter whose right to repudiate is at issue. There must be at least as many instances where the state would want to sue the private contractors for breach of contract. Yet if there is to be no subrogation in the contract, this must hold for both sides of it. What attitude will a court of the successor state take toward a private contractor who pleads in defense the frustration of the contract upon independence, and argues that the only damages that the state can claim are those accrued before the date of the change? One might hazard the guess that the defense would not succeed, and if research into actual cases were exhaustive, support for this might be forthcoming.

It is significant that in the *Lighthouses* Arbitrations conducted in 1956,[39] Verzijl, who is a known supporter of the view that international law protects contractual performance, took it for granted that the relevant contracts were unaffected by the change of sovereignty. And as a matter of practice, there has been no recorded instance since the Boer War of succession states claiming the right forthwith to repudiate a contract upon the change of sovereignty.[40] Rather, the repudiation has come at a later date and has all the characteristics of an ordinary expropriation or nationalization. Indeed, the most obvious instance, that of Indonesian expropriation of Dutch property, occurred despite a treaty guaranteeing the performance of the contracts. Indonesia was, legally, in a far more dubious position as affected by the treaty than if she had accepted as a matter of customary law her automatic succession to contracts, for then her liabilities under international law would have depended upon what remedies existed under Dutch law for breach of contract.

Once the fear is allayed that, by accepting succession to contracts as the norm states are disabled from expropriation, a dispassionate approach to the question is suggestive of a conclusion in favor of succession, at least where the contract was that of an autonomous local administration. The American cases of the nineteenth century misled most writers into believing that once succession was acknowledged the private rights persisted in perpetuity.[41] This occurred in the United States only because the rights, once vested, fell under the protective provisions of the Constitution. No implications as to the international-law rule need or should be drawn. Similarly, the famous enunciations in favor of the doctrine of acquired rights by the International Court in the 1920's are not to be taken as inhibiting the successor state's competence to expropriate, because that competence was in the actual cases affected by treaty.[42] In short, a doctrine of succession to contracts would place the successor state in no different legal position from the predecessor state with respect to performance, and in most instances national interest can be preserved by resort to the ordinary law of expropriation, even if this means an increase in the measure of damages.

It must also be borne in mind that the problem of state succession is not only a problem of continuing legal relationships between governmental authorities and alien vested interests, but also, and more immediately important, a problem of the survival rights of local inhabitants who become nationals of the successor state. If contracts expire, this means contracts of nationals, as well as of aliens. It is sociologically unsatisfactory that independence should produce this sort of legal upheaval, and indeed it is only because the question of succession has been confused with the question of how to get rid of inconvenient alien control of natural resources or public utilities that it is contemplated at all. The confusion has been confounded by the English doctrine of Act of State, which has prevented English property and contractholders from pursuing in English courts the question of the survival of their interests following the acquisition of territory by the Crown.[43] This, in its results, assimilated the problem of the national with that of the alien, and gave the impression, erroneous but widespread, that upon change of sovereignty all claims lapse.

Again it is necessary to propose that succession to governmental contracts upon independence should be the norm and not the exception. The conclusion can be made with some confidence if the localization of the contracts resulting from the autonomy of the colonial administrations can be regarded as analogous with the localization of debts. There is a well-settled rule that local debts are unaffected by a change of sovereignty. When a contract has been performed and payment only is awaited, this is a local debt, which the successor state must satisfy. Why, when the contract is still in part executory, should not performance in ways other than payment also be expected?

III. SUCCESSION TO DELICTUAL CLAIMS

It has always been taken for granted that a successor state is not liable for the delicts of its predecessor.[44] That the problem is topical in the case of independence in Africa is demonstrated by events in the Congo. Whichever political authority ultimately inherits Katanga will be confronted with a legacy of violence, and to make the fate of claims dependent upon a decision whether Katanga is an instance of state succession or of succession of governments is to overformalize the whole issue. No one has yet sufficiently analyzed the proposition that there is no succession to delicts, and upon analysis it might well be found that the doctrine is spurious. The first point to be settled is whether it is an international delict that is referred to, or a municipal law tort. Let us take the first alternative first: An international delict is an injury for which a state is responsible. It need not be an injury arising out of revolutionary violence involving the destruction of alien property or physical assault on alien persons. It may be a mere breach of contract, in which case the problem is one of contractual performance. Or it may be a misapplication of law or a misdemeanor of the courts. The important thing is that until local remedies are denied the injured party there is no international responsibility; therefore, every international delict consists of a denial of local remedies, or, so it is technically called, a denial of justice.

When it is said that there is no succession to an international delict, this can surely not mean that there can be no succession with respect to any denial of justice, for this would exclude succession even in claims arising under contracts that survive the change of sovereignty; it would mean that the successor state could disclaim responsibility for, say, delivery of defective goods under the contract before the date of the change, when the courts of the predecessor had wrongfully frustrated pursuit of a remedy, even though in the outcome the performance of the contract as a whole is affected.

Perhaps the proposition that there is no succession to delictual claims is limited to cases of violence, or the municipal-tort situation, and to cases of judicial misdemeanor. The difficulty with this is that both violence and procedural denial of justice may amount to a substantive interference with acquired rights. The *Robert E. Brown* Claim admirably illustrates the artificiality of the whole doctrine.[45] Brown, it will be remembered, took the necessary steps under Transvaal law to acquire a mining license, but this was refused. The courts, under executive pressure and in violation of the law, supported the refusal. Brown's claim against Great Britain was rejected by the tribunal on the ground of nonsuccession to delict, the delict in this case, presumably, being the procedural denial of justice. But the effect was to cancel out Brown's mining rights acquired under Transvaal law. The case is thus authority for the proposition that the successor state is never required to restore private property taken from an alien by the predecessor in violation of the local law. If this is actually the state of international law, then it can only be deplored.

If, in addition, the proposition means that there is no succession to the liabilities of the predecessor state under situations characterized by municipal law as tortious, it is of dubious validity. Surely succession cannot be made to depend upon the accidents of municipal-law systems, which may vary in their characterization. In any event, it is surely nonsense to suggest that, although the legal system survives a change of sovereignty, claims of negligence against the Board of Works lapse. For this reason the suggestion criterion of liquidated, as distinct from unliquidated claims, when only the former survives the change of sovereignty, is, perhaps, unrealistic.

IV. Succession to the Legal System

It is said that the private law survives a change of sovereignty, but the public law does not. The suggested distinction was made by French authors in the nineteenth century. No doubt to the French lawyer it is a clear and workable distinction, though he makes it on somewhat different premises from the German or the Dutch lawyer. To the English or American lawyer, however, it is a purely verbal distinction, for the common law does not recognize a division between public and private functions, and the statute law is based on premises that do not support it. In the case of independence with the British Commonwealth, therefore, the suggestion that the distinction between public law and private law is the touchstone for determining which legal institutions survive is utterly misleading.

Take the doctrine of Act of State, for example.[46] This denies an English court competence to entertain suits against the Crown arising out of the acquisition of territory by the Crown. Has this doctrine been inherited as part of the corpus of common law by the independent states so that nobody—not even a new national of those states—can set up against the new sovereign property rights that he enjoyed under the Crown?

The doctrine has its public aspects, inasmuch as it is concerned with a transfer of political power, and it rightly figures among those disparate legal institutions assembled in the textbooks under the heading of constitutional law. But as a common law, and not statutory doctrine, it no doubt passes with the whole corpus of English law. It means that, save where a succession is statutorily provided for, as in the case of India,[47] no one can sue the successor government in tort or contract or enforce property rights.

Similarly, the whole doctrine of the royal prerogative is inherited by the successor state so long as it remains a monarchy; and, so long as it maintains a parliamentary form of government, all the law relating to parliamentary privilege and institutions of review of executive action, such as certiorari, mandamus, or prohibition, are likewise inherited. One is forced to the conclusion that it is only in matters of franchise and the like, affected by independence, that there is a lapse of law at all.

The problem of the distinction between public law and private law—and, indeed, its general irrelevance—is highlighted by the particular case of employment of civil servants. In the English system, civil servants have vested rights only inasmuch as they enjoy them under statute. If the distinction means that when such a statute expires civil servants lost their rights, this must be one of the very few instances of a lapse of a legal institution upon a territory's attainment of independence. In civil-law systems, the employment of civil servants is ordinarily an instance of vested rights, and in consequence is characterized as a case of mixed public and private law. It constitutes an exception to the rule of nonsurvival of political institutions, and hence termination of employment engages a duty to compensate. Furthermore, most territories upon attainment of independence had a local administration, at least in the lower echelons, and the argument for continued employment is strong. The Dutch East Indies, for example, were an autonomous administration. Naturally, the new states cannot be expected to continue to employ alien officials, and their political and moral right to discharge them must be undisputed. The proper method, when vested rights occur, is for legislation of the mother state to deal with the matter, and this is, in fact, the case where a solution is not possible within the framework of existing statute law. The point, then, is that the distinction between public law and private law is of little value in solving the problem of the fate of civil servants.

V. The Problem of inter se Relations in the Commonwealth

Many states that were once Crown colonies are now members of the Commonwealth. The question that arises is whether their relations *inter se* are governed by the ordinary rules of international law, or fall under some system of constitutional law, or exclude the operation of rules of law altogether. The problem is complex and can only be adverted to here. Three questions will be discussed:

1. May the Commonwealth countries claim sovereign immunities in each other's courts?
2. Does signature by two Commonwealth members of multilateral treaties bring these into operation *inter se*?
3. May one member maintain diplomatic claims against another?

The questions are relevant to state succession inasmuch as they raise all manner of implications as to legal continuity through the process of independence.

Sovereign Immunities

The Commonwealth Relations Office has certified to English courts that Pakistan is an "independent sovereign State," and should enjoy full sovereign immunities.[48] In 1952 the High Commissioners of Commonwealth countries and of Ireland, their staffs, servants, and property, were declared identical in the United Kingdom, in most respects, with those of non-Commonwealth countries,[49] and this legislation has been copied throughout the Commonwealth. So far as armed forces are concerned, these have been treated as "visiting armed forces" since 1932,[50] though the common allegiance to the Crown has prompted certain common implications from the royal prerogative. In 1942 the Australian High Court decided that when seamen were seconded from the Royal Australian Navy to the Royal Navy, they fell under United Kingdom statutory discipline, and not Australian. This principle may have been altered by the acquisition of powers to legislate repugnant to United Kingdom statutes.

The problem of visiting warships and other governmental vessels is opaque. An Australian warship would have been immune from the jurisdiction of New Zealand courts, not because it enjoyed sovereign immunity, but because it fell under the privilege of the

Crown. The issue raised by the divisibility of the Crown is not likely to trouble a court in the case of warships in the new Commonwealth because these would in any event now have international immunity, but the case would be different with government merchant ships should English law decide not to include them in this immunity. Then the question of prerogative immunity would call for decision. The problem is tricky, however, inasmuch as before the ships can be potentially public, the operating instrumentality must be held to fall under the "shield of the Crown."

Treaties inter se

Since World War II, agreements between member-states of the Commonwealth have been registered with the United Nations as treaties, although the mutual understandings arrived at in Commonwealth consultation and not recorded in agreement form are still regarded as outside the scope of international law, and hence as unaffected by the Ihlen doctrine. An immensely complex structure of treaty relationships *inter se* has, however, been inherited from the prewar Commonwealth and its practices and attitudes. It was decided at the 1926 Commonwealth Conference that treaties should not operate *inter se*, and that when the Crown became a signatory to a Head of State treaty, this was to be understood as a joint commitment on behalf of all the members not bringing the Convention into operation *inter se* but only vis-à-vis nonmembers. The Warsaw Convention on Air Carriage was one such convention, but it has now been brought into operation *inter se* by each member's legislating to declare the others high contracting parties. There is now little doubt that multilateral conventions do operate *inter se*, but there is still doubt as to the extent to which those inherited from the United Kingdom and contracted before the war do so.

Incidentally, the manner of implementing the Warsaw Convention is of interest to the topic of the localization of treaties. It was specifically brought into operation between listed colonies and the high contracting parties by Order in Council under the Carriage by Air Act. It was thus a treaty contracted specially for each named colony.

The system of imperial preference was long regarded as outside the ordinary rules of most-favored-nation preference. Therefore, it has been considered that a foreign nation with a most-favored-nation agreement with the United Kingdom could not in virtue of it claim the same tariff privileges as Ghana. So long as uniformity of tariff policy was a feature of organic Commonwealth unity, the understanding that this was a matter of domestic concern could be defended, but once the members began raising tariffs *inter se*, the danger of outside states attempting to claim equal privileges increased, and was only warded off by a particular application of the *inter se* doctrine. Since this may now be taken to have disappeared, the exclusion of Commonwealth preference from the system of most-favored-nation preference has been rationalized on the quite different argument that the Commonwealth is a customs union, the Ottawa Agreement constituting its charter, and that customs unions are outside the scope of most-favored-nation clause operation.[51] That the argument was not made confidently may be gathered from the fact that in her commercial agreement entered into after the Ottawa Conference in 1932, the United Kingdom specifically excluded from the operation of the clause any agreements made between territories under the sovereignty of the Crown. The intriguing thought now arises that the other parties to these treaties may claim the same privileges as are accorded those countries of the Commonwealth that have become republics. Indirectly, then, state succession may have stimulated quite unexpected patterns of treaty operation.

Disputes between Members of the Commonwealth

The declarations submitted by members under the Optional Clause, with two exceptions, still reserve disputes *inter se* from the jurisdicion of the International Court of Justice, but the Court has been given jurisdiction *inter se* in many treaties operating *inter se*. The reason why this reservation is persisted in is to exclude the jurisdiction over those understandings that lie at the heart of Commonwealth cooperation, and that are never intended to be the subject of rules of law. The jurisdiction of the other organs of the United Nations cannot be ousted *inter se*, as the Kashmir dispute demonstrates.[52]

However, the most interesting area for state-succession study is that of the fate of claims upon independence of colonial territories, and the relevance of a continued common British nationality. The United Kingdom Nationality Act of 1948 [53] aims at preserving the common status of British subjects by means of the "common clause," which provides that persons defined as citizens of another Commonwealth country shall be recognized by the enacting country as having the status of British subjects or Commonwealth citizens. The clause has not been enacted uniformly by all Common-

Independence and Problems of State Succession

wealth countries, but the net result of all the legislative devices employed is that no citizen of one Commonwealth member is to be classed as an alien by another. Actually, this is meaningful only so long as aliens are the only persons to suffer legal disabilities, but since the right to reside, vote, or hold public office is coming increasingly to depend upon citizenship and not British nationality, it is clear that the pre-eminent distinction is between citizenship and noncitizenship, and not between nationality and alienage. Allegiance remains as a consequence and not an occasion of both citizenship and nationality, with implications concerning the allegiance of British subjects to a Commonwealth country of which they are not citizens.

From an international-law point of view the shift in emphasis from British subject to citizen is significant, for it could be that the bond of association that for international purposes is defined as nationality is citizenship, and not British nationality in its domestic sense. It is significant that the Act of 1948 disclaims jurisdiction over British subjects or Irish citizens who are not United Kingdom citizens, in respect of acts performed extraterritorially, except where it would lie over aliens.[54] The New Zealand, Australian, and Southern Rhodesian acts have similar provisions. The implications are contradictory, for while in matters of extraterritorial jurisdiction noncitizens are equated with aliens, it seems that in matters of intraterritorial jurisdiction they are in respect nonaliens. The 1948 Act in fact has been held to perpetuate in England not only the benefits of British nationality previously enjoyed by Irish citizens but also its burdens, including liability to conscription.[55]

This resulted from a literal interpretation of the section that provided that any law in force at the date of the Act would continue to affect Irish citizens.[56] In the case of citizens of member countries of the Commonwealth, the same result seems to be arrived at, at least where relevant statutes are not construed to the contrary. All British subjects ordinarily resident in the United Kingdom are liable to conscription, and though the international-law rules on conscription of nonnationals are not clear, the fact that conscripts are obliged to take an oath of allegiance to the Crown of the United Kingdom is significant in ascertaining the international implications of nonalienage. It is not unreasonable to argue that for jurisdictional purposes British subjects who are not citizens may be treated as if they were citizens. The argument is maintained by reference to the facility with which citizenship is interchangeable. It is to be noticed that Ireland is prepared to grant citizenship to persons of Irish descent who have no other connection with the country, and that persons availing themselves of this privilege may at the same time retain United Kingdom or New Zealand citizenship.

The results of the argument could, however, be startling. Suppose a United Kingdom citizen has his property confiscated by Ghana. Would a claim by the United Kingdom be met with the argument that between members of the Commonwealth claims do not lie, or that the person affected was not an alien in the eyes of international law and thus not protected by international law? Considering the real political and social separation of the United Kingdom and Ghana, such a conclusion would be disturbing. Yet if it be rejected, it may be difficult to sustain the view that one member of the Commonwealth may diplomatically protect the citizens of another. Until World War II the United Kingdom not only made its diplomatic facilities available to Australians, for example, but was prepared to represent them internationally as it represented a resident of the Irish Free State against Panama. At the time, however, citizenship within the Commonwealth had not been devised, and though the Dominions were international persons, it could be contended that the mother country, as the fountainhead of British nationality, could represent them diplomatically. Also, the practice at the time perhaps owed much to the unitary concept of the Crown, which was a corollary of the concept of a united Empire. Theory, and to some extent practice, has now altered. A British consulate, for example, will not register the birth of a New Zealand citizen even when no New Zealand agency is available. There is, therefore, some argument in favor of the view that only the country of citizenship may extend diplomatic protection.

And yet this conclusion also has its unrealistic aspects, at least so far as citizens of the "European" Members of the Commonwealth are concerned, for migration among them is frequent, and the social bond of attachment is often more with the country of residence than with the country of nominal citizenship. If the argument that only the country of citizenship may protect diplomatically is pursued to its conclusion, it could result, through the operation of the rule of continuous nationality (if there is such a rule) in the conclusion that a person who avails himself of the simple procedure of change of citizenship after he becomes vested with an international claim will lack any country competent to pursue it. A person who changed his citizenship from United Kingdom to Nigerian could find himself in this position, which the designers

Independence and Problems of State Succession 39

of multicitizenship could scarcely have contemplated. The anomaly becomes even more obvious if one examines some of the categories of persons who avoid this fate. Certain persons remain British subjects but not citizens of any member state under interim provisions of the 1948 Act.[57] Others are British-protected persons on the most technical of grounds, with far less social bond of attachment to the United Kingdom than New Zealanders resident in London.[58] Clearly the United Kingdom may represent them internationally.

A different attitude to the problem may be expected from a New Zealander, with his more intimate sense of the British connection, than from a Pakistani or even a Canadian, yet it is difficult to distinguish between the Commonwealth members as a matter of logic. Perhaps a distinction is possible between the monarchies linked in a personal union and the republics, and though the doctrine of the divisibility of the Crown imposes some obstacles, the distinction is supported by the bond the union manifests, a bond at once sociological and juridical. The analogy with Austria-Hungary, which, despite a measure of international personality in its two Kingdoms, was one entity for nationality purposes, is unhelpful because it is a case of real union, whereas the Commonwealth monarchies exhibit the characteristics of a personal union. The pre-eminent consideration, however, is that international law does not rigidly insist upon citizenship as a precondition of international nationality, but only upon a claim to subjection that is ordinarily but not necessarily formulated as domestic nationality.[59] Such a claim is clearly made by all the members of the Commonwealth with respect to each other's citizens. Whether the United Kingdom is prepared to represent a New Zealander internationally will be a matter of discretion, and one may well anticipate reluctance to do so. But it by no means follows that the United Kingdom is disbarred. A sufficient social link exists between a New Zealander and the United Kingdom where he is resident to sustain a claim to nationality internationally, and common British nationality is its formal aspect. Pursued to its end, this argument disposes of the problem of continuous nationality for litigation purposes.

Should it be admitted that one Commonwealth member may represent the citizens of another, the argument must then return to the problem of one Commonwealth country pursuing a claim against another. Is this possibility excluded by the implications of non-alienage? The case of Ireland is perhaps the clearest with which to test the problem. It is not very difficult to suppose that Ireland could represent a citizen against the United Kingdom, although that citizen was for domestic purposes treated as a British subject. Wherein could a distinction be drawn in the case of Commonwealth members—on the ground of their membership, or on the ground of the "common clause"? Since membership of the Commonwealth seems to involve no noticeably tighter legal links than exist between Ireland and the United Kingdom, it may be concluded that it is irrelevant to the point. As for the problem of common status as a British subject, this would seem to be disposed of by the rules concerning litigation between two states that both regard the claimant as their national. If an offended resident of Ghana seeks the protection of the United Kingdom Foreign Office, it would seem correct to ask with which of the two countries he has had the more effective connection. This approach allows for the possibility of claims between Commonwealth members without detracting from the significance attachable to common British nationality.

There must come a point, however, when international law frowns on reciprocal nationality for jurisdictional and representational purposes. The case of South Africa's withdrawal from the Commonwealth raises the issue. Until amendment of the British Nationality Act, the withdrawal would have no effect on the status in the United Kingdom of South Africa's citizens as British subjects, though in South Africa, because of the drafting of its "common clause," all Commonwealth citizens became aliens. The result is that for jurisdictional purposes South Africans remained non-aliens in the United Kingdom although South Africa became as much a foreign country as the United States. Wherein does the social bond of attachment referred to in the *Nottebohm* decision lie?[60]

VI. Conclusions

The object of this paper has been to explore realistically the relevant doctrines of state succession in their application to the recent cases of colonial independence. Serious doubts have been cast upon the cogency of these doctrines, and the exception traditionally admitted of continuity of local obligations seems to have become the norm, or is in process of doing so. It remains for the jurists to reflect the pressures in this direction and not retard them.

It has become obvious that concrete problems are to be solved much more by techniques of construction than by resort to abstract principles, and a study of state succession that does not emphasize the devious and technical inquiries that must be made through the processes of municipal law is unrealistic. Far more attention has been paid in this paper to problems of imperial constitutional law than to international law, for appreciation of the problem is a matter of constitutional law, which thus forms the backdrop to the operation of rules of international law. The inquiry is made possible because the author has some experience in this field of imperial constitutional law, and the lesson is that similar detailed inquiries must be made by people with technical knowledge of French, Italian, Belgian, and Dutch law before a complete structure of the contemporary law of state succession can possibly be erected. This endeavor will be a notable contribution to the legal and political education of the new states.

2. MILITARY SERVITUDES AND THE NEW NATIONS

BY ALBERT J. ESGAIN

The recent emancipation of numerous subject territories whose culture and institutions are alien to those of Western civilization has given rise to myriad complex legal and political problems.[1] The emergence of these territories as new states has intensified efforts of both East and West to extend to them their political ideologies. For this purpose, certain states have sought to establish themselves physically within the territory of the new states. In some instances these states have sought to accomplish their ends by infiltrating political agents and military personnel into the new states,[2] or by the conclusion of agreements that would permit them, for one purpose or another, permanently or for a term of years, either to station troops within, or otherwise to use the territory of, the new states for their military aims.[3]

The desire to achieve such particular political and military objectives has revived among scholars and publicists interest in, and support for, the concept of servitudes of international law generally, and military servitudes in particular[4]—a concept long ago jettisoned by many scholars as fallacious because there existed no evidence that it had ever been recognized or substantiated by international practice.

It was natural that the emancipation of subject territories in unprecedented numbers would give new importance and significance to the concept of servitudes of international law. If the recognition of servitudes in the practice of states could be substantiated, the emancipating states could, by concluding appropriate conventional arrangements with the newly emancipated states, retain a preferential status and some—or perhaps even all—of their prior prerogatives, including the continued use for their own purposes of the territory of the emancipated state. Furthermore, under this concept, states that had enjoyed certain rights in subject territories prior to their emancipation, under treaties concluded with the

Military Servitudes and the New Nations

emancipating states, would legally be entitled to assert the continuation of such rights against the emancipated states themselves. The emergence of an independent Morocco and the British grant of independence to several colonies in the West Indies have provided recent and significant instances in which the contentious doctrine of military servitudes of international law has been put to the test of state practice.[5]

Our purpose in this study is to determine whether the recent practice of states recognizes the doctrine of military servitudes either as it has traditionally been defined or as it has more recently been redefined.[6] The characteristics that have been attributed to military servitudes will therefore be considered in some detail, and the instances in state practice that are alleged to constitute recognition of such servitudes will be examined.

I. THE DOCTRINE OF INTERNATIONAL SERVITUDES

An international servitude has been defined as an "exceptional restriction made by treaty on the territorial supremacy of a State by which a part or the whole of its territory is in a limited way made perpetually to serve a certain purpose or interest of another State." [7]

There is no concept of international law that is less understood or more contentious than that of international servitudes.[8] It has been stated that:

> The "servitude" of international law is the scapegoat of international jurisprudence. There is hardly any other concept or doctrine of international law which has suffered such contemptuous criticism and blunt rejection, and at the same time enjoyed such unsubstantiated approval and wanton praise. It has been accused of being the obsolete vestige of medieval, patrimonial, feudal and—last but not least— Roman law. It has been attacked as being the hybrid product of a servile adaptation of private law concepts, it has been indicated as being a superfluous and artificial construction, apt to deform international law and to introduce the utmost confusion therein. It has been dealt even the deadliest blow which can be given to any scientific conception. . . . Its existence has been denied.[9]

Those who espouse this concept of servitudes of international law maintain that it constitutes in theory and practice an important and distinct category of legal relationships governed by special rules that differ materially from those applicable to conventional arrangements generally.[10] They allege that resort to the concept fosters the sovereignty, security, and general welfare of states and that it provides the environment and the legal stability required for the proper functioning of an interdependent community of nations.[11]

Those who deny[12] the existence of servitudes of international law maintain that these are in fact nothing more than normal, conventional restrictions of territorial sovereignty that are personal in nature[13] and governed by precisely the same rules that are applicable to international conventions generally. They deny that the concept of international servitudes has been recognized by the practice of states, and they maintain that its recognition would not only frustrate the attainment of results that are acceptable in the practice of states but would be incompatible with the best interests of the international community.[14]

These contentions indicate that any attempt to determine whether military servitudes are recognized in international law[15] must be predicated upon a critical analysis and evaluation of the concept of international servitudes; of treaty relationships that have been characterized as international servitudes; and of the pertinent decisions of international jurists, arbitral tribunals, and international courts.

The definition of international servitudes that is utilized for the purpose of this study[16] is the one generally recognized by the proponents of the doctrine of servitudes as being accurate. International servitudes may be categorized according to their subject matter or objective, e.g., economic, commercial, political, or military. These categorizations are indistinct, not mutually exclusive, and, in some respects, descriptive only. Writers have not categorized the same instances of so-called servitudes similarly, due in part to their zeal to substantiate or deny their existence. This paper will focus upon military servitudes, which may be properly defined as restrictions imposed by conventional arrangements on the territorial supremacy of a state by which a part or the whole of its territory is in a limited manner made perpetually to serve a certain military purpose or interest of another state. These so-called servitudes of international law may, in turn, be classified according to their nature (arising from either bilateral or multilateral agreements concluded voluntarily[17] or involuntarily[18]), their form (either positive[19] or negative[20]), and the benefit they serve (either that of the dominant or the servient state or of both).

Although much has been written about international servitudes and their characteristics, only one author has given favorable and particular consideration to military servitudes of international law.[21] At least one exponent[22] of international servitudes, however,

Military Servitudes and the New Nations 45

has expressly denied the existence of military servitudes. Other exponents have expressed doubt as to the propriety of applying the term "international servitudes" to relationships other than those economic in character.[23] Those who deny the existence of international servitudes have, of course, had no reason to differentiate between them.

It should be noted that the legal principles advanced in this consideration of military servitudes of international law are those applicable to all servitudes of international law. As such, the general conclusions reached would also be generally applicable to other types of international servitudes.[24]

Reid has summarized the characteristics and principles of international servitudes, as espoused by their proponents as follows:

> On the basis of reason and authority [apparently the holding of the Arbitral Tribunal in the *North Atlantic Fisheries* case between the United States and Great Britain in 1910] we may say that an international servitude is a real right, whereby the territory of one state is made liable to permanent use by another state, for some specific purpose. The servitude may be permissive or restrictive, but does not involve any obligation upon either party to take positive action. It establishes a permanent legal relationship of territory to territory, unaffected by change of sovereignty in either of them, and terminates only by mutual consent, by renunciation on the part of the dominant state or by consolidation of the territories affected.[25]

Under this concept sovereign nations can, by conventional arrangements, establish "real" or absolute rights that, being permanently attached to the land, forever bind not only the contracting states but all states. These rights, once established, are not terminated by a substitution of sovereigns and are not subject to unilateral denunciation by the servient state or its successor under the *clausula rebus sic stantibus*—a principle of international law that is recognized by many as being available to states by an implied provision of all conventions.[26]

The proponents of international servitudes suggest that since the elements and fundamental principles of these servitudes are substantially similar to those of servitudes of private law, and are applicable to similar relationships, the private-law terminology may, by analogy, legitimately be applied to international relationships.[27] Such individuals aspire, by using the term "servitudes," to endow the treaty rights and obligations they so designate with a sanctity greater than that which they would otherwise enjoy, and seek thereby to immunize certain rights and obligations from the general existing legal exemptions and qualifications regarding the binding force and effect of treaty provisions.

Those who deny the doctrine maintain that no conventional arrangement is subject to such particular principles, and that the use of the term "servitude" is improper, misleading, and confusing.[28]

Váli, in a recent study [29] of rights in foreign territory, has attempted to establish the general existence of servitudes of international law, and the existence of military servitudes in particular. In his efforts to establish the recognition of servitudes in state practice, he materially modifies the essential characteristics of the traditional concept. He justifies his modifications by asserting that no consensus exists among writers as to the "real meaning" or "extent" of the concept and its characteristics.[30]

For Váli's purpose, servitudes of international law are conventional arrangements, either temporary or permanent in duration,[31] that create rights and obligations, which, being directly attached to a specific portion of a state's territory,[32] create rights that are "available against the world at large"[33] and obligations that bind all states that succeed to the encumbered territory,[34] whether the succession be by conquest, or otherwise. In his discussion, however, Váli in effect denies that the rights created by international servitudes, (in contradistinction to the obligations) descend by operation of law to the successor of grantee states. He asserts that "as to the descent of the right, no clear statement is available amongst the writers, and owing to the absence of a definable *praedium dominans* it would be difficult to see [by analogy to private-law servitudes] how the right could be localized on the part of the grantee State." [35] As to the applicability of the *clausula rebus sic stantibus* to servitudes of international law, Váli states that "there is no precedent up to now which would support the permissibility of the unilateral denunciation of a right in foreign territory in the case of intervening territorial changes of a nature to frustrate the original *raison d'être* of the concession." [36] He is of the further opinion that should the *clausula* eventually be recognized by the practice of states "as a permissible means of terminating treaties," it would "not be possible to establish a general rule for its application which would close the door to possible abuse." [37] It is Váli's view, contrary to that of other exponents of international servitudes, that servitudes are rendered inoperative during a war between a grantor and a grantee state.[38] But he believes, as do the other exponents of international servitudes, that servitudes "are generally not annulled by a supervening war be-

Military Servitudes and the New Nations   47

tween the parties."[39] On the issue of whether a neutral state burdened with a servitude may, during a war between the grantee state and a third state, continue to fulfill obligations "which offer great military advantage to the grantee State,"[40] Váli's view is that the practice of states provides no definite answer.[41]

The attributes of Váli's concept of international servitudes bear little substantive resemblance to those of the traditional concept generally approved by the proponents of international servitudes. Under Váli's concept, a servitude need not be in perpetuity, but may be created for a period of years only. This, of course, is a very significant expansion of the traditional concept that requires that the rights and obligations of servitudes be in perpetuity. Váli's broadened concept might apply to practically all conventional arrangements in which land is involved. Furthermore, under Váli's concept, (1) the obligations—but not the rights—established by servitudes descend to successor states; (2) servitudes would be terminable under the *clausula rebus sic stantibus* should the *clausula* eventually be recognized by the practice of states (Váli's position on this matter is difficult to comprehend for he considers a servitude to be dispositive); and (3) military servitudes remain operative during wars between the dominant state and a power other than the servient state.

An analysis of Váli's concept of international servitudes indicates that his ultimate goal is to extend to all conventional relationships concerned with the utilization of the land of one state by another state a greater sanctity than that extended by the practice of states to conventional arrangements concerned with matters unrelated to land and its use. It is submitted that the practice of states has never recognized the particular sanctity or the quasi-dispositive effect that Váli seeks for conventional arrangements concerned with the temporary use of land.

The consequences of international conventions depend on whether they are construed as establishing "real" rights (servitudes) or personal obligations. If a convention is interpreted as creating a servitude, the rights and obligations created are perpetual and invariable. If it be not so interpreted, it establishes personal rights and obligations that bind only the contracting parties for the period of time specified by the convention and that may be unilaterally denounced under the *clausula rebus sic stantibus*.[42]

Logically, it would appear that the use of the term "military servitudes of international law" would be justified only if it served to designate, in situations analogous to those of private law, the rights, obligations, and principles applied to private-law "servitudes."[43] The appropriateness of such terminology for international law should therefore be considered in the light of the history and development of the private-law servitude.

II. HISTORY AND DEVELOPMENT OF THE PRIVATE-LAW SERVITUDE

The Servitude of the Roman Law

During the classical period of Roman law, ownership was considered to be an accumulation of rights—for example, the right of user and the right of enjoyment—any one of which could be detached and vested in another person without any impairment of the superior right of the owner.[44] These rights, *jura in re aliena*, were divided into two groups: *Praedial*, or real, servitudes, and personal servitudes.[45] *Praedial* servitudes were specific rights perpetually [46] attached to land by which the owner thereof was entitled to some advantages from, or to a certain use of, adjacent or neighboring land owned by another. This right was enforceable against anyone for all time.[47] Consequently, third parties who acquired either the dominant or the servient land, whether by descent or purchase, took those lands subject to all the benefits or restrictions that applied to the land under the previous owner. A *praedial* servitude, a *jure in rem*, was thus a perpetual, or "real" and absolute right.[48]

Praedial servitudes could not create obligations requiring positive action.[49] They could only require tolerance or abstention on the part of the servient tenement. Servitudes were classed as being either positive or negative. The former class permitted actual interference with, or activity upon, the servient land—for example, a right of way. The latter permitted no activity on the servient land and required the owner of servient land to abstain only from certain activities on his land—for example, to refrain from erecting a building.[50] *Praedial* servitudes were terminable only by agreement, renunciation by the owner of the dominant tenement, confusion, nonuse, in the case of positive servitudes, destruction of either the dominant or servient *praedium*, or such an alteration in the servient tenement that it was impossible to have a servitude on it.[51] *Praedial* rights were protected and enforced by law, and one in the peaceful enjoyment of a servitude, whether or not entitled, could obtain an interdict against anyone disputing or interfering with his right.[52]

But personal servitudes, on the other hand, although they could relate to land as well as to personal property, attached to an individual personally, and were good only against a specific person or group of persons. These servitudes, *jura in personam*, could legally be granted to an individual for life only and, as such, were personal rights that terminated upon the death of the possessor.[53]

The Servitude of the German Public Law

The servitude of the Roman law [54] passed into the public (constitutional) law of the old German empire. During this period the first known use of the word "servitude" in relationships under the public law occurred. It appeared in a treaty of the year 1281 between the Knight of Lichtenstein and the free city of Speyer:

> I, John, Knight of Lichtenstein, in my castle known as Knopfsberg, one-half of which I obtained from H., Knight of Hohenecke, institute this right of servitude in favor of the magistrates and citizens of Speyer namely that they shall have the right of entering my castle aforesaid and of issuing thence with armed men, of fighting whomsoever they wish or as often as they may wish from the fortifications of this my castle aforesaid with any enemies of theirs whatsoever without distinction of persons and of taking the spoils of the enemy to the castle aforesaid and of doing all other things that may to them seem expedient against their enemies and foes. . . .[55]

The development of the concept of servitudes in German public law in the eighteenth century was fostered to compensate for the theoretical character of the power of the German emperor. The real power during this period was dispersed among more than 300 member states,[56] mostly small principalities and city states that also lacked effective power because their territory was not contiguous. Even the larger of these member states possessed only small and widely separated parcels of land.[57] The existence of the member states therefore depended on mutual assistance in both peace and war. Under these circumstances, matters of common interest among the various member states—such as access to the sea, and rights of passage and pasturage—required regulation. Eventually, the regulation of the relationships gave rise to rights resembling in some respects the servitude of private law. It was thus natural for the jurists of the period to resort to the analogy of the Roman-law servitude in developing rules applicable to relationships among the various states of the German Empire.[58]

It is easy to comprehend why, during this primitive period of juridical science dominated by private-law concepts, the principles of private-law servitude were applied with little or no change to public rights. In the various subdivisions of the German empire, the sovereign was in most instances the largest, and in some instances the only, landowner. As such, he was considered as having a *dominium*, an ownership of the land over which he ruled, which, though not identical to that of the private law, was somewhat analogous to it. On this basis it was possible to consider that rights acquired by sovereigns in and over each other's lands constituted rights that attached to the land itself.[59] Consequently, rights available to a sovereign within the territory of another sovereign, during this period, whether concerned with land or commercial activities, were almost without exception classed as servitudes.[60] The analogy between servitudes of private law and "real" servitudes in public law, originally one of nomenclature only, was soon extended to embrace the classifications and the essential characteristics of the Roman-law servitude,[61] and, eventually, even to an acknowledgment of the "real" or absolute character of these public-law servitudes.[62] The term servitude, carried over from the domain of private law into German law,[63] was then transmitted to the law of nations, where its existence continues to be a matter of controversy.

III. THE DOCTRINE OF MILITARY SERVITUDES OF INTERNATIONAL LAW

The principles, the characteristics, and the consequences of the private-law servitudes are such that the use in international law of the term military servitudes cannot be substantiated by analogy to them.[64] The term "military servitudes" is truly a misnomer.[65]

Lauterpacht, an ardent exponent of international servitudes, in effect concedes this point by his qualified statement that:

> . . . international lawyers . . . [should] exercise a greater . . . restraint in classifying as servitudes different restrictions of sovereignty, preferably to . . . recognising as servitudes *only economic or quasi-economic* restrictions of territorial sovereignty. . . . Thus it may be doubted whether the widely adopted class of military servitudes, especially the negative ones admits of any analogy to servitudes of private law or whether it can be defined at all with any approach to exactitude. . . .
> Here, as in many other cases, conceptions of private law prove to be vicious and misleading only if resorted to for purposes of metaphor or when made to support certain debatable political assertions. [italics added] [66]

Váli, on the other hand, although denying an analogy between the concept of servitudes in private and in international law,[67] be-

Military Servitudes and the New Nations

lieves that it would be "totally illogical to argue that a legal concept is wrong or non-existent because its name is a bad one or bears a different meaning in another branch of law. . . . If the concept itself is good and conforms to law, it exists, even if its name is entirely wrong and misleading. . . ."[68] In his view, the question whether there are international servitudes, and whether they constitute rights analogous to the rights *in rem* of private law, is independent of the special real character that is attributed to institutions of private law.[69] He states "that international servitudes, if they are to be regarded as an independent concept, must necessarily possess a character different from other 'conventional relations' and the difference must be 'essential' and not 'artificial'."[70] He believes that the concept of international servitudes possesses this special, and essentially different, character, and he specifies that his reason "for separating international servitudes from other legal relations is their territorial, 'real' character"[71]: the fact that the obligations created by servitudes relate to land only; that they are "attached to certain territory within a foreign State," and that they are "absolute," that is, available against the world at large.[72]

On examination, the special character Váli attributes to international servitudes will be seen to be purely illusory, for conventional arrangements characterized as being purely personal in nature can also relate to land and, for the period of time specified in such conventions, these are likewise "good against the world at large" for very much the same purposes and in the same sense as that for which Váli uses this terminology, for he states that the "mere descent or the way of the descent" of the rights and obligations of international servitudes "cannot rightly be made the only criterion of the existence or justification of the concept, although, as actually happens, exceptional rules may follow from the territorial character of the relationship."[73] The *Principium Individuationis* of Váli's concept of international servitudes is not, as he alleges, the territorial character of the rights and obligations created thereby, and their effectiveness against the world at large, but the alleged invulnerability of these rights to changes in sovereignty over the territory of the servient state, and the inapplicability of the *clausula rebus sic stantibus* to such rights: the very characteristics that the traditional concept attributes to international servitudes. Váli's definition of international servitudes, therefore, contains no new, different, or essential characteristics that would warrant its recognition as a separate concept. In truth, Váli's proposed concept is dependent upon and predicated upon exactly the same "touchstone" as the traditional concept of international servitudes: the alleged descent by operation of law of the obligations of international servitudes upon states that succeed to servient land, no matter how the succession takes place.

As regards the permissibility of analogy between private-law servitudes and those that are alleged by the traditionalists to exist in the practice of states, it has been argued, persuasively, that the juridical construction of international servitudes is logically impossible, as "real rights" relate to *dominium* only—not to *imperium*, and that states possess only the latter.[74] As one author puts it:

> As long as sovereignty over territory was thought to be suitably expressed as the "proprietary right" of the State it could be regarded as perfectly logical to call rights in foreign territory "servitudes" following the private law nomenclature, but without being compelled . . . to adopt its substantive rules. Calling territorial sovereignty "property" has—rightly or wrongly—been abandoned nowadays and the appellation has been replaced by other terms. The logic of terminology requires a certain proportion and appropriateness of the various terms. If the term "property" has been successfully dropped in international law and at the same time the term "servitude" has not . . . it cannot be doubted that there is a certain discrepancy in phraseology which, if not misleading, is surely embarrassing. From this point of view the name "servitude" in international law is a misnomer.
>
> Even the argument of analogy between the concept of servitudes in private and in international law cannot obtain against these reasons of unsuitability.[75]

More specifically, the term military servitudes of international law implies that similar juridical relationships existed or could have been established under private law, and that their fundamental elements and characteristics are substantively identical to those of the private-law servitude. Such an implication is, of course, erroneous, for military servitudes were unknown in private law. Furthermore, the private law governed internal relationships only, and these relationships were forcibly controlled by superior authority that recognized neither title to nor any other interest in property that has been acquired by force or coercion.[76] The object of the private-law servitude was to protect peaceful pursuits and to foster voluntary relationships, so that the property of some, more marginal than that of others, would in the general interest of the community be rendered more valuable. International law, to the contrary, applies to external relationships that are not subject to superior authority, and it recognizes title to, and other interests in, property that is acquired by conquest, subjugation, and coercion [77]—even those that may be contrary to the general interests and security of the community of nations.[78] In fact international law "disregards the effect of coercion in the conclusion of a treaty imposed by the victor upon the vanquished. . . ."[79]

Although the term "military servitudes" is technically a misnomer, its use in international law might nevertheless be warranted if it could be established that the practice of states recognizes rights and obligations that reflect the essential legal characteristics of the rights and obligations of private-law servitudes.[80] As previously stated, international servitudes are territorial rights and obligations [81] established by conventional arrangements between sovereign states.[82] If the following essential characteristics attributed by doctrine to international servitudes could be established, the use of the term international servitudes would be sufficiently justified, and its use in international law appropriate: (1) the creation of perpetual territorial rights and obligations that survive changes in sovereignty over both the dominant and servient territory, and (2) the creation of rights and obligations that are not terminable because of vital changes in circumstances, or by a war between the dominant and the servient states, or by a war between the dominant state and a third state.

IV. Significant Aspects of the Problem of International Servitudes

General Restrictions Imposed by Customary International Law

It is worthy of note that general restrictions upon the territorial sovereignty of states, being restrictions imposed by customary, and not conventional, international law, are binding upon all states alike, because of their membership in the community of nations. The binding effect of these general restrictions, therefore, may not properly be considered as servitudes of international law, for their binding effect is not attributable to the "real" or absolute character of treaty obligations. Particular restrictions upon territorial supremacy, on the other hand, arise out of conventions that impose restrictions that are peculiar to the contracting states and, as a general rule, binding only upon the contracting states.

Conventions Binding Noncontracting States

The creation by convention of rights and obligations that are allegedly binding on noncontracting nations defines a significant aspect of the problem of international servitudes. Under generally accepted legal principles, treaties can neither bestow enforceable rights nor impose liabilities upon third states (*Pacta tertiis nec nocent nec prosunt*).[83] Even treaties the purpose of which is in part to establish rights for the benefit of "all nations" do not thereby confer benefits or impose obligations upon third states.[84] It has been asserted, however, that this latter principle has certain qualifications, that, although recognized, are not yet well defined. McNair[85] asserts that "two classes of treaties have a law-creating effect beyond the immediate parties to them." The first consists of "treaties which form part of an international settlement," for example, World War I peace treaties; the second consists of "treaties which regulate the dedication to the world of some new facility for transit or transportation," for example, the right of world navigation upon a river formerly closed.

In support of his contention, he quotes Roxburgh:

> It frequently happens that a treaty becomes the basis of a rule of customary law, because all the states which are concerned in its stipulation have come to conform habitually with them under the *conviction* that they are legally bound to do so. In this case third states acquire rights and incur obligations which were originally conferred and imposed by treaty but which have come to be conferred and imposed by a rule of law.[86] [italics added]

Although a "conviction" by third states that such a treaty legally binds them is a matter of proof that is difficult, if not impossible, to establish when the imposition of burdens is involved, it is said that this "conviction" is to be presumed for treaties designated as international settlements.[87] But it is more probable that it is not the implied "conviction" of third states that gives these treaties whatever binding effect they may have upon noncontracting States, but rather the preponderant strength of the signatory states, which third states cannot successfully challenge, or which they decline to challenge because of the risk of combat, adverse public opinion, political repercussions, or economic retaliation.[88]

Some proponents of international servitudes designate military and economic restrictions upon territory that are intended to accomplish a "territorial settlement" as international servitudes. Oppenheim, for example, in discussing treaties of international settlement, states: "It is particularly in connection with those treaty restrictions upon the use of State territory, which many writers (including the author . . .) call 'servitudes,' that parties other than parties of the original treaty are likely to acquire an interest in their preservation." [89]

Even if it were to be conceded that "lawmaking" treaties that establish an international regime or status in the general interest of the community of nations have, for reasons mentioned above, some binding effect upon third states, they could not on that basis properly be characterized as international servitudes. In contradistinction to private-law servitudes, a "lawmaking" treaty is allegedly binding upon parties that are not signatories, beneficiaries thereof need not be specified, its signatories are bound by its provisions even though they may not have voluntarily consented to them, and its alleged binding effect is not derived from, nor protected by, the prerogative of superior authority.[90] Such a treaty is subject to denunciation under the *clausula rebus sic stantibus*.

Real or Absolute Rights and Obligations

It is asserted that the rights and obligations of international servitudes are perpetually attached to the territory itself and, as such, are good against the world for all time.[91] Since these rights and obligations are allegedly "real" or absolute, all third states that acquire servient lands, whether by purchase, conquest, or otherwise, would necessarily take such lands subject to all the restrictions or benefits that existed thereon under previous sovereigns. Oppenheim takes this position. He states: "Since State servitudes ... are rights inherent in the object with which they are connected (rights *in rem*), they remain valid and may be exercised however the ownership of the territory to which they apply may change. Therefore, if, after the creation of a State servitude, the part of the territory affected comes by subjugation or cession under the territorial supremacy of another State, such servitude remains in force." [92]

Lauterpacht is of the opinion that "the classification as servitudes carries with it all the implications of a real right; the term itself would otherwise serve no useful purpose." [93]

O'Connell considers treaties that are alleged to create real rights, including those that are alleged to have created military servitudes, to be dispositive, and that the restrictions that are imposed by such treaties "constitute equitable property in the beneficiary State." Treaties of this nature are, in his view, "conveyances" under which the state that accepts "the dispositive obligations possesses for the future no more than the conveyance assigned to it, and a Power which subsequently succeeds in sovereignty to the area in question can take over only what its predecessor possessed. This basis of the restrictions imposed on the territory is therefore not destroyed by the change of sovereignty, or even by lapse of the treaty." [94]

The dispositive character that Oppenheim and certain other proponents of international servitudes have attributed to treaties is fallacious and illusory, for they consider them to be concluded subject to the *rebus sic stantibus* rule.[95] O'Connell believes that the distinction between "personal" and "dispositive" treaties is virtually irrelevant save in form between state succession and governmental succession and that in most instances burdensome treaties can be got rid of quite conveniently by the ordinary processes of treaty law.[96] Logically, it would appear that the term "dispositive" is proper for application only to treaties that effect a full transfer of real property, and that the real rights that are allegedly created by treaties are nothing more than concessions that are made in the grantor's best interest and sustained by his own will.[97] As Judge Huber put it in the decision of the arbitral tribunal in the *Island of Palmas Case*:

> Sovereignty in the relation between States signifies independence. Independence in regard to a portion of the globe is the right to exercise therein, to the exclusion of any other State, the functions of Government. The development of the national organization of States during the last few centuries and, as a corollary, the development of international law, has established this principle of the exclusive competence of the State in regard to its own territory in such a way as to make it the point of departure in settling most questions that concern international relations.[98]

Lord McNair, in "So-Called State Servitudes," submits that "the main object of the champions of state servitude in asserting that doctrine is . . . to establish for the territorial restrictions to which they give that name a sphere of operation wider than they would receive as treaty obligations of a personal character governed by the maxim *pacta tertiis*. . . . In fact, the object is to make them bind third parties into whose hands the so-called dominant or servient territories may come." [99] Under this view, third states would of course succeed to the "real" rights of their predecessors to the same extent that such rights were transferred to individuals who took dominant tenements under private law.[100]

This statement places in perspective the most important of the three controlling considerations that have motivated those who seek the recognition of military servitudes in international law. The other two considerations reflect a desire to preclude the unilateral

Military Servitudes and the New Nations 57

denunciation of so-called real rights and obligations because of vital changes in circumstances, and to render the law of neutrality inapplicable to lands that are utilized by a dominant state in time of war between it and a state other than the servient state. There are no other benefits of any particular significance that could be derived from the doctrine of international servitudes that could not also be attained by treaties of a personal nature.

It is submitted that so-called international servitudes establish relationships that are dependent upon the identity of the parties and are binding on third states only upon their consent.[101] As Keith puts it:

> A servitude, though in a sense a right *in rem* yet essentially involves a relation of one state to some other state or states which must be of a contractual character. . . . On the theory of singular succession it must be held that the substitution of the new power causes the quasi-contractual relation to cease, and if the relation is renewed it is a new quasi-contract and not a continuance of the old.[102]

A consideration of the consequences that would result in the case of so-called military servitudes should the theory of universal succession[103] be considered applicable clearly confirms its inapplicability. Consider the situation of a state that is the beneficiary of a so-called military servitude under which it is permitted to have a garrisoned base upon the territory of another state, and assume further that the servient territory is lawfully conquered by a state hostile to the state in whose favor the military servitude exists. Could it be held that there exists a rule of law obligating the conquering state to recognize the servitude? It is inconceivable that there could be such a rule, and the practice of states negates its existence.[104] The same conclusion would apply to the situation in which the conquered state is the beneficiary of a positive military servitude upon the territory of a state hostile to the conqueror. Under such circumstances, the servient state could not, in the interest of its own security, permit the conqueror to be subrogated to the rights of the conquered to the use of its territory.[105]

As a practical matter, so-called military servitudes are "too essentially of a contractual nature to be treated in international law as a right *in rem*." [106] Agreements between states that relate to their particular military interests in fact create military alliances: political rights and obligations of a purely personal nature.[107] It cannot be assumed that a grantor state ever intended under conventional arrangements to grant rights that, in the event of a war between the grantee state and a third state in which the grantee state was conquered and annexed, would descend by operation of law to a conquering state hostile to the grantor state. There is no rule of international law that recognizes the descent of rights under these circumstances, even where it can be established that the contracting parties intended such a result and their intent to accomplish this end is expressly set forth in the agreement between them. Such a rule of international law is inconceivable, for it would jeopardize the very objects that it seeks to protect and promote: the peace and security of the international community.[108] International law in fact denies states the bilateral right to contract in a manner that would impose upon third states, no matter how their sovereignty over an alleged servient state might be acquired, obligations or restrictions of a military nature that could jeopardize their security or be contrary to their best interests, or that would require them to assume obligations that are, or could be, incompatible with their obligations under the laws of neutrality or the Charter of the United Nations.

It is very possible that these ramifications of the concept of international servitudes have motivated the various judicial bodies that have considered this concept to refuse either to give it express recognition or to lay down any criteria that would be precise enough to sustain it.[109] International judicial bodies have on four separate occasions passed on rights and obligations that were asserted as servitudes. On all occasions these judicial bodies have refused to give express recognition to the concept. In the *North Atlantic Fisheries Case*,[110] the Permanent Court of Arbitration in 1910 rejected the doctrine of servitudes *in casu* but admitted its possibility. In the *Aaland Islands Case*,[111] the report of a committee of jurists appointed by the Council of the League of Nations in 1921 rejected the doctrine of international servitudes. The committee declared that "the existence of international servitudes, in the true technical sense of the terms, is not generally admitted." But since it chose to rest its opinion on the existence of a rule of "European" law, rather than on an alleged servitude, it did not wholly or definitively disavow the concept of international servitude. In the case of the *S.S. Wimbledon*,[112] the Permanent Court of International Justice in 1923 refrained from considering the matter. In the case of the *Free Zones of Upper Savoy and the District of Gex*,[113] the Permanent Court of International Justice in 1932 refused to commit itself on the question of international servitudes.

These cases were concerned with relationships typical of those that are alleged to constitute international servitudes. In the first case, the question was whether the inhabitants of the United States had an absolute right, pursuant to a treaty of 1818 with Great Britain that employed the word "forever," to fish off the Coast of Newfoundland. In the second case, the question was whether the provision of a multilateral treaty of 1856, demilitarizing the Aaland Islands, was binding upon Finland, then sovereign of the Aaland Islands, although it was not a signatory of the treaty of 1856. In the third case, the question was whether a neutral state, Germany, was bound to permit munitions ships bound for belligerent states to pass through its territorial canal pursuant to the Versailles Treaty, which specified that the canal "shall be maintained free and open to the vessels of commerce and war of all nations at peace with Germany on terms of entire equality." In the fourth case, the question was whether the provisions of a treaty of 1815 establishing a free customs zone between France and Switzerland was a territorial arrangement from which Switzerland, a third party, derived enforceable rights.

The conclusion to be drawn from the decisions in these cases is that the doctrine of international servitudes is so inconsistent, and its implications are so startling and dangerous, that the jurists have refused to give it any express recognition. These decisions, often criticized and interpreted in a manner contrary to the actual holding,[114] were indeed judicious. They were based upon the only principle proper for application in the determination of such matters—the general well-being, the security, and the best interests of the international community—not by recourse to inflexible rules of private law that can serve no useful purpose in international law. The tribunals, cognizant of the implications of the doctrine of servitudes in private law, could not properly have endorsed the doctrine in international law. The question in cases of this nature is not whether a particular treaty establishes a servitude that is binding on third states, but whether the particular rights and obligations in issue are such that the best interests of the international community require that they be so binding, and binding for such time as political interest or economic considerations, whichever be the case, require a binding effect.

The decision of the Supreme Court of Cologne in 1914, in the case of *Aix-la-Chapelle, R.R. Co.* v. *Thewis and the Royal Dutch Government, Intervener*,[115] has often been cited in support of international servitudes. In this case, the owner of dwellings in

Germany damaged by mining operations sued the lessee of the mine, who held his lease from the Dutch Government, owner of the mine pursuant to the provisions of a Prusso-Netherlandish Boundary Treaty of 1816, which specified that: "Neither under pretext of instructions issued to its engineers, nor by imposts or other burdens may . . . Prussia interfere with or restrict the mining of coal or the bringing of the coal mined to the surface, nor may it place any hindrance in . . . its being marketed." [116] The court, in denying the concessionary nature of this right, held that the treaty gave Holland certain sovereign territorial rights: "Because of this fact, a sort of international servitude has arisen by which Holland is . . . entitled . . . in the matter of this mine, to exercise its own legislative authority and police supervision . . . it has real sovereign rights with respect to the object situated within . . . the foreign state." [117]

Under the text of this arrangement, this municipal decision could not, without disregarding the specific language of the treaty provisions, have concluded that the Dutch Government had no sovereign rights in Germany. Therefore, and because no third state was involved, the decision may be considered to hold no more than this: (1) The treaty set up a contractual obligation that expressly precluded Germany from exercising any sovereign rights over the mine, and (2) no vital change in circumstances had occurred to warrant application of the *clausula rebus sic stantibus*.

McNair correctly states that:

> The advocates of this theory [international servitudes] have not made good their contention. To enumerate a list of territorial restrictions and to call them servitudes proves nothing at all. To pick out a very few of them and to point out that in spite of changes of territory they continue to survive and to be recognized as restrictions proves next to nothing, unless it is further shown (a) that this result is purely automatic and happens because the creation of the right confers a fragment of imperium or at least dominium upon the party entitled, and (b) that there are no subsequent treaties between the new parties recognizing or renewing the restrictions other than treaties purely declaratory of the continuance of the restrictions which would survive without them.
>
> A brief analysis of the instances of the permanence of so-called servitudes demonstrates, I submit, that their champions are unable to produce this evidence.
>
> It is believed that most, if not all, of the cases in which a so-called servitude has not been merely asserted by textwriters to have a "real" character but has actually met and successfully survived the test of a

change of sovereignty over the dominant and servient territory can upon analysis be assigned to one of these two classes of treaties [lawmaking treaties which form part of an international settlement and those which regulate the dedication to the world of some new facility for transit or transportation].[118]

The instances that have been advanced to support the "real" character of military servitudes of international law are discussed below. Suffice it to say, a priori, that the instances cited do not support the *de jure* descent of rights and obligations in the practice of states. They indicate that the passing over of treaty rights and obligations occurred either because (1) the convention that established them was essentially equally advantageous to both of the parties concerned and, being so, was tacitly renewed by continued action consistent with the original treaty provisions; or (2) because the rights and obligations of the original convention were expressly adopted by a separate treaty or were otherwise renewed informally; or (3) because the rights and obligations of the original convention were not contested because political or other considerations made it inadvisable for the burdened governments to insist upon their legal rights.

Termination of International Servitudes

One of the three essential characteristics of the concept of "military servitudes"—the continuity of the territorial rights and obligations despite changes in sovereignty over both the dominant and servient territory—has been considered. The other essential characteristics necessary for the justification of the concept are invulnerability of the rights and obligations to the *clausula rebus sic stantibus*, and invulnerability to the laws of neutrality. It has been mentioned that by doctrine, servitudes can only be terminated by agreement, renunciation by the dominant state, or consolidation of the territories concerned. This contention has given rise to two controversial matters: (1) the effect upon a servitude of a war between the dominant and the servient states, or between the dominant state or the servient state and a third state, and (2) the unilateral right of a servient state, under unusual circumstances, to denounce a servitude.

WAR BETWEEN SERVIENT AND DOMINANT STATES

Generally, the supporters of international servitudes allege that the "real" rights created thereby are not extinguished by the outbreak of war between the servient and the dominant state. War, they suggest, may temporarily suspend, but can never terminate, a servitude.[119] Those opposed assert that all conventional relationships are terminated by war except (1) pacts concluded specifically for use in case of war—where war is the condition required to bring them into force and effect, as in treaties on the neutralization of certain portions of the territory belonging to the belligerents, or in treaty provisions on the conduct of warfare or the treatment of prisoners of war, and (2) universal and "lawmaking" treaties that set up an international regime or status[120] in the general interest of the community of nations.

The political nature of military servitudes is evident. It is clear from the practice of states manifested in various treaties of peace that treaties of a political nature are considered either to have been terminated or to have lapsed on the outbreak of war between the parties,[121] to be revived only by express treaty provisions. After the war between Greece and Turkey in 1897, both countries were agreed that the treaties of capitulation, and all other conventions concluded between them, had been dissolved by the war.[122] The peace settlement after World War I also recognized that political treaties among the belligerents had been terminated by the war. After World War II, the Treaties of Peace of 1947 with Italy,[123] Romania,[124] Bulgaria,[125] Hungary,[126] and Finland [127] specified that each Allied or Associated Power was to notify each of the five states as to which of the bilateral treaties in effect between them before the war it desired to continue in force or to revive. Treaties on which the defeated nations received no notification of intent from the Allied or Associated Powers were to be regarded as abrogated. These provisions indicate that the victorious powers deemed, on the basis of principles and considerations not disclosed, certain treaties to have been automatically terminated by the outbreak of war.

This pattern was repeated in the Treaty of Peace with Japan, 1951, Article 7(a) of which provides that each of the Allied Powers is to notify Japan as to which of its bilateral treaties it wishes "to continue in force or revive, and any treaties . . . so notified shall continue in force or be revived subject only to such amendments as may be necessary to ensure conformity with the present Treaty." [128] The recent State Treaty for the Re-Establishment of Independent and Democratic Austria of 1955[129] clearly indicates that all bilateral treaties between the Allied and Associated Powers and Austria were terminated by the war. It should be noted that the Agreements and Protocol whereby Germany regained the status of a sovereign state on May 5, 1955,[130] make no mention of the status of either the bilateral or multilateral treaties to which the Three Powers and the German Reich were parties prior to the war, and on which neither the Governments of the Three Powers, the occupation authorities, nor the Federal Republic of Germany had taken any action. The United States took the position that its Treaty of Friendship, Commerce, and Consular Rights of 1923 with the German Reich had not survived the war.[131] This treaty, however, was "restored to full force and effect . . . as a provisional measure pending the conclusion of a more comprehensive modern treaty" by the Treaty of Friendship, Commerce, and Consular Rights of October 22, 1954.[132] France also considered its treaties with the German Reich terminated by the outbreak of war.[133]

WAR BETWEEN A DOMINANT STATE AND A THIRD STATE

The pertinent question here is whether a servient state burdened with a so-called military servitude may, without violating its duties as a neutral, continue to fulfill its obligations thereunder during a war between the dominant state and a third state. The resolution of this problem requires a consideration of the impact that the General Treaty for the Renunciation of War, of 1928, and the Charter of the United Nations, of 1945, had upon the status of neutrality in international law. Although it has been stated that the traditional conception of neutrality is no longer compatible with the principles of international law established by these instruments,[134] an examination of their provisions shows that the General Treaty for the Renunciation of War had no direct effect upon the law of neutrality[135] and that the Charter of the United Nations, even though it may have modified the right of U.N. members to remain neutral, did not abolish that right. This is true even regarding wars between states that are U.N. members. It is clear, furthermore, that the Charter did not substantially modify the law of neutrality for member states that assume a status of neutrality either in compliance[136] with, or in derogation of, their obligations under the Charter.

The General Treaty for the Renunciation of War. The General Treaty for the Renunciation of War [137] consists of two articles. In Article I, the signatories "declare . . . that they condemn recourse to war for the solution of international controversies and renounce it as an instrument of national policy in their relations with one another." In Article II, they "agree that the settlement or solution of all disputes or conflicts, . . . which may arise among them, shall never be sought except by pacific means." This treaty did not abolish among the signatories the lawful recourse to war as a means of self-defense or as a measure of redress for the international wrong occasioned by a recourse to war in violation of its provisions. Neither did the treaty render war among signatories and nonsignatories unlawful.[138] Since the treaty imposed no obligations upon the signatories to abandon any of their duties of neutrality toward a signatory that breaches its obligations, and contains no provision for the enforcement of such obligations, it did not impair the law of neutrality. It may, however, by denying to states the unrestricted right to wage war, have undermined the principle of absolute impartiality inherent in the traditional conception of neutrality, and may thus have laid the basis for its eventual modification.[139]

The Charter of the United Nations. Article 2, paragraph 5, of the Charter imposes an obligation upon all members to "give the United Nations every assistance in any action it takes in accordance with the present Charter" and to "refrain from giving assistance to any State against which the United Nations is taking preventive or enforcement action." The Charter vests in the Security Council of the United Nations the "responsibility for the maintenance of international peace and security" (Article 24) and provides that its decisions in this respect must be accepted and carried out by all members (Article 25). The decisions of the Security Council on substantive matters, however, must "be made by the affirmative vote of seven members including the concurring votes of the permanent members," the five Great Powers. This provision (Article 27), referred to by some as the "right to veto," established the groundwork for the survival of the law of neutrality within the framework of the system of collective security established by the Charter, because unanimity among the five Great Powers was likely only with respect to minor and geographically delimited conflicts.[140]

Under the specific provisions of the Charter, there exist numerous circumstances in which a U.N. member may properly assume a position of absolute neutrality. For example, although Article 39 makes the Security Council responsible for determining the existence of any threat to the peace, breach of the peace, or act of aggression, the Council can so determine only by a majority vote of seven members, which includes the concurring vote of all the permanent members (Article 27). In all instances—obviously many—in which such a vote is not obtained, member states may properly, without contravening the Charter, maintain a status of neutrality. Article 39 provides, additionally, that the Security Council shall decide on the nonmilitary or military measures that are to be taken "to maintain or restore international peace and security." [141] Since such a decision requires the majority vote specified in Article 27, member states would also be free, in all instances where the required vote is not secured, to assume a status of absolute neutrality without violating the Charter.[142] Pursuant to Article 48, the Security Council may carry out its decisions for the maintenance of peace by directing all or only some of the members to take action. Here again, in instances where action is to be taken by some members only, the other members may validly maintain a status of absolute neutrality.[143] Article 51 expressly recognizes the exercise of legitimate self-defense until the Security Council, by the majority vote specified in Article 27, has taken measures to restore peace. Failing such a vote, a defensive war could continue, and the members would be under no obligation to abandon a status of absolute impartiality toward the belligerents.[144] Similarly, Articles 52 and 53 permit, and may even require, that members not belonging to a particular regional organization adopt an attitude of absolute impartiality toward the disputing states.[145]

Since the Charter cannot impose legal obligations on third states,[146] it should be noted that the right of third states to maintain a neutral status and to be governed by the traditional law of neutrality remains unimpaired.[147]

Thus the principle of absolute neutrality has not been rendered ineffective or obsolete by the system of collective security created by the U.N Charter.[148] The law of neutrality is now as applicable to states burdened with so-called military servitudes as it was before the Charter, in most instances, during wars between states that are the beneficiaries of such servitudes and third states.

The Law of Neutrality and So-called Military Servitudes. Exponents of international servitudes are in general agreement that, to the extent that servitudes are not precluded by the U.N. Charter, it is not a breach of neutrality for a nonbelligerent servient state to permit a belligerent dominant state to use its territory or its resources for military operations.[149] They are committed to this view because they consider treaties that they allege to have established military servitudes as "conveyances" under which the servient state has forever alienated specific rights regarding its territory. They maintain that treaties establishing military servitudes are "dispositive," and thus establish a status that is "indefeasible" and "independent of the existence or will of the contracting parties." [150] Westlake, for example, states:

> There is a class of treaties called transitory or dispositive . . . which dispose of . . . things by transferring or creating rights in or over them . . . such as treaties which . . . [create] a servitude or easement . . . a transferee or annexing state takes the territory as it stands, that is, subject to all the rights which have been impressed on it in favor of third parties by the treaties which have disposed about it. . . .[151]

Vattel puts it this way:

> If . . . a nation granted in perpetuity to a neighboring prince the right . . . to keep a garrison in one of his fortresses, the prince does not lose his rights even though the Nation from which it has received them should happen to be conquered by . . . a foreign Power. His rights do not depend upon the continued existence of the State from which he received them, for the latter alienated them, and its conqueror could only take over what is actually possessed.[152]

This position is clearly contrary to the law of neutrality, and is, as such, untenable. Neutrality has been defined "as the attitude of impartiality adopted by third States toward belligerents and recognized by belligerents, such attitude creating rights and duties between the impartial States and the belligerents."[153] Among other matters, this attitude of impartiality denies to a neutral the right to permit a belligerent (1) to occupy a neutral fortress or any portion of neutral territory;[154] (2) to use a portion of its territory or any of its facilities whatsoever for military purposes;[155] or (3) to erect or to maintain on neutral territory depots and factories or arms, ammunitions, and military provisions.[156] It is Oppenheim's view that pursuant to the provisions of:

> Hague Conventions V and XIII, which deal with neutrality in land and sea warfare respectively, it becomes quite apparent that any facility whatever directly concerning military or naval operations, even if it consists only in granting passage over neutral territory to belligerent forces, is illegal, although granted to both belligerents alike. The duty of impartiality comprises abstention from any active or passive cooperation with belligerents.[157]

These rights are denied a neutral even though a treaty previously concluded between it and a belligerent may have provided for such activities.[158] It would be illegal, therefore, for a nonbelligerent state to permit a belligerent state that is the beneficiary of a so-called military servitude upon its territory to exercise its rights thereunder. Therefore, treaties concluded in time of peace, except treaties of alliance, which accord a dominant state any military use of servient territory during a war with a third state, are properly to be considered as being illegal *ab initio*. Military servitudes of this nature, unless they are suspended by war (a view the proponents of servitudes generally deny) or are considered as treaties of alliance (necessarily personal in nature), have as their object or result a breach of the law of neutrality. But it is a principle of international law that obligations contrary to its generally recognized rules cannot legally be the object of a treaty.[159]

Thus, all positive military servitudes[160] (except, in certain instances, those under which action is compatible with the U.N. Charter) are void, and so being, are not binding upon third states and are not enforceable between the parties themselves. Although there are no judicial opinions substantiating this view,[161] McNair's [162] assertions do support this position. He states "that a treaty between two States the execution of which contemplates the infliction upon a third State of what customary international law regards as wrong is illegal and invalid *ab initio*." Hall also supports this position. It is his view that:

> The due conclusion of an international contract also affects third parties. A state of things has come into existence which, having been legally created in pursuance to the fundamental rights of states, other countries are bound to respect, unless its legal character is destroyed by the nature of its objects, or unless it is evidently directed, whether otherwise legally or not, against the safety of a third State, and except in so far as it is inconsistent with the rights of states at war with one another. So long therefore as a contract is in accordance with law, or consistent with the safety of the states not parties to it, the latter must not prevent or hinder the contracting parties from carrying it out.[163]

The statements that have been made on the illegal nature of positive military servitudes apply equally to negative servitudes that would preclude a servient state from taking the action that the law of neutrality requires of it. It therefore would be a breach of neutrality for a servient state, because of the provisions of an alleged military servitude under which it is not to maintain troops within certain portions of its territory, not to comply with its obligation to prevent breaches of its sovereignty, or with its obligation to accord neutral asylum to belligerent personnel and war material.[164]

On this basis, it would appear that military servitudes—(excluding those that may in certain instances be compatible with the U.N. Charter, a circumstance under which the servient state could occupy a status of "qualified neutrality")[165]—are in fact either conditional treaties of alliance or political treaties that are purely personal in nature.[166] The recognition by certain authors that military servitudes are stayed or suspended by operation of law upon the outbreak of war between a dominant state and a third State in itself denies the alleged "real" character of a servitude.

EFFECT OF A VITAL CHANGE IN CIRCUMSTANCES UPON MILITARY SERVITUDES

Under the doctrine of international servitudes, the rights and obligations thereof are not affected by a radical change in the political situation, such as that occasioned when the sovereignty of either the dominant or the servient state passes to a third state.[167]

Those who consider servitudes to be treaty stipulations of a purely personal character consider them to be subject to all the rules and principles that are applicable to treaties generally—one of which allows their denunciation when a vital change of circumstances, whether internal or international in nature, has materially altered the situation that existed between the contracting parties at the time that they concluded the agreement. This principle, known as the doctrine of *rebus sic stantibus*, and considered by many [168] to be a sufficient basis for the voidability or the denunciation of a treaty, has been explained in these terms: "Neither party to a contract can make its binding effect dependent at his will upon conditions other than those contemplated at the moment when the contract was entered into, and on the other hand a contract ceases to be binding as soon as anything which formed an implied condition of its obligatory force at the time of its conclusion is essentially altered." [169]

Hall,[170] listing implied conditions under which a treaty is made, states that a treaty originally consistent with the right of self-preservation becomes voidable as soon as it is dangerous to the existence of, or is incompatible with, the independence of a state, unless those effects were contemplated at the time of its conclusion. He further states that the freedom of will of the parties at the time of signature with respect to subject matter is to be presumed unless the treaty is a restraint upon liberty. Subordination of a state by conquest and annexation by a third state would render the treaty voidable on the option of the third state, since it cannot be assumed that a state would subordinate its will to another state except under the pressure of necessity or vital need, as in treaties that are made under compulsion at the end of a war.[171]

Some supporters of international servitudes have departed from strict theory to admit that the *clausula* constitutes an implied provision of treaties that set up so-called servitudes. Rivier[172] and Oppenheim,[173] for example, admit that treaties establishing international servitudes are to be regarded, though dispositive, as being concluded on the condition *rebus sic stantibus*. Labrousse[174] admits of the denunciation of servitudes in the case of modifications in the servient state's constitution. Oppenheim, although denying that servitudes may be extinguished because of a change in sovereignty over the territory of the servient state, does state: "But it is difficult to understand why, although State servitudes are called into existence through treaties, it is sometimes maintained that the clause *rebus sic stantibus* cannot be applied in case a vital change of circumstances makes the exercise of a State servitude unbearable."[175]

The acquisition of sovereignty by a third state, which is hostile to the dominant state, over the territory of the servient state, which is subject to a military servitude, would doubtless establish a most unbearable situation. Indeed, could there be a situation more susceptible to proper application of the *rebus sic stantibus* rule?

Although the practice of states is not conclusive as to the applicability of the *clausula rebus sic stantibus* to conventional arrangements, including those that are alleged to create international servitudes, the *clausula* has been applied and confirmed by state practice on numerous occasions. When France and Geneva were united in 1798, France renounced all treaties of alliance that Geneva had concluded with foreign countries.[176] The classic example of the repudiation of treaty obligations on the grounds of an essential change of circumstances was Russia's repudiation in 1878 of that portion of the Treaty of Paris of 1856 that neutralized the Black Sea and placed restrictions on her regarding the keeping of armed vessels there. Russia stated that a material change in conditions contemplated by the treaty had occurred through the subsequent union of the Danubian principalities, acquiesced in by the Great Powers, as well as by the changes in naval warfare occasioned by the use of ironclad vessels. When the Powers met at

London at the close of the Franco-Prussian War, Russia was allowed her way.[177]

Again, in 1866, Russia closed the port of Batum, contrary to the express provision of Article 59 of the Treaty of Berlin of 1878, which provided for the freedom of that port.[178] All signatories except Great Britain appear to have tacitly consented to the denunciation.

Germany in 1936 unilaterally renounced her obligations under the Treaty of Versailles regarding the disarmament and demilitarization of the Rhineland on the grounds that it was incompatible with the Franco-Soviet Pact of 1935.[179]

In the case of the *Free Zones of Upper Savoy and the District of Gex,* France during the period 1929-32 maintained before the Permanent Court of International Justice that the provisions of the treaties of 1815 and of other supplementary acts concerning the customs-free zone of the District of Gex should, due to vital changes in circumstances, be considered by the court to have lapsed. Although the court found that the changes were insufficient to substantiate France's claim, the fact that the court answered on its merits a claim based on the doctrine of *rebus sic stantibus* indicates that the nature of Switzerland's rights did not preclude a resort to that doctrine. As the dispute arose concerning an alleged servitude, it may be said as well that the court by its consideration of the doctrine (properly applicable by analogy to personal obligations only) inferentially denied the existence of a servitude in this case.[180] The United States in 1941 renounced its obligations under the international Load Lines Convention of 1930 on the grounds of "changed conditions" that were alleged to confer on the U.S. "an unquestioned right and privilege under approved principles of international law" to declare the treaty inoperative.[181]

In the case of *Luzern* v. *Aargau* (1882), the Federal Swiss Tribunal recognized the doctrine of *rebus sic stantibus* in a dispute between two Swiss cantons about the extinction of a conventional public-law servitude. The court held that it was a universally recognized principle of law that a contract may be denounced by unilateral act as soon as its continued existence is incompatible with the self-preservation of an independent state, or when a change has occurred in the tacit conditions originally intended by the parties as necessary for the existence of the treaty.[182]

Thus, there is precedent that the practice of states recognizes that treaties establishing so-called servitudes are susceptible to denunciation when, due to unforeseen changes in circumstances, an obligation imperils the existence or development of the burdened state.[183]

As neither general rules of international law nor the decisions of international judicial bodies substantiate the doctrine of international servitudes generally, or of military servitudes in particular, instances of alleged military servitudes must be examined to determine whether the practice of states recognizes their existence. Only if the practice of states shows that territorial restrictions upon the sovereignty of a state for the military interests or purposes of another state have survived a change of sovereignty and have passed to the new sovereign of the servient state, over his opposition (assuming that the successor had not been subject to any kind of coercion or duress), can it be said that the rights and obligations concerned are in fact "real" or absolute in nature. Although instances have been cited by Váli and others in support of the recognition of the absolute nature of the rights and obligations of military servitudes in the practice of states, an examination of the facts and circumstances of such instances fails to substantiate such recognition.

V. The Practice of States

It has been observed that the basis of an international rule "is the consent of nations; and of this their practice is the evidence." [184] The practice of states recognizes that a state commences its independent existence in the community of nations, whether peacefully or by force of arms, free of the encumbrances that have previously been placed upon it by treaties that were concluded by its former master, and that it is free as well to conclude whatever international agreements it considers to be in its best interests.[185] It is said, however, that the practice of states recognizes several exceptions to this general rule, one exception existing in the case of states emerging to full sovereignty from a semisovereign or self-governing status.[186] It is stated that the treaties that were previously concluded by their former sovereign, protector, or constitutional superior, on behalf of, or as the agent of the semisovereign or self-governing states, are personal to the new states and are therefore binding upon them. Another exception is said to exist for states that succeed, by conquest or otherwise, to territory that is encumbered with a servitude of international law. It is alleged that states are bound by operation of law to assume the obligations of servitudes, for the treaties that create them are dispositive in nature, and the obligations involved are real or absolute.[187] The review of the practice of states, however, shows that such practice does not substantiate the descent by operation of law of the rights and obligations of international servitudes to successor states. Even Váli, in his extended discussion of treaties (under his expanded concept of international servitudes) concerned with military matters, presents no cogent evidence that would substantiate the recognition of military servitudes in the practice of states.[188]

Although Váli lists many agreements relating to military matters or purposes that he apparently considers to have established military servitudes, most, if not all of them are by their express provisions clearly personal in nature, or are agreements the alleged "real" obligations of which were never subjected to the tests of either succession, war, or vital change of circumstances.

A consideration of instances in the practice of states that, although cited as military servitudes, were never put to the test of succession would, of course, be fruitless. Consideration must be directed to treaties of a military nature that have been characterized as military servitudes in the recent practice of states and that have been subjected to the test of succession—in particular, the 1950 agreement between the United States and France under which the United States established military bases in Morocco;[189] the agreement between the United States and Great Britain under which the United States established military bases in the West Indies;[190] and those of less recent date that have repeatedly been held out as having satisfied the a priori test laid down for military servitudes: their descent by operation of law to successor states, and their invulnerability to war, the law of neutrality, and vital changes in circumstances.

For convenience, these so-called military servitudes will be considered according to their form: first, the positive military servitudes, whereby the dominant state is authorized to take positive action for its military purposes within the territory of another state; and second, the negative or passive servitudes, whereby the servient state is restrained, in the military interests of the dominant state, from performing certain acts within its own territory.

Positive Military Servitudes

MILITARY RIGHTS OF THE UNITED STATES IN MOROCCO

The agreement concluded between the United States and France in 1950 under which the U.S. maintained five military bases in

Morocco has been cited as one that established a military servitude in favor of the U.S., thereby continuing to bind Morocco after its independence from France.[191] Evidence for such a conclusion was implicit in the fact that the United States had continued to man its bases in Morocco after Morocco became independent in 1956.[192] It was inferred from this fact that the U.S. military rights in Morocco had by operation of law become obligatory upon Morocco, the successor state, and, as such, could lawfully be terminated only by a U.S. renunciation of them, or pursuant to an agreement between the two countries.

An examination of the circumstances under which the United States acquired its bases in Morocco and the conditions under which Morocco attained its independence refutes the idea of the creation of a military servitude on behalf of the U.S. in Morocco, or the idea that Morocco or France considered the U.S. right to maintain bases in Morocco to be other than a purely personal right that would, unless expressly recognized by Morocco, lapse upon Morocco's attainment of full sovereignty over the territory.

The Treaty of Fez of March 30, 1912, which made Morocco a French Protectorate, pertinently provides:

> Article II: His Majesty the Sultan consents that henceforth the French Government, *after it shall have notified the makhzen, may proceed to such military occupation of the Moroccan territory as it might deem necessary for the maintenance of good order* and the security of commercial transactions, *and to exercise every police supervision on land and within the Moroccan waters.*
>
> Article VI: The diplomatic and consular agents of France shall be *charged with the representation and protection of Moroccan subjects and interests abroad.* His Majesty the Sultan pledges himself not to conclude any act of an international nature without the previous approval of the French Republic. [italics added] [193]

It was pursuant to Article II of the Treaty of Fez that France established bases and stationed its forces in Morocco, and, presumably, it was under the authority of both Article II and Article VI that France concluded the 1950 agreement authorizing the United States to garrison and utilize five bases in Morocco. Although it is not known whether the French Government ever notified the makhzen that it contemplated the conclusion of such an agreement with the U.S., it is clear that the Moroccan Government never considered this agreement to have been concluded on its behalf or for its benefit, or that it would be obligated in the absence of its express consent, to respect its provisions after attaining its independence.[194]

Treatises on the law of state succession recite that the general principle that a new state does not inherit the treaties of its predecessor is inapplicable to states emerging to full sovereignty from a semisovereign or self-governing status: Treaties concluded for such communities by their suzerain, protector, or constitutional superior are considered to have been concluded by them as the agent of these communities, and, as such, are considered personal to these communities.[195] Furthermore, it is possible that even if these treaties cannot be upheld as personal to the autonomous or semiautonomous regions, they could, nevertheless, if dispositive in nature, bind these regions after their independence. A treaty that is alleged to have established a military servitude, for example, is considered dispositive, and, as such, binding upon the parties irrespective of their will.[196]

But Morocco never considered the French-American Agreement of 1950 to be personal to it. The circumstances of this agreement, furthermore, negate the creation of a military servitude the alleged real rights and obligations of which would be binding on Morocco. The Treaty of Fez was terminated by a Joint French-Moroccan Declaration of March 2, 1956,[197] when authority for the maintenance of French bases in Morocco ceased. The Declaration provided that pending the conclusion of new agreements "which will define the inter-dependence of the two countries . . . especially in matters of defense, foreign relations. . . ." Franco-Moroccan relations would be founded on the provisions of the Protocol annexed to the Joint Declaration. The Protocol (Article II) states only that "the present status of the French Army in Morocco shall remain unchanged during the transitional period." [198] The Joint Declaration and the Protocol, therefore, effectively transferred to Morocco whatever title France may have possessed to state-owned property in Morocco. Under general principles of international law, the title to such property vested in Morocco. The Declaration and the Protocol also removed the basis on which the U.S. rights in Morocco were predicated, unless, of course, the Agreement between France and the United States of 1950 could be regarded as one that was personal to Morocco, or unless the continuation of the U.S. rights in Morocco could be substantiated on the basis of their "real" or absolute nature, and the dispositive nature of the 1950 agreement. In the Diplomatic Accord between France and Morocco signed May 20, 1956,[199] Morocco (Article II) would assume "the obligations resulting from international treaties passed by France in the name of Morocco, as well as those resulting from international acts relating to Morocco which have not been subject to observations on its part." Morocco, which had consistently challenged the validity of the U.S. and French Bases Agreement of 1950 and had decried the danger to which it would subject Morocco in event of war, informed the French Government in a note dated May 20, 1956, that the Moroccan Government "completely reserves its position on whatever relates to the French-American Agreement of December 22, 1950." [200] A note from the French Government of the same date advised the Moroccan Government that France had taken cognizance of the Moroccan reservation and confirmed "in this respect that this agreement does not enter into the category of the acts and treaties alluded to in Article II of the Diplomatic Agreement between France and Morocco." [201]

This exchange of notes is conclusive of the fact that neither the French nor the Moroccan governments considered that there was a descent by operation of law of the obligations that were contained in the agreement of 1950, or that this agreement was personal to Morocco. It is also evident that neither France, Morocco, nor the United States considered the treaty to have established a military servitude the alleged "real" obligations of which would be binding upon Morocco by operation of law, or considered the agreement to be other than one of alliance between France and the United States, and, as such, a purely personal treaty that was incompatible with Morocco's newly acquired sovereignty.

As early as November 25, 1957, the United States indicated its desire to pursue negotiations on the status of its installations in Morocco "with full respect for the sovereignty of Morocco" to the "appropriate adjustments of present conditions regarding the armed forces of the United States in Morocco" [202] and to the continued "recognition of the United States of Moroccan sovereignty over the American bases." [203] The Moroccan Government promptly initiated negotiations for the expeditious departure from Morocco of both French and U.S. forces. In 1959 the United States agreed to withdraw all its forces from Morocco by the end of 1963,[204] and, in March, 1961, the French Government agreed to withdraw most of its troops by October, 1961.[205]

Although the 1950 Military Bases Agreement would be categorized under Váli's concept as a military servitude of international law, it is evident that none of the parties to the agreement considered that they could support, on the basis of state practice, the position that the treaty of 1950 was dispositive, or that it had created "real" rights—even for a period of years—that would bind a successor state.

It is logical to assume that both France and the U.S., if they considered the possible application of the doctrine of servitudes under the agreement of 1950, realized that it would be detrimental to their international posture and prestige if they were to assert in an era in which colonialism has been completely repudiated—and attempts to preserve vestiges thereof bitterly denounced—the alleged real nature of the rights established by the agreement. As one author has observed, both internal and external politics and influences militate against the acceptance by states of an absolute inheritance of obligations. The solution of the problem of state succession is in fact a practical one dictated and governed by policy, not by confused and unsubstantiated legal principles.[206]

LEASED NAVAL AND AIR BASES IN THE WEST INDIES, NEWFOUNDLAND, BRITISH GUIANA, AND BERMUDA

The agreement between the United Kingdom and the U.S. of March 27, 1941,[207] relating to naval and air bases in the West Indies, Newfoundland, British Guiana, and Bermuda, which the U.K. on September 2, 1940,[208] had leased to the U.S. for a period of ninety-nine years, has been cited as an agreement creating military servitudes of international law.[209] Regarding the servitude created in Newfoundland, it is stated that it is "considered as a further precedent to prove that such undertakings of a territorial character descend to the successor State." [210] Such an assertion is completely groundless. Recent events have established the purely personal nature of the leased air and naval bases agreements.

The very text of these agreements reflects their personal nature. First, the notes exchanged between the U.K. and the U.S. that granted air and naval facilities to the U.S. in the British transatlantic territories specify that the grant is for a period of ninety-nine years, not in perpetuity. Second, the agreement between the U.K. and the U.S. that pertains to the use of bases provides expressly (Article XXIII) that the "United States will not assign or underlet or part with the possession of the whole or any part of any Leased Area, or of any right, power or authority granted by the Leases or this Agreement." This language is unequivocal. It is not susceptible to varying interpretations; it negates in express terms the devolution by succession of the rights granted to the U.S.[211] Third, the purpose for which the leases were concluded, mutual defense, conclusively established the political and, as such, personal nature of the agreements establishing the leases. They are in fact agreements of alliance, as reflected by the exchange of notes that state that the leases are granted "to strengthen the ability of the United States to cooperate effectively with the other nations of the Americas in the defense of the Western Hemisphere." Additionally, the agreement relating to the use of these bases specifies (Article II) that "when the United States is engaged in war or in time of other emergency, the Government of the United Kingdom agrees that the United States may exercise in the Territories and surrounding waters or air space all such rights, power and authority as may be necessary for conducting any military operations deemed desirable by the United States. . . ."

It is a generally recognized principle of international law that "treaties of alliance . . . or of neutrality or of any other political nature fall to the ground with the extinction of the State which concluded them. They are personal treaties, and they naturally, legally, and necessarily presuppose the existence of the contracting State." [212] In this connection, it should be noted that all the territories in which the leased bases were established were, when the U.S. acquired the bases, colonies of Great Britain. All these territories were therefore then fully subject to British rule, and the treaties and agreements that were concluded by Great Britain on the use of the territory of these colonies were concluded solely for the purposes and interests of Great Britain, not the colonies. It cannot be argued, therefore, that the Leased Bases Agreement in fact imposed a personal obligation on the colonies themselves, as it could be argued had the territories involved been protectorates of Great Britain and had the agreements been concluded on their behalf and in their interests. If any uncertainty existed as to the real or personal character of the obligations of the Leased Bases Agreement, it recently was definitively resolved by the practice of states.

When it became evident that Great Britain would soon grant independence to the West Indies Federation, the question arose as to whether the Leased Bases Agreement with the United Kingdom would, by operation of law, and in the absence of a specific undertaking by a sovereign West Indies Government, carry over and remain binding upon the West Indies Federation when it achieved its independence. It was open to the United States whether to argue the continued effectiveness of this agreement against a sovereign West Indies Federation on the ground that it created a servitude of international law, the real obligations of which were binding upon the Federation, or whether to seek its continuance by other means. To adopt the position that the agreement had created real obligations and was, as such, dispositive would not have been persuasive, or for that matter legally tenable, because of the purely political nature of the agreement. Recourse to possibly more attractive alternatives that might prove practically more effective was also available to the United States for the purpose of retaining the rights it had enjoyed under the Leased Bases Agreement. The United States could, for example, demand on valid legal grounds that the United Kingdom respect its obligations toward the U.S. under the Agreement by requiring, as a condition of its independence, that the West Indies Federation be required to accept the U.K. obligations under the Agreement. Should the United Kingdom consider this proposal infeasible, as being incompatible with, or repugnant to, the sovereignty that a new state should in fact enjoy under a grant of independence, the United States could have recourse to still other measures to ensure the continuity of its rights: It could refuse to recognize the West Indies Federation upon its independence if it did not assume the obligations of the Leased Bases Agreement. Action of this nature, however, would undoubtedly have repercussions, for it would in all probability be viewed by the international community as both improper and arbitrary, and as an attempt to continue to subject the West Indies to restrictions that had been imposed upon its territory while it was in a colonial status. The espousal of such a position would have subjected the United States to criticism detrimental to its international posture. It would undoubtedly have been viewed as conduct incompatible with the prior pronouncements of the United States on the evils of colonialism and the entitlement of colonial areas to full sovereignty.[213] As a practical alternative, the United States could, prior to the independence of the West Indies Federation, initiate negotiations with the United Kingdom in which the representatives of the West Indies Federation would, with the U.K.'s consent, not only participate but, under a delegation of authority from the United Kingdom, would on behalf of the Federation also be authorized to sign an agreement under which the Federation would voluntarily assume the U.K. obligations under the Leased Bases Agreement.

From subsequent developments it appears that on balance the United States and the United Kingdom concluded that the latter alternative provided the most feasible means of securing to the United States its rights in the West Indies. Although the voluntary assumption of the obligations of the United Kingdom under the Leased Bases Agreement by the West Indies Federation prior to its independence under an entrustment from the U.K. could not result in an agreement that would be legally binding on the Federation thereafter,[214] unless the Government of the West Indies Federation after its independence accepted the agreement, this situation did not pose a serious practical problem. It is normally U.K. practice toward dependent territories to which it grants independence to have an exchange of notes under which the new state agrees to assume the international obligations of the U.K. relating to its territory.[215] Under such an exchange of notes, the Federation would thereby assume the U.K. obligations in the West Indies on the basis of an agreement that it had itself concluded in its sovereign capacity under conditions which, by having signed the agreement under a delegation of authority from the U.K., it had previously indicated to be acceptable. This approach may have been dictated in part by the notice that the West Indies Federation gave to the U.S. and the U.K. prior to the commencement of negotiations on the revision of the 1941 Leased Bases Agreement, that the "West Indies considers that on its independence it should have the right to form its own alliances generally and to determine for itself what military bases should be allowed on its soil and under whose control such bases should come." [216] The West Indies in its statement of policy also enunciated the principle that the "West Indies on the achievement of independence would have the right to reject the agreement if it thought fit or to elect to accept the 1941 agreement as a basis for negotiation." [217]

On November 3, 1960, negotiations on the revision of the 1941 Leased Bases Agreement were begun in London among representatives of the United Kingdom, the United States, and the West Indies Federation, who discussed in broad outline the review of the 1941 Leased Bases Agreement.[218] These negotiations formed the first of three stages through which negotiations progressed before the "Agreement Between the Government of the Federation of the West Indies and the Government of the United States of America Concerning United States Defense Areas in the Federation of the West Indies" was concluded on February 10, 1961.[219] The Agreement was signed by the West Indies Federation under a delegation of authority granted to it for this purpose by the U.K.[220] A joint communiqué issued at the conclusion of the first stage of the negotiations reflects the fact that none of the parties to this agreement considered that the Leased Bases Agreement of 1949 constituted in any way a military servitude that the West Indies Federation would, as a successor state, be obligated to assume by operation of law. This communiqué stated: "There was assumption by all parties of the basic principle that the West Indies were independent, would have the right to form its own *alliances* and to conclude such agreements as it thought fit regarding military bases on its soil. It was agreed, however, that the review of the Leased Bases Agreement should proceed on the basis that the West Indies, in the exercise of such rights would be both willing and anxious to cooperate in whatever would strengthen the mutual security and contribute to the continuing defense of the Western Hemisphere, as part of the defense of the democratic world." [italics added] [221]

Under the "Defense Areas" Agreement that was concluded on February 10, 1961, the United States was granted the rights, power, and authority, in accordance with the terms and provisions of the agreement, necessary for the development, use, operation, and protection for military purposes of the defense areas that were particularized in the Annex to the Agreement. The Agreement, which is to last for sixteen years, provides for its review to determine the desirability of its modification in 1968, and again in 1973.[222] Should it not be agreed before the end of 1973 that a defense area is to be continued as such, the agreement, and any modification thereof, is to continue to apply to such area until the end of 1977.[223]

It is clear from the foregoing that the recent practice of states does not recognize the existence of military servitudes of international law and that it refutes the doctrine that it is possible, by an agreement that relates to military activities, to create real rights and obligations (so-called military servitudes of international law) that would descend to successor states by operation of law. State practice correctly views agreements of this nature as treaties of alliance that are personal to the signatories, having no binding effect upon successor states.

It is noted that two of the ten British colonies [224] in the Caribbean that were formed into a Federation by the British in 1957, Jamaica and Trinidad-Tobago, voted to secede from the Federation[225] and that the West Indies Federation that was scheduled to become independent on May 31, 1962, was dissolved by Great Britain on that date.[226] On August 6, 1962, Jamaica assumed an independent status within the British Commonwealth.[227] On August 7, 1962, by an exchange of letters, the Government of Jamaica agreed to assume, as of August 6, 1962, all the obligations and responsibilities of the U.K. Government that arose "from any valid international instrument (including any such instruments made by the Government of the Federation of the West Indies by virtue of authority entrusted by the Government of the United Kingdom) . . . in so far as such instruments may be held to have application to Jamaica." [228] Trinidad and Tobago assumed an independent status within the British Commonwealth on August 31, 1962.[229] On the same day, by an exchange of letters, the Government of Trinidad and Tobago agreed to assume all the obligations and responsibilities of the U.K. Government that arose "from any valid international instruments (including any such instruments made by the Government of the Federation of the West Indies by virtue of authority entrusted by the Government of the United Kingdom) . . . in so far as such instruments may be held to have application to Trinidad and Tobago." [230] As for the rest of the territories of the West Indies Federation that remain dependent territories of Great Britain, an internal understanding will undoubtedly be reached under which the dependent territories are to carry out their obligations under the 1961 "Defense Areas" Agreement.

On the bases in Newfoundland, under the Leased Bases Agreement of 1941, the obligations of Great Britain were assumed by Canada, with Canadian consent, when Newfoundland became the tenth province of Canada on April 1, 1949. The Canadian consent, which was given subject to minor modifications in the agreement, was later embodied in a special exchange of notes dated February 13–March 19, 1952.[231] Váli cites it as evidence for the descent of such duties to the successor state after a change of sovereignty over the burdened territory.[232] The fact that the Canadians assumed the obligations of Great Britain regarding Newfoundland under the 1941 Leased Bases Agreement, and that this consent was affirmatively reflected in an exchange of notes, refutes the conclusion that the obligations of this agreement descended upon Canada by operation of law. It confirms that the practice of states regards the obligations of military agreements as personal to the contracting state —and binding upon successor states only with their consent.

The obligations regarding the Leased Bases Areas in Bermuda and British Guiana remain those of Great Britain. Should these territories be granted independence or be transferred to another sovereign, the British, in accordance with their normal practice, will undoubtedly require, as a condition of independence or transfer, that the new state or sovereign assume the British obligations thereunder. Should these areas fall to another state by conquest, the conquering state could properly assume sovereignty thereover free of the political and other personal obligations that the Leased Bases Agreement of 1941 imposed on Great Britain.

AGREEMENTS BETWEEN THE UNITED STATES AND THE UNITED KINGDOM ESTABLISHING A LONG-RANGE PROVING GROUND FOR GUIDED MISSILES IN THE BAHAMAS.

The U.S. "Long-Range Proving Ground" for guided missiles in the Bahamas [233] and the Dominican Republic,[234] and the British "Practice Bombing Range" near Cuxhaven, in Germany,[235] have each been cited as examples of "international relationships establishing servitudes." [236] The agreements with Great Britain and the Dominican Republic, under which the United States operates the Long-Range Proving Ground across British and Dominican territories, have been further characterized as an "outstanding example of rights in foreign territory of an absolute character. The territorial rights of the grantee necessarily apply *erga omnes*." [237]

The agreement between the United Kingdom and the United States of July 21, 1950, which authorizes the United States to establish a long-range proving ground for guided missiles in the Bahama Islands,[238] provides that it is to be used by the United Kingdom and the United States "for testing the flight of guided missiles and for training with such missiles and equipment." It further provides that the "details of its practical application shall be arranged by friendly co-operation." This agreement is to remain in force for a period of twenty-five years and thereafter until one year from the day on which either government gives notice to the other of its intention to terminate it. The agreement expressly forbids the U.S. to assign its rights under it. An agreement between the United States and the Dominican Republic dated November 26, 1951, extended the proving ground through a portion of the territory of the Dominican Republic, and the provisions of this agreement were made applicable to the U.K. by an exchange of notes dated November 26, 1951.[239]

The express limitations in the agreements as to their duration (twenty-five years) and as to the nonassignability of rights preclude a designation of the rights and obligations of these agreements as "servitudes of international law" as that term has traditionally been defined: The rights and obligations are neither in perpetuity nor dispositive in the sense that the grantees may make such use of their rights as they see fit. The rights and obligations of these agreements are in fact purely personal and are governed by general treaty rules. In any event, the allegation that these agreements established military servitudes of international law proves nothing because they have never been subjected to the test of succession.

It will be remembered that for Váli's purposes a "military servitude of international law" can be established by an agreement effective for any period of time, if the provisions thereof authorize the grantee to make use of foreign territory for his military purposes or deny the grantor the right to use his territory for his own military purposes. Under his definition military rights granted for a term of years are absolute in nature and "necessarily apply *erga omnes*"[240] merely because they are available, for a stated period of time, against the grantor states. He implies, however, that the obligations assumed by the grantor descend to successor states by operation of law and that these obligations are not terminable because of vital changes in circumstances. There exists no need to use the term "military servitudes of international law," a word of art that has a very special technical meaning, to differentiate from other treaty rights and obligations those relating to use or nonuse of territory for the military purpose of a grantee for a stated period of years. If it is Váli's intent and it appears that it is—to attribute to his "military servitudes of international law" the real and absolute attributes of servitudes of international law as that law has traditionally been defined (the descent of the rights and obligations thereof by operation of law, their invulnerability to vital changes in circumstances, and the other characteristics attributed to servitudes), his terminology is completely inappropriate and entirely fallacious. His views have furthermore been unequivocally repudiated by the practice of states.

As indicated above, the Agreement between the Federal Republic of Germany and Great Britain concluded by an exchange of notes on September 9, 1952,[241] under which Great Britain is authorized to use the "Sandbank Range" near Cuxhaven, Germany, as a practice bombing range, is also considered by Váli to be a servitude of international law. The duration of this agreement is limited to five years. The agreement also specifies certain conditions that may, if they occur, terminate it. This agreement has never been subjected to the test of succession. There is thus no evidence to substantiate the conclusion that it constitutes a military servitude. Furthermore, it may be said that the conditions that are spelled out in the agreement in fact anticipate and reflect the circumstances under which the *clausula rebus sic stantibus* would properly be applicable.

Váli discusses other agreements concerned with military rights and bases,[242] none of which has ever been put to the test of state succession, and few of which could be properly characterized as servitudes as that term has traditionally been defined. Without exception, the agreements that he cites are either treaties of alliance or are otherwise purely personal in nature. In fact, certain of these agreements, for example, that between Egypt and the U.K. of October 19, 1954,[243] relative to the use of Egyptian territory by U.K. troops in the event of an armed attack by an outside power on any country that is a party to the treaty of Joint Defense between Arab League States of April 13, 1950, or on Turkey, was denounced, without repercussions, by Egypt on January 1, 1957.[244]

THE PROVINCES OF CHABLAIS AND FAUCIGNY

The Swiss right to station troops in the provinces of Chablais and Faucigny is the most frequently cited instance of a positive military servitude.[245] The Final Act of the Congress of Vienna of 1815 [246] provided that the two northernmost provinces of Savoy, Chablais and Faucigny, and all territory north of Ugine, then territory belonging to Sardinia, were to participate in the permanent neutralization of Switzerland and that no fortifications were to be erected or forces garrisoned there in time of war.[247] Additionally, pursuant to Article 92 of the Final Act of the Congress of Vienna, Switzerland was authorized to occupy the neutralized provinces in the event of a European war, and the King of Sardinia was permitted the right to withdraw his forces through Valais to Piedmont in the event of such a war.[248]

The territory in question was ceded to France by Sardinia by the Treaty of Turin on March 24, 1860, subject to all the conditions under which Sardinia had held that territory.[249] After World War I, Switzerland agreed to the termination of the neutral zones of Savoy and to the termination of its right to position troops therein. Article 435 of the Treaty of Versailles, recognizing that these rights were "no longer consistent with present conditions" and taking "note of the agreement reached between the French . . . and the Swiss Government for the abrogation of the stipulations relating to this Zone," provided that the stipulations "are and remain abrogated."

It has been claimed that prior to the agreement to terminate the neutral zones in Savoy and the Swiss right to station troops in those zones, there existed a servitude for the benefit of the Swiss that survived the change in sovereignty over the zones that had been accomplished by the Treaty of Turin between Sardinia and France of March 24, 1960. The facts and circumstances of this instance, however, refute this allegation. It will be noted that France, under the provisions of Article II of the Treaty of Turin, voluntarily had recognized and agreed to abide by the restrictions applicable to the province of Savoy to which Sardinia had been subjected by the Treaty of Vienna of 1815. It was not, therefore, by operation of law—not because "real" rights and obligations were involved—that France was obligated to respect Swiss rights in the province of Savoy. It was because she had voluntarily assumed Sardinia's obligations under the provisions of the treaty between them. Furthermore, in 1883, France had again in a formal exchange of notes with the Swiss expressly recognized these obligations and stated that it would respect the neutralized territory. France's continued respect for the neutralized and demilitarized status of the provinces of Chablais and Faucigny and the Swiss right to occupy these provinces may be predicated as well on the fact that a failure on the part of France to respect these provisions would have constituted a repudiation of her obligations under the Treaty of Vienna of 1815 —a "lawmaking" treaty that set up an international regime to which she, Sardinia, Austria, Prussia, Russia, and Great Britain were signatories—to guarantee the neutrality of, and the passage of troops through, the Savoy area.[250]

COALING STATIONS IN THE PACIFIC ISLANDS

A positive military servitude is said to have been established in the Islands of the Carolines and Palaos by a treaty between Germany and Spain in 1889.[251] By Article 5 of a treaty of 1885, Spain authorized Germany to maintain in the Islands of the Carolines or the Palaos a naval station and a coaling station. Four years later Spain ceded the Islands to Germany, specifying: "Spanien wird ein Kohlendepot für die Kriegs und Handelsmarine in dem Karolinen Archipel, ein gleichen in dem Palau—und ein drittes in dem Marianen—Archipel errichten und auch in Kriegszeiten behalten können." [252]

Although the duration of the Spanish rights to establish three coaling stations for use in time of war was not delimited, these rights completely disappeared after World War I. The mandate over these islands that was conferred on Japan by the League of Nations makes no mention of the Spanish rights, nor does it contain a general reservation for rights possessed therein by third states. Furthermore, the Treaty of Peace with Japan of 1951,[253] under Article II of which Japan renounced ". . . all rights, title, and claim in . . . the . . . Mandate System," and recognized the action of the United Nations Security Council of April 2, 1947, which extended the trusteeship system to the Pacific Islands formerly under mandate to Japan, makes no mention of, and contains no provision for, the rights that third states might have regarding these islands.

The facts on this alleged instance of a military servitude establish the personal and political nature of the agreement.[254]

PANAMA CANAL

The provisions of the Hay-Bunau-Varilla Treaty of November 18, 1903,[255] between the United States and Panama have been cited as "definitely permanent grants, based upon a peculiarly close relationship between the territories concerned, and possessing all the elements essential to constitute an international servitude." [256]

Article II of this treaty "grants to the United States in perpetuity the use, occupation and control of . . . land . . . for the construction, maintenance, operation, sanitation and protection of said canal . . . extending . . . five miles on each side of the center line . . . of the canal to be constructed."

Article III grants to the United States perpetual "use, occupation and control of any other lands and waters outside of the zone above described which may be necessary and convenient," for the purposes specified in Article II.

Article XXIII states that: "If it should be necessary at any time to employ forces for the safety or protection of the canal, or of the ships that make use of the same, or the railroads and auxiliary works, the United States shall have the right at all times and in its discretion, to use its police and its land and naval forces or to establish fortifications for these purposes." [257]

This alleged military servitude has never been put to the test of a succession in either the grantor or grantee state. There is thus no support for the conclusion that it established "real" rights and obligations running with the land. In fact, the treaty is properly to be considered a treaty of alliance,[258] and, therefore, a treaty that created only personal rights and obligations.[259]

CUBA

It has been said that the "United States possesses in Cuba a permanent real right, . . . an international [military] servitude," and that "geography alone would . . . indicate a sufficient *causas perpetuas* for such a territorial relationship, and "that the explicitly permanent nature of the . . . treaty of May 22, 1903, serves to strengthen that interpretation." [260]

By an agreement of February 16–23, 1903, Cuba leased to the United States, "for the time required for the purpose of coaling and naval stations," designated "areas of land and water" at Guantanamo and Bahia Honda. It also authorized the United States:

> . . . the right to use and occupy the waters adjacent to the said areas of land and water . . . and generally to do any and all things necessary to fit the premises for use as coaling or naval stations. . . . While the United States recognizes the continuance of the ultimate sovereignty of the Republic of Cuba over the described areas. . . . Cuba consents that during the occupation . . . the United States shall exercise complete jurisdiction and control. . . .[261]

From the language of the agreement of February 16–23, 1903, on the rights of the United States to "coaling and naval stations" at Guantanamo and Bahia Honda, it may be said that these rights are personal, for they are to last only so long as the specifically designated beneficiary, the U.S., requires them for specified purposes, and that the rules applicable to treaties generally apply to this agreement.[262]

Negative Military Servitudes

WISMAR

Old agreements pertaining to the status of the City of Wismar have sometimes been cited [263] as having established a negative military servitude.

At the peace of Westphalia in 1648, the City of Wismar, one of the most effectively fortified points of the Baltic, was ceded to Sweden. During the war of 1715, the fortresses of the city were destroyed, and at the peace of Stockholm of 1720, Sweden agreed that the city was never to be fortified. By the Treaty of Malmö of 1830, Sweden hypothecated the City of Mecklenburg-Schwerin for a hundred years. Article 15 of this treaty specified:

> . . . le roi de Suède se trouvant engagé par une ancienne stipulation encore subsistante . . . de ne jamais fortifier la ville et le port de Wismar . . . ct les hautes parties contractantes étant persuadées qu'une cession hypothécaire ne saurait invalider cette obligation stipulée par un traité antérieur . . . le duc de Meclembourg-Schwerin transfère la dite obligation de sa Majesté Suèdoise pleinement . . . sur sa personne et sur celles de ses descendants, pendant toute la durée du terme hypothécaire.

Article 16 provided that "Le port de Wismar ne sera jamais constitué port de guerre."

These terms were respected. In 1903 [264] Sweden chose not to take back the City of Wismar and ceded it to Germany. The act of cession did not mention the prohibition to fortify. The Swedes, in lieu of demanding a guarantee of demilitarization from Germany, decided to bring the Malmö clause relative to the demilitarization of Wismar to the attention of the signatories of the Malmö Treaty. The City of Wismar was later fortified by the Germans, who had no doubt that the restrictions imposed on the City of Wismar by the Treaty of Malmö had been extinguished by their acquisition of the city.

That the city had not been fortified and its port never used as a naval base during the period of its hypothecation can best be explained on the basis of the subsequent and expressly personal obligation that the Duke of Mecklenburg, the pledgee, assumed in this respect. The actions of Germany and Sweden after 1903 confirm the fact that the original obligation not to fortify the city constituted a personal obligation, since Germany's fortification of the city occurred without repercussion, without the consent of the signatory powers to the Malmö Treaty, and without any action, either formal or informal by the signatory powers under the treaty to specifically renounce these rights.

THE PORT OF ANTWERP

Article 15 of a treaty signed at Paris between France, Austria, Russia, England, and Prussia on May 30, 1814, which provided that "Dorénavant, le port d'Anvers sera uniquement un port de commerce," has been cited as a negative military servitude.[265]

Although Article 14 of the Treaty of 1839 between Belgium and the Low Countries separating their respective territories provided that "Le port d'Anvers conformément aux stipulations du traité de Paris du 30 Mai 1814, continuera d'être uniquement un port de commerce," Belgium, nevertheless, sometime after 1839, made Antwerp a strong fortress. It is clear, therefore, that Belgium as a successor state did not consider herself bound by the political obligations of her predecessor under the Treaty of May 30, 1814. Had this treaty established "real" rights that descended to her by operation of law, Article 14 of the treaty would have been unnecessary, and Belgium could not, without fear of repercussion, have disregarded a bilateral commitment binding her not to fortify Antwerp.

HÜNINGEN

The prohibition to fortify the City of Hüningen is probably the most frequently cited instance of a negative military servitude. Article 3 of the second Treaty of Peace of Paris of November 20, 1815, provided on behalf of the Swiss confederation, a nonsignatory power, that France should not restore the fortifications of the Alsatian town of Hüningen and that its fortifications should not be replaced by new ones within three leagues of the city of Basle.[266] The duty not to fortify survived the cession of the town to Germany by the Treaty of Frankfort in 1871, and its cession back to France by the Treaty of Versailles in 1919.[267]

The binding effect of these obligations upon Germany can be readily explained without attributing a "real" character to them.[268] Furthermore, their binding effect upon Germany was never actually put in issue or decided, since Germany, for reasons best known to herself, never manifested any desire or intention to refortify the town. If Germany believed herself bound to respect her obligations under the Treaty of Paris, it was not because of their "real" nature, but because she, having succeeded voluntarily to the obligations of Prussia, believed herself bound by the promise Prussia (a signatory of the Treaty of Paris of November 20, 1815) gave to the Swiss Confederation that it, together with the other signatories, would ensure the destruction of the fortification of the town of Hüningen and prevent its refortification.[269]

THE PROVINCES OF CHABLAIS AND FAUCIGNY

The alleged negative military servitudes arising from the Final Act of the Congress of Vienna of 1815, relative to the status of the Provinces of Chablais and Faucigny and the territory north of Ugine (the permanent neutralization of this area and the prohibition to fortify it in time of war), have been considered above.[270]

STRAITS OF MAGELLAN

Article 5 of the Treaty of 1881 between Chile and the Argentine Republic,[271] which provides that no fortifications or military defense shall be erected that could interfere with "the liberty and neutrality of the Straits of Magellan" that are "forever" guaranteed by the treaty, has been cited as a military servitude of "non-fortification burdening Chile for the benefit of Argentina." [272]

Since the provisions of this treaty have not been subjected to the test of succession, no evidence exists to substantiate the alleged real or absolute nature of the military rights concerned.[273]

STRAITS OF GIBRALTAR

Article 7 of the Anglo-French Declaration (part of the Entente Cordiale of 1904), which provides that, "in order to secure the free passage of the Straits of Gibraltar, the two Governments agree not to permit the erection of any fortifications or strategic works" as to a particular portion of the Moroccan coast, has been asserted by some to constitute a negative military servitude.[274] Suffice it to say that the territory concerned has never been subjected to a change of sovereigns.

TREATY OF PORTSMOUTH

Article 9 of the Treaty of Portsmouth of September 5, 1905, whereby "Japan and Russia mutually agree not to construct in their respective possessions on the Island of Sakhalin or the adjacent islands any fortifications or other similar military works . . . [or to] engage . . . [in] any military measures which might impede the free navigation of the Strait of La Perouse and the Strait of Tartary," [275] has been cited by some as a military servitude.[276]

Pursuant to Article 2(c) of the Treaty of Peace of 1951, between Japan and the Allied Powers, Japan renounced "all right, title and claim . . . to that portion of Sakhalin and the islands adjacent to it over which Japan acquired sovereignty as a consequence of the Treaty of Portsmouth." [277] This treaty makes no reference to the alleged permanent demilitarized status of Sakhalin. It would appear, therefore, that only personal rights and obligations had been established.

TREATY OF STOCKHOLM

The Treaty of Stockholm (Karlstad) of October 26, 1905, which dissolved the union between Sweden and Norway, and established a perpetual neutral zone, where all military operations were forbidden and all fortifications were to be dismantled, has also been cited as a negative military servitude.[278] But this treaty has never been put to the test of state succession, and there is no evidence to substantiate its recognition as a military servitude in state practice.

TREATY OF VERSAILLES OF 1919

The provisions of the Treaty of Versailles of 1919, a "lawmaking" treaty, whereby "Germany is forbidden to maintain or construct any fortifications either on the left bank of the Rhine or on the right bank to the west of a line drawn 50 kilometres to the East of the Rhine," [279] or on the Island of Heligoland,[280] or "in the area comprised between latitudes 50°27′N. and 54°00′N. and longitudes 9°00′E. and 16°00′E. of the meridian of Greenwich, nor install any guns commanding the maritime routes between the North Sea and the Baltic" [281] have often been cited as instances of an agreement that "clearly constitutes an international servitude, designed to assure the security of France and Belgium from attack from across the Rhine, and to guarantee the uninterrupted use of the Kiel Canal and the other maritime routes to the Baltic." [282]

An examination of the facts on these so-called negative military servitudes disproves them. On March 7, 1936, Germany unilaterally repudiated her obligations relative to the demilitarization of the Rhineland [283] on the grounds that such demilitarization was incompatible with the Franco-Soviet Pact of May 2, 1935.[284] The Council of the League of Nations denounced this action as a breach of international law,[285] which recognizes as an essential principle that no state can relieve itself of its treaty obligations or modify the provisions of treaties except by the mutual consent of the contracting parties—a principle that is, of course, as applicable to treaties of a personal nature as to those establishing so-called servitudes. On November 14, 1936, Germany denounced Articles 380–86 of the Treaty of Versailles, which provided that the Kiel Canal and its approaches should be equally free and open to the vessels of commerce and war of all nations at peace with Germany. The majority of the interested signatory powers of the Treaty of Versailles made no express protest about this denunciation.[286]

By the beginning of World War II, Germany had completely disregarded all the provisions of the Treaty of Versailles that were in any way restrictive about her military activities within her territory.[287]

Because of the present political alignment of the Federal Republic of Germany with the North Atlantic Treaty Powers,[288] many of the military restrictions (so-called servitudes) that were imposed upon Germany by the Treaty of Versailles have now been considered infeasible and have already been relegated to the sphere of historic facts, and this without the consent, either express or implied, of the signatories to the Versailles Treaty or of all of the parties at the unconditional surrender of Germany.

TREATY OF DORPAT

Staël-Holstein[289] is of the opinion that the following provisions of the Treaty of Dorpat of 1920 established a series of diverse negative military servitudes, representing gradations of demilitarization, all of which show a "real" character: Article 6, prohibiting Finland from fortifying the coast of Petchenga; Article 13, whereby Finland agreed to neutralize militarily specified islands in the gulf of Finland; Article 14, whereby Finland agreed to the military neutralization of Hogland; Article 15, providing for the disarmament of the fortifications of d'Ino and Puumala, the coast between Styostudd and Inonniemi, and the coast between Ino and the mouth of Rajoki; and Article 16, neutralizing the Ladoga and its banks, and the rivers and canals emptying into the Ladoga.

These provisions are territorial restrictions alleged to be so framed that they will subsist forever. But they have never been put to the test of state succession. It is submitted that if they are tested by succession, they will survive, if at all, only by the consent of the successor state.

TREATIES OF PEACE WITH ITALY AND BULGARIA OF 1947

The Treaty of Peace with Italy in 1947 [290] provides that Italian fortifications along the Franco-Italian frontier shall be destroyed or removed;[291] that Italian fortifications along the Italian-Yugoslav frontier shall be destroyed or removed;[292] that there shall be no fortifications in the Apulian Peninsula east of longitude $170°45'E.$;[293] that Pantellaria, the Pelogian Islands (Lampedusa, Lampione, and Linosa), and Pianosa shall remain demilitarized;[294] and that in Sardinia all permanent coastal defense artillery emplacements and all naval emplacements located within thirty kilometers from French territorial waters shall be removed or destroyed.[295]

The Treaty of Peace with Bulgaria of 1947 [296] prohibits Bulgaria from maintaining permanent fortifications to the north of the Greek-Bulgarian frontier capable of firing into Greek territory.[297]

Neither of these treaties, cited as having established negative military servitudes,[298] has ever been subjected to the test of succession. Whatever binding effect these treaty provisions may have can be credited to the fact that they are "lawmaking" treaties.

The instances cited above, many of a "lawmaking" nature, cover all the important conventional arrangements that have been characterized as military servitudes of international law as that term has traditionally been defined.

An examination of the many published bilateral treaties concluded during the unprecedented political instability of the period 1940–62, by which states in the interest of mutual security have granted to other states the right to utilize their territory for military purposes or have denied to themselves the right to use their territory for their own military interests, discloses no treaty or agreement that can be said to have established either a positive or negative military servitude the alleged "real" obligations of which have been recognized in the practice of states. Without exception, these conventions expressly reflect their political (personal) character, for they specify their mutual-defense purposes and contain express provisions on duration. "The personal character of the relationship is decisive." [299]

Judging from the recent practice of states, it is submitted that the concept of military servitudes is fictional, and that the nature and instability of international organization—its lack of discipline and control—negate the possibility that military servitudes of international law can be created. Changing international political affiliations and interests preclude a principle of law under which treaty rights of one state that impinge upon the territorial sovereignty of another state can be considered "real" in nature.

It has been said that, since territories in most instances undergo a change of sovereignty only under the pressure of brute force and not because of contracts freely entered into, an absolute right can, in the face of such force, be no more resistant, no surer, than a relative right.[300] The recent practice of states substantiates the truth of this statement.

VI. Is There a Necessity for a Concept of Military Servitudes in International Law?

It is asserted that the importance of the concept of military servitudes in international law:

> lies in its possible use as a safeguard of sovereignty by permitting a foreign state to exercise the right necessary to its own interest, perhaps to the advantage of the whole world without modifying the nationality of the territory in question. For instance, there are two ways of assuring permanent and uninterrupted access to the sea for the benefit of a landlocked state: one is the actual cession of a strip of territory connecting it with the coast; the alternative is the grant

of a servitude of passage, leaving intact the territorial sovereignty of the neighboring states. Which is to be preferred? [301]

International servitudes concerned with distribution are particularly important, it is said, because their objective is "to alter the arbitrary distribution of physical resources affected by national boundary lines." [302]

The untenability of these statements is reflected when they are taken to their logical conclusion. They imply that states endowed with natural physical advantages or resources not possessed by neighboring states are somehow under an obligation to share these endowments with such states, and, in fact, that they must, if they desire to safeguard their sovereignty, either cede a portion of their territory to the other states or grant to them limited sovereign rights for a portion of it. The fact that these natural conditions exist, however, imposes neither a legal nor a moral obligation upon the states that "have" to share with those that "have not." Certainly, states are not endowed with an inalienable right to share or benefit from the natural advantages, resources, or prosperity of other states. Neither are states bound to impoverish themselves for the benefit of others. Furthermore, there is no assurance that a permanent grant of access to the sea or a permanent partial grant of sovereignty over particular territory for military purposes would not eventually result in the subjection of the grantor state, or that it would in any way satiate the aggressive designs of neighboring states. Rights of access to the sea, rights of transit, and economic and commercial benefits are all proper objectives of treaties, but such treaties establish only personal obligations that have no binding effect upon successor states.

As for the assertion that military servitudes are necessary because their object or result is "to increase security," [303] it is obvious that a converse result is just as probable. Its partisans recognize that the doctrine of military servitudes may be abused, and "even misused as a weapon of oppression and aggression," but blandly submit that the "remedy for any such possible perversion lies in the enlightened self-interest of the States concerned, controlled and directed by an enlightened public opinion, rather than in the mere discarding of a legal term." [304]

It has also been stated by some that the concept of servitudes is especially useful with respect to total or partial transmission of territory, since the servitude necessarily follows with the land and is transmitted with it.[305] By this technique, therefore, a state could, ostensibly, grant independence to a former subject territory without in fact divesting itself of the rights that it actually desires to retain perpetually within the territory of its former subject. It could assert the rights not only against the grantor, but against his successors as well, on the basis of their alleged "real" nature and the dispositive character of the convention that created them.

So-called military servitudes are, therefore: conducive to disguised aggressive intervention and possible annexation;[306] a source of armed conflicts;[307] a danger to universal peace;[308] and a hindrance to the development of liberty and to the accomplishment of the humanitarian interests of nations.[309] As Funck-Brentano and Sorel put it: "Ces traités de servitude sont en général une source de conflicts, un moyen d'abus pour l'État le plus fort, une cause de vexation pour l'État le plus faible, une menace enfin et une atteinte à son indépendance. Il est sage de les éviter." [310]

The concept of military servitudes serves no useful purpose, but is in fact inherently dangerous to the independence of states and to world peace. It is a myth that security derives from so-called military servitudes. They can prove a subterfuge for conquest, and cannot deter brute force any more effectively than can military rights and obligations of a personal nature.

VII. Conclusions

The concept of "military servitudes" has been refuted by the recent practice of states. An examination of conventional arrangements, the military rights and obligations of which are asserted to be "real" or absolute because they were alleged to have survived changes in the sovereignty of the servient state, discloses that in fact none of these arrangements survived contrary to the will of the successor state—or, in other words, devolved by operation of law. An analysis of the alleged military servitudes discloses that those that did survive a change of sovereignty did so only because the successor state had formally assumed the obligations pursuant to a new and subsequent treaty; had informally consented to the continuance of the obligations; or, as a matter of political expediency, had tacitly renewed the obligations of their predecessors by continued action consistent with the original treaty establishing them.

The position taken by the proponents of servitudes of international law is superficial, unrealistic, and juristically untenable. They seek by recourse to archaic theories and principles that were effective in solving the constitutional problems of the German empire to resolve the vastly different, complex international problems of a new and highly sophisticated era. The resolution of the present-day problems of state succession rests in large measure upon the principle of self-determination, the necessity to preserve and enhance the security and the welfare of the international community, and the need for a flexible and effective approach to the revision of treaty provisions that have become outmoded or odious because of changing conditions. Such an approach is essential for military arrangements in the case of state succession. The nature of the international community, including its political instability and its lack of discipline and constitutional authority, precludes the recognition in international law of the alleged real rights and obligations of treaties concerned with military activities. Changing international political affiliations and interests dictate the personal nature of such rights and obligations.

International judicial bodies have refused to give the concept of military servitudes recognition because its endorsement would in effect permit states an unrestrained liberty to create military rights and obligations that could jeopardize the independence of states and the security of the community of states. Both practice and opinion refute the view that international law is composed of abstract doctrines and inflexible principles that are impervious to power, social progress, and legitimate national aspirations.[311]

Treaties that are alleged to have established so-called positive military servitudes are in fact treaties of alliance and, as such, are purely personal in nature. In most instances they are concluded with the eventuality of war in mind. No other reason could motivate their conclusion or substantiate their existence. Unless these so-called military servitudes are considered as conditional treaties of alliance, necessarily political, and, therefore, personal in nature, or unless they are suspended during wars between dominant and third states, treaties that accord to a dominant state any military use of servient territory during a war with a third state have as their purpose a breach of the law of neutrality—a purpose that, being contrary to generally recognized rules of international law—is not a valid treaty object. Such treaties are void *ab initio*, binding neither signatories nor third states. This illegality exists as well for so-called negative military servitudes that would preclude servient states from taking the action required of them by the law of neutrality and the U.N. Charter.

History has demonstrated that the concept of military servitudes serves no useful purpose. It is, as we have said, a concept that is inherently dangerous to the independence of states and to world peace. The belief that security is assured by so-called military servitudes is fallacious, because they can in fact prove a subterfuge for conquest. Practically, security can be more effectively ensured by personal treaties that are responsive to changing interests and conditions than by treaties alleged to create military servitudes.[312] Territories most generally undergo changes in sovereignty only under the pressure of a preponderantly aggressive force. As such, military servitudes can no more effectively deter such force than can security or defense arrangements of a personal nature.[313] Furthermore, it is highly improbable that a dominant state could derive any real benefit or use from a military servitude to which the servient state objects because the so-called right or obligation has become odious to it.

The intent of the parties to a conventional arrangement is in large measure the key to the question of the so-called military servitudes of international law. Almost invariably the parties concluding military arrangements intend only to resolve problems personal to themselves or to ensure thereby only their own immediate military interests. It cannot be assumed that parties concluding such arrangements contemplated, or had any interest whatsoever in fostering, the military objectives of possible successor states the military requirements of which would in all probability be materially different from their own. Under these circumstances, there exists an almost irrebuttable presumption that understandings on military matters are personal in nature. The rights and obligations of international conventions are properly to be considered as binding successor states only when—and for only so long as—the security and the welfare of the international community so mandate. The problem is essentially a practical one—most certainly not one that can be resolved on the theoretical and artificial bases of the "real" or personal nature of the rights and obligations involved.

3. UNITED STATES RECOGNITION POLICY TOWARD THE NEW NATIONS

BY WILLIAM V. O'BRIEN AND ULF H. GOEBEL

A study of U.S. recognition policies toward the new nations makes it possible to treat simultaneously two subjects that deserve attention. The first is the contemporary state of recognition—surely one of the most chaotic subjects in an increasingly unsettled body of law. One reason for the chaos is that there is still comparatively little accurate, comprehensive reporting on state recognition practice. International-law authorities have rendered a most elusive subject even more complex by imposing their own unsubstantiated theories on a record of practice that is murky enough already and that often becomes further distorted by subjective analyses. The appearance of close to fifty new states since World War II has provided us with a mass of new data to be collected, analyzed, and compared with existing data on earlier recognition practice and with fashionable theories as to the nature, criteria, and forms of recognition.

Second, the emergence of so many new states, virtually all in Asia and Africa, has naturally caused speculation on the effect of all of these non-Western states on international law and diplomacy. One side of the subject, and possibly the most important in the long run, concerns the behavior of the new nations themselves. It is still rather early, however, to develop this side in depth. On the other hand, a study of the recognition policies of the established international persons toward the new nations is already possible. It would appear to be well worthwhile to assess what, if any, discernible impact the sudden avalanche of new nations has had on one of the most characteristic institutions of traditional international law and diplomacy—recognition. This study examines the attitude and behavior of the United States, the acknowledged leader of the West, yet in many respects a power independent of the colonialist heritage of its Western allies and friends, in the realm of recognition policy toward the new nations.

After World War II, the monographs of Lauterpacht and Chen revived ancient, inconclusive debates over the place of recognition in international law.[1] In these, as in earlier attempts to analyze recognition scientifically, efforts were made to combine a priori theories or dispositions on the nature of recognition with expositions of state practice, the latter supposedly supporting the former. Without attempting a full-scale critique of such efforts, one may make the following critical observations:

In the case of the works of Lauterpacht and Chen, the supporting evidence was drawn mainly from the most abundant sources, British and American diplomatic practice and judicial decisions. But, as Percy Corbett has pointed out, seemingly impressive evidence of state practice must often be taken cautiously indeed.[2] The very concern for the rule of law that at times has favored the development of international law in the Anglo-Saxon countries, for example, has also favored the loose, and even at times hypocritical, use of legalisms, of legalistic "double-talk," and of sweeping, rhetorical platitudes couched in legal terms, none of which offers much more than confusion to the "scientific" analyst. Thus the discount rate for the conservative appraisal of legalistic verbiage on recognition is a high one. The legal thinker who begins with a strong doctrinal bias, who is inclined to believe that state practice *will* support his theories, naturally tends to interpret the sweeping, imprecise language of diplomatic practice to fit his own hypotheses. But a rival theorist may do the same. We are thus treated to the spectacle of Scholar A citing a certain Secretary of State or Minister of Foreign Affairs to be of the Constitutive school and Scholar B insisting the same person to be of the Declaratory persuasion, whereas in fact the poor man may have been ignorant of both theories, trying only to put a good respectable face on his government's purely pragmatic recognition policies.

Even more precarious, however, is the established Anglo-American custom of "proving" recognition theories by quoting from domestic judicial decisions. The reason for this practice is obvious: The abundance of competently reported case law provides the scholar with a great bulk of primary legal material that is seemingly relevant and highly authoritative. Yet both the relevance and the authority of much of this case law is open to question. As Anglo-American courts are usually eager to proclaim, they have no direct role in the conduct of foreign affairs, only taking cognizance of the decisions and policies of the Executive, and, where appropriate, spelling out the legal consequences within their own jurisdictions.

What they say, therefore, about the nature of recognition as an institution in public international law, or about the criteria for recognition, or the forms or degrees appropriate to different kinds of recognition, is usually *obiter* and sometimes rather inexpert and confused.[3] (To make up for this, the Executive is sometimes unclear, sometimes almost coy, in giving guidance to the courts in matters of recognition.)

Yet we have read statements by scholars, public officials, domestic court justices, and members of international arbitral tribunals reeling off "the law" on recognition with the confidence of a veteran municipal court judge reiterating the law of his jurisdiction on a question of contract that had been settled for a hundred years.

In these circumstances, what is needed above all is the record of international practice on recognition. It is increasingly apparent that, whether for some of the reasons suggested or for others, there is no consensus on the theoretical nature of recognition, and there is no indication yet that the study of practice will prove anything more than that practice is variable and contradictory, supporting no general theory of recognition.

Yet recognition is a subject from which the international lawyer cannot escape. Whatever the vagaries of its "nature" or "function," whether legal, political, or a mixture of both, recognition has important legal effects in international as well as in municipal law. It would appear that the task confronting this generation of international-law scholars is to compare the vast disarray of theories, definitions, distinctions, and procedural institutions that have grown up and have been accepted by international-law texts with the actual practice of states in a period when occasions for recognition have proved extremely numerous.

This task must be carried out by scholars in all countries, and, obviously, it must go beyond the scope of the recognition of new states to deal with the recognition of governments, and beyond recognition policies toward new nations to embrace all diplomatic intercourse. But it was thought useful to limit this study to the recognition policies of one state, the United States, toward the so-called new nations that have emerged since 1943. (By starting in 1943, rather than 1945, several interesting case studies can be included.) Austria, which some contend was extinguished in 1938, will not be considered. This is not because of an uncritical acceptance of the view that Austrian international personality survived the German absorption of 1938, but because Austria presents none of the problems that are typical of the new nations that emerged from the former colonial areas, problems characteristic of virtually all the new nations here discussed.[4]

Section I of the study will very briefly review some of the prevailing theories on the nature of recognition, not to reopen old and, it is believed, often fruitless controversies, but to provide a context for the treatment of a very practical subject, the criteria for recognition.

Section II will summarize the different types of recognition that have been granted, and analyze the entities accorded recognition. Here the question will be raised as to what difference it makes whether recognition is *"de facto"* or *"de jure."*

Section III will analyze the modes of granting recognition. Special attention will be given to the changes in traditional practice that may have resulted from improvement in international communication and transportation facilities.

Section IV discusses methods of recognition.

Section V, in the light of the foregoing sections, will report in summary form on the record of U.S. recognition practice toward the new nations; subsequently, a brief interpretive commentary will be offered. It is appropriate at this point to pay tribute to the wise and scholarly work on United States recognition policy toward the new nations presented by Denys P. Myers in the *American Journal of International Law* of July, 1961.[5] The present study builds on the ground covered so thoroughly and precisely by Mr. Myers, a veteran practitioner of international law in the U.S. Department of State, and a respected scholar.

I. THE FUNCTION OF RECOGNITION AND THE CRITERIA
FOR RECOGNITION OF NEW STATES

Is the act of recognition predominantly legal or political? What considerations should govern a government's decision to recognize a new state? Lauterpacht held that each government should be conscious of a legal duty of objectivity in its recognition policies. The recognizing state was to be aware that it was executing a legal function on behalf of the decentralized international juridical order, namely, the creation of a new international person.[6] Jessup and others would extend this approach further and assert that since recognition is precisely the legal means of creating a new international person, it should be a collective function, preferably carried out by the United Nations as a representative of the whole international legal community, rather than by the variable and arbitrary decisions of many individual states.[7]

The traditional Constitutive theory, of course, denied that in the realm of recognition a sovereign independent state was under any overriding obligation imposed by a superior international community. Each sovereign had an unrestricted right to vote for or against the membership of an applicant to the exclusive club of sovereigns.[8] The Declaratory theory, on the other hand, divorced the institution of recognition from the question of the objective legal criteria of actually existing states. It tended toward the belief that recognition is essentially a political institution.[9]

However, there are more dimensions to the question than "legal" and "political." The term *political*, in the context of the debate over the nature of recognition and the proper criteria for granting it, has implied mainly "power political self-interest." Yet there is a further dimension that may be in part either legal or political but that transcends both in their ordinary connotations. Depending on one's judgment or sympathies, this dimension is moral—or moralistic, based on justice or some higher law—or, to use that all-pervasive twentieth-century adjective, ideological. In our time, it appears increasingly that recognition practice is not justified, either explicitly or implicitly, in terms of performance of legal duties enjoining complete "objectivity," or in terms of power-political leverage to obtain selfish political, economic, or other advantages. In an age of profound ideological conflict, recognition has become an ideological weapon. This is not an entirely new development, since recognition has often been used as a power-political weapon, and the two phenomena overlap.[10] Yet, it is submitted, both the depth and scope of recognition as a weapon in the cold and hot wars of this century raise problems that render the old "legal-political" dichotomy inadequate as a basis for analysis of recognition and determination of the criteria for recognition.

The history of U.S. recognition policy in particular abounds with examples of the use of recognition—and nonrecognition—as a means to further some "higher purpose." Presidents and secretaries of state, often with popular support, have accorded or withheld recognition as a means of supporting the good, the democratic, the constitutional, or the anti-Communist, and of punishing or combating the evil, the totalitarian, the unconstitutional, or the Communistic.[11] Thus a high degree of *subjectivity* has characterized much of modern U.S. recognition policy, in contrast to the tolerant objectivity enjoined by the original Jeffersonian theory of recognition.[12] And, as if to underscore the complexity of this "political," or, at least not "strictly legal," element in recognition, American policy has not lacked for critics who have contended that these "moralistic" policies have actually depreciated from the national interest, whatever their standing among those who hold that recognition ought to be a strictly legal, nonpolitical function.[13] Thus, for example, it is possible to envisage a two-pronged criticism of U.S. nonrecognition of Red China by, on the one hand, Lauterpachtians who might say that the United States is not acting objectively in the name of the decentralized juridical order, and, on the other, by straightforward advocates of power politics who might contend that the U.S. is unrealistically neglecting a power-political need to come to terms with Red China to indulge instead in a hopeless, "moralistic punishment" of evildoers and to express a desire to avoid their company.

Are such subjective, moralistic approaches in fact incompatible with Lauterpacht's concept of objective, legal recognition of entities that ought to be accorded international personality? Perhaps not entirely. An American idealist might argue, in the manner of Henry Stimson, that it is precisely on behalf of the international legal order that the United States has refused to recognize would-be states and governments constituted in flagrant violation of the fundamental law of that order, whether the League Covenant, the Kellogg-Briand Pact, or the U.N. Charter.[14]

Certainly this explanation cannot be lightly brushed aside. But although, in principle, opposition to the violation of the international legal order is admirable, the question is whether manipulation of the institution of recognition is an appropriate means of sanctioning the law. Lauterpacht argued that the basic purpose of recognition is the identification of the subjects of international law.[15] Every legal order, he reasoned, must have a means of identifying the parties holding rights and duties under it. This is particularly true of a primitive, decentralized legal order such as that governing the family of nations. The principal object of recognition, then, is to clarify the possessors of international rights and duties. Presumably, frequent use of recognition as an ideological weapon would seriously detract from the usefulness of recognition as a legal means of conferring international personality.[16]

Lauterpacht's theory of recognition has not, of course, been generally accepted. But it serves as a good starting point for the comparison of attitudes toward recognition that emphasize the need for disinterested objectivity in the discharge of what is essentially a legal function and those attitudes that supercharge the institution of recognition with subjective elements and purposes that, as we have said, may range from the purely selfishly political to the "higher" ends and purposes of the ideological. Finally—and most relevantly to U.S. policy from Wilson's time to the present—we must contrast the view that recognition, as a legal institution, is exclusively a means of according international personality with the view that, whatever the normal function of recognition, its manipulation may be a legitimate legal sanction against violators of international law and order.

In order to judge the consequences of alleged misuse of the institution of recognition, we must recall the logic underlying views, such as Lauterpacht's, that recognition is a legal function. This argument would appear to rest securely on the classic concept of a globe divided into areas of sovereign jurisdictions with high seas in between. The concomitant of what was, in principle, absolute sovereign jurisdiction was complete international responsibility for occurrences within a state's physical domain. Such a system obviously could not long countenance vacuums of sovereign jurisdiction and responsibility. The task of the recognizing state, viewed from this perspective, was the largely factual task of identifying the particular political society that in fact exercised jurisdiction and that therefore ought to be legally responsible within a given portion of the globe.[17]

There is yet a further aspect to this argument for objectivity in recognition policies. It may be argued that not all states share a common practical necessity for identifying actually existing international persons all over the world. If one does not accept Lauterpacht's contention that there is a legal duty to make recognition policies conform to the exigencies of the decentralized international legal order, it may be argued that a state may follow subjective, nonlegal recognition policies to the extent that its actual need for intercourse with other parts of the world permits. But the whole trend of modern history and of contemporary social thought speaks against such a subjective, selfish attitude.

With the shrinking of the world, the enormously heightened pace of communication among peoples, and, above all, with the spread of international conflict into all corners of the world and the omnipresence of nuclear weapons, the essential universality of human interests is becoming strikingly clear. Such widely divergent realizations as fear of nuclear destruction and awareness of the requirements of international social justice are rendering untenable an attitude of indifference toward the identification of the actual holders of power in the international community. From all the factors mentioned flows a normative imperative to maintain *communication* among the nations of the world. Thus recognition must be viewed not only as an instrument for identifying the accredited, legally competent actors on the international scene, but also as the indispensable means of ensuring continuous, orderly communication among the nations of the world.

Implicit in the foregoing is the dichotomy between the world of political reality and the international legal scene as it is pieced together by the community of international persons that creates, interprets, and applies international law. The historical background for our discussion has been characterized by the phenomenon of nonrecognition of political societies or of governments that patently did exist, exercising all the usual powers of sovereignty. The other side of this coin, of course, has been the continued recognition of political societies or of governments that no longer existed in fact at all. As we analyze the recognition practices of the older states vis-à-vis the new nations, we shall be interested in the degree to which they are objective, to which they unite actual status with legal status, and, in the light of our recent history of subjective recognition policies, we shall have to be alert to both the forms of subjectivity that have characterized our times, namely, nonrecognition of what exists in fact and recognition of what does not exist in fact.

The practical focal point for the analysis of recognition policies is in the realm of the *criteria* for recognition. Since this study is limited mainly to recognition of states, our treatment of this subject will likewise be limited to the criteria for recognition as an international person, not as a new government of an existing international person.

Here all of our theorizing about the nature of recognition is of practical importance. If recognition or nonrecognition is viewed as a free-wheeling means of advancing the national interest, or as an instrumentality of ideological conflict, or even as a sanction for international law, it would not seem feasible to prepare a list of criteria for recognition. The criteria would be as infinite as the diverse interests pursued in all of international relations. Yet, interestingly, most treatises and monographs dealing with recognition provide us with rather circumscribed lists of criteria. They are almost all substantially the same. Regardless of their differences over the nature of recognition, theorists agree that only entities meeting the traditional political-science definition of the state, namely, a sovereign, independent government exercising effective control over a population in a definable territory, should even be considered for recognition as full international persons.[18]

The traditional question is, "Does a state exist?" (In the case of recognition of a new government, the question is, "Does it have effective control of the population and territory of the state?") To Lauterpacht, these conditions were substantially "definite and exhaustive." However, as subjective criteria gained prominence, the question became increasingly, "*Should* this state, which seems to enjoy a real existence in the material sense, exist as an international person?" The "should" could be couched in the context of political, legal, or even moral norms. Thus the U.S. refused recognition for sixteen years to the Soviet Union, despite its clear establishment as an independent entity by, at the latest, the early 1920's.

The U.S. has justified such policies by adding to the traditional criteria for recognition the requirement that the entity's government be able and willing to abide by international law.[19] The very positing of this criterion, of course, makes possible at least a threefold breakdown of international entities:

1. Full international persons, entities possessing the elements of a sovereign state *and* evidencing an ability and willingness to comply with international law.

2. Occupants of a legal limbo, entities possessing the elements of a sovereign state, but failing to evidence an ability and willingness to accept the obligations of international law.

3. Less than full international persons, entities not possessing the traditional prerequisites for statehood.

It is true that, thus far, the weight of authoritative opinion and the practice of states seem to deny the validity of "willingness" to accept international obligations as a criterion for international personality and that insistence upon it has been almost entirely confined to the practice of the United States.[20] Moreover, Lauterpacht is probably right in suggesting that the "ability" to meet international-law obligations is properly a part of the "effective control" that is the necessary characteristic of the independent government of a sovereign state.[21] But still this criterion remains embedded in the practice of the most powerful state in the West. Thus far it has been applied mainly to the question of recognition of new governments rather than to recognition of new states. But there is no reason to believe that its application might not preclude recognition of a new state that otherwise clearly met the standards of statehood.

This subject is not without its importance for the new nations.

There is always the distinct possibility that a new state will appear that, in principle, rejects the foundations of international law as a development from Western Christendom. This, of course, was the case with the Soviet Union, and practical as well as doctrinal questions were raised that have yet to be adequately answered, by the West or by the Soviet Union and its legal theorists themselves.[22] One early objection to the American criterion of willingness to accept obligations under international law was that it was superfluous—that all new international persons automatically fell under the scope of all existing institutions and rules of international law.[23] It seems at least questionable whether most of the new nations accept the deeper implications of this view, or, at least, whether they are unwilling to endorse it openly.[24] Thus, it is not inconceivable that we may find a fundamental unwillingness on the part of some new nations to accept existing international law—its "Western" normative foundations—or their specific rights and duties under it, without profound alterations. In such cases, the American criterion of willingness and ability to submit to international law (as understood by the U.S.) might once again prove the object of debate.

In summary, we may say that the criteria that are expressly or implicitly applied in determining whether a new state should be recognized should provide some insight into the nature of recognition itself. What, then, has been the pattern of U.S. recognition policy toward the new nations? Has it been highly legalistic and objective—has the United States insisted on a rigorous scrutiny of facts and on the prompt recognition of the existence of the prerequisites for statehood and, consequently, the prerequisites for international personality? Or has the United States abstained from recognizing political societies that did not meet the traditional requirements for statehood? Has the peculiarly American condition of willingness and ability to abide by international law been widely applied?

Or, has recognition seemingly been used as a power-political tool, a lever with which to extract political, strategic, economic, or other advantages? Beyond this, have ideological considerations, particularly reflections of the Cold War, dominated U.S. policy? Have some new considerations appeared that introduced new dimensions to the categories of "political" and "ideological" recognition policies, again to the detriment of a strictly legal, objective approach? These questions should be kept in mind as the record of U.S. recognition policy toward the new nations is unveiled.

In addition to these points, this study will examine, in the light of current U.S. practice, a second category of questions concerning the types and degrees of recognition accorded; the modes that they take; and the methods employed in granting them. What, if any, difference does it make whether a state is granted *de facto* or *de jure* recognition? Is the distinction always clearly made? Does the mode or the method serve to distinguish degrees of certitude or of enthusiasm concerning the recognized state? On the other hand, to what extent are the procedures of recognition in an age of proliferation of new sovereigns the product of practical necessities rather than of legal or diplomatic niceties? Let us now proceed to examine these questions.

II. THE OBJECTS AND TYPES OF RECOGNITION

The Objects of Recognition: Entities

Green H. Hackworth points out that "Recognition of new states usually carries with it recognition of the government of the state so recognized, since states can speak and act only through their governments." [25] Yet, a distinction should be made between the recognition of a state and that of its government, first, because newly established governments in already existing states are often recognized, and, second, because the U.S. Government has, on occasion, made a distinction between the simultaneous recognition of a newly independent nation and of its government. As a third reason for such a distinction, the Indian case might be cited. Implicit recognition was extended to the Government of India long before it was granted the status of independent statehood by Great Britain.[26]

Since 1943, the U.S. has extended recognition to a great variety of dependent, as well as independent, states. First, a distinction should be made between new states that remained autonomous or entirely independent members of the British Commonwealth of Nations or the French Community and those that have chosen at least formal independence in the absolute sense of the word. While the former have retained some ties with the European nations from which they received independence or autonomy, the latter have accepted neither formal nor informal qualifications of their international status. This distinction may appear as rather fictional, since members of the British Commonwealth and the French Community are probably no less independent legally and politically than the "completely independent" new nations. Yet, the U.S. Government has, in fact, made a clear and express distinction in several instances of recognition. This was probably done purely out of courtesy to the metropole and may have had little more than formal value; still, the fact remains that it was done.[27]

Most states recognized by the United States during the past twenty years come under the categories discussed in the previous paragraph. For the rest, there has been recognition of nations that were not "newly" independent, but existent as autonomous entities for decades and possibly centuries before their acceptance by the U.S. as members of the international community. The reason for such retarded action has usually been a lack of contact by these states with the civilized world.[28] In addition, there has been at least one instance of implicit, but clearly intended, recognition of a dependent nation and its government.[29] The United States has also on occasion recognized a change in the nature of a state, as, for example, the conversion of a constitutional monarchy into a republic.[30] And finally, the Department of State has had to consider recognizing the establishment of a federation by several previously autonomous or independent units, the dismemberment of a federation, the fusion of two political entities into a single and unitary state, and the changing political status of a nation that had not yet attained its independence.[31]

This study is not concerned with the recognition of new governments in states that already existed prior to 1943. It is sufficient here to point out that the United States has managed publicly to evidence an awareness of the fact that a given government had been established either by legal or illegal, constitutional or unconstitutional means. Of sufficient significance to deserve mention is the formal recognition of a newly established government in a nonindependent state. Reference is made here to the formal recognition of the government of Austria, which at the time was still under Allied occupation and had as yet regained very few attributes of an independent state.[32] There has also been at least one instance of extending recognition to a constitutional change in the character or form of a government.[33]

The Objects of Recognition: Situations

The objects of recognition discussed so far have been described as "entities." It remains now to mention two instances in which recognition was extended to what might best be described as a "situation." For example, in 1949 the United States expressly recognized the *de facto* authority of the Republic of Indonesia within a specified area. Although it may be validly held that the United

States, in this instance, recognized the government of that republic or even the republic as such, the wording of the formal act of recognition is certainly ambiguous enough to permit a very different, more limited, interpretation. In fact, only the situation of the existence of an authority within an area was formally recognized. It cannot be maintained that there was express recognition of an entity in this case. Secondly, the United States has taken cognizance of the unilateral proclamation of neutrality on the part of a state to which recognition of independence had previously been extended. In noting the proclamation of neutrality of the Austrian Government, the United States again did not recognize an international entity. The Austrian Government and State had already received recognition. Consequently, this act was also the recognition of an international situation.[34]

As for other types of recognizable situations, the United States appears not to have recognized a state of either belligerency or insurgency, or the acquisition of new territory, during the period under discussion.

The Types of Recognition

No attempt will be made in this section to consider the controversies over the nature and legal or political value of recognition. We shall refer to only a few of the international-law authorities who have written about this highly complex subject. More than such select reference is beyond the scope of this study, which purports to analyze U.S. practice, but does not attempt a comprehensive analysis of the various views on the nature of recognition.

Let us begin our examination of the various types of recognition found in U.S. practice by considering the distinction between implied and express recognition. Implied recognition is usually extended by some act that contains a clearly perceived intention to recognize a specified entity or situation but that does not involve an explicit expression of this intention. As Lauterpacht states, implied recognition, although not expressly referring to recognition, leaves no doubt "as to the intention to grant it."[35] Express recognition, on the other hand, refers to an oral or written statement on the part of the U.S. Government in which the word "recognition," or words of identical meaning, are expressly used, and that leaves no doubt about the intention of the Government. It takes place through formal notification or by a declaration of the intention to recognize.

A second distinction is that between *de facto* and *de jure* recognition. *De jure* recognition generally constitutes an acknowledgment that the entity recognized fulfills the requirements laid down by international law. *De facto* recognition, on the other hand, has been described as recognition of a new authority that, although it actually exists independently in a specific area of land, has not achieved stability and does not fulfill all the criteria established by general international law. *De facto* and *de jure* recognition have also been contrasted by classifying *de facto* recognition as temporary. It is said to be subject to withdrawal if the absent requirements of recognition fail to materialize. *De jure* recognition, on the other hand, is said to be permanent in nature.[36]

In preparing this study the authors operated under the assumption that the *de facto-de jure* dichotomy still prevailed in U.S. recognition practice. However, as the study was being concluded, the appearance of Volume II of Miss Whiteman's *Digest* added new dimensions to the subject. The authors had concluded that the United States probably intended the *de jure* recognition of most of the states recognized since World War II, even though this was usually not expressly stated. However, Miss Whiteman explains current usage as follows:

> While the terms "*de facto* recognition" and "*de jure* recognition" are frequently employed, the expressions "recognition of a *de facto* government," situation, etc., and "recognition of a *de jure* government," etc., are preferable. The character of the object recognized may be recognized as "*de facto*" in existence or control. In prevailing practice, when the United States extends recognition, it is recognition *per se*, not "*de facto*" recognition. The United States may, however, should it so desire, recognize a *de facto* situation, government, state, etc.; that is to say, recognize that the situation, government, state, etc., in fact exists.[37]

Thus, what the authors interpreted to be implicit *de jure* recognition of new states is termed recognition "per se" by Miss Whiteman. We will return to this increasingly complicated problem of terminology at the end of the study.

In any event, there have also been governments to which "recognition" was extended with a simultaneous expression of disapproval of the way in which that government came to power. This type of recognition should be referred to not as *de jure* but as *de facto* recognition. The difficulty of making an accurate distinction, however, lies in the fact that the United States has only on rare occasions explicitly stated that it was recognizing an entity either *de facto* or *de jure*. In most instances, only the fact that an act of recognition took place has been made express. The delicate matter of the degree or nature of that act is usually left to the imagination of the observer.

In addition to the types of recognition reviewed so far, the United States has accorded recognition of several subsidiary or related types. In the case of Israel, for example, "full" recognition was expressly granted to the State of Israel. Of course, this may have meant the same as *de jure* recognition. On another occasion, the U.S. Government extended "diplomatic" recognition to entities that it apparently did not want to recognize outright as *de facto* or *de jure*, but with which it wanted to have diplomatic contacts.[38] "Official" recognition is another term that has been used, and, in at least one instance, there has been express conditional recognition.[39] Also of significance have been acts referred to as completion of recognition, and supplementation of recognition of a provisional or interim government by a formal announcement.[40]

III. The Modes of Recognition

The preceding analysis has served to demonstrate the complexity of recognition practice and procedure. An additional categorization of modes and methods of recognition would at first sight appear to serve no other purpose than that of further complication. Some types of recognition come close to being both modes and methods. There really is no clear dividing line between these three categories. The very coining of the words "types," "modes," and "methods" is rather arbitrary. Yet valid distinctions can be made. Accordingly, the reader is asked to overlook a certain degree of arbitrariness and duplication, so that the formulation of distinguishable analytical categories may be permitted to make its contribution to the better understanding of a highly complex subject matter.[41]

First, the U.S. has made extensive use of the mode of express declaration. When this mode was employed—sometimes after implied recognition had already taken place by other means—recognition was usually definitive and conclusive. The qualifying word "usually" is used because, as in the Austrian case, even an express declaration of recognition may contain an expressly stated condition. A second mode of recognition that can be either express or implied is that of the bilateral treaty.[42] According to Chen, a treaty that regulates more or less permanent relations of a general character would constitute recognition, while the same could probably not be said for a nonpolitical treaty that merely regulates business relations.[43] A third mode that generally implies recognition is the exchange of diplomatic representatives.[44] There certainly cannot be such exchange without the presumption that the foreign state exists, either independently or in some state of dependence.

Fourthly, the U.S. has participated in recognition by conference. What is meant here is not the recognition of a newly established state by members of an international conference as a result of the admittance of the new state to the conference, but the deliberate setting up of a conference in order to arrange formal transfer of sovereignty to the new entity, and thus the objective recognition of the new entity brought into being through the instrumentality of the conference. The Round Table Conference that terminated in the transfer of sovereignty from the metropole of the Netherlands to the emancipated colony of Indonesia is an excellent example of this mode of recognition. Finally, the United States has engaged in a type of collective recognition sometimes referred to as collective recognition "in substance." Collective recognition "in form" would be an express declaration on the part of the recognizing states, incorporated in either a multilateral treaty or declaration. It appears that the United States has not employed this formal mode of collective recognition since World War II. But collective recognition "in substance"—consultation among the recognizing states before they separately and unilaterally recognize the new state—has been practiced extensively in the Western Hemisphere and elsewhere.[45]

The five modes of recognition that have just been examined have been found in U.S. practice during the period under discussion. But they are not the only possible modes. Some authors, for example, contend that acceptance into the U.N. constitutes implied recognition by all members of the U.N., since statehood is one of the primary qualifications for admission, according to the Charter.[46] However, admission to the U.N. will not here be considered tantamount to recognition. The matter should be discussed, but it is a major question in itself, and beyond the purview of this study. Another possible mode of recognition is the signing of a multilateral treaty. Although a provision of express recognition in a multilateral treaty or the signing of a multilateral treaty by an unrecognized state would probably constitute recognition of that state by the signatories of the treaty, this possible mode of recognition has not been employed by the United States during the past two decades and is therefore not relevant here. The United States has emphatically denied that recognition is automatically accorded when both the U.S. and a state or government that the U.S. has not recognized adhere to a multilateral treaty. This issue was raised with respect to the adhesion of East Germany to the Nuclear Test-Ban Treaty of August 5, 1963.[47] Lastly, the contention that the granting of an *exequatur* to the consul of an unrecognized government or the receipt of an *exequatur* for the U.S. consul from an unrecognized government constitutes implied recognition must be mentioned. But, such action will again not be considered as constitutive of recognition here.[48]

IV. THE METHODS OF RECOGNITION

In a study of practice and procedure, the objects and various characteristics of action are obviously important factors and deserve appropriate analysis. But by far the most important component of practice is methodology—the way things are done, or the method of implementing action in the concrete individual case.

In order to examine the methodology of American recognition practice, we propose to divide it into three subdivisions according to the locus of the particular method's implementation. First, those methods of recognition will be considered that can be effected in Washington, D.C. Second, an attempt will be made to outline the various methods that have been or could have been made use of in the capital of the nation or government about to be recognized. Finally, we shall examine those methods that lend themselves to the utilization of modern means of communication between the two capitals concerned. It must again be said, however, that these divisions are arbitrary, and that the full process of recognition usually makes use of several interrelated methods of all three categories at the same time or in succession.

The process of recognizing a new international entity begins in Washington. The initial decisions are made here and the subsequent directives are sent to United States representatives abroad from this location. On occasion the process of recognition is also effected and terminated in Washington. In addition to commencement and direction of action, the capital city of the United States has served as effective base for the implementation of various methods of recognition. The simplest and most obvious of these, one which is also most frequently used, is the announcement at a White House or Department of State press conference, or in a press release, of the fact that the United States has decided to recognize a certain international entity. Another method that may be employed is the reception, on the part of the President, of the continuing foreign representative of a nation in which a change of government has taken place for the purpose of his making an oral announcement of that change to the President. The purpose of the reception would obviously be the important criterion in this case. If such a reception were informal and if its purpose were merely a communication by the President to the representative of a revolutionary government that the United States would enforce the protection of the rights of its nationals in that country, the reception would not necessarily constitute recognition of that government. Another method that has been employed by the President during the period under discussion is the official reception of the envoy of an unrecognized nation or one that is in the process of being recognized for the purpose of accepting his letter of credence. Again, the purpose of the meeting would determine its legal effect. Another method that the President has employed is the formal acknowledgment of a letter sent to him by the head of the new foreign government in which letter the assumption of authority on the part of that government was announced.[49]

In addition to the President, the Secretary of State and his Department have also been instrumental in the first category of recognition methodology. The Secretary of State has occasionally sent a congratulatory message to the ambassador of the newly independent nation concerned, when such ambassador happened already to have established himself in Washington before his country actually achieved full independence. It has also happened that the Secretary of State has formally replied to a note received from the ambassador of an already recognized nation, the constitutional government of which had been replaced by some type of unconstitutional regime. Lastly, in the event recognition had been granted to a provisional or interim government, such recognition has occasionally been supplemented by a formal announcement after the provisional government had been replaced by a constitutional or permanent one.[50]

For the second category of recognition methodology, the locus of the act shifts to the foreign capital. As Whiteman points out, "Recognition is usually extended to a new government or state by means of a formal communication addressed to the Foreign Office of the government or state by the highest ranking diplomatic officer of the state extending recognition, acting under the instruction of his government."[51] In other words, the process of recognition is usually effected or terminated in the foreign capital. Nevertheless, the methods used here have in general been secondary or complementary to the initial procedure originated in Washington. They may be enumerated as follows:

1. The Department of State has on occasion instructed the American diplomatic representative at the foreign capital to enter into relations with the new government established there and to notify the new government of this decision.[52]

2. In at least one case, the U.S. consul general at the capital of a newly independent nation has, under instruction from the Department of State, sent a formal message of recognition to the head of the new nation.[53]

3. The Department has made use of the presence of a liaison officer at the capital of a newly independent nation by instructing him to inform the head of the new government that the U.S. intended to establish relations with that government at an early date.[54]

4. Another method that has found application in the period under consideration has been formal reply by the U.S. ambassador at the capital of a country in which a political upheaval has taken place to a note received from a member of the newly established government.[55]

5. Raising the status of a consulate or consulate general in the capital of a newly independent nation to that of a legation or embassy and appointing the consular officer as chargé d'affaires, minister, or ambassador has been an effective method.[56]

6. The accreditation of such newly elevated diplomatic post and person to several bordering and also newly independent nations has been utilized as an expedient method.[57]

7. On another occasion, the Department of State elevated a commissioner who had been the U.S. representative at a conference or U.N. Commission for a particular nation to the status of ambassador to the nation for the sake of which the commission or conference had been established.[58]

8. A further method made use of by the Department in the foreign capital has been the appointment of a liaison officer at the capital in question as chargé d'affaires ad interim, in order to gain sufficient time to commission and send an ambassador.[59]

9. The U.S. Government has sent official diplomatic delegations to attend either the independence ceremonies at the capital of the newly independent nation or the inauguration ceremonies of a new government about to assume power by constitutional means.[60]

10. As an example of a tenth method, the Korean case, where

recognition apparently took place as the result of the signing of a bilateral treaty with the Republic of Korea, may be cited. However, Whiteman would apparently discount such implied recognition and would not recognize the signing of a treaty here by the special U.S. representative as constitutive of recognition. According to Whiteman, whether any act "may be construed as recognition depends, of course, upon the intent to recognize in the attendant circumstances." [61] It should be added that the methods of recognition described in the preceding paragraphs are exhaustive only of the period and source materials covered by the research for this study.

Before concluding the analysis of methodology, let us look at two ways in which the United States has made use of international means of communication for the purpose of recognizing a new international entity. At the risk of being overly repetitious, it must again be said that the categories abstracted here might well have been fitted into the analysis already completed, and that they make sense only when they are thought of in terms of their relation to the methods employed in the two capitals involved.

The first means of international communications used has been the physical sending of a diplomatic representative to the foreign capital for the purpose of delivering a formal message of recognition and in order to institute permanent diplomatic relations with the new government or nation.[62] Second, the United States, and especially the American President, has employed modern international communications facilities for the sending of messages of good wishes or congratulations to heads of new nations or governments.[63] The subsequent delivery of these messages falls into a slightly different category of methodology.

In the light of these categories, forms, modes, and methods of recognition, let us now turn to the record of U.S. recognition practice toward the new nations during the period from 1943 to 1964. The reader may validly object that the problem area of nonrecognition should be considered first. What has U.S. policy and practice been in this area? Has it been determined by legal or political criteria? What are the entities or situations that have expressly been refused recognition? These important questions constitute a whole study in themselves. The task of selecting would-be international persons whose existence might or should have been recognized is a rather subjective one. It also involves formidable requirements with respect to fact-finding and political-legal analysis of the facts. It has not been possible to include these tasks within the scope of this study. Moreover, it is believed that the principal problems of United States nonrecognition policies arise with respect to new governments of recognized international persons (e.g., Red China), rather than toward seemingly viable new states.

V. The Record of United States Recognition Practice Toward the New Nations, 1943–64

The "new nations" of earlier times often established themselves by force of arms in revolutionary wars like those of the U.S., the Latin American states, and Italy, Germany, and the Balkans. While guerrilla and other forms of irregular warfare have been well known for centuries, the older tradition of wars of independence involved meeting and defeating the governing state's regular forces on the battlefield. More recently, as in the case of the Irish wars of independence, the imbalance between the means available to an established modern government and those within the capabilities of rebel forces has tended to be so great that a combination of guerrilla warfare and political, economic, and psychological action, often accompanied by propaganda campaigns to win international support, became necessary for a successful revolution.

Accordingly, a problem presents itself for those attempting to make some rough divisions among the different categories of new nations. Briefly, the ranks of new nations include those that won their independence almost exclusively by force of arms; those that achieved independence in a relatively peaceful manner under the auspices of the U.N.; those that established themselves on comparatively orderly and peaceful terms with their former rulers, but only after exerting heavy pressures; those that achieved independence without much struggle; and those that enjoyed particularly friendly relations with their former rulers, parting as definitely close friends. The differences in degree among the last three categories are probably not significant.

Why is it necessary to distinguish such situations? The reason will become more clear as our summary of practice proceeds, but this much may be said from the outset. Most of the new nations have come into existence by virtue of a formal proclamation of independence, either in the form of a decree of the former sovereign or, in the case of a mandate or trust territory, the joint action of the U.N. and the mandatory power; or, as the result of some kind of international agreement, whether bilateral or multilateral, usually ending a period of strife between the aspiring new nation and the former ruler. It will be contended in this study that the very existence of the power to bring pressure on the old ruler, whether in the form of open warfare or in some more subtle form, will tend to confirm the existence of elements in the new nation capable of molding it into a sovereign state. But, of course, this does not always happen. There may be enough power to overthrow and tear down, without sufficient unity and stability to govern in turn and to rebuild.

On the other hand, some new nations appear to have been "unloaded" rather precipitously, their present readiness or even ultimate capacity for independence being far from evident. Where this is the case, there will often appear to be little really serious pressure for independence—bluntly, little willingness to work or even die for it. When such is the case, a question arises as to the advisability of according automatic recognition on the date set for its independence by the former ruler to every entity that is certified as a sovereign independent state. Let us now examine the practice of the U.S. Government in this respect.

Independence by Force of Arms

It is, of course, difficult to draw a line between independence that results mainly from force of arms and more peaceful cases of independence. In this section, Algeria, Cyprus, Indonesia, Israel, and Jordan are considered. Throughout this and the two succeeding sections, simple alphabetical order has been used.[64]

ALGERIA

The National Front of Liberation in Algeria proclaimed the establishment of the Provisional Government of the Algerian Republic on September 19, 1958, in Cairo, Tunis, and Rabat. The Provisional Government was declared to be responsible "to the National Council of the Algerian Revolution." On the same day that this proclamation was made the Department of State informed United States missions abroad and certain foreign missions in Washington that the United States "did not intend to recognize the Algerian Provisional Government-in-Exile." The reasons for this act of express nonrecognition are summarized by Whiteman:

> The Department of State, in elaborating the statement that the Algerian government-in-exile did not possess the attributes of legal government, explained that other considerations underlying the non-recognition of the Algerian government-in-exile were that it did not measure up to the standards that the United States generally applied in determining the question of recognition, namely: (1)

whether a government is in possession of the machinery of state (*de facto* control); (2) whether it appears to have the assent of the people (public acquiescence or stability); and (3) whether it is willing to fulfill its international obligations and responsibilities as a sovereign state under treaties and international law.[65]

Almost three years later the "Democratic and Popular Republic of Algeria" became formally independent. On July 3, 1962, the United States was informed by the Government of France that the Algerian people had chosen independence by a referendum on self-determination that had been conducted on July 1, 1962. The French Government also informed the United States that it recognized the independence of Algeria as of July 3, 1962.[66] While the State of Algeria thus came into existence on that date, a national government was not formed until sometime in September of 1962.

In recognizing the new state of Algeria, the U.S. employed a very hesitant and somewhat ambiguous procedure. On July 3, the official date of independence, the White House released a congratulatory statement made by President Kennedy. It stated that "This moment of national independence for the Algerian people is both a solemn occasion and one of great joy," and that the United States congratulates the Algerian leaders and their French colleagues "on the wise statesmanship, patience, and depth of vision they showed in paving the way for this historic event." [67] The President further stated that the United States wishes "to strengthen and multiply the American bonds of friendship with the Government and people of Algeria" in the coming days. Did this statement constitute recognition of Algeria's independence? It appears so. One does not congratulate the coming into existence of a phenomenon that one does not wish to recognize. At least this is how the statement appears to have been construed by Secretary of State Dean Rusk at his press conference on July 12, 1962. He was asked what held up United States recognition of the Algerian Government. His answer was that:

> there is nothing on our side which holds up further action in this regard. We have recognized the independence of Algeria as a state. We are prepared to transform our Consulate General there into an Embassy, and to appoint a Chargé. But the problem has been an uncertainty on the part of the responsible Algerian authorities as to how they would want foreign governments to proceed in this matter. As far as we are concerned, we are ready to proceed at any time. Meanwhile, our official representatives are there, and do have contacts with the local authorities, and are in a position to act in support

of American interests and to take care of American citizens whose needs might arise.[68]

So far then, only the independence of the Algerian state appears to have been recognized. The type of recognition appears to have been little more than *de facto*. Procedures were not even graced with the establishment of an embassy or the dispatching or accreditation of official diplomatic representatives. The mode was that of express announcement, and the method involved little more than the formal statement issued by President Kennedy.

After a functioning national government came into existence, another phase of the recognition process began. On September 29, 1962, the Department of State announced that "The United States today recognized the newly established Government of the Republic of Algeria." [69] Congratulatory messages were sent by both President Kennedy and Secretary of State Rusk to the chief officials of the new government in Algiers. They were delivered to Prime Minister Ahmed Ben Bella and Foreign Minister Mohammed Khemisti by the American Consul General in Algiers, William J. Porter. It was also announced that Algerian agreement had been requested to the elevation of the American consulate general to the status of an embassy, with Porter as chargé d'affaires ad interim. The Presidential message to Prime Minister Ben Bella warmly congratulated the Prime Minister on his assumption of office and referred to the desire of the American people "to foster and extend the cordial relations that exist between" Algeria and the United States. Similar pleasantries were contained in Secretary Rusk's message to the Foreign Minister of Algeria.

Express *de jure* recognition appears to be the correct designation of U.S. procedure and intention. The modes of recognition were again express declaration and the exchange of diplomatic representatives. The latter was confirmed by the appointment of Chargé d'Affaires Porter as Ambassador to Algeria.[70] The methodology included announcements in Washington, the sending of congratulatory messages, and the utilization of personnel already in the foreign capital.

CYPRUS

Violent hostilities between Greeks and Turks broke out in this former British Protectorate and (subsequent to 1925) Crown Colony, when in 1955 the Greek-Cypriot underground movement for political union with Greece launched an all-out campaign against the Turks. As a result, in August of that year negotiations between Britain and Cyprus for limited self-government were initiated. But these came to an unfruitful end in 1956. In 1958, Archbishop Makarios proposed that Cyprus become independent and that guarantees be given against both partition and union with Greece. A series of negotiations ensued, culminating in the London-Zürich Agreements of February 19, 1959. "These agreements prohibit both union of the island with Greece and its partition between Greece and Turkey; and they provide that Greece, Turkey, and the United Kingdom be the guarantors of the Republic's independence, territorial integrity, and security; moreover, they, as guarantors, have the right to take collective or individual action to fulfill this obligation." [71]

Independence was formally proclaimed following agreement with the United Kingdom on August 16, 1960.[72] A week prior to this date, on August 9, 1960, Secretary of State Herter recommended that President Eisenhower send an "Independence Day Message" to the President of Cyprus. His memorandum to President Eisenhower, as quoted by Whiteman, reads as follows:

> Steps already taken and now in process indicate that, on the date of independence, there will be in Cyprus a democratically elected Government in effective control of the country.
>
> The Treaty Concerning the Establishment of the Republic of Cyprus, which was initialed on July 6 by all parties to the Cyprus settlement and will be signed on Independence Day, provides that all international obligations and responsibilities of the Government of the United Kingdom shall, in so far as they may be held to have application to the Republic of Cyprus, be assumed by the Government of the Republic of Cyprus.
>
> We believe that it would be in the interests of the United States to recognize the Republic of Cyprus when it is established. . . . We consider it desirable that recognition be effected by means of a congratulatory message from you to the President of Cyprus, Archbishop Makarios.[73]

President Eisenhower acted on this memorandum; his congratulatory message was delivered to His Beatitude Archbishop Makarios on August 16, the date of independence. Having extended the most cordial "greetings and felicitations" to the Government and people of Cyprus in his own name and on behalf of the people of the United States, President Eisenhower stated in his official message that "The Government and people of the United States welcome the independent and democratic Republic of Cyprus to the family of nations, and look forward to maintaining close and cordial relations with the Government and people of Cyprus."[74] Also on the day of independence, the Department of State announced in a press release that "concurrent with the achievement of independence by the Cypriot people and the establishment of the Republic of Cyprus, the United States Government is extending recognition to the Government of Cyprus and elevating its Consulate General at Nicosia to Embassy status, effective August 16."[75] L. Douglas Heck was appointed chargé d'affaires ad interim, pending the arrival of the first U.S. ambassador. This temporary arrangement was terminated with the confirmation of Frazer Wilkins as American Ambassador to Cyprus on September 19, 1960.[76]

Express declaration and the exchange of diplomatic representatives were the modes of recognition. The methodology involved a formal announcement by the Department of State and activity in the foreign capital, including the delivery of an official congratulatory message from President Eisenhower. The act of recognition itself, that is, the type of recognition, was express in every sense of the word. "Recognition" was extended to the Government and Republic of Cyprus. Such terminology, and the sending of diplomatic representatives, again, appear to point to a U.S. intention to recognize Cyprus not only *de facto* but *de jure*.

INDONESIA

On August 17, 1945, shortly after the Japanese surrender, Indonesian independence was proclaimed by Sukarno and Hatta, and the Republic of Indonesia was established. During four years of warfare and negotiations, the Dutch attempted unsuccessfully to re-establish control. In the Linggadjati Agreement, signed by the Netherlands and the Republic of Indonesia in March, 1947, the Netherlands finally recognized the *de facto* authority of the Republic of Indonesia in Java, Sumatra, and Madura.[77] On September 26, 1949, the *Department of State Bulletin* announced that the United States had welcomed this agreement and had also recognized the *de facto* authority of the Republic of Indonesia. Thus recognition of the Indonesian proclamation of independence was secured in part through the use of armed force. What makes this case doubly significant, however, is subsequent U.N. mediation, the convocation of a conference, and the resultant collective act of recognition.

The Security Council of the United Nations had become involved in the Indonesian case in 1946, when the Ukrainian Republic had complained that the British were using Japanese troops to resist the Indonesian independence movement. When hostilities continued after the Linggadjati Agreement had been signed, India appealed to the Security Council under Articles 34 and 35 of the Charter. Other interested countries having been invited to the Council Table, a resolution was passed by the Security Council on August 1, 1947, calling for the immediate cessation of hostilities and the settlement of differences by arbitration or other means of peaceful settlement. A Consular Commission was established to report on the implementation of the cease-fire order. Its report led to a further cease-fire order from the Security Council on November 1, 1947. Previous to this, a Committee of Good Offices had also been established by the Council. Its efforts resulted in the signing of a truce agreement between the warring parties on January 17, 1948, aboard the American naval vessel *Renville*.

Fighting broke out again in 1948, however, and the Security Council found it necessary to re-establish the Good Offices Committee, this time under the name of United Nations Commission for Indonesia.[78] The latter was instrumental in bringing the Netherlands and Indonesia together for the Round Table Conference at the Hague. Negotiations were held from August 23 to November 2, 1949, and resulted in the Charter of the Transfer of Sovereignty from the Kingdom of the Netherlands to the Republic of the United States of Indonesia and other agreements.[79] On November 3, 1949, Secretary of State Acheson issued a statement, commemorating the termination of the Round Table Conference, detailing the history of the evolution toward Indonesian independence, and concluding as follows:

> The United States will be gratified to welcome into the community of free nations the United Republic of Indonesia and looks forward to Indonesia's membership in the United Nations which the Netherlands has undertaken to propose. With their record of genuine nationalism, the Indonesian people may be expected successfully to resist all efforts of aggressive foreign dictatorships to subvert their newly won independence.[80]

In other words, the United States announced its intention to recognize Indonesian independence almost two months prior to the actual transfer of sovereignty, which took place on December 27, 1949. On the following day, December 28, H. Merle Cochran, the former United States Representative on the United Nations Commission for Indonesia, who had been commissioned United

U.S. Recognition Policy Toward the New Nations

States Ambassador to Indonesia, presented his credentials in Djakarta to President Sukarno and delivered to him a personal message from President Truman, congratulating the people and President of Indonesia "on the attainment of Indonesian independence."[81] Also on that day the Secretary of State and President Truman issued statements of felicitations welcoming the newly independent republic to international society.[82]

It is of note that two distinct phases of recognition appear in this case. In 1947, the United States recognized the *de facto* authority of the Republic of Indonesia in certain areas. Exactly what entity or situation was recognized here is hard to determine, but it certainly appears to have been something more than the mere recognition of a state of belligerency or insurgency. On the other hand, in view of the formal recognition accorded in 1949, it is difficult to regard the 1947 recognition as that of a newly independent state. Yet, in one of its publications the Department of State has given August 17, 1945, as the date of independence for the Republic of Indonesia.[83] Thus it may well be that the original recognition of the *de facto* authority of the Republic in certain areas was recognition of the situation of *de facto* independence of Indonesia. This *de facto* recognition was later changed to implicit *de jure* recognition of the international entity of Indonesia by the formal declaration of December 28, 1949. The mode of recognition was that of express declaration in both cases; however, in the latter instance, the mode of exchanging diplomatic representatives and the mode of collective action were added to the mode of express declaration. In the first instance, the method was simply one of announcement. In the second instance, the announcements were made conclusive by the commissioning of the U.S. Representative on the U.N. Commission for Indonesia as ambassador to the Republic that had been formally established and by having him deliver a message of felicitations.

ISRAEL AND JORDAN

Force of arms was by no means the sole determining factor in the attainment of independence by Israel, and was of little significance in the Jordanian case. But, U.S. recognition of these two nations is almost inseparably interrelated, and acts of open warfare against the surrounding Arab states served to ensure the formal independence of Israel for which provision had been made in the U.N. General Assembly Resolution of November 29, 1947.[84]

When the United Kingdom recognized the independence of

Trans-Jordan on March 22, 1946, through a treaty of the U.S. Alliance that became effective on June 17, the Secretary of State stated that the Department of State considered recognition of Trans-Jordanian independence as premature, even though Trans-Jordanian independence did not violate any treaties between the United States and Great Britain and did not deprive the United States of any rights in Trans-Jordan.[85] According to Whiteman, "political implications within the United States" were the reason for the delay in United States recognition of Trans-Jordan. A May, 1946, message from the minister of Foreign Affairs of the Hashemite Kingdom of Trans-Jordan, announcing Trans-Jordanian attainment of independence, was acknowledged by the Department of State, but such acknowledgment was not considered to constitute recognition.[86]

Such a cautious procedure was not followed when the problem of Israel's recognition arose. On May 14, 1948, President Truman received a note from the agent of the Provisional Government of Israel in which he was informed that the State of Israel had proclaimed its independence as a republic, within the boundaries approved by the General Assembly in a resolution of November 29, 1947. The Israeli note also proclaimed that the Provisional Government of Israel was established to ensure law and order in Israel, to ward off aggression, and to discharge Israel's obligations under international law. Independence was to be effective one minute after six o'clock in the evening, Washington time, of the day the note was delivered. At eleven minutes after six o'clock, President Truman replied to the Israeli note, announcing that he recognized the Provisional Government of Israel "as the *de facto* authority of the new State of Israel." [87]

According to Denys P. Myers, President Truman approved a Department of State memorandum of August 30, 1948, suggesting that *de jure* recognition be granted to an elected Israeli Government.[88] On October 24, 1948, the President announced that *de jure* recognition would promptly be given to a permanent Israeli Government when it should be elected. This announcement may have stimulated doubts about the nature of the recognition extended to Israel on May 14, 1948, for on December 17, 1948, Professor Philip Jessup, U.S. Representative at the Security Council of the U.N., explained that U.S. recognition of the State of Israel had been "immediate and full," that there had been no qualification, and that it had not been *de facto* recognition, even though the recognition of the Provisional Government of Israel had been *de facto*.[89]

A Department of State Memorandum of January 27, 1949, recommended simultaneous *de jure* recognition of Israel and Trans-Jordan; it was approved by President Truman. On January 31, 1949, the White House released the texts of the two messages by which the President had extended simultaneous *de jure* recognition of the governments of Israel and Trans-Jordan and at five o'clock in the afternoon of that same day these messages were telegraphed to Tel Aviv and Amman. A White House press release stated that *de jure* recognition had been extended to the Government of Israel because the President had announced on October 24, 1948, that he would extend *de jure* recognition to a permanent government in Israel when it was elected.[90] The press release further stated that elections had been held in Israel on January 25, 1949, and that the United States had been officially informed of their results. Concerning Jordan, the press release announced that *de jure* recognition was extended to the Government of Trans-Jordan, that informal and friendly relations had existed between the United States and Trans-Jordan for some time, and that the U.S. was supporting this newly recognized nation for membership in the U.N.[91]

On February 28, 1949, the U.S. liaison officer at Amman, Trans-Jordan, was commissioned chargé d'affaires, and on March 18, 1949, the United States special representative at Tel Aviv was elevated to the rank of ambassador.[92]

The types of recognition and of entities recognized in this case are several. First, there was the "full" recognition of the State of Israel on May 14, 1948, according to Professor Jessup's statement to the Security Council. There was also *de facto* recognition of the Provisional Government of Israel and the explicit announcement that recognition of the State of Israel was neither *de facto* nor conditional. Thus the newly established state appears to have been implicitly recognized *de jure* by the initial act of recognition. It might also be said that an implicitly conditional element was contained in the *de facto* recognition of the Provisional Government, for President Truman made it quite clear that he would be willing to extend *de jure* recognition if and when a "permanent" government had been "elected." When this condition was fulfilled, the promised consequence was presently granted. With respect to Trans-Jordan, the situation was somewhat simpler. Although the new nation had actually received its independence in 1946, the U.S. had refused to consider its recognition at that time. Consequently there was apparently no express or implied recognition before President Truman's formal act of *de jure* recognition of the

"Government" of Trans-Jordan. Prior to this act, the relations between the two countries had been kept on an "informal" level. When *de jure* recognition of the government was proclaimed, however, it undoubtedly also implicitly included *de jure* recognition of the State of Trans-Jordan. As for the modes of recognition of both governments, they were express declaration, strengthened by the mode of exchanging diplomatic representatives, in both cases. Of interest are the methods employed. In the first instance of the recognition of Israel, the President himself, acting apparently on his own counsel, hastily responded to a request for recognition on the part of the newly established Provisional Government of the newly established State of Israel. Recognition was granted exactly ten minutes after independence became effective. Few persons, if any, were advised of the President's intentions in advance. In the second instance of recognition of both Trans-Jordan and Israel, the decision of the White House was announced at a press conference and the texts released at the conference were telegraphed to the capitals of the two nations concerned. The telegrams were then supplemented by the later commissioning of diplomatic representatives to both countries.

Independence Under United Nations Auspices

BURUNDI AND RWANDA

Burundi or, as it was formerly known, Urundi, is typical of many newly independent states. Having at one time been an ill-defined ancient kingdom, it became an administrative district in German East Africa prior to World War I. Under the League of Nations, it was assigned as a mandate to Belgium, and in April, 1949, it was integrated into the Belgian-administered United Nations Trust Territory of Ruanda-Urundi. It acquired independence along with the Republic of Rwanda by the termination of the trusteeship on July 1, 1962.[93]

In this case, as in many others involving the independence of former colonial dependencies, the U.S. Government set in motion the procedure of recognition and made known its intentions before the formal date of independence. The American Representative to the General Assembly of the U.N. announced the support of his government for the General Assembly Resolution concerning the independence of Rwanda and Burundi of June 27, 1962, stating that in his view it was clear that "Both Rwanda and Burundi should achieve their separate sovereign independence on the 1st of July," and that the Assembly should to that end "decide to formally terminate the Rwanda-Urundi trusteeship agreement as of that date. . . ." [94]

On June 28, still three days prior to the proclamation of formal independence, President Kennedy dispatched messages of congratulation to Mwami Mwambutsa IV of the Kingdom of Burundi and President Grégoire Kayibanda of the Republic of Rwanda. In these messages, released to the press on June 30, President Kennedy voiced his pleasure and that of the people of the U.S. to be able to extend his congratulations "on the attainment of independence of Burundi" and "on the occasion of Rwanda's accession to independence." The independence of both new nations thus was expressly recognized in both messages. Each also specifically mentioned the U.S. desire to establish cordial relations with Burundi and Rwanda.

The messages of June 28 were followed by a Department of State announcement, on June 29, that the United States was to establish embassies in Kigali, Rwanda, and Usumbura, Burundi, on July 1, the formal date of independence. Herbert V. Olds, U.S. Consul General at Usumbura, was appointed chargé d'affaires ad interim to Burundi and David J. S. Manbey was appointed chargé d'affaires ad interim to Rwanda, both pending the appointment of ambassadors. On October 27, this temporary arrangement was remedied in Burundi by the appointment of Donald Dumont as minister to that country.

The entire procedure of recognition in the case of Burundi and Rwanda appears to have taken place before the actual date of independence. Even though the word "recognition" does not seem to have been mentioned, the U.S. expressly did recognize the independence of both countries, and the type of recognition, again without explicit mention, was undoubtedly *de jure*. The mode of recognition was express declaration and exchange of diplomatic representatives. The methodology involved announcements in Washington, international communications, and activity in the foreign capitals.

CAMEROON

By a decree of April 16, 1957, Cameroun, formerly an associated territory under the French Union, became a state, at the same time remaining under French trusteeship. On June 12, 1958, the Cameroun Legislative Assembly requested that the independence of Cameroun be recognized by France upon termination of the trusteeship, and, on December 5, 1958, the U.N. General Assembly formally took note of the declaration of the Government of France that the Cameroun under French administration was to achieve independence on January 1, 1960.[95]

On the same day, the General Assembly requested a report from the Trusteeship Council. Having received and examined this report and a report of the Visiting Mission on the Cameroons under French administration, the General Assembly adopted a resolution on March 13, 1959, in agreement with France, that the Cameroon Trusteeship Agreement approved by the General Assembly on December 13, 1946, was to be terminated on January 1, 1960.[96] On that date, the independence of the State of Cameroun was proclaimed by its Prime Minister and Chief of State, Ahmadou Ahidjo.

On November 29, 1959, the Secretary of State received an airgram from the American Consul General at Yaoundé, Cameroun, in which he was informed of an accord between France and Cameroun that provided as follows: "Cameroun accepts all international agreements now applicable to Cameroun. They are to remain in effect unless formally denounced." [97] On the following day, Secretary of State Herter dispatched a memorandum to President Eisenhower, advising him as follows:

> In accordance with your approval of the establishment of an American Embassy in the Republic of Cameroun on January 1, 1960, the date on which the United Nations Trusteeship of the Cameroun, under French administration, terminates and Cameroun becomes independent, the Department has sent instructions to the Consulate General at Yaoundé providing for the elevation of that post to the status of an Embassy. Formal recognition of the new state will be achieved by notification from the Consulate General to the Cameroun authorities.
>
> However, in view of the increasingly important role being played by the independent states of Africa, particularly in the United Nations, and in view of the fact that the independence of Cameroun represents the successful conclusion of a United Nations Trusteeship, I believe it especially desirable that a telegraphic message of both congratulations and recognition be sent by you to the Prime Minister of Cameroun. It is recommended that this message be delivered by Henry Cabot Lodge during his stay in Cameroun in his capacity as your Personal Representative, with the rank of Special Ambassador, to the ceremonies in connection with the achievement of independence by the Cameroun.[98]

President Eisenhower responded with a message to Prime Minister Ahmadou Ahidjo that was subsequently telegraphed to the American Consulate General at Yaoundé by Secretary of State Herter. President Eisenhower's message read as follows:

> Recalling with pleasure our meeting during your recent visit to Washington, I extend in my own name and on behalf of the people of the United States most cordial greetings and felicitations to you and your countrymen upon the occasion of the independence of Cameroun. That the birth of an independent Cameroun constitutes the successful conclusion of a United Nations Trusteeship is a source of pride and satisfaction to the United States and to all countries that have sought to make the United Nations an effective instrument of world peace and progress. The Government and people of Cameroun and the Administering Authority, through their dedication to the social and economic advancement of the Cameroun, have earned the gratitude of all free nations.
>
> The Government of the United States looks forward to close and friendly relations with the Government of the Cameroun.[99]

On December 29, 1959, the White House announced "the appointment of the official United States delegation to the independence ceremonies in Cameroun on January 1, 1960." Henry Cabot Lodge, U.S. Representative to the U.N., was designated as the President's personal representative with the rank of special ambassador and was to be accompanied by a delegation of other notable persons. In addition, Mason Sears, U.S. Representative on the U.N. Trusteeship Council, was appointed as the President's representative, with the rank of special ambassador, to the independence ceremonies in Cameroun.[100] On January 6, 1960, Secretary of State Herter received a telegram from the American Consulate General at Yaoundé informing him that President Eisenhower's congratulatory message had been delivered to the Prime Minister of Cameroun on January 3.[101] The delivery of this message and the presence of an official American delegation headed by Ambassador Lodge constituted the first step by the U.S. in the recognition of the independence of Cameroun,[102] a procedure that had been set in motion considerably prior to the actual date of formal independence. The type of recognition was certainly *de jure* and express.

On January 5, 1960, the Department of State announced that the American Consulate General at Yaoundé, Cameroun, had been elevated to an embassy on January 1, "upon formal attainment of independence by the former United Nations Trust territory under French administration." [103] By this announcement the "independence" of the new nation was again expressly recognized. The elevation of the consulate to an embassy was merely a supplementary act. The mode of recognition was one of express declaration,[104] and of dispatching diplomatic representatives. In this case, however, even though preparations were made prior to January 1, 1960, formal recognition did not take place until after the attainment of actual independence.

With the adoption of a new constitution on March 4, 1960, the state of Cameroun became a republic and, subsequent to a plebiscite held on February 11, 1961, the Southern Cameroons, the part of the former Trust Territory administered by Britain, joined with the Republic of Cameroun forming, on October 1, 1961, the Federal Republic of Cameroun. No record has been found of the express or implied recognition of these changes by the United States.

GHANA

Subsequent to receipt of a report by the United Nations and United Kingdom Plebiscite Commission that a majority of native persons were in favor of the union of the Trust Territory of Togoland (which was under British administration) and the British colony of Gold Coast, and having been informed that the U.K. was to grant independence to the latter colony on March 6, 1957, the U.N. General Assembly expressed its approval of the Union and resolved that the Togoland Trusteeship Agreement of December 13, 1946, was "to cease to be in force" after the union and the independence of the Gold Coast had come into being.[105]

On February 14, 1957, the Department of State announced the appointment of an official delegation that was to accompany Vice-President Nixon to the ceremonies from March 3 to 10 marking the independence of Ghana. The U.S. consul general at Accra was designated to serve as adviser to this official delegation. On leaving for Accra, the Vice-President stated that "the United States by sending this delegation to the ceremonies is indicating its support and its friendship for this new nation as it enters into the activities in which it will engage in the years ahead as an independent member of the British Commonwealth."

Whiteman has recorded the following interesting information:

> On February 20, 1957, the Ghanaian Foreign Minister gave assurances to the United States that the Government of Ghana would consider Treaties and Agreements between the United Kingdom and the United States of America affecting Ghana as remaining in

effect for a period of 3 months following March 6, 1957. On June 28, 1957, the Government of Ghana informed the United States that it considered the informal undertaking still in force. The undertaking on the part of Ghana was continued indefinitely, when by a note of December 21, 1957, the United States was informed that there had been formally transferred to Ghana as of March 6, 1957, the rights and obligations of Treaties and Agreements between the United Kingdom and others in so far as the nature of these rights and obligations admitted such transfer.[106]

On March 5, one day prior to the attainment of formal independence, the Department of State announced that the U.S. Government "has officially recognized the new state of Ghana, which becomes independent and a member of the British Commonwealth on March 6." It was also announced on the same day that "with the permission of the Government of Ghana, the American consulate general at Accra will be raised to the status of an embassy at 1 minute past midnight on March 6," and that Donald W. Lamm, Consul General of the United States in Accra, would be named chargé d'affaires pending the appointment of an ambassador to Ghana. Lastly, it was stated that the U.S. Government has informed "the Government of Prime Minister Kwame Nkrumah that it would welcome the establishment of a Ghanaian embassy at Washington as soon as practicable." [107]

U.S. recognition of Ghana's independence was enhanced by the Senate's confirmation of Wilson C. Flake as ambassador to Ghana on May 20, 1957,[108] by U.S. support for admitting Ghana to U.N. membership,[109] and by two Congressional and one state legislative resolutions congratulating Ghana on the attainment of its independence. These were communicated to the American Embassy at Accra for transmittal to the Foreign Minister of Ghana.[110]

On July 1, 1960, the Dominion of Ghana became a republic. On the occasion of the celebration of this change and of the inauguration of Kwame Nkrumah as President of the new Republic of Ghana, President Eisenhower sent a message to President Nkrumah, extending his "most cordial greetings and felicitations [on the] accession of Ghana to status of Republic." [111]

This case is significant because the entity recognized was, in the first instance, a newly independent dominion and member of the British Commonwealth of Nations. In the second instance, the transformation of this dominion into a republic was recognized. The type of recognition, while not expressly *de jure*, was certainly so in substance. The Department of State announced that Ghana had been "officially recognized." The mode of recognition was express declaration in both cases, and the exchange of diplomatic representatives in the first instance. The methodology involved announcements in Washington, the sending of international messages, the dispatching of a delegation and representatives to the foreign capital, and the elevation of a consulate general to the status of embassy. It is interesting to note also, of course, the messages of congratulations from both houses of Congress and from the Michigan State legislature.

KOREA

President Truman issued the following statement on the liberation of Korea from Japan on September 18, 1945:

> The surrender of the Japanese Forces in Seoul, ancient Korean capital, heralds the liberation of a freedom-loving and heroic people. Despite their long and cruel subjection under the warlords of Japan, the Koreans have kept alive their devotion to national liberty and to their proud cultural heritage. This subjection has now ended. The Japanese warlords are being removed. Such Japanese as may be temporarily retained are being utilized as servants of the Korean people and of our occupying forces only because they are deemed essential by reason of their technical qualifications.
>
> In this moment of liberation we are mindful of the difficult tasks which lie ahead. The building of a great nation has now begun with the assistance of the United States, China, Great Britain, and the Soviet Union, who are agreed that Korea shall become free and independent.
>
> The assumption by the Koreans themselves of the responsibilities and functions of a free and independent nation and the elimination of all vestiges of Japanese control over Korean economic and political life will of necessity require time and patience. The goal is in view, but its speedy attainment will require the joint efforts of the Korean people and of the Allies.
>
> The American people rejoice in the liberation of Korea as the Tae-gook-kee, the ancient flag of Korea, waves again in the Land of the Morning Calm.[112]

Reflected in this statement is the determination of the United States to assist the Korean people in the attainment of their independence with all deliberate speed. It is the same policy that was reaffirmed by Secretary of State Marshall before the General Assembly of the United Nations on September 17, 1947. Referring to the question of Korean independence, he stated that:

At Cairo in December 1943, the United States, the United Kingdom, and China joined in declaring that, in due course, Korea should become free and independent. This multilateral pledge was reaffirmed in the Potsdam Declaration of July 1945 and subscribed to by the Union of Soviet Socialist Republics when it entered the war against Japan. In Moscow in December of 1945, the Foreign Ministers of the U.S.S.R., the United Kingdom, and the United States concluded an agreement designed to bring about the independence of Korea. This agreement was later adhered to by the Government of China. It provided for the establishment of a joint U.S.–U.S.S.R. Commission to meet in Korea and, through consultations with Korean democratic parties and social organizations, to decide on methods for establishing a provisional Korean government. The Joint Commission was then to consult with that provisional government on methods of giving aid and assistance to Korea; any agreement reached being submitted for approval to the four powers adhering to the Moscow agreements.

Secretary of State Marshall then pointed out that no progress had been made toward Korean independence in two years and that no solution appeared to be possible through further attempts at bilateral negotiations with the Soviet Union. For this reason, he stated, it was "the intention of the United States Government to present the problem of Korean independence" to the General Assembly.[113]

On November 14, 1947, the General Assembly of the United Nations acted on Secretary of State Marshall's statement by passing resolutions concerning the re-establishment of Korean national independence. These resolutions stipulated that "immediately upon the establishment of the new government, pursuant to elections held under the observation of the United Nations Temporary Commission on Korea, an agency of the General Assembly, certain steps should be taken with respect to the transfer of functions of government in Korea," including the withdrawal of occupation forces.[114]

On August 9 and 11, 1948, General Hodge, the United States Commanding General in Korea, and President Syngman Rhee of the newly established elected government in South Korea exchanged notes providing for the termination of the military government on the date of the inauguration of the new Korean Government, August 15, 1947.[115] The note General Hodge received from President Rhee reads as follows:

> I have the honor to inform you that, in consequence of the deliberation and acts of the Korean National Assembly, which was

constituted as a result of the election held on May 10, 1948, under the observation of the United Nations Temporary Commission on Korea, there was formed as of August 5, 1948, the Government of the Republic of Korea. In accordance with paragraph 3, of Resolution II of the United Nations General Assembly Resolutions on Korea of November 14, 1947, the United Nations Temporary Commission on Korea was notified on August 6, 1948, of the formation of this government.

In furtherance of the United Nations General Assembly Resolutions on Korea, particularly paragraph 4, of Resolution II, I have the honor further to inform you that the Government of the Republic of Korea, after consultation with the United Nations Temporary Commission on Korea, will be prepared to take over the functions of government. To that end, your cooperation and assistance are requested in transferring to the Government of the Republic of Korea all such functions now exercised by you as Commanding General United States Army Forces in Korea, including the direction of all police, coast guard and constabulary units now in being.

The Government of the Republic of Korea recognizes that it will be necessary for you to retain control over areas and facilities of vital importance to you (such as ports, camps, railways, lines of communication, airfields, etc.), as you deem necessary in order to accomplish the transfer of authority to the Government of the Republic of Korea and the withdrawal of United States Occupation Forces from Korea in accordance with the United Nations General Assembly Resolutions on Korea. During this period, the personnel of your command, both military and civilian, including their dependents, shall remain under your exclusive jurisdiction.

In the interest of providing a progressive and orderly transfer of full governmental responsibility and authority from the United States Army Forces in Korea to the Government of the Republic of Korea and to accomplish the purposes set forth above, I am prepared to name Mr. Lee Bum Suk, Mr. Yun Tchi Young, and Mr. Taik Sang Chang to consult with representatives of your command.[116]

Several days later, on August 12, 1948, the official position of the United States concerning Korean independence was announced in a Department of State press release. The Korean Government established in accordance with the General Assembly Resolutions of November 14, 1947, was held to be

> entitled to be regarded as the Government of Korea envisaged by the General Assembly resolution of November 14, 1947. Pending consideration by the General Assembly at its forthcoming Third Session of the report of the United Nations Temporary Commission on Korea, the United States, pursuant to its responsibility as occupying

power, is sending to Seoul a special representative who will be authorized to carry on negotiations with that Government, in consultation with the United Nations Temporary Commission on Korea, concerning the implementation of the further provisions set forth in paragraph 4, of the second of the General Assembly resolutions of November 14, 1947. As such special representative the President has named John J. Muccio of Rhode Island, who will have the personal rank of Ambassador.[117]

On the occasion of the inauguration of the New Government of the Republic of Korea, August 14, 1948, General Hodge made the following significant statement:

> Effective at midnight tonight, the United States Military Government in Korea ceases to exist and a civil affairs section of the headquarters of the United States Forces in Korea is established. This civil affairs section will complete the turning over of essential controls to the new Korean Government, and will carry on residual duties of Military Government during the transition period.[118]

Apparently, President Rhee regarded this as United States recognition of his Government. In his inaugural address he expressed his "heartfelt gratitude" for "recognition of our government." [119] However, the United States was not yet prepared to recognize Korean independence. In a letter to President Rhee, transmitted to the American Representative in Seoul on August 26 by Secretary of State Marshall, President Truman expressed his "congratulations on the progress made" by Korea "toward the attainment of freedom and independence. . . ." [120] Nevertheless, beginning on August 24, 1948, the United States concluded several agreements and treaties with the Rhee Government that clearly imply *de facto* recognition of Korean independence. On August 24, an Executive Agreement, providing for the regulation of interim military and security matters, was signed by General Hodge and President Rhee.[121] On September 11, Special Representative Muccio concluded an agreement on initial financial and property settlements with the Rhee Government, the status of which was still pending final United Nations action.[122] A month later, on December 10, another agreement, in many respects a preliminary treaty of commerce, was signed by the United States and Korea.[123]

Not until December 12, 1948, did the Third General Assembly pass the resolution by which it recognized that a lawful government had been established in the Republic of Korea, that this government had effective control in the area to which the Temporary

United Nations Commission had access, and that it was based on the will of the people.[124] The resolution also recommended that all troops of occupying forces be withdrawn and that countries take into consideration the findings of the General Assembly in the establishment of relations with the new republic. In the light of this action, the United States extended full recognition to the "Government of the Republic of Korea" on January 1, 1949, and announced that it anticipated the raising of the mission of the U.S. special representative in Korea to embassy rank in the near future. This was accomplished when the Special Representative of the United States to Korea was commissioned as Ambassador on April 7, 1949. On March 25, 1949, almost two weeks prior to this elevation of the American Special Representative to Ambassador, Dr. John M. Chang, the newly appointed Korean Ambassador to the United States, made the following statement on the occasion of the presentation of his letter of credence to President Truman:

> We remember particularly, with profound gratitude, your very gracious action in according the first *de jure* recognition to the Republic of Korea on January first of this year, thereby restoring the position of our country to an international standing as a duly qualified member of the community of the freedom-loving nations.[125]

It is interesting that Denys P. Myers, formerly of the State Department, does not accept the official date of the formal recognition of the Republic of Korea as the valid date of recognition. He contends that the United States recognized the new republic implicitly long before January 1, 1949, and regards September 11, 1948, the date of the signing of the agreement of initial financial and property settlement, as the correct date of recognition.[126] One might even go further and say that recognition was implied in the Agreement of August 24, 1948.

Myers' argument demonstrates how vastly complicated the Korean case is. The types of entities recognized are a newly independent nation, on the one hand, and a newly established government, on the other. Classification of the type of recognition is somewhat more difficult. First, the formal recognition on January 1, 1949, was certainly express and probably implicitly *de jure*, although it is referred to as "full" recognition. At any rate, it was regarded as *de jure* recognition by the Korean Government. On the other hand, if Myers is correct, the actual act of recognition—the act from which legal consequences flowed—was implied in the agreement on initial financial and property settlement. It is no less difficult to determine the modes of recognition in this case, or as argued by the authors of this study, by the Agreement of August 24. The formal act of recognition would be classified under the mode of express declaration and probably as one of collective recognition, since there was similar action on the part of other U.N. members. But if Myers is correct, the modes were exchange of diplomatic representatives and bilateral treaty. As for the methods employed, it is interesting to note the mission of the United States Special Representative who was unconfirmed, but who had the rank of ambassador. It is true that the intention in sending this ambassador was not to recognize the newly established republic through him but merely to employ him in negotiations. Nonetheless, his actions brought about an act of implicit recognition, setting in motion the legal consequences that flow from such an act under international law. Later actions made this initial implicit act conclusive. The formal declaration and the elevation of the U.S. special representative to the rank of ambassador certainly left little doubt about the fact that the newly established Republic of Korea had been recognized by the U.S. as an independent state.

LIBYA

This former Italian colony, administered jointly by France and Britain subsequent to World War II, became fully independent on December 24, 1951, when the Government of the United Kingdom, in collaboration with the French Government and the United Nations Commissioner for Libya, transferred all remaining powers to the Libyan Government, making possible the proclamation by King Idris I of Libyan independence. By resolution of November 21, 1949, the General Assembly of the United Nations had recommended that Libya be constituted "an independent and sovereign State" no later than January 1, 1952.[127] After a United Nations Commissioner for Libya had been appointed and reports from the administering states had been received, the General Assembly adopted a further resolution on November 17, 1950, recommending that a National Assembly be convened in Libya before January 1, 1951, which in turn would bring into being a National Government to which all sovereign powers were to be transferred progressively. The final transfer of powers actually took place a week prior to the date recommended by the General Assembly. Instead of January 1, 1952, the effective date of Libyan independence was December 24, 1951.

On that day, the Department of State announced that the Government of the United States was "extending full recognition to the new Government" of Libya.[128] Andrew G. Lynch, who was designated to serve as chargé d'affaires until a minister should arrive, informed the Libyan Foreign Minister of the recognition of his Government by the United States and of the elevation of the Consulate to the status of Legation. The text of his message is as follows:

> My government has received the announcement that Libya has been proclaimed an independent state in accordance with the decision of the United Nations General Assembly, and has instructed me to inform Your Excellency that the Government of the United States is pleased to extend full recognition to the Government of the United Kingdom of Libya as of this date.
> I am pleased also to inform Your Excellency that my government has approved the elevation of the Consulate General to the status of Legation effective immediately. I have been designated as First Secretary and Consul General and as Chargé d'Affaires *ad interim* until the new Minister arrives, and have been instructed to enter into relations with your government.[129]

In addition to these steps, President Truman sent a message to King Idris I, informing him that the U.S. supported the U.N. decision, and congratulating him. There was also a message from Secretary of State Acheson, in answer to a telegram received by him announcing the proclamation of Libyan independence. He welcomed Libya to its "rightful place" among nations and stated that the United States would urge the immediate admission of Libya to the U.N.[130]

The language of the announcement in Washington and of the message delivered by Consul General Lynch is interesting. "Full" recognition was extended to the new "Government" of Libya. No mention is made of the recognition of a newly independent state. Nevertheless, the meaning is clear. "Full" recognition undoubtedly is identical with *de jure* recognition. Furthermore, a government is not usually recognized without extending implicit recognition to the state it governs. We note also that Secretary Acheson welcomed "Libya" and not only the "Government of Libya" to its "rightful place" among nations, and that President Truman's message makes reference to the "independence of Libya." The mode of recognition was express declaration, through an announcement, messages, and the exchange of diplomatic representatives. As for the method employed, the United States here made considerable use of the services of its consul general at Tripoli. But Washington and international communications were also involved. On February 7, 1952, this procedure was supplemented by the commissioning of a minister to Libya.

SOMALI REPUBLIC

In 1949, the U.N. adopted a resolution placing former Italian Somaliland under the international trusteeship system for a period of ten years, and designating Italy as the Administering Authority. At the termination of this period, Italian Somaliland was to become an independent state. The date for independence was later set for July 1, 1960. At that time British Somaliland was also approaching self-government and was granted independence on June 26, 1960, so that it could form one independent nation with Italian Somaliland on July 1, 1960.

The United States was aware of these developments and of Britain's intention in granting independence to Somaliland on June 26, 1960, and the recognition of this new nation, which was soon to merge with another, took the form of a single brief message from Secretary of State Herter to the Council of Ministers of Somaliland. Best wishes, congratulations, and warmest regards were extended on the occasion of Somaliland's independence.[131]

A more elaborate procedure was employed in the recognition of the Somali Republic, the result of the merger. On June 30, one day prior to its coming into existence, the Department of State announced that the U.S. would welcome the Somali Republic into the family of nations on July 1 and that the President of the U.S. had sent a warm message of good will and an official delegation, headed by the President's Personal Representative, Secretary of Commerce Fred H. Mueller, to attend the independence ceremonies at Mogadiscio.[132] The President's message extended greetings and congratulations on the independence of the Somali Republic. Also on June 30, it was made public that the American consulate general at Mogadiscio was to be elevated to the status of embassy on July 1, and that Andrew G. Lynch, the Consul General, had been nominated as the first U.S. Ambassador to the Somali Republic.[133] Shortly thereafter, by way of enhancing its decision to recognize the new state, the United States supported the admission of the Somali Republic to U.N. membership.[134]

Recognized in this case was the independence of a new state and the merger of that state with another newly independent state, the latter not having been separately recognized. The type of recognition was express, even though the word recognition was not employed, and certainly again *de jure*. The rapidity with which recognition took place and the absence of conditions qualifying the act of recognition provide reasonable assurance that *de jure* recognition was intended. The modes of recognition were express declaration and the exchange of diplomatic representatives, including the dispatching of an official delegation, and the methodology involved announcement in Washington, the sending of international messages, the elevation of a consulate to the status of embassy, and the attendance of a personal representative of the President at the independence ceremonies.

TANGANYIKA

Formerly a portion of German East Africa, Tanganyika was a British mandate under the League of Nations subsequent to World War I and a U.N. trust territory from 1946 to 1961. It became Africa's twenty-ninth independent nation at one minute past midnight on December 9, 1961. The trusteeship was dissolved, effective December 9, by resolution of the General Assembly of the United Nations on November 6, 1961.[135]

This recognition was implicitly but not explicitly *de jure*. It was also express recognition. Following the recommendation of Acting Secretary of State Chester Bowles "that the United States recognize Tanganyika" and White House approval of this recommendation, the Department of State announced on the date of Tanganyika's independence that the Consulate General at Dar-es-Salaam had been elevated to the status of embassy and that William Duggan, the U.S. Consul General, had been named chargé d'affaires ad interim.[136] So far, the mode of recognition had been one of exchanging diplomatic representatives. Added to this was the mode of express declaration. F. D. Roosevelt, Jr., was sent to Dar-es-Salaam at the head of an official delegation as President Kennedy's personal representative, with a message from President Kennedy to Prime Minister Julius Nyerere and to the government and people of Tanganyika congratulating them on their attainment of independence and their assumption of equal status among nations.[137] The express declaration of recognition was contained in the Presidential message and in the congratulatory telegram from President Kennedy.[138] The procedure described so far was supplemented by Ambassador Adlai E. Stevenson's statement before the U.N. Security Council on December 14, 1962, to the effect that the U.S. would be happy to welcome the application of Tanganyika for U.N. membership.[139]

(For a discussion of the subsequent merger of Tanganyika and Zanzibar into the United Republic of Tanzania, see p. 223.)

TOGO

Togo was formerly a part of the German protectorate Togoland, which after World War I became under the League of Nations a mandate territory administered by both Britain and France. In 1946, it was placed under the trusteeship system. British Togoland later became part of Ghana. French Togoland, on the other hand, became an autonomous republic within the French Union, as the result of a plebiscite held on October 28, 1956. Pursuant to a resolution of the U.N. General Assembly of December 18, 1959, complete independence from both France and the U.N. was achieved on April 27, 1960. Until this date the trusteeship had remained in effect.[140]

Whiteman describes an interesting sequence of relations between the United States and Togo that might be said to constitute anticipatory recognition of this new nation:

> On March 1, 1960, Sylvanus Olympio, Prime Minister of the Government of Togo, addressed a letter to President Eisenhower, inviting him (or, if he could not be present in person, an official U.S. delegation) to attend the ceremonies to be held at Lomé on April 27, 1960, on which date "the National Independence of the Togolese people will be solemnly proclaimed." On March 30, 1960, President Eisenhower acknowledged receipt of the letter, stating that he had followed with deep interest the developments leading to "the independence" of the Prime Minister's country and would be honored to designate a delegation to "the independence ceremonies." At the same time he states: "I send to you and to the people of Togo my warm congratulations and best wishes on this historic occasion."
>
> Subsequently, on April 7, 1960, Secretary of State Herter stated in a memorandum to the President that he believed that "it is in the best interest of the United States to recognize the Republic of Togo as an independent state on April 27, 1960, and to elevate our Consulate at Lomé, Togo, to the rank of Embassy on the same day." He added: "The Department is taking steps to satisfy itself that the new Government of Togo will observe its international obligations so that we will be in a position to extend recognition to that government by an exchange of ambassadors." [141]

On April 14, 1960, the Department of State announced the appointment of an official U.S. delegation to the independence ceremonies in Togo. William P. Rogers, U.S. Attorney General, was designated as personal representative of the President and commissioned with the rank of special ambassador.[142] This was two weeks prior to the actual date of independence. On April 27, the Department of State further announced that the U.S. consulate at Lome, Togo, had been elevated to the status of embassy on that day, the official date of independence. Lastly, it was announced that Jesse M. MacKnight had been named chargé d'affaires.[143] During the independence day ceremonies in Togo, Attorney General Rogers delivered a personal message of greetings and felicitations from President Eisenhower, on "the accession to independence of the Republic of Togo," to Prime Minister Olympio.[144]

All the preparations for the final official communication of United States recognition were made well in advance and were well publicized. With the exception of the note from the Secretary of State advising that the Department of State was taking steps to satisfy itself that the new Government of Togo would abide by its international obligations, no conditions were stated for the publicly announced intention of the United States to recognize the independence of Togo on April 27. While recognition was not legally effective until the date of independence, of course, an interesting question is whether the United States had not incurred a legal obligation by its anticipatory announcements and whether it would not have been difficult to change the policy of recognition toward Togo at the last moment.

WESTERN SAMOA

Having been mandated to the British Crown, on behalf of New Zealand, by the League of Nations in 1920, Western Samoa became a U.N. trust territory in 1946. It acquired its independence "in accordance with an agreement between the Government of New Zealand, the Samoan leaders, and the Trusteeship Council of the United Nations.[145] Western Samoa accepts no diplomatic representatives from any nation and has not applied for U.N. membership. The reason for this, according to a Department of State official,[146] is the prohibitive cost of diplomatic relations and of the inevitable obligations resulting from an active participation in world politics. Therefore, the "Independent State of Western Samoa" conducts its foreign relations through New Zealand.

Independence celebrations took place from January 1 through 5, 1962. Present there, among other dignitaries and representatives, was Senator Oren E. Long, at the head of the U.S. delegation and as Personal Representative of President Kennedy.[147] He delivered a personal message from President Kennedy to "Their Excellencies, Tupua Tamasese Mea'ole, and Malietoa Tanumafili II, Heads of State of Western Samoa," which in part read as follows:

> It gives me particular pleasure to extend my congratulations and good wishes on the occasion of the independence of Western Samoa.
>
> The people of my country have long felt a special friendship for the people of Western Samoa. As your close neighbors in American Samoa, and as members of the United Nations Trusteeship Council, we have watched with deep interest your steady progress toward independence. Now that you have achieved this goal, we welcome you as our partner in the world community of nations. Your country's independence is indeed a tribute to you, the people with whom you have worked, and the Government of New Zealand. I look forward to seeing the friendly ties already established between our two countries grow even stronger in the years ahead.[148]

Implied in this message and in the presence of Senator Long, as President Kennedy's Personal Representative, at the independence ceremonies is *de jure* recognition on the part of the United States of the independence of Western Samoa, a state that is not even sufficiently independent financially to be able to conduct its own foreign affairs. Precisely what this act of recognition means in real, as opposed to merely formal legal terms is an interesting question. The legal scholar might well express doubt that the term recognition, as we know it today, has retained much of the meaning and significance ascribed to it in many of the treatises on international law.

Independence by More-or-Less Peaceful Action of the Metropole

BURMA

Burma came into existence as a relatively autonomous unit of the British Empire in 1937, when it was separated from British India and granted a constitution providing for a considerable degree of self-government. In 1947, Burma was presented with the opportunity of joining the British Commonwealth of Nations. This was rejected in favor of independence without formal association with the Commonwealth. Subsequent to conversations in London, an agreement had been signed between Burma and the United Kingdom on January 27, 1947, leading to the establishment of a republic on June 17, 1947, and the adoption of a new constitution on September 24, 1947. Independence was granted by Britain on January 4, 1948, pursuant to a treaty between the Provisional Government of Burma and the United Kingdom signed on October 17, 1947, and coming into force on the date of independence. The Burma Independence Act was approved on December 10, 1947.[149]

On January 28, 1947, the day following the conclusion of the London conversations between Burma and the British Government, the Department of State made the following announcement:

> The Department of State welcomes the announcement that the conversations between the British Government and Burmese political leaders in London have ended with a mutually satisfactory settlement. We look forward to increasingly cordial relations with this emerging Asiatic country.[150]

This was followed by an exchange of notes between Secretary of State Marshall and Thakin Mya, Chairman of the Burma Constituent Assembly in June of 1947. Marshall's message was read before the Burma Constituent Assembly on June 10, 1947:

> On this historic occasion, I extend to you as Chairman of the Constituent Assembly and through you to the Burmese people the sincere good wishes of the United States Government and the people of the United States of America for a successful conclusion of the important task you are about to undertake. Burma's peaceful and steady progress in rehabilitation is being watched with sympathetic interest. Freedom-loving people throughout the world hope that you will lay the foundation for a stable and peaceful nation.[151]

Chairman Thakin Mya answered Secretary Marshall's message in a letter dated June 13, 1947, expressing his gratitude and stating that free Burma would "regard it as its special duty and privilege to maintain most cordial and friendly relations" with the United States.[152]

On September 18, 1947, it was announced that the government of Burma and the government of the United States of America had "agreed to exchange representatives with the rank of ambassador." In addition, the following statement was made:

> The Consulate General of the United States in Rangoon is being raised to the status of Embassy, and the present Consul General, E. L. Packer, will act as Chargé d'Affaires ad interim until the appointment of an ambassador by the United States Government.[153]

On the following day, September 19, 1947, several months prior to the attainment of independence, Chargé d'Affaires ad interim

Packer presented his credentials to the Burmese Government and made the following statement:

> The establishment of diplomatic relations and the exchange of diplomatic representatives between the United States and Burma is a milestone in the development of relations between the two countries, signifying American recognition of Burma's changing political status.
>
> The Government of the United States is deeply interested in developments in Burma and westcoast Asia and looks forward to Burma's resulting possibilities for international collaboration in a peaceful world.[154]

This step was followed by the institution of more formal diplomatic relations through the appointment of an ambassador to Burma on October 17, 1947. His credentials were not presented in Rangoon until March 3, 1948, however. Meanwhile, a formal note of recognition was dispatched on December 29, 1947. The instructions were to deliver this message from President Truman to Sao Shwe Thaike, Saophe of Yawnghwe, the President of the Union of Burma, on January 1, 1948.[155] It contained references to Burma's independence and its reception among the "family of nations" and interestingly was delivered three days before the actual date of independence. In contradistinction, a message from Acting Secretary of State Robert A. Lovett to the ambassador of Burma on the occasion of the flag-raising ceremonies at the Burmese Embassy in Washington was not released to the press until January 4, 1948.

The types of entities recognized here are both a dependent state developing toward independence and a newly independent state. Recognition was express in both instances and undoubtedly by intention *de jure* of the achievement of independence on January 4, 1948. Again, the modes of recognition were express declarations and the exchange of diplomatic representatives. The methods included the sending of a chargé d'affaires, the appointment of an ambassador, the dispatching of a message of congratulations (containing in so many words an express statement of recognition), the delivery of that message in the foreign capital, and the presentation of a congratulatory message from the Secretary of State at an already existing Burmese Embassy in Washington.

CAMBODIA, VIETNAM, AND LAOS

Independence came to these three nations by way of an extended and complex process. On February 2, 1950, the French National

Assembly approved the instruments that had been concluded with Vietnam on March 8, 1949; with Laos, on July 19, 1949; and with Cambodia, on November 8, 1949, regarding the independence of these countries carved out of former French Indochina. Their independence or, more accurately, their autonomy, was defined "as associated states within the French Union" that had been established by Article 61 of the French Constitution of 1946.[156] This was the first step in the process that was to lead to the ultimate transfer of final powers on December 29, 1954.

The U.S. recognition extended to this qualified grant of independence was problematical. To begin, Vietnam was singled out with a special congratulatory message from Secretary of State Acheson on January 27, 1950. It was addressed to His Majesty Bao Dai and delivered to him by American Ambassador-at-Large Jessup on the same day. The message read as follows:

> The Secretary of State, Dean Acheson, has instructed me to express to Your Majesty the gratification of the United States Government at the assumption by Your Majesty of the powers transferred by the French Republic at the beginning of this year, and its confident best wishes for the future of the State of Vietnam with which it looks forward to establishing a closer relationship. . . .[157]

According to Whiteman, this message "was interpreted in the Department as merely intending to imply that the United States intended to extend recognition at a time when French ratification of the agreements and other factors should permit, at the same time stating that the Secretary looked forward to establishing a closer relationship with Vietnam." [158]

On February 7, 1950, the Department of State announced that "the Government of the United States has accorded diplomatic recognition to the Governments of the State of Vietnam, the Kingdom of Laos, and the Kingdom of Cambodia." [159] This clearly is an express statement of recognition. But what does "diplomatic recognition" mean? According to Denys P. Myers, a former State Department official and expert on these matters, diplomatic recognition is "obviously different from *de facto, de jure* or plain recognition" and "seems to have been a hedge in view of the situation in Indochina." [160] It should also be noted that the governments of these various states were recognized, not their independence. Did the U.S. then recognize dependent entities, members of the French Union?

The supplementary steps taken by the United States at this time were no less problematical. In the same press release that contained the statement of formal recognition, it was further announced that the President of the United States had instructed the American consul general at Saigon to inform the heads of the governments of the states in question that diplomatic recognition had been extended and that the U.S. was looking forward "to an exchange of diplomatic representatives between the United States and these countries." [161] By way of explanation, it was stated that "Our diplomatic recognition of these Governments is based on the formal establishment of the State of Vietnam, the Kingdom of Laos and the Kingdom of Cambodia as independent states within the French Union." It was argued that "this recognition is consistent with our fundamental policy of giving support to the peaceful and democratic evolution of dependent peoples toward self-government and independence." The political mechanics that preceded ratification by the French National Assembly were also referred to.[162]

So far then, the United States was extremely cautious and appears not to have been altogether certain of what precisely was being recognized here. The methodology is clear. An express statement of recognition was made, and the consular personnel in Saigon were instructed to proceed with the notification of the governments concerned. But regarding the substance, their appears to have been considerable concern with justifying the steps the U.S. took. To be sure, an exchange of diplomatic representation was mentioned as desirable, but diplomatic relations in the full and formal sense of the word, that is, diplomatic relations clearly implying *de jure* recognition, did not come into existence until 1952, in the case of Vietnam and Cambodia, and 1955, in the case of Laos.[163] It is true that Donald Heath was commissioned as minister to Vietnam, Laos, and Cambodia on June 29, 1950, and that a legation was established in Saigon. But a minister is not an ambassador, and a legation is not an embassy. That the U.S. attached significance to this terminology is indicated by the fact that the legation in Saigon was elevated to the status of embassy on June 25, 1952, that an embassy was established in Phnom Penh, Cambodia, on that same date, and that a third embassy was established in Laos on July 27, 1955. According to Myers, undiluted recognition was probably not effected until these acts had taken place.

During this same period, a full-scale war was being fought in Indochina. It was terminated by the Geneva agreements of July 20 and 21, 1954, between the Franco-Laotian Command and the Command of the People's Army of Vietnam, the Royal Khmer

Army Command and the People's Army of Vietnam, and the Franco-Vietnamese Command and the Command of the People's Army of Vietnam. At the occasion of this agreement, the U.S. expressed apprehension over the partition of Vietnam and stated its hope "that the agreements will permit Cambodia, Laos, and Vietnam to play their part in full independence and sovereignty, in the peaceful community of nations, and will enable the peoples of that area to determine their own future." [164] This statement was made by Under-Secretary Walter B. Smith at the conclusion of the Indochina Plenary Session at Geneva on July 21, 1954. It was supplemented by a White House news conference statement by the President on the same day, to the effect that "as evidence of our resolve to assist Cambodia and Laos to play their part in full independence and sovereignty, in a peaceful community of free nations, we are requesting the agreement of the Governments of Cambodia and Laos to our appointment of an Ambassador or Minister to be resident at their respective capitals." [165] The fact that a chief of mission already existed in Saigon was referred to, and it was stated that this "embassy" would of course be maintained.

It will be remembered that the transfer of final powers to all three countries did not occur until December 29, 1954. In October, 1954, the United States reaffirmed its intention "to support the complete independence of Cambodia, Laos, and Vietnam," and on October 2, 1954, two months prior the transfer of final powers, Robert McClintock presented his credentials as American Ambassador to Cambodia, where a chargé d'affaires had been resident in the American Embassy in Phnom Penh since 1952. At this time, it was also announced that "The assignment of a resident ambassador at Phnom Penh constitutes further recognition by the United States of the completion of Cambodian independence through the full assumption by Cambodia of the powers of self-government." But these powers were not finally transferred until December 29. What, then, does this granting of "further recognition" mean? Was not full recognition implied in the establishment of the embassy at Phnom Penh in 1952, as Myers would have it? Or were some elements of recognition still missing? And why was there such a time-lag between the "undiluted" recognition of Cambodia and Vietnam and the completion of the process of recognizing Laos through the establishment of an embassy there in 1955? That is, President Eisenhower had received the letter of credence of the first Laotian Minister to Washington on July 13, 1953, and an American diplomatic mission had existed in Laos prior to 1955. However,

U.S. Recognition Policy Toward the New Nations 151

it was not until 1955 that both of these missions were elevated to embassy status.[166] The United States does not appear to have been certain as to when and how Cambodia, Vietnam, and Laos emerged as truly independent nations in the international arena. According to the explicit statement of the U.S. Government, the accreditation of an ambassador to Cambodia constituted "further" recognition of the "completion" of Cambodian independence. Then Cambodia must still have been a "dependent" state when the United States established an embassy in Phnom Penh. Is there a precedent for this in international law and relations? It does not appear so.

Of interest here is Whiteman's somewhat uneven discussion of U.S. recognition of Vietnam, Laos, and Cambodia. She does not speculate, of course, as to when U.S. recognition was effective in each case. She refers to the express statement of "diplomatic" recognition and in the case of Cambodia and Vietnam appears to consider the Geneva Conference of 1954 as conclusive collective recognition of the two countries. In the case of Laos, however, she adds a description of Prince Souvanna Phouma's visit to Washington in 1958 as though this made U.S. recognition of Laos conclusive.[167]

At any rate, over the period of time extending from 1949 to 1955, the United States appears to have accorded express and *de jure* recognition to each of the three states carved out of former French Indochina. The traditional methodology of sending ministers and ambassadors, dispatching messages of congratulations, and making formal announcements was employed, but with a considerable degree of greater caution and hesitation than in most other cases of recognition.

CENTRAL AFRICAN REPUBLIC, CHAD, REPUBLIC OF CONGO-
BRAZZAVILLE, AND GABON

The former overseas territory of Ubangi-Shari, part of French Equatorial Africa, became an autonomous member of the French Community on December 1, 1958, and, on that occasion, received the name of Central African Republic. Chad, Congo, and Gabon received their autonomy on November 28, 1958. Independence was attained by all four states pursuant to the Agreements of Transfer of Power and Cooperation that were signed in Paris on July 12, 1960. Since the Central African Republic, Chad, Congo, and Gabon had formed a customs union on January 17, 1959, it had been more or less expected that they would become independent as a single entity. However, they opted for separate existence as sovereign states and attained full independence individually between August 11 and 17, 1960.

There appears to have been no U.S. recognition of the attainment of autonomy by these states in 1958. The record shows only that effective August 15, 1960, the American consulate at Brazzaville, Republic of Congo, was "elevated in rank to mission status"; that this "Embassy" was also accredited to the Republic of Chad, the Central African Republic, and the Republic of Gabon;[168] that the U.S. announced on October 13 its intention to open embassies in the near future in Fort Lamy, Chad Libreville, Gabon, and Banqui, Central African Republic;[169] that these embassies were in fact established in January, 1961; that subsequently William W. Blancke was appointed as U.S. ambassador to the Republic of Congo; and that messages of congratulation, on the occasion of the attainment of independence, were sent and delivered to the governments of all four states by President Eisenhower.

In the case of the Central African Republic, Alan W. Lukens, the American Consul at Brazzaville, Republic of Congo, delivered President Eisenhower's message of congratulations and, implicitly, recognition to Prime Minister David Dacko while presenting his letter of credence as chargé d'affaires.[170] The same procedure was followed in the case of Chad, the Republic of Congo, and Gabon. On August 11, 1960, Consul Lukens presented his credentials as chargé d'affaires to Prime Minister Tombalbaye of Chad and read to him President Eisenhower's letter of implied recognition.[171] Four days later, on August 15, Consul Lukens, who also became chargé d'affaires to the Republic of Congo, delivered a similar message of congratulations and implied recognition to President Fulbert Youlou of the Republic of Congo.[172] On August 17, again while presenting his credentials as chargé d'affaires, Consul Lukens delivered to Prime Minister Léon M'Ba of Gabon a message of felicitations and implied recognition very similar to those he had delivered to the other three states discussed here.[173]

It is evident that the type of recognition intended in each case was again *de jure*, or *per se*, if we employ Whiteman's terminology, even though these words were not mentioned in the messages referred to. Recognition was effected through the mode of express declaration, supplemented by the mode of exchanging diplomatic representatives. The accreditation of one chargé d'affaires and embassy to all four countries does not in any way appear to have signified a qualified legal act short of full recognition. The reasons for this method of quadruple accreditation of one chargé d'affaires were probably purely practical.

Of particular interest in this case is the language of the original announcement of the elevation of the Brazzaville consulate. In contradistinction with the language employed in the long-drawn-out procedure of recognizing Cambodia, Vietnam, and Laos, no distinction is made here between a "mission" and an "embassy." This fact points to the importance of determining precisely what the intent of the United States Government was in each particular case. The terminology acquires meaning only when it is measured against such intent.

CEYLON

The former British Crown Colony of Ceylon became an independent member state of the British Commonwealth of Nations on February 4, 1948, in accordance with the provisions of the Ceylon Independence Act of 1947.[174]

The procedure of recognizing this newly independent state was relatively simple. On February 3, 1948, one day prior to the formal transfer of final powers, President Truman addressed a message to Sir Henry Moore, the Governor General of Ceylon. In it, he extended his good wishes on the attainment of Dominion status by Ceylon in the British Commonwealth of Nations.[175] On the same day it was also announced that Henry F. Grady, U.S. Ambassador to India, had been designated as the President's personal representative, with the rank of Special Ambassador to Colombo and that he would attend the Ceylonese independence celebration in Colombo from February 10 to 14.

So far then the type of recognition was express, and, in so many words, probably *de jure*. This is again indicated by the fact that the mode of express declaration was combined with that of the exchange of diplomatic representatives. This latter mode was confirmed by a Department of State announcement of April 26, 1948, to the effect that the governments of the United States and Ceylon had agreed to initiate diplomatic relations and exchange ambassadors. It was also announced on that date that Felix Cole had been appointed as first U.S. ambassador to Ceylon. As for methodology, the sending of a message and of an official delegation to be present at the Ceylonese independence ceremonies sufficed to make U.S. recognition complete.

Of special significance is the terminology employed by President Truman in his message to Sir Henry Moore. Specific mention was made of the fact that a dominion and member of the British Commonwealth of Nations was being recognized here. That is, the object of recognition was not only a newly independent state, but also a Commonwealth dominion.

CONGO-LEOPOLDVILLE

Independence came to this former Belgian colony subsequent to, and in accordance with, the agreement of January 27, 1960, between Congolese and Belgian officials. Provision was made for the holding of general elections in the Congo on May 31, 1960. These having been held, a Treaty of Friendship and Collaboration was concluded between Belgium and the Congo on June 29, 1960. The proclamation of independence followed on the next day, June 30, 1960.[176]

U.S. recognition was effected through the elevation of a consulate general to the status of embassy, the sending of an official delegation to the independence ceremonies with a message of congratulations, and the commissioning of an ambassador. In short, an already familiar pattern was repeated. The type of recognition may be said to have been express—even though the word recognition was not used—and, as a result of the most probable intent of the U.S., *de jure*. The mode was one of exchanging ambassadors and of express declaration. The methods of procedure involved the foreign capital, international communications, and Washington.

On June 28, 1960, the Department of State announced that the American consulate general in Leopoldville would be elevated to the status of embassy on June 30, the date of formal independence.[177] On that day, a White House Press release made public a message from President Eisenhower to Joseph Kasavubu, Chief of State of the new republic. The President extended "cordial greetings and felicitations" on the occasion of the transfer of final sovereign powers.[178] This express statement of U.S. recognition of Congolese "independence" was read to President Joseph Kasavubu of the Congo by Robert D. Murphy, personal representative of President Eisenhower and head of the U.S. delegation to the Congolese independence ceremonies, while presenting his credentials to President Kasavubu.[179] This procedure was further enhanced by the Senate's confirmation of Clarence H. Timberlake as Ambassador to the Republic of the Congo on July 2, 1960.[180]

The speed with which recognition was granted and the formal expressions of U.S. friendship clearly indicate that recognition was by intention unqualified and *de jure*.

DAHOMEY, NIGER, UPPER VOLTA, AND IVORY COAST

On December 4, 1958, the French Overseas Territory of Dahomey became an autonomous Republic in the French Community. Niger attained this status on December 19 of the same year, and the Republic of Ivory Coast on December 4, the date of Dahomey's accession to autonomy. The Volta Republic, which changed its name to Republic of Upper Volta on March 2, 1959, became autonomous on December 11, 1958. There appears to have been no U.S. recognition of the attainment of autonomy on the part of these four republics. It is interesting to note the difference between the dependent autonomy of Dahomey, Niger, Upper Volta, and Ivory Coast and the grant of "independence" to the subsequently associated states within the French Union of Vietnam, Laos, and Cambodia in 1949. The United States extended "diplomatic recognition" to the latter.

U.S. recognition was not extended to Dahomey, Niger, Upper Volta, and Ivory Coast until formal and complete independence was proclaimed following accord with France. The official dates of the transfer of final powers are August 1, 1960, for Dahomey, August 3 for Niger, August 5 for Upper Volta, and August 7 for Ivory Coast.[181] Having received notice that independence was to be attained on these respective dates, the Department of State announced on July 29, 1960, that the U.S. consulate in Abidjan, Ivory Coast, was to be elevated to the status of embassy on August 7, 1960, and that the new embassy was to be accredited to all four new states, which on May 29, 1959, had organized the Conseil de l'Entente.[182] Donald R. Roland, U.S. Consul at Abidjan, was named chargé d'affaires, also to each of the four states. This action was supplemented on October 13, 1960, by the Department of State announcement that the U.S. would in the near future open embassies in Porto Novo, Dahomey; Niamey, Niger; and Ouagadougou, Upper Volta.[183]

Recognition so far, even though undoubtedly again *de jure*, was not explicit but implied in the action of elevating a consulate to embassy status and accrediting a diplomatic representative. This procedure was supplemented in each case by an express note of congratulation or felicitation by President Eisenhower to each of the new states in the Conseil de l'Entente. The word "recognition," however, did not appear in these messages

In the case of Dahomey, the American Consul at Abidjan delivered a message from President Eisenhower to Prime Minister

Maga of Dahomey on the day of independence, August 1, 1960. The message stated that President Eisenhower extended greetings and felicitations to the Prime Minister and people of Dahomey "on the occasion of the independence of the Republic of Dahomey," in his own name and on behalf of the United States.[184] The same American Consul whose elevation to chargé d'affaires had been announced on July 29 delivered a message from President Eisenhower to Prime Minister Houphouet-Boigny of the Republic of the Ivory Coast during the independence ceremonies on August 7, 1960, the date of that Republic's attainment of sovereignty.[185] Both this message and those delivered during the course of Niger's and Upper Volta's independence ceremonies to Prime Minister Dicri of Niger and to Prime Minister Yameogo of Upper Volta "extending recognition to the new State" of Niger and "in recognition of the independence of the Upper Volta," as Whiteman puts it, were very similar in content and wording.[186] They amounted to an express statement of recognition in substance. As was already indicated, such messages had become part of a familiar pattern of recognition procedure.

In the case of Niger, a further supplementary act is recorded. On December 6, 1961, more than a year after the formal transfer of final sovereign powers from France, the Department of State announced that President Kennedy had named an official delegation, the members of which had the rank of special ambassador, to be present at the celebrations commemorating the independence of the Republic of Niger, December 16 to 18. Secretary of Labor Arthur Goldberg was appointed head of this delegation and personal representative of the President.[187]

GUINEA

Because of the special circumstances under which Guinea achieved its sovereign independence from France, its recognition by the U.S. does not fit into the "pattern" of practice of which we have been speaking. This pattern has not been inflexible, applying in the strict sense only to the "new nations" that have come into the international arena since 1957. Since Guinea became independent on October 2, 1958, it would seem that rightly the "pattern" should have been applied to it. That is, its American consulate should have been elevated to the status of embassy on the date of independence, diplomatic representatives should have been exchanged, and there should have been a message of congratulations

U.S. Recognition Policy Toward the New Nations 157

and possibly a delegation to the independence ceremonies. But an exception was made.

The reasons were the political factors surrounding Guinea's attainment of independence. Instead of becoming an autonomous member of the French Community in 1958, as did the four states discussed in the previous section, Guinea rejected French administration and a proposed French constitution in a public referendum on September 28, 1958. Independence followed on October 2, 1958. As Myers points out, because of the delicate situation this created, "the United States withheld recognition while studying that situation until November 1 and did not open an embassy at Conakry until February 18, 1959." [188]

President Eisenhower received a communication from Prime Minister Sékou Touré of Guinea on October 2, 1958, informing him that the National Assembly of Guinea had on that day proclaimed the Republic of Guinea and that the newly established Government of the sovereign and independent State of Guinea desired to enter into diplomatic relations with the United States.[189] A second message was addressed to President Eisenhower by Prime Minister Touré on October 13. It contained the following significant statement:

> Owing to the urgency of certain decisions of international significance, the establishment of embassies and of economic relations, the Government of the Republic of Guinea, earnestly desiring to protect American interests and hoping for the development of economic and cultural relations with the United States has the honor to request your excellency to reply to our message of October 2. In the interest of the United States and the Republic of Guinea, please agree to cooperation between our two countries through international relations. [190]

While President Eisenhower had not personally replied to these messages, they had been acknowledged by an official of the American Government. On October 8, 1958, the American Consul General at Dakar, who was accredited to French West Africa, had addressed the following "interim" message to Prime Minister Touré.

> I have been instructed by my Government to acknowledge receipt of your telegram of October 2, to the President concerning your desire to establish diplomatic relations with the United States. My Government has asked me to assure you that your proposal will re ceive its most serious consideration and that a final reply will be

transmitted to Your Excellency when all aspects of the juridical position of Guinea are clarified. I have also been asked by my Government to extend to Your Excellency its sincere good wishes for the future of Guinea.[191]

To this message the Prime Minister of Guinea replied on October 9, 1958, "that his country intended to assume the attributes of sovereignty without limitation in conformance with the principles of international law." [192] This was followed by the October 13 message to President Eisenhower, which was also not ignored by the U.S. Government. Again the American Consul at Dakar was directed to communicate the following message to Prime Minister Touré on October 18:

The United States Government is giving due consideration to the question of the recognition of your country as an independent state. I can assure Your Excellency that the Government and people of the United States have the warmest friendship for the people of Guinea and are looking forward to giving full expression to their feelings through lasting ties of a political and cultural character.[193]

On November 1, 1958, the President of the United States finally replied personally and officially to the messages of Prime Minister Touré with a statement of formal recognition, which was released to the press on November 2. President Eisenhower stated that it gave him "great pleasure to renew" his sincere good wishes "for the future of Guinea," which had been conveyed to President Touré through the American consul general at Dakar, and that it was his pleasure to extend to the Government of Guinea, "the formal recognition of the Government of the United States." [194] The supplemental mode of exchanging diplomatic representatives or the method of establishing an embassy in Conakry was not effected until February 18, 1959.[195] Previous to that date—at the time of President Eisenhower's "formal recognition" of the "Government" of Guinea—there was neither an elevation of the American Consulate to embassy status nor the appointment of a chargé d'affaires.

President Eisenhower's delay in answering the two messages from President Touré appears to indicate an intentional policy of nonrecognition. This is substantiated by the messages of the American consul general at Dakar, which might be said to constitute express statements of nonrecognition. For political reasons, the new state of Guinea appears not to have been considered fit for recognition. When President Eisenhower finally answered President Touré's notes, the type of recognition was probably intended to be no more than *de facto*. The words used were "formal recognition" and only the "Government" of Guinea was mentioned as the object of U.S. recognition. Furthermore, no embassy was established, and no diplomatic representatives were accredited until several months later. Recognition then does not appear to have been completed until February 18, 1959, when the mode of exchanging diplomatic representatives was finally employed, and when the type of recognition was apparently changed from *de facto* to *de jure*. The nuances of U.S. policy were reflected in methodological techniques ranging from the employment of the American consul general at Dakar to deliver the message of temporary nonrecognition to the accreditation of diplomatic representatives, and the establishment of an embassy.

INDIA AND PAKISTAN

India acquired international status on January 10, 1920, as a member of the League of Nations and confirmed this status later as a participant in World War II. On July 24, 1941, President Roosevelt accredited a commissioner with the rank of minister to the Government of India, with reciprocal representation in Washington, and, on December 18, 1942, a senior foreign service officer with the rank of ambassador was assigned to India "partly with the intention of forwarding the country's independence." [196] The incumbent commissioner to India was named chargé d'affaires ad interim on December 17, 1946, and a full ambassador was accredited to the Governor General of India on April 10, 1947. Two months earlier, the United States had taken steps in the direction of recognizing the Interim Government of India, which had been formed on September 2, 1946, by receiving India's first Ambassador to the United States.[197] This Ambassador's credentials had been signed by the British Crown.

Under the Independence Act of August 15, 1947, India and Pakistan became dominions of the British Commonwealth of Nations, and the Governor General, "as Viceroy of the British Crown," became the head of state in both nations. Up until this time, Pakistan had not existed as a separate entity.[198] On August 14, 1947, the Department of State announced that the U.S. Government and the newly independent Dominion of Pakistan had agreed to exchange ambassadors effective August 15 and that the American consulate in Pakistan was to be raised to the rank of embassy.[199] On August 15, the U.S. ambassador to India was reaccredited to the Governor General, who was now the head of the independent Dominion of India as well as Viceroy of the head of the British Commonwealth of Nations.[200] Furthermore, on the same day President Truman telegraphed messages of congratulations to the Governors General of both new Dominions.[201]

Denys P. Myers contends that India had been treated as a state for years before she was granted formal independence in 1947. He mentions, for example, that India signed the Lend-Lease Agreement on November 11, 1941, and also the Declaration by the United Nations in 1942. India also participated fully in the drawing up of the Charter of the U.N. and became an original member of the organization.[202] Thus Myers feels that U.S. recognition of India and Pakistan was "really superfluous and in fact was informally accorded." [203] This is not entirely accurate. Let us see what conclusions we can reach through an analysis of the facts.

The types of entities recognized were, first, two newly independent dominions of the British Commonwealth of Nations; second, a dependent entity acting like a full member of the international community, and, third, the government of that dependent entity. This interpretation of the facts is substantiated by the contents of the notes sent to the Governors General of the newly independent dominions on August 15, 1947. In his note to India, President Truman recognized the "new and enhanced status" of an entity that, by this very terminology, was implicitly considered as having been recognized as possessing some degree of international personality before the formal date of independence. The note to the Pakistani Governor General presents a striking contrast to the Indian note. Here President Truman expressly recognized the "emergence among the family of nations of the new Dominion of Pakistan." As for the types of recognition, that of India before August, 1947, was implied, and could be referred to as having a *de facto* character.[204] However, recognition of India's new status as an independent dominion was certainly express, and, by implication, *de jure*. The same applies to the express recognition of Pakistan. The modes of recognition were more complex. When the U.S. implicitly recognized the status of India as an international person, the mode of recognition was that of exchanging diplomatic representatives, and when India's independence was recognized, the mode was one of express declaration. Pakistan was also recognized by express declaration and by the exchange of ambassadors. As for the methodology, it is interesting to note that the express declarations of formal recognition were made in the form of telegraphed

U.S. Recognition Policy Toward the New Nations 161

messages of congratulations from the President of the U.S. to the heads of the newly established governments. The pattern of recognition later developed toward the new states attaining independence after 1957 is already anticipated here.

Myers' contention then that the formal act of recognition in 1947 was "really superfluous" would seem to be inaccurate. Pakistan was recognized both as a new international entity and a newly independent Dominion on August 15, 1947, and this recognition must be regarded as the act from which legal consequences flow under international law. Regarding India, the matter is a little more complicated. It is true that India was recognized as an international entity before 1947, and that the act of accrediting a senior foreign service officer with the rank of ambassador to India probably constituted a legally valid act of recognition. However, this was only the recognition of an international entity and of the government of an entity that had not yet attained full and formal independence in international society. Thus the telegrams of congratulations from President Truman to the Governor General of India constituted the formal act of recognizing the independence of an international person that had hitherto existed in a dependent, or at least formally dependent, condition.

The correctness of this analysis is put into question by the 1954 Circuit Court of Appeals decision in *Murarka et al. v. Bachrack Bros. Inc.*[205] Consequently, the objective validity of Myers' contention must be granted. We continue to argue, nevertheless, that recognition of India's independence was not formally effected until August 15, 1947, and that the previous acts of implied recognition had as their object a dependent nation and its government. In the *Murarka* decision the Circuit Court of Appeals held as follows:

> It appears from a State Department communication which was before the lower Court that although our Government did not formally recognize India as an independent nation until August 15, 1947, it took steps to recognize the Interim Government of India after its formation on September 2, 1946, by receiving in February 1947 India's first ambassador, whose credentials were signed by the British Crown, and accrediting the first United States ambassador to India in April 1947.
>
> The parties have not directed our attention to any further act of recognition which occurred after the exchange of ambassadors, and we view the statement in the State Department communication to the effect that India did not become independent until August 15,

1947, as being rather in the nature of a legal conclusion which adds little more to the significance of the already existing relations between that Government and our own.

Whether the position of India be viewed as of July 14, 1947, when the complaint was filed, or as of January 14, 1953, when the complaint was amended, we think that at both times its international status was such as to give Indian citizens the right to sue in our Federal Courts. True, as of July 14, 1947, our Government had not yet given India *de jure* recognition, but its exchange of ambassadors in February and April 1947 certainly amounted at least to *de facto* recognition, if not more. To all intents and purposes, these acts constituted a full recognition of the Interim Government of India at a time when India's ties with Great Britain were in the process of withering away (see U.S. Foreign Relations 1913, p. 102), which was followed a month later, when partition took place between India and Pakistan, by the final severance of India's status as a part of the British Empire. The significance of these events is not lessened by the fact that the credentials of the first Indian Ambassador to the United States were signed by the British Crown. We think that in its setting the act is more properly to be regarded as a mere expediency rather than as a significant act of sovereignty in the usual sense of that term. Unless form rather than substance is to govern, we think that in every substantial sense by the time this complaint was filed India had become an independent international entity and was so recognized by the United States.[206]

Of further interest in the Indian case is the proclamation of January 26, 1950, changing the status of India from Dominion to "sovereign Republic." This constitutional change, as in the case of Ghana, was expressly recognized by the United States. "On the occasion of the coming into effect of the Constitution of the Union of India and the inauguration of its republican form of government, Secretary of State Acheson sent a message of felicitation to Pandit Nehru." [207] With this last officially recorded act, the involved process of United States recognition of India appears to have come to an end.

JAMAICA

In 1958, several British dependencies in the Caribbean formed the West Indies Federation, to which the United Kingdom was to grant independence in May, 1962, subsequent, and subject to, a popular referendum in Jamaica. The referendum was held in Sep-

U.S. Recognition Policy Toward the New Nations 163

tember, 1961, but the results proved contrary to expectation. Jamaica voted itself out of the Federation, which was then abandoned. Jamaica, as a separate entity, attained independence, with Dominion status in the Commonwealth of Nations on August 6, 1962.

On the occasion of Jamaica's attainment of independence, President Kennedy addressed a message to Prime Minister Sir Alexander Bustamante and to the people of Jamaica, sending "greetings" and expressing gratification at seeing "a newly independent state joining the family of nations." [208] This express statement of recognition in substance was supplemented by further official acts, indicating intended *de jure* recognition. There is no record, however, of the accreditation of a chargé d'affaires or the elevation of a consulate to embassy status at the time of Jamaican independence.

On August 5, 1962, one day prior to the date of Jamaica's official independence, Vice-President Johnson announced that the U.S. Government would present a $75,000 scholarship fund to Jamaica as an "independence gift," and that this gift was to be presented to Prime Minister Bustamante at the ceremonies commemorating the granting of "Commonwealth status to the Caribbean island." [209] It was also announced at this time that Vice-President Johnson would be President Kennedy's official representative at the independence ceremonies in Kingston.

In accordance with these announcements, Vice-President Johnson, Representative Adam C. Powell, and New York State Senator James E. Watson arrived in Jamaica for the ceremonies, the Vice-President bringing greetings from President Kennedy.[210] The gift introduces an interesting element into recognition techniques. The sending of a special representative was later supplemented by the appointment to Washington of an ambassador of the Jamaican Government, Neville Noel Ashenheim, and the reception of his credentials by President Kennedy on October 23.[211] The *de jure* character of U.S. recognition was further indicated by the Department of State announcement on June 22, more than a month prior to the date of independence, "that Sir Alexander Bustamante, Premier of Jamaica, would arrive at Washington on June 27 to call on President Kennedy and to meet with other officials" of the U.S. Government. It might even be argued that this reception of the head of state of a dependent nation was tantamount to recognition.

KENYA

The newly independent nation of Kenya is composed of a former British Crown Colony and a Protectorate. The area was under Portuguese control from the sixteenth to the seventeenth century, but during the nineteenth century it was subjected to increasing British influence.

Britain granted Kenya independence on December 12, 1963. U.S. recognition followed the already familiar pattern described in several of the preceding case studies. Type of recognition was express and probably *de jure*. The mode was express declaration, and the act of recognition itself was anticipatory, even though it was clearly intended to have effect on the official day of independence. On December 10, 1963, it was announced in a White House press release that Secretary of the Interior Stewart L. Udall, in his capacity as personal representative of the President with the rank of special ambassador, had on that day delivered a congratulatory message from President Johnson to Prime Minister Jomo Kenyatta. The note is reproduced here in its entirety because it is typical of those dispatched to various newly independent states and it is a relatively recent example of such congratulatory messages of recognition.

> Once again, as has happened so frequently in these exciting years, a new nation has appeared in the family of mankind. And once again, the people of the United States of America see in that event a reaffirmation of the ideals which were embodied in their own struggle for freedom. As our own freedom for all our citizens was proclaimed to the world by our Declaration of Independence, so Kenya's freedom begins with her declaration of independence today.
>
> The United States, under President Kennedy, welcomed and supported the growth of free and independent nations in Africa, and American policy will continue along the same lines. Our ultimate goal is a world dedicated to peace and freedom. To help achieve such a world, we will continue to combat those age-old enemies of world peace—illiteracy, illness, malnutrition, and poverty. We also are deeply committed to the attainment of basic human rights by all men. And we are irrevocably determined to speed that process by assuring equal rights to all Americans as quickly as we are able. In essence, then, the United States is devoted to the same basic human aspirations as those of the people of Kenya—and, indeed, as those of people of good will throughout the world.
>
> To the courageous people of Kenya, the American people and I send the warmest good wishes as you enter into nationhood. Just as the infant United States was encouraged and strengthened by the

sympathy of those throughout the world who loved liberty, so your young and vigorous nation will have the understanding support of free men in every land. Good fortune in the years ahead. May the responsibilities of freedom wake the best that is in you, and may its benefits be known by generations yet unborn.[212]

This message of express recognition and congratulations was later supplemented by the appointment of an ambassador. On February 24, 1964, the Department of State announced that William Attwood had on that day been sworn in as the first ambassador to Kenya, and would arrive in Nairobi on February 28, 1964.[213] In addition, Adlai Stevenson, U.S. Ambassador to the United Nations, made an official welcoming statement on the date of Kenya's admission to the U.N.[214]

KUWAIT

According to an agreement of January 23, 1899, between Great Britain and Kuwait, the Sheik of Kuwait pledged and bound "himself, his heirs and successors not to receive the Agent or Representative of any Power or Government at Kuwait or at any other place within the limits of his territory, without the previous sanction of the British Government.[215] In other words, a protectorate was established.

The United States appears to take the position that the independence of Kuwait was regained sometime before World War II. G. Etzel Pearcy, an official of the Department of State, argues that "no basis exists for placing" Kuwait among the states that attained full sovereignty since 1943, "though conceivably its independence has in part at least materialized since World War II by force of a series of bilateral and unilateral actions, no one of which sharply defines the newly found autonomy." [216]

However that may be, not until June 19, 1961, celebrated as the official date of independence in Kuwait, did the British Government officially recognize the full independence of the small sheikdom. On that day the "state of Kuwait" received a note from the United Kingdom, in which the relationship between the former metropole and protectorate was set out:

> 1. The Agreement of the 23rd of January, 1899, shall be terminated as being inconsistent with the sovereignty and independence of Kuwait.
>
> 2. The relations between the two countries shall continue to be governed by a spirit of close friendship.

3. When appropriate the two Governments shall consult together on matters which concern them both.

4. Nothing in these conclusions shall affect the readiness of Her Majesty's Government to assist the Government of Kuwait if the latter requests such assistance.[217]

That Kuwait had received a degree of recognition as an international person prior to the date of this note is indicated by the fact that it signed the constitution of UNESCO on November 18, 1960, and that the acceptance of this signature was deposited on the same day.[218] What is more, by way of bilateral agreement, the U.S. extended a form of implied recognition to Kuwait. On December 11 and 27, 1960, an agreement relating to the reciprocal granting of nonimmigrant passport visas was effected by exchange of notes between the U.S. and Kuwait. This agreement entered into force on December 27, 1960, and became operative on January 26, 1961.[219]

The implication then is that the United States recognized Kuwait some time prior to 1943, but "just when this recognition began is almost impossible to determine," according to Pearcy.[220] The mode of this implied recognition was probably that of a bilateral agreement. That such recognition took place is also implied by the fact that official listings of newly independent states since 1943 by the Department of State do not include Kuwait.[221] Nevertheless, all other indications that Kuwait attained independence prior to its official recognition by the British Government on June 19, 1961, are missing. There was a U.S. Consulate in the sheikdom, but no diplomatic representatives.

A further indication that the United States does not appear to have considered Kuwait fully independent until that status had been expressly recognized by Britain is a Department of State press release of September 22, 1961. On that date it was announced that, "Effective immediately the United States Government has agreed to the establishment of diplomatic relations with the Government of Kuwait and, pending the assignment of an ambassador, has designated the present American consul in Kuwait, Dayton Mak, as Chargé d'Affaires." [222]

Thus the previously implied recognition was apparently made *de jure*. In view of the facts, it is strange that Kuwait is not listed among the "newly independent nations," but is nevertheless considered fully independent. It is doubtful that by any reasonable interpretation it can be held to have attained independence prior to or during World War II. A minimal status of international personality may very well have been bestowed on Kuwait by the acts of the Allied powers. Bilateral agreements subsequent to 1945 may have confirmed this limited status, short of full sovereignty. But the fact remains that Kuwait recognizes June 19, 1961, as its official date of independence, and that Britain had not expressly abrogated its protectorate agreement of 1899 until that date.

In other words, implied *de jure* recognition, by way of elevating a consulate to embassy status, was followed by an express statement of congratulations in which the word recognition was again not used, but the tone of which clearly indicated recognition. The exchange of diplomatic representatives supplemented the mode of express declaration. That is, the *de jure* character of United States recognition in this case is evidenced by the employment of several methods, such as announcement in Washington, the dispatching of an official message, and the elevation of a consulate to the status of embassy.

Whiteman now informs us that:

> In July 1961 the Department of State explained that it had for some time recognized Kuwait as a sovereign state as evidenced by U.S. consular offices in Kuwait receiving exequaturs from the Ruler of Kuwait, and by the conclusion in 1960 of an agreement respecting visas directly with the government of Kuwait. It was added that the United States Government would, of course, support Kuwait's application for membership in the United Nations.
>
> It was explained that the Secretary of State's exchange of felicitations with the Ruler of Kuwait on June 19, at the initiative of the United States, and President Kennedy's and Secretary of State Rusk's exchanges with the Ruler and State Secretaries, respectively, on July 4, 1961, at the initiative of Kuwait, were not intended to suggest a new status for Kuwait; rather, that they simply represented normal exchanges by the United States with an already recognized independent state on the occasion of a national holiday.[223]

MALAGASY REPUBLIC

Independence came to the Island of Madagascar in an already familiar way. A French dependency, the Overseas Territory of Madagascar became an autonomous member of the French Community on October 14, 1958, and received the name of Malagasy Republic. Following agreements with France, signed in Paris on March 26, 1960, and ratified on June 25, 1960, full independence was proclaimed on June 26, 1960.[224]

U.S. recognition procedure likewise conformed to an established pattern. On June 24, two days prior to the transfer of final powers, the Department of State announced that the American consulate at Tananarive, Madagascar, would be elevated to the status of embassy on the date of formal independence and that John Roland Jacobs had been named chargé d'affaires to the Malagasy Republic.[225] On June 26, it was made known that President Eisenhower had formally congratulated Philibert Tsiranana, President of the newly independent republic, extending "cordial greetings and felicitations." [226] This action was supplemented by an announcement of July 25, 1960, to the effect that the United States had recommended the Malagasy Republic for U.N. membership.

MALAWI

On July 6, 1964, Nyasaland, former member of the Federation of Rhodesia and Nyasaland, became the thirty-seventh African state to attain its independence. Along with British colonial rule it also discarded its former name, choosing that of Malawi instead.[227]

United States recognition of this most recently established independent state followed the by now generally accepted procedure of anticipatory preparation and immediate official relations and felicitations. On June 26, 1964, more than a week prior to the date of independence, the White House announced that the President had nominated Samuel Patrick Gilstrap as United States Ambassador to Malawi and that he would be one of President Johnson's two personal representatives at the independence ceremonies. He would have the rank of Special Ambassador.[228] On the same day, in a separate press release, it was announced that the second personal representative of President Johnson would be Dr. Rufus E. Clement, President of Atlanta University, that he would also have the rank of Special Ambassador, and that he would head an official delegation, the members of which would be G. Mennen Williams, Assistant Secretary of State for African Affairs, and Ambassador Gilstrap.

To the mode of exchanging diplomatic representatives was added that of express declaration in substance. On July 3, three days before the final powers were transferred, the Department of State made public the statement that Dr. Clement would deliver while presenting the United States independence gifts to Malawi on July 6, 1964. The gifts were broadcasting and medical equipment, and their official presentation certainly constituted implied anticipatory recognition. Dr. Clement's statement, reproduced below in full, is indicative of the changed character of recognition and the function that this legal institution, by bringing into existence not only the legal relationship, but also certain social and political consequences of such a relationship, now plays in the international arena:

> It is a great privilege and a joy for me to be here in this lovely land, among the people of Malawi, as we celebrate your great move into the community of independent nations.
>
> One hundred and eighty-eight years ago this day, July 4, 1776, the United States of America shed its colonial bonds. As Americans at home and abroad commemorate our national independence, I have a special honor. President Lyndon B. Johnson has asked me, as his Personal Representative and as America's Special Ambassador, to present to you, Mr. Prime Minister, our country's independence gifts to the people of Malawi.
>
> Our gifts are radio broadcasting equipment and mobile health facilities which are intended respectively to expand Malawi's mass communications and popular education services and to help increase the physical welfare and general well-being of your people.
>
> Mindful of Malawi's need for nationwide communications, we are presenting to you two medium-wave radio broadcasting transmitters as well as relay equipment and towers. To help assure effective operation of these installations, my country's gifts also comprise a certain number of related technical training scholarships.
>
> With these new facilities, which will begin operation next October, Malawi will have a greatly increased capacity to see that its citizens in all regions know more about their homeland and about the events shaping their continent and the world in which we live. A related and equally important potential of this broadcast equipment is that of popular instruction by radio, which accords with Malawi's educational development program.
>
> Mindful of your desire to improve the health and thereby the productive capacity of your people, our gift of a mobile medical unit combines a self-sufficient X-ray unit with mobile medical clinic facilities.
>
> These gifts reflect the United States' desire to help Malawi speed its development. Politically and economically strong nations in Africa, we believe, are in the best interests of the people of Africa and of the United States.
>
> In its careful pursuit of independence, Malawi has clearly indicated its desire for a nationhood in which all of its peoples' welfare

will be increased. It is with much pleasure that I now present these gifts to the Government and people of Malawi. May they serve you well.[229]

United States *per se* recognition of Malawi, to use Whiteman's terminology, appears to have been concluded and made official by the presence of Assistant Secretary Williams, Ambassador Gilstrap, and Dr. Clement at the independence ceremonies on July 6.[230] There is no further record, as of the time of completion of this study of other customary modes and methods of recognition.

MALAYA

The Malayan Union, established in 1946, became the Federation of Malaya, under British administration, on February 1, 1948. An agreement, signed on February 8, 1956, provided for the creation of an independent Malaya. Final powers were transferred as the result of a second agreement, signed in Kuala Lumpur on August 5, 1957, putting an end to British supremacy on August 31, 1957.[231]

In a press release of July 24, 1957, the Department of State announced that in view of the fact that the Federation of Malaya would attain independence "within the Commonwealth of Nations" on August 31, the American consulate general at Kuala Lumpur would be raised to an embassy and the consul general appointed chargé d'affaires on the same date to serve until an ambassador should arrive.[232] This preceded by a month the actual date of independence. Two weeks later, still well ahead of time, the Department of State made public the plan of Under Secretary of State Christian Herter and Ambassador James P. Richards to attend the official independence celebrations of the Federation "as personal representatives of President Eisenhower with the rank of special ambassador." [233]

These acts of anticipatory implied recognition were followed by a letter, dated August 31, 1957, from Secretary of State Dulles to Prime Minister Tunku Abdul Rahman, through which, according to Whiteman, "the United States extended recognition to the new State of the Federation of Malaya." [234] The letter reads as follows:

> It is with great pleasure that I offer you the congratulations and the warm good wishes of the Government and people of the United States of America on the occasion of the independence of the Federation of Malaya. May the Federation enjoy to the fullest the benefits of freedom and prosperity, and may you continue to enjoy the blessings of health and success in your high position.

U.S. Recognition Policy Toward the New Nations

The Federation's transition to full independence, which you have so skillfully led, provides an impressive example of the fruits of honest negotiation by men of high purpose meeting in peace and amity at the council table. I look forward with pleasure to the establishment and cultivation of the ties of cordial friendship between our two nations.[235]

There is little doubt that the anticipatory acts of implied recognition and Secretary of State Dulles' letter together constituted *de jure* recognition of the newly established federation. The mode of exchanging ambassadors and the methods of dispatching an official mission to the independence ceremonies and a congratulatory message to the head of state were probably supplemented by an express statement of recognition on the part of Under Secretary Herter on his being received by Prime Minister Rahman. What is significant about this elaborate procedure is that preparations for exchanging representatives and other acts implying recognition were made so far in advance.

MAURITANIA

The Islamic Republic of Mauritania, a former French Overseas Territory, attained autonomous status within the newly established French Community on November 28, 1958. Independence was not granted until November 28, 1960, however, after an agreement between France and Mauritania had been signed in Paris on October 19, 1960, "whereby France signified her full accord to international sovereignty and independence for the Islamic Republic of Mauritania in West Africa." [236] This agreement was subsequently ratified and independence was proclaimed on November 28.

Until the publication of the second volume of Whiteman's *Digest* no public record could be found of United States implied or express recognition of Mauritania as a new nation. Apparently this was due to the delicate political situation called into existence by Mauritania's accession to independence. The only indication that Mauritania had been recognized was a report in the *New York Times* of December 6, 1960, that Henry S. Villard, United States Ambassador to Senegal, had also been accredited to Mauritania.[237] Now, however, Whiteman has published an "independence day message" from President Eisenhower to Prime Minister Daddah and details concerning the accreditation of Ambassador Villard. President Eisenhower's message read as follows:

> I am happy to extend, both for myself personally and on behalf of the people of the United States, most cordial greetings and felicita-

tions to you and your countrymen upon the accession to independence of the Islamic Republic of Mauritania.

As Mauritania takes its place in the family of nations, I am confident that it will remain attached to the high principles expressed in its constitution and that its leaders will devote their talents and energies unstintingly to the cause of world peace.

The Government and people of the United States share your pride in this occasion and look forward to amicable relations between our two countries.[238]

Whiteman describes the accreditation of Ambassador Villard:

In recognition of the Islamic Republic of Mauritania having achieved its independence, President Eisenhower named Henry S. Villard, American Ambassador to Senegal, as his personal representative, with the rank of Special Ambassador, to attend the independence day ceremonies. Special Ambassador Villard also presented his credentials as Ambassador to Mauritania on November 28, and for that purpose was received by the Prime Minister.[239]

On December 13, 1960, almost two months after the official transfer of final sovereign powers to Mauritania, the *New York Times* commented that President Eisenhower "underscored United States recognition of the new African Republic of Mauritania" on that day by receiving Premier Daddah in Washington.[240] This statement was made against the background of the Soviet veto of Mauritania's application for admission to the U.N. and the U.S. concern over "the neutralism of Morocco, which claims sovereignty over Mauritania." On December 4, the day on which Soviet opposition prevented Mauritania's entry into the U.N., the U.S. Representative to the U.N. made a strong plea on behalf of Mauritania, giving further indication of the official position of the U.S. Government toward Mauritania. The American delegate stated: "The traditional policy of the United States is to support applications for membership from states which accept the obligations of the Charter and which are able to carry out these obligations. In keeping with this traditional policy, the United States will vote in favor of the resolution recommending the admission of the Islamic Republic of Mauritania to membership in the United Nations." [241] The delegate went on to state that in doing so the United States "is confident that the people of Mauritania, as they take their place in the family of nations, will remain dedicated" to the principles of the Charter and to peace. The U.S. was thus pleased to extend "its friendly greetings to this newest African country," welcoming the "opportunity to vote in favor of the resolution" for admission.

U.S. Recognition Policy Toward the New Nations 173

Even though *de jure* recognition was certainly implied in the independence day message from President Eisenhower to Prime Minister Daddah and in the accreditation of Ambassador Villard, the United States apparently avoided publication of these official acts. Not until the Soviet Union vetoed Mauritania's entry into the United Nations did the United States openly espouse the position that in the eyes of Washington Mauritania was a sovereign and independent state. However that may be, United States recognition procedure followed the established pattern about which we have spoken. The United States was represented at the independence day ceremonies, an ambassador was accredited, and there was a message of felicitation from the American President. The American Ambassador's appointment to Mauritania appears to have been made permanent on June 22, 1961, when Ambassador Villard was replaced by Philip M. Kaiser as American Ambassador to Senegal and Mauritania.[242] That is, on that day Ambassador Kaiser's appointment was confirmed.

MOROCCO

In the strict sense of the word, Morocco is not a "newly independent nation." A descendent of the Alouite dynasty, established in 1649, still occupies the Moroccan throne. Yet, for a time Morocco was subjected to French and Spanish administration, its status being that of a protectorate. What took place in 1956 then was the removal of limitations on Moroccan independence that had been established in the present century. This renewed attainment of full independence and sovereignty was recognized by the United States in several ways.

Even prior to establishment of the Protectorate in 1912, the U.S. had been deeply involved in the affairs of Morocco. It had Moroccan "protégés" under the convention of July 3, 1880. The United States signed the Act of Algeciras, dealing with customs, police, bank, revenues, and public service in Morocco. Americans also participated in the government of the International City of Tangier. Up to 1912, there had been an American Legation in Morocco, but this was discontinued with the establishment of the French Protectorate. Nevertheless, diplomatic agents-consuls general "were regularly accredited to the Protectorate at Tangier after the International Statute of December 18, 1923." [243]

On March 2, 1956, the French Government "solemnly" affirmed "its recognition of the independence of Morocco" and renounced the Protectorate Treaty of March 30, 1912, which it considered as "no longer consistent with the requirements of modern life."[244] The U.S. reaction was a formal announcement in a press release of the fact that France had recognized Moroccan independence, and the sending of a congratulatory message both to the acting Foreign Minister of France and to "His Cherifian Majesty Mohammed V.[245] The latter message, delivered by Julius Holmes, Diplomatic Agent of the United States to Morocco, on March 7, 1956, informed Sultan Mohammed that Holmes had "been instructed" by his Government to convey to His Majesty and his Government "and to the Moroccan people warmest congratulations on the recognition of Morocco's independence, as embodied in the Franco-Moroccan Declaration of March 2, 1956."[246]

A similar procedure followed the announcement on April 10, 1956, that on April 7 the Foreign Minister of Spain and the Prime Minister of Morocco had signed a joint declaration in which the independence and unity of Morocco was recognized. In other words, Spain here renounced the agreement of November 27, 1912, by which its right to administer a Moroccan zone along the Mediterranean had been established. U.S. congratulations were extended to both Spain and Morocco. The wording of these messages was almost identical with that of the messages dispatched on the occasion of French recognition of Moroccan independence. The U.S. diplomatic agent in Tangier was again employed to deliver personally the congratulatory message of his government.[247]

On July 21, 1956, the United States commissioned an ambassador to Morocco; on August 1, Congress repealed laws establishing consular jurisdiction in Morocco; and, on October 6, the American Ambassador "informed Morocco of the relinquishment of the relevant portions of the bilateral treaty of 1836, the Convention of 1880 and the Algeciras Act of 1906."[248] A further move was the acceptance on September 5, 1956 of El Mahdi Ben Mohammed Ben Aboud's credentials as Moroccan ambassador to the U.S.[249] Thus the process of recognition of Morocco's changed international status was completed.

What was recognized was not the independence of a new state, but the removal of limitations on the independence of an old state. The express statements of recognition made no mention of the type of recognition intended. But again the elaborate procedure leaves no doubt that it was *de jure*. Express declaration and the exchange of diplomatic representatives were the modes employed. The methodology of recognition involved Washington, the foreign capital, and international communications between the two capitals. Particular notice should be taken of the manner in which Congress cooperated in the process of recognizing Morocco's independence by repealing legislation connected with the Protectorate.

NIGERIA

The Federation of Nigeria is composed of the former British Colony and Protectorate of Nigeria and the Northern Cameroons, part of the United Nations Trust Territory of the Cameroons administered by Britain. While the Southern Cameroons voted to join the Federal Republic of Cameroon, the Northern Cameroons voted, in a plebiscite held on February 11, 1961, for union with the Federation of Nigeria. The formal unification took place on June 1, 1961. By this time, however, the Federation had already attained full independence, final powers having been transferred on October 1, 1960. U.S. recognition of this initial accession to independent status is on the public record. But there appears to have been no special recognition of the later act of federation with the Northern Cameroons.

The type of recognition extended by the United States was by implication *de jure*. On September 24, 1960, a week prior to the formal attainment of independence, President Eisenhower appointed Joseph Palmer II as ambassador to the Federation of Nigeria,[250] and on September 30, still one day in advance, the Department of State announced in a press release that the American consulate general at Lagos, Nigeria, would be elevated to the status of embassy on October 1, on Nigeria's accession to independence.[251]

So far the United States had employed the mode of exchanging diplomatic representatives. The *de jure* character of the final act of recognition resulting from the two announcements was implied by the fact that they had been made so well in advance of the actual date of independence. This implication is further substantiated by the messages of congratulations sent by President Eisenhower and Secretary of State Herter. On October 1, the White House announced in a press release that the President had extended his "heartiest" congratulations to Nigeria in a message dated September 30.[252] Secretary Herter's message, also dated September 30, introduced a new method of recognition. In a Department of State press release, it was announced that the message had been recorded for transmission by the Voice of America.[253] In other words, public radio communications, instead of diplomatic wires, were used. Added to this already elaborate methodology of recognition was the appointment of Governor Nelson Rockefeller as Personal Representative of President Eisenhower, with the rank of Special Ambassador, to head a United States delegation to be present at the Nigerian independence ceremonies. Governor Rockefeller called on Prime Minister Sir Abubukar Tafawa Balewa of Nigeria on October 2 and delivered President Eisenhower's message of congratulations to him.[254]

PHILIPPINES

In accordance with the Tydings-McDuffie Act or the Philippine Independence Act of March 24, 1934, which changed the status of the Philippines from "overseas territory" to that of a self-governing commonwealth, and provided for a transitional period at the end of which independence was to be granted, the United States transferred the remaining vestiges of sovereignty to the Republic of the Philippines on July 4, 1946.[255] During the intervening period, the Commonwealth of the Philippines acquired international status as a belligerent, fighting on the side of the Allies during World War II, and as one of the original members of the U.N.

United States recognition of Philippine independence was unique; for the first and only time both the granting and the recognizing authority of the new state's independence occurred in Washington. In a White House press release of July 4, 1946, President Truman made public his proclamation of Philippine independence.[256] The United States, he stated, had promised to relinquish sovereignty over the Philippines as soon as that emerging nation had been prepared to assume the obligations of independence and had demonstrated a capacity for self-government. These conditions, he continued, had been met, and he therefore proclaimed that "in accordance with and subject to the reservations provided for in the applicable statutes" of the United States, "the United States of America hereby withdraws and surrenders all rights of possession, supervision, jurisdiction, control, or sovereignty now existing and exercised by the United States of America in and over the territory and people of the Philippines." President Truman further announced that on behalf of the United States he by this proclamation recognized "the independence of the Philippines as a separate and self-governing nation," and that the United States acknowledged "the authority and control over the same of the government instituted by the people thereof, under the constitution now in force."

This, then, was the official act of granting and recognizing Philippine independence. There is no doubt that this express recognition was intended to be *de jure*. It is, however, interesting to note that there is a qualifying clause in the proclamation. Independence was granted "in accordance with and subject to the reservations provided for in the applicable statutes" of the United States. To this mode of express declaration, actualized by a simple public statement in Washington, the following supplementary activity was added. Both President Truman and Acting Secretary of State Acheson made separate statements concerning Philippine independence, and it was announced that President Truman's proclamation would be read in Manila on July 3, 1946, a day prior to the official transfer of sovereignty. Thus the foreign capital was drawn into the methodology of recognition. There was also to be a special short-wave radio program, saluting the granting of independence and transmitting messages from President Truman and other government officials to the Philippines. Lastly, it was announced that an American embassy was to be established in Manila on independence day, thus adding the mode of exchanging diplomatic representatives. The Philippines reciprocated by accrediting Joaquin M. Elizalde as ambassador to the United States. His credentials were presented to President Truman on July 24, 1946. Even prior to this, however, as reported by Myers, "a provisional agreement and a treaty of general relations were signed at Manila on July 4 by a United States ambassador whose credentials were dated June 21." [257]

SIERRA LEONE

The British Colony and Protectorate of Sierra Leone attained independence subsequent to, and in accordance with, the London Constitutional Conference of April 20 to May 4, 1960. Sierra Leone retained membership in the British Commonwealth of Nations.

U.S. recognition of the newly independent Commonwealth member followed the familiar pattern: an express statement of recognition, without mention of either the words "recognition," "*de jure*," or *de facto*"; the elevation of a consulate general to the status of embassy; and the appointment of an American chargé d'affaires. Familiar types, modes, and methods of recognition are contained in these acts.

The Department of State having recommended that Sierra Leone be recognized by the United States as an independent state on

April 27, 1961, and a communication having been received from the British Embassy in Washington inviting United States representation at the independence celebrations in Sierra Leone on April 27, 1961, President Kennedy, on April 22, 1961, addressed a letter to Queen Elizabeth II, stating that, "in recognition of Sierra Leone having received its independence within the British Commonwealth," he had "made the choice of Thurgood Marshall" as his "Personal Representative, with the rank of Special Ambassador, to attend the ceremonies incident to the celebration of the independence of Sierra Leone." [258] President Kennedy also addressed the following message to the Prime Minister of Sierra Leone, for delivery by the American Consul General at the time of the ceremonies.

> I am delighted to extend, both personally and officially, cordial greetings and heartfelt congratulations upon the independence of Sierra Leone.
> My country has noted with admiration the statesmanship exhibited by you and other leaders of Sierra Leone in guiding your nation through the successive stages leading to independence, and we congratulate Sierra Leone for having attained this goal in harmony and friendship with the United Kingdom.
> As Sierra Leone takes her place in the family of nations, I am confident that she will remain devoted to the democratic principles embodied in her constitution and that her people will give generously of their talents and energies in the cause of world peace.
> The Government and people of the United States share deeply in your joy in this occasion and look forward to lasting friendship with your Government and people.[259]

According to a White House press release of April 26, 1961, the attainment of independence having been scheduled for the following day, President Kennedy extended "heartiest congratulations and warmest wishes" to the Government and people of Sierra Leone on the occasion of their independence.[260] One day later, while independence was being celebrated in Sierra Leone, the Department of State announced that the American consulate general at Freetown was being elevated to an embassy on that day and that Herbert Reiner, a career Foreign Service Officer, having held the position of consul and consul general in Freetown since 1958, had been designated chargé d'affaires.[261] In turn, President Kennedy accepted Richard E. Kelfa-Caulker's credentials as Sierra Leone's Ambassador to Washington on July 18, 1961.[262]

SUDAN

British and Egyptian agreement to a declaration of the Sudanese Parliament of December 19, 1955, that Sudan would become a fully independent republic on January 1, 1956, formally ended the Anglo-Egyptian condominium over the Sudan.

On the day final sovereign powers were transferred, the U.S. had a liaison officer in Khartoum, Sudan. One day later, on January 2, 1956, it was made public that President Eisenhower had sent a message to the President of the Supreme Commission of Sudan on the occasion of U.S. recognition of Sudanese independence. This message was delivered by American Liaison Officer Arthur E. Beach on the same day in Khartoum. The message stated that it gave the President "great pleasure to extend, on behalf of the American people, warmest greetings on the attainment of Sudanese independence." [263]

On the same day, the Department of State announced that "the United States has extended recognition to the Sudan as an independent sovereign state. This action followed termination of the Anglo-Egyptian condominium in the Sudan and recognition of Sudan's independence by Egypt and the United Kingdom." [264] It was also announced that Liaison Officer Beach presented a letter to the President of the Supreme Commission of the Sudan in which it was stated that he had been requested by his Government to inform the President of the Supreme Commission that the U.S. "has noted the declaration on December 19, 1955, by the Parliament of Sudan proclaiming the Sudan as an independent sovereign state and is pleased to extend its formal recognition. The Government of the United States contemplates the establishment of appropriate means for the conduct of formal diplomatic relations at an early date." [265]

This is one of the rare instances in which the U.S. expressly employed the term "recognition." Still, no mention was made of its *de jure* or *de facto* character. Yet, the elaborate procedure again indicates that that character could only have been the former. The mode of recognition was express declaration through both the President's message and the letter of formal recognition that were delivered by the American liaison officer in Sudan. This mode was later supplemented by that of exchanging diplomatic representatives. On February 17, 1956, more than a month after independence had been attained, the Department of State announced that the liaison office in Khartoum had been elevated to the status of embassy and that Liaison Officer Beach had been appointed chargé d'affaires.[266] Of interest in the methodology is the unique use of a "liaison officer." It also appears to have been the intention of the U.S. to leave no doubt that the new state had been recognized. This is indicated by the elaborate character of the procedure.

TRINIDAD AND TOBAGO

The West Indies Federation, of which both Jamaica and Trinidad and Tobago were members, was officially dissolved on May 31, 1962. The stage was thus set for the establishment of the independent Dominion of Trinidad and Tobago on August 31, 1962.

Because of the political situation surrounding the emergence on the international scene of this new nation, U.S. recognition procedure displays unique characteristics. Evidently, Washington was prepared to extend immediate recognition to the West Indies Federation when final powers would be transferred. On February 14, 1962, the Department of State announced that in view of a statement issued by the British Government on February 6, 1962, that legislation was to be introduced in Parliament to dissolve the West Indies Federation, "the Department of State decided to terminate its mission in Port-of-Spain effective March 1, 1962" and to revert its status to that of consulate general.[267] The elevation of a consulate to the status of mission then had already taken place, indicating that the process of recognizing the independence of the Federation had been set in motion and, when independence was not forthcoming, had to be stopped. Of course, without the necessary supplementary acts, the procedure did not constitute recognition; it was merely a beginning.

Regarding Trinidad and Tobago, on August 29, 1962, two days prior to the official date of independence, it was announced in a Department of State press release that Judge William Hastie, Federal Judge of the Third Circuit Court of Appeals, had been named by President Kennedy to "head the United States Delegation to the ceremonies which will establish the independence of Trinidad and Tobago." [268] Judge Hastie stated that his mission "will be to symbolize to the people and Government of this new nation the strong bonds of friendship which we Americans feel for them upon their becoming an independent state." The fact that a mission was sent is itself sufficient to indicate that U.S. recognition was *de jure* in intent. In addition, "on August 30, 1962, President Kennedy addressed a communication to Dr. Eric Williams, Prime Minister of Trinidad and Tobago, extending greetings to the Prime Minister and to the people of Trinidad and Tobago on the occasion of attainment of independence, and, in the name of the American people, welcoming the new State into the family of nations." [269]

The probable *de jure* character of U.S. recognition in this case is substantiated both by President Kennedy's message and by subsequent supplementary acts of recognition. On September 12, 1962, Adlai E. Stevenson, U.S. Representative to the United Nations, announced in the Security Council American support for admission of Trinidad and Tobago to the U.N.[270] About one month later, on October 10, the U.S. Senate confirmed the nomination of Robert G. Miner as ambassador to Trinidad and Tobago, and on October 29 "the newly appointed Ambassador of Trinidad and Tobago, Ellis Emmanuel Innocent Clarke, presented his credentials to President Kennedy." [271] Thus was added the mode of exchanging diplomatic representatives.

TUNISIA

The medieval beylic of Tunis, having been under Turkish regency for centuries, became a French Protectorate on May 12, 1881. That is, French jurisdiction was established on that date. It was not formally referred to as protectorate until June 8, 1883. On December 17, 1952, the General Assembly of the U.N. adopted a resolution calling for "free institutions" in Tunis, and on July 31, 1954, France recognized "the self-government of the Tunisian State." [272] Negotiations followed, culminating in the signing of a general convention on June 3, 1955. This abrogated the protectorate article of the 1883 convention and "set up a Tunisian governmental authority" to which French recognition of March 20, 1956, "was simply a formal ratification." [273]

U.S. recognition of the newly independent Kingdom of Tunisia was extended through two messages of March 22, 1956. The first message was from the United States Consul General in Tunis, Morris N. Hughes, to the Bey of Tunis, Sidi Mohammed Lamine Pasha. It stated that the U.S. Government "wishes to convey to His Highness the Bey, to the members of the Tunisian Government and to the people of Tunisia its congratulations on the signature of the Protocol of agreement of March 20 between the Government of Tunisia and France and on the recognition of Tunisian independence as embodied therein." [274] The other message was from the U.S. ambassador in France to the French Foreign Office. Its content was congratulatory.[275]

In other words, express and implicitly *de jure* recognition was extended to the newly independent kingdom through the methodology of having American consular and diplomatic representatives deliver congratulatory messages, signed not by governmental officials in Washington but by the representatives themselves, to the governments of both the metropole and the former protectorate. To this was later added the mode of exchanging diplomatic representatives. On June 5, 1956, the Department of State announced that the American Consulate General had been elevated to the "rank" of embassy.[276] On September 6, 1956, Mongi Slim, the newly appointed ambassador of Tunisia to the United States, presented his credentials to President Eisenhower.

This effectively concluded the U.S. recognition of Tunisian independence. But the independence recognized had been that of a kingdom. Thus, on July 30, 1957, the United States found it necessary to extend formal recognition to the "new Republic of Tunisia." On that date the Department of State announced U.S. recognition of the change in the status of the Government of Tunisia from kingdom to republic, as set forth in the resolution of the Tunisian National Constituent Assembly dated July 25, 1957. The recognition will be conveyed in a note to be delivered by Ambassador G. Lewis Jones to the Tunisian Government." [277] Methodology and intent are clear. As in the case of Ghana's change of status from dominion to republic, it was evidently regarded necessary to extend formal recognition to the change in the nature of the Tunisian state, because in the strict legal sense the entity to which independence had originally been granted no longer existed.

UGANDA

A British Protectorate since 1894, Uganda became fully self-governing locally in March, 1962. General elections were held in April of the same year, and sovereign independence was granted on October 9, following a constitutional convention in London.

U.S. recognition again followed the familiar pattern established toward the new nations since 1957. On October 8, a White House press release made public a message from President Kennedy to Prime Minister A. Milton Obote of Uganda. It was dated October 5 and stated that the President congratulates the Prime Minister and his people "upon Uganda's independence. The government and the people of the United States wish Uganda a prosperous future as a sovereign nation." [278] This message, dated four days in advance of the actual attainment of independence, and delivered by President Kennedy's personal representative at the Ugandan independence day ceremonies, Senator Benjamin A. Smith II, was followed by a Department of State announcement "that the United States would elevate its consulate general at Kampala, Uganda, to an embassy upon the independence of that nation on October 9, 1962." [279] It was further announced that Olcott H. Deming, until then American consul general in Kampala, would become chargé d'affaires ad interim on the same day.[280]

Full, express recognition was consummated by these acts. Implicitly, it was *de jure* recognition. The mode and methods are familiar. Significant again was the rapidity with which recognition was extended; all acts discussed above took place prior to the actual attainment of independence.

The *de jure* character of U.S. recognition of Uganda's independence is also indicated by the fact that the American Representative at the United Nations, Adlai E. Stevenson, recommended on October 15, 1962, before the Security Council, that Uganda be admitted to the U.N.[281] In addition, according to a White House press release of October 18, Prime Minister A. Milton Obote was to be President Kennedy's guest in Washington on October 22 and 23. The statement read: "Prime Minister Obote's visit is warmly welcomed by the President as an opportunity to establish without delay the most cordial relations with this new African nation. It will provide an opportunity for the President to express once more the best wishes of the United States for a prosperous future for Uganda, which achieved its independence through application of self-determination in cooperation with the United Kingdom." [282]

ZANZIBAR

The British Protectorate of Zanzibar, composed of two islands off the East African coast, became independent on December 9, 1963. U.S. recognition of Zanzibar was not anticipatory, as it was for Kenya, to which independence was granted three days later. However, it came on the day final powers were transferred. On December 9, the White House announced that Governor Philip H. Hoff of Vermont had been appointed personal representative of President Johnson, with the rank of special ambassador, and had on that date delivered a message of congratulations to His Majesty Seyyid Jamshid bin Abdulla, the Sultan of Zanzibar.[283]

Recognition in this case was clearly express and *de jure* by intention. A diplomatic representative was dispatched to the independence ceremonies and a note containing what amounted to an express statement of recognition was delivered.

Soon after independence was attained by Zanzibar, a revolution brought the Sultanate to an end. The People's Republic of Zanzibar was proclaimed. In recognizing the government that was subsequently established, the U.S. was more cautious. On February 23, 1964, "recognition of the Government of Zanzibar headed by President Abeid Amani Karume" was formally announced by the Department of State. However, it was specifically stated in this announcement that other nations, among them the governments of members of the British Commonwealth, had already extended recognition to the Karume Government; that "consultations were held with a number of governments including those African governments most immediately concerned"; and that "recognition of the new Zanzibar Government" had already been announced by the following African states: Tanganyika, Kenya, Uganda, Ethiopia, Ghana, and the United Arab Republic.[284]

In the same press release, it was also announced that the U.S. foreign service officer who had been designated to be chargé at the American Embassy in Zanzibar had been instructed to convey to the Karume Government "the decision of the United States to recognize the new government and to establish diplomatic relations." Significantly, before this step was taken, U.S. Ambassador William Leonhart, Jr., apparently appointed to Zanzibar prior to the revolution (even though there is no record of this in Department of State press releases) met with President Karume and members of his cabinet to discuss the question of recognition.

In view of its proximity to independence, U.S. recognition of the revolutionary government could be interpreted as a supplementary act to the original recognition of Zanzibarian independence. (For a discussion of the subsequent merger of Tanganyika and Zanzibar into the United Republic of Tanzania, see p. 223.)

Some Special Cases

ARAB UNION

On May 19, 1958, the American Diplomatic Missions in Baghdad and Amman were informed by the Ministry of Foreign Affairs of the Arab Union that the Arab Union between Iraq and the Hashemite Kingdom of Jordan had come into existence and had established a government.[285] Five days later the American Embassy in Baghdad, under instructions from the Department of State, addressed a note to the Ministry of Foreign Affairs of the Arab Union, referring to the latter's note of May 19 and stating that the

"Government of the United States, having taken note of the assurances of the Arab Union Government that it intends to respect and observe its international obligations, including all international obligations of the Kingdoms of Jordan and Iraq, respectively existing at the time of the formation of the Arab Union, is pleased to extend its good wishes to the Arab Union." [286]

It is interesting to note that this express act of recognition on the part of the United States contains conditional overtones. Washington appears to have put off notifying the American Ambassador in Baghdad of United States recognition of the new Arab Union Government until after the various assurances mentioned above had been received. This conditional element of United States recognition *per se* (for all intents and purposes identical with *de jure* recognition) was to be ignored a few days later, however.

On May 28, 1958, the Ministry of Foreign Affairs of the Arab Union explained in yet another note that treaties binding on the parties to the Union prior to the establishment of the Union would remain binding on Jordan and Iraq respectively, but would not be binding on the Union. Only for the purpose of international treaties, pacts, and agreements concluded after the establishment of the Union would the members "be under the jurisdiction and authority of Arab Union Government." The American Embassy confirmed the receipt and understanding of this note on the same day.[287]

In addition, on May 28, the same day that the exchange of notes described above took place, the United States announced the recognition of the "establishment" of the Arab Union in Washington. This was done apparently both to complete and legally to put on record the process of recognition that had begun on May 24. The announcement read as follows:

> The Government of the United States of America has today [May 28] recognized that the necessary constitutional and legislative measures have been taken by Iraq and by the Hashemite Kingdom of Jordan for the establishment of the Arab Union and has extended its good wishes to the Union on this occasion.
> The Government of the United States has been informed that until the time when the Union takes over the central functions of the two Kingdoms, pursuant to the provisions of the constitution of the Arab Union, their external affairs will remain as they are at the present time. The matter of the accreditation by the United States of an ambassador to the Arab Union and by the Arab Union to the United States does not, therefore, arise for the present.[288]

The Arab Union was destined never to become fully established as a viable international unit. On July 14, 1958, after a revolutionary government had come to power in Iraq, Jordan announced that the Arab Union had been dissolved and that "a decree issued by the Jordanian Cabinet, confirmed by His Majesty the King, has brought the Hashemite Kingdom of Jordan to function as a separate state in accordance with the Constitution of Jordan, effective from the 1st of August 1958." [289]

ICELAND

In the strict sense of the word, Iceland is not a "newly independent" state. Denmark and Iceland recognized each other as "free and Sovereign States" under a common King by the "Act of Union" of November 30, 1918, effective December 1, 1918.[290] During the period that the Act of Union was in force, the two states were formally independent and bound together only by their common sovereign, as were the United Kingdom and Ghana prior to the latter's change in status from Dominion to Republic. Until World War II, however, the foreign policy of Iceland continued to be conducted largely through the Danish Foreign Ministry.[291] On April 10, 1940, the Icelandic Parliament passed two resolutions. The first stated that, due to the situation then obtaining in Denmark, it was impossible for the King of Iceland and Denmark to exercise the executive power vested in him with respect to Iceland and that the Icelandic Cabinet was therefore entrusted for the time being with such power. The second provided that, since Denmark was not in a position to safeguard the foreign affairs of Iceland or to carry out fishery inspection in accordance with the Union Act, the Icelandic Parliament for the time being "would take over entire charge of such affairs." [292]

The Act of Union was abrogated by a plebiscite held from May 20–23, 1944, and a new Constitution was approved, pursuant to Article 18 of the Act of Union and a resolution of the Icelandic Althing of February 25, 1944. The new Constitution was ratified by the Althing on June 16, 1944, and the Republic of Iceland was formally proclaimed on June 17, 1944.[293] What actually happened then at this time was the effectuation of an internal constitutional change and not the coming into existence of a new state. Formally, Iceland had been "free" and "sovereign" since 1918. It appears, however, that the United States did not recognize Iceland as formally independent until 1944, even though qualified recognition was extended much earlier and for all intents and purposes constituted the *de jure* recognition of Iceland's sovereignty and government.

Beginning in 1933, letters of credence for American diplomatic personnel were addressed to the King of both "Denmark and Iceland" and even prior to this date treaties had been entered into by the United States with the King of "Denmark and Iceland" on behalf of the "Government of Iceland." [294] After Iceland had assumed the exercise of its own sovereign powers in the international arena in 1940, it proposed and subsequently postponed the establishment of an Icelandic Legation in Washington and the appointment of a consular representative in New York. Secretary of State Hull replied as follows to this proposal:

> The establishment of direct diplomatic and consular relations between the Government of Iceland and the Government of the United States in the existing circumstances will be welcomed by my Government. . . .
> As a first step in reciprocating direct relations between our two Governments, my Government is anxious to open a Consular Office in Reykjavik. . . . .[295]

The negotiations leading to the Agreement for the Defense of Iceland by United States Forces, ratified by the Icelandic Regent in Council on July 10, 1941, reveal an interesting exchange of notes between Reykjavik and Washington. On July 1, 1941, the Prime Minister of Iceland addressed a message to President Roosevelt, stating that the Government of Iceland was willing to accept United States protection, but only under the condition that the United States promise not to interfere in Iceland's internal affairs, to withdraw its military forces after the war, and "to recognize the absolute independence and sovereignty of Iceland." [296] The concluding paragraph of the Prime Minister's communication read as follows:

> This decision is made on the part of Iceland as an absolutely free and sovereign state and it is considered as a matter of course that the United States will from the beginning recognize this legal status of the country, both states immediately exchanging diplomatic representatives.[297]

President Roosevelt's almost immediate answer to the Prime Minister's message, also dated July 1, 1941, can be construed as a statement of *de jure* recognition. He stated that the United States "promise to recognize the absolute independence and sovereignty of Iceland and to exercise their best effort with those powers which will negotiate the peace treaty at the conclusion of the present war in order that such treaty shall likewise recognize the absolute independence and sovereignty of Iceland." So far the President appears to have promised future recognition of a not yet independent state. Yet, his message also contains the following statement:

> You further state that this decision is made on the part of Iceland as an absolutely free and sovereign state and that it is considered as a matter of course that the United States will from the beginning recognize the legal status of Iceland, both states immediately exchanging diplomatic representatives.
>
> I take pleasure in confirming to you hereby that the conditions set forth in your communication now under acknowledgment are fully acceptable to the Government of the United States and that these conditions will be observed in the relations between the United States and Iceland. I may further say that it will give me pleasure to request of the Congress its agreement in order that diplomatic representatives may be exchanged between our two countries. . . .
>
> The steps so taken by the Government of the United States are taken in full recognition of the sovereignty and independence of Iceland.[298]

On September 30 of the same year, the first United States Minister presented his credentials to the Regent of Iceland and on the occasion of the presentation of his letters of credence made the following statement:

> I am profoundly sensible of the privilege accorded me to initiate the diplomatic representation of my country here, and to labor to draw still closer, and to develop in all fruitful ways, the understanding which has existed immediately between our two peoples.[299]

A little over a month later, on November 19, 1941, the first Minister of Iceland to the United States presented his letters of credence to President Roosevelt as Envoy Extraordinary and Minister Plenipotentiary near the Government of the United States.[300]

It would seem then that by 1941 express recognition had been extended to Iceland by the United States, subsequent to implied recognition through the mode of bilateral treaty and supplemented by the mode of exchanging diplomatic representatives. Yet, the procedure of formal United States recognition of the proclamation of the Republic of Iceland on June 17, 1944, was quite elaborate. The question is and remains, of course, whether this was simply the recognition of a change in Iceland's Constitution or whether it constituted the previously promised recognition of Iceland's "absolute independence."

On March 25, 1944, the Department of State Bulletin published an announcement that Louis G. Dreyfus, Jr., had been confirmed as American Minister to Iceland.[301] He was to replace Leland Morris, the previous American Minister. His letters of credence were presented to the Regent of Iceland on June 14, 1944, at which time he stated that he had been designated Envoy Extraordinary and Minister Plenipotentiary by the President of the United States on the "eve of the establishment of the Republic of Iceland." Implied in this action was the forthcoming recognition of the Republic of Iceland when it came into existence. A further indication of such advance implied recognition was given by President Roosevelt's appointment of Minister Dreyfus as Special Representative with the personal rank of Ambassador, to attend the ceremonies to be held in Iceland on June 17, "incident to the establishment of the Republic of Iceland."

When the Republic finally came into existence on June 17, President Roosevelt and Secretary of State Cordell Hull dispatched messages of congratulations to President Sveinn Bjornsson and Minister of Foreign Affairs Vilhjalmer Thor, respectively. President Roosevelt's message to President Bjornsson read: "Please accept my heartiest congratulations on your election to the high office of President of the Republic of Iceland and my best wishes and those of the people of the United States for the continued prosperity of the Icelandic nation." [302] The wording of Secretary Hull's message was similar. On the same day Ambassador Dreyfus stated at the inauguration ceremonies in Iceland that he had the honor "to welcome the Republic of Iceland as the newest republic in the family of free nations." [303]

The type of recognition here is clearly express and by implication *de jure*. There is little extraordinary about the modes and methods employed, for the acts discussed so far. What is significant, however, is the emphasis that was placed on the word "new republic." It appears to have been clear that the change of status to that of a republic was at issue here, not so much the attainment of formal independence.

What is most significant about the recognition of Iceland as a new republic is the exchange that took place between the legislative bodies of the United States and Iceland. On July 26, 1944, the Secretary of State delivered to Thor Thors, Minister of Iceland to the United States, a copy of a concurrent resolution of the American Congress, "congratulating the Icelandic Althing on the establishment of the Republic of Iceland." [304] Appreciation of the Icelandic legislative body, the Althing, was conveyed to the American Legation at Reykjavik by the Minister of Foreign Affairs in a note of June 22, 1944. In this note he significantly stated that the President and Government of the U.S. had been the first power to promise recognition in advance, should the "independence" of Iceland be fully solved during the year of 1944. He also stated that the U.S. was the first nation to send a special representative of highest standing to be present at the inauguration of President Bjornsson. Thus an unusual participation of the legislatures in the process of recognizing Icelandic independence or the establishment of the Republic of Iceland clearly revealed the intention of the U.S. Government to extend *de jure* recognition to the state of Iceland that now existed without qualification as an independent nation.

LEBANON AND SYRIA

The states of Lebanon and Syria, formerly several administrative divisions of the Turkish Empire, began to emerge from the mandate of Syria, assigned to France at the San Remo Conference on April 26, 1920, during the interwar period. Grand Liban or Greater Lebanon was formed in August, 1920, and the first Syrian Federation was established in June, 1922. Both states proclaimed their independence shortly after British and Free French forces had entered Syria in June, 1941, and Lebanon on November 26, 1941. Yet formal independence was not attained until several years later. Lebanon has declared November 22, 1943, as the date of its accession to full sovereignty. In view of the factual situation, this is somewhat unrealistic. Not until December 27 was an agreement signed between representatives of the French National Committee of Liberation and Lebanon, transferring most of the mandate powers to the government of that country on January 1, 1944. The withdrawal of foreign troops was not completed until December, 1946. The situation was similar for Syria. An agreement transferring most of the mandate powers exercised by France to Syria was signed on the same day they were transferred to Lebanon, December 27, 1943. Thus Syria, unlike Lebanon, more realistically claims January 1, 1944, as the date of its independence. Still, the last French troops were not withdrawn until April, 1946.[305]

U.S. recognition of these two states reflected the delicate political situation surrounding their emergence to full independence.

Initially, relations between the U.S. Consul General at Beirut and officials of the Syrian and Lebanese governments were expressly restricted to informal or "personal" exchanges.[306] On November 29, 1941, the Department of State announced that it had received inquiries regarding the attitude of the U.S. Government toward the proclamations of independence issued in Damascus on September 27 and in Beirut on November 26.[307] The Department's answer was that the American people had sympathy for the "natural and legitimate" aspiration of the people of Syria and Lebanon, and that the United States welcomed any steps toward the realization of these aspirations. It was further stated, however, that the Convention between the United States and France of April 4, 1924, and the French mandate over Syria and Lebanon, which embodied the "idea" of independence, must be regarded as continuing in effect until new instruments could be negotiated. In other words, recognition of Syrian and Lebanese independence was refused at that time.

In May, 1942, the possible appointment of a Diplomatic Agent and Consul General to the governments of Syria and Lebanon was discussed in the Department of State. In considering the accreditation of such an agent, "in anticipation of formal recognition," when duly constituted independent governments would be established in both countries, a State Department official summarized the situation as follows:

This Government has refrained so far from recognizing the independence of these areas, principally:
(1) in order to avoid further complicating our relations with Vichy;
(2) because of possible prejudice to existing American rights in those areas;
(3) because genuine independence had not been granted; and
(4) because the governments set up in Beirut and Damascus have no constitutional basis and, according to many indications, are not widely representative of the desires of the peoples of the areas.

The first consideration has doubtless lost much if not all of its significance. The second need not prevent our extending recognition if such extension is accompanied by an understanding regarding the maintenance of our treaty rights. The third and fourth considerations, however, remain valid reasons for withholding formal recognition at present, in the opinion of this division.

It has been the policy of this Government in the past to accord recognition only to governments which are in substantial *de facto* control of the areas over which they claim jurisdiction. The Governments of Syria and Lebanon do not exercise such control, since the

Free French officials there have refused to surrender any significant authority to them. No actual independence therefore exists, and recognition by us would be contrary to fact.

Furthermore, the Governments which have been set up in Beirut and Damascus have been hand-picked by the Free French, and would doubtless be unable to maintain their positions without foreign support. Even Iraq, a neighboring Arab state, which has taken a leading part in endeavoring to gain independence for Arab states, has announced its decision not to recognize Syria and Lebanon until constitutionally elected governments are set up.

If the American Government should extend full recognition to Syria and the Lebanon at this time, when independence is not a fact and with what amounts to puppet governments in office there, we would not only do violence to the high standard we have set in international relations but our prestige would suffer in the very area we are endeavoring to influence. However, it would be helpful in furtherance of the war effort for this Government again to assure the Syrians and Lebanese of our willingness to extend recognition as soon as they gain actual independence, and to state that in anticipation of such recognition we are accrediting a Diplomatic Agent and Consul General to Damascus and Beirut at once. Such action would follow precedents set in the cases of Egypt and Morocco, and would be adequate, I believe, for the immediate purpose of encouraging Arab support to the cause of the United Nations.[308]

A similar policy statement was made by Under Secretary of State Sumner Welles in a memorandum addressed to President Roosevelt on September 1, 1942. Even though the British and Free French authorities had recognized Syria and Lebanon as independent states and had requested American recognition of these states, Welles argued as follows:

Independence for areas such as Syria and the Lebanon would be in accord with the traditional policy of this Government to favor self-determination, as the Department pointed out in a statement issued to the press on November 29, 1941, a copy of which is attached. In the present instance, however, we are faced with the fact that neither Syria nor the Lebanon in actuality enjoys an independent status. The local Governments in Beirut and Damascus have been appointed by the Fighting French, and exercise only a very limited degree of sovereign independence. It may be doubted that the exigencies of the military situation will permit their being granted full independence during the war. General de Gaulle has even expressed the view recently that Syria and the Lebanon may not be ready for full independence "for many years."

The American Government enjoys an enviable reputation with

U.S. Recognition Policy Toward the New Nations 193

Arab peoples for honest and fair dealing. If we should take the action of according full recognition to Syria and the Lebanon when it is well known throughout the Near East that the two Governments have very limited powers, we would be participating in an action which would not only be contrary to the facts in the case but would also, I believe, lower our prestige with the Arab peoples and therefore not serve to encourage their support for the United Nations.

It would accord, however, with the existing situation for this government to elevate its Consulate General at Beirut to a Diplomatic Agency and Consulate General, and I recommend that this action be taken. In the past, Diplomatic Agents have been sent to areas enjoying a status of less than full independence, such as Morocco at the present time, and Egypt and Bulgaria when those countries enjoyed certain autonomy but were under the suzerainty of the Ottoman Empire.[309]

These memoranda and another that had been drawn up by a Near Eastern Affairs official of the Department of State on May 15, 1942, were subsequently acted on by the President and the Senate. "On October 9, 1942, the Senate confirmed the nomination of George Wadsworth of New York to act as Diplomatic Agent and Consul General of the United States of America near the Government of the Republic of Lebanon, at Beirut, and near the Government of the Republic of Syria, at Damascus." [310] In view of the Department of State recommendations reproduced above, this action clearly was not intended to constitute recognition.

The formal granting of express recognition to both Lebanon and Syria took place on September 19 and 20 of 1944. It was introduced by a note from U.S. Diplomatic Agent and Consul General Wadsworth to the Ministers of Foreign Affairs of both Lebanon and Syria on September 7, 1944, nine months after France had transferred most of the powers she had held under the Mandate to these countries.[311] Wadsworth stated that it was his honor to inform the governments of Lebanon and Syria that the United States Government "has observed with friendly and sympathetic interest the accelerated transfer of governmental powers to the Syrian and Lebanese Governments since November 1943 and now takes the view that the Syrian and Lebanese Governments may now be considered representative, effectively independent and in a position satisfactorily to fulfill their obligations and responsibilities." [312] Therefore, he continued, the United States is "prepared to extend full and unconditional recognition" of the independence of Syria and Lebanon, on the receipt of assurances that the existing rights of the

United States and its nationals would be fully recognized and would continue to be protected. Following the receipt of such assurances, the United States would be prepared to appoint an Envoy Extraordinary and Minister Plenipotentiary as American representative near the Syrian and Lebanese Governments and "would be pleased to receive in the United States a diplomatic representative of" the same grade.[313] The respective foreign ministers replied with the requested assurances. Thus, on September 20, President Roosevelt was able to announce that he had sent the name of George Wadsworth to the Senate for confirmation as envoy extraordinary and minister plenipotentiary, and that the United States was extending recognition to the Republics of Syria and Lebanon. "Recognition," he stated, "of the independence of Syria and Lebanon by the United States Government is a step in which I, like every American, can take wholehearted pleasure." A similar statement was made by the Secretary of State on September 19.[314] The confirmation of Ambassador Wadsworth was announced in the *Department of State Bulletin* of September 24.[315]

The type of recognition was "full and unconditional" or *de jure*. The mode was express declaration and the exchange of ambassadors. Concerning the methodology, it is interesting to note that political and policy considerations again caused the United States to hesitate with the recognition of states that had been granted their independence by the former metropole.

MALAYSIA

In accordance with the Manila Agreement, the Federation of Malaya, Indonesia, and the Philippines sought the assistance of the Secretary General of the U.N. to ascertain the wishes of the people of Sabah (North Borneo) and Sarawak regarding the planned establishment of a Federation of Malaysia, toward which Britain had been working for some time. On September 14, 1963, the Department of State announced that it had received a report issued by the Secretary General that concludes that the majority of the people of Sabah and Sarawak "desire the inclusion of their two states in Malaysia, to be proclaimed on September 16." The Department then stated that "the United States welcomes Malaysia and looks forward to close and cordial relations between our two nations." [316]

Thus was clearly indicated the U.S. intention to recognize the new federation. Yet the political situation was delicate, and the United States was cautious. There was no press release on the recog-

U.S. Recognition Policy Toward the New Nations 195

nition of Malaysia. A conversation with a Department official disclosed that the United States did not regard Malaysia as a new nation, but merely as an already recognized state, the status of which had changed because of the addition of federated territories. However, when questioned at the daily Department of State press briefing whether the United States had extended recognition to Malaysia, the briefing officer replied that Deputy Under-Secretary U. Alexis Johnson had been named the President's special representative and that he was present at the inaugural ceremonies that began on September 16, the date on which the Federation officially came into existence. He stated that this "is an indication of the importance we attach to the formation of Malaysia and a sign of our recognition of the new government." [317] Regarding the establishment of an embassy, he pointed out that the U.S. already had an embassy in Kuala Lumpur, and that this would be reaccredited to the Federation. When a reporter persisted in questioning whether the United States had "recognized" Malaysia, the briefing officer said that the sending of a special representative to the inaugural ceremonies was "a form of recognition." [318]

So far, the public record discloses no further acts of recognition. It is apparent, however, that the United States has effectively recognized the new Federation. As was pointed out earlier, *de jure* recognition was probably extended to Malaya when it first became independent. The caution with which the United States then recognized the Federation of Malaysia might indicate that this recognition was only *de facto* in character. Yet a special representative was dispatched, and diplomatic relations were maintained at the highest level. If the Federation is successful, the acts described above can probably be held to constitute full and *de jure* recognition. If not, it can as well be argued that the United States had not yet completely committed itself to Malaysia and that its recognition was merely temporary and *de facto* in nature.

MALI FEDERATION, MALI, AND SENEGAL

Because of the peculiar circumstances surrounding the independence of Mali and Senegal, they will be considered in this section. The Republic of Senegal and the Republic of Soudan became autonomous members of the French Community on November 25 and 24, 1958, respectively. As such, they formed the Federation of Mali on April 4, 1959. This is the political entity to which France granted sovereign independence on June 20, 1960. It turned out that the Federation, to which recognition was extended by the

United States, was to be short-lived. On August 20, 1960, Senegal seceded from the Federation of Mali and on August 25 adopted a new constitution. The official date of Senegalese independence is August 20. Mali, on the other hand, claims September 22 as its date of independence. It was on this date that the Republic of Mali was officially proclaimed. Thus, within a period of three months, the United States was confronted with the establishment of an independent federation, on the one hand, and that of two independent republics, on the other.

United States recognition of the Federation of Mali (not when it was first established, but when it became independent) followed the familiar patterns revealed in this study. There was an express statement of recognition, in the form of a message from President Eisenhower to Modibo Keita, President of the Government of the Federation of Mali.[319] From this message and from the official acts of the American Consul General at Dakar, performed under instruction from Washington, may be deduced the *de jure* character of American recognition in this case. Whiteman describes what happened at Dakar as follows:

> On June 13, 1960, the American Consul General at Dakar, Donald A. Dumont, in compliance with instructions, addressed a letter to the French High Commissioner asking him to inform the government of Mali of the intention of the Government of the United States to recognize the new State and Government of Mali on the day of the proclamation of its independence, of the desire of the Government of the United States to raise its Consulate General to the status of an Embassy effective the day of the proclamation, and to request the Government of Mali to accept accreditation of himself as Chargé d'Affaires, effective the same date.[320]

The Mali Federation Government replied favorably and on June 20, 1960, the day final powers were transferred to the Federation, the Department of State announced that the American consulate general at Dakar, Federation of Mali, had been elevated to the status of embassy on that date, "upon formal attainment of independence by the Federation." [321] In a way, this last statement also constitutes express recognition. The mode of exchanging diplomatic representatives was completed by the appointment of career Foreign Service Officer Donald A. Dumont as chargé d'affaires to the Federation of Mali. This exchange was elevated to the highest level of diplomatic intercourse by the naming of Henry S. Villard as ambassador to the Federation on July 18. Ambassador Villard's confirmation was announced on September 19, after the fragmentation of the state to which he had been accredited.

On September 24, 1960, after the proclamation of the Republic of Mali, the U.S. announced "its recognition of the Republic of Mali and the Republic of Senegal." In a White House press release it was made public that the American Consulate at Bamako, Mali, had been elevated to the status of embassy, and that "the President has indicated his intention to appoint Henry S. Villard, who was formerly appointed Ambassador to the Federation of Mali, as the first Ambassador to the Republic of Senegal, subject to the approval of the Senegalese Government."

On the day preceding this announcement, September 23, 1960, "the Department of State instructed the American Consul at Bamako that, when the Malians were informed on that day of the decision of the United States to recognize the Republic of Mali on September, 24, 1960, assurances as to that country's intention to fulfill its international obligations should be obtained." [322] In Senegal, the already established American Embassy at Dakar "informed the Foreign Minister of Senegal of recognition on the part of the United States of the Republic of Senegal" on September 24.[323] Pending the arrival of a U.S. ambassador, the former consul in Bamako, John Gunther Dean, was appointed as chargé d'affaires to the Government of Mali. This pattern of action was supplemented by the appointment of Thomas K. Wright as ambassador to the Republic of Mali on November 5, 1960,[324] the appointment of Henry S. Villard as ambassador to the Republic of Senegal on October 10, and the official reception by President Eisenhower of the credentials of Ousmane Soce Diap, the newly appointed ambassador of the Republic of Senegal to the United States on December 8. According to Whiteman, the United States had waited more than a month after Senegal had proclaimed its independence to recognize the two new states, "since the matter was still under discussion within the French Community." [325]

It appears that the recognition of the two republics was clearly *de jure*. First, there was the express statement of recognition. Second, there was the elaborate procedure of establishing embassies and accrediting or reaccrediting ambassadors. There were also stated conditions for recognition, which were apparently complied with.

NEPAL

The Kingdom of Nepal, lying to the north of India, entered into the international community with the recognition of its independence by Great Britain through the Treaty of Friendship concluded on December 21, 1923. Ministers were not exchanged between the former metropole and the newly independent state until 1934 and active participation in international relations by Nepal came only after World War II.[326]

Whiteman describes the early relations between the United States and Nepal:

> In October 1945, General Shingha, Minister of Nepal to London, called at the Department of State and informally requested American economic assistance for Nepal and indicated that the Nepalese Government would welcome a good will mission from the Government of the United States. In June 1946 the Department of State had concluded that the principal task of such a good will mission to Katmandu on the part of the United States would be to negotiate a provisional commercial agreement, including provisions for the exchange of diplomatic and consular representatives, and that the good will mission should, as a preliminary step, transmit to the sovereign of Nepal a formal document embodying official recognition by the Government of the United States of the absolute and complete independence of Nepal. In November 1946 George R. Merrell, Chargé d'Affaires ad interim, in New Delhi, India, acting under instructions, proceeded to Nepal to present the Legion of Merit, Degree of Chief Commander, to his Highness, Padma Shum Shere Jung Bahadur Rana, Maharaja of Nepal, and to arrange for the sending of an American good will mission to Nepal to negotiate a provisional commercial agreement. Mr. Merrell found that elaborate plans had been made for his reception in Nepal, including a durbar at which the decoration was presented to His Highness the Maharaja, and a durbar at which Mr. Merrell had a formal audience with His Majesty the King. The Nepalese Government extended a formal invitation for the good will mission to visit Nepal in March or April 1947 to negotiate a provisional commercial agreement and to arrange for the exchange of diplomatic representatives. It was learned that the Nepalese were particularly interested in the export of jute, linseed, and other products to the United States; the importation of American capital goods; and the possibilities of obtaining an American loan.[327]

These early relations between Nepal and the United States were followed on March 21, 1947, by an announcement on the part of the Department of State:

Joseph C. Satterthwaite, veteran Foreign Service Officer now assigned to the Department of State, has been designated by the President as his personal representative with the rank of Minister to be chief of a special United States diplomatic mission to the Kingdom of Nepal. Mr. Satterthwaite will depart from Washington at the end of the month on the special mission, the purpose of which is to conclude an agreement of commerce and friendship with the Government of Nepal and to make arrangements for the exchange of diplomatic and consular representatives between the United States and Nepal. . . .

The proposed inauguration of diplomatic relations between the United States and Nepal arises from a series of informal contacts between officials of the two countries beginning in 1945 when American technical experts attached to the office of the United States Foreign Economic Administration at New Delhi were invited to visit Nepal to discuss informally the economic development of that country and the possibility of establishing direct trade with the United States. At about the same time the Nepalese Minister at London visited the United States and called on several high American officials including the President. In July 1946 a Nepalese goodwill mission spent several weeks in the United States as guests of the Department of State and the War Department.[328]

On the same day that the Department of State made this announcement, President Truman dispatched a personal letter, formally delivered by Minister Satterthwaite, to the King of Nepal, in which he extended express recognition to the Kingdom of Nepal:

> Mindful of the many generations during which Your Majesty's ancestors have been Maharajadhirajas of Nepal, and of the independence which your Kingdom has long enjoyed under Your Majesty's rule, I take pleasure in informing Your Majesty that the Government of the United States recognizes the absolute and complete independence of Nepal and by this letter makes known its intent to accord you and Your Majesty's Government the privileges of such recognition to endeavor to promote friendly relations between our two countries.[329]

It may be inferred from the close relations between the United States and Nepal during the years preceding this express declaration of recognition that *de facto* recognition had taken place long before April, 1947, at which time it was made *de jure*. The process of bringing into being the highest level of diplomatic relations between Nepal and the United States was, however, to take another four years. On April 25, 1947, three days after President Truman's note of recognition had been delivered, the agreement "respecting friendship and commerce" was finally entered into; it came into effect through an exchange of notes, signed at Katmandu, Nepal, by the Chief of the United States Special Diplomatic Mission to Nepal and the Prime Minister and Supreme Commander-in-Chief of Nepal.[330] More than four years later, in a press release of August 27, 1951, the Department of State announced that the respective diplomatic missions of the United States and Nepal had been raised to embassy status.[331] This does not add anything to President Truman's formal and complete act of recognition in 1947. It may, however, be said to give us a further indication of the *de jure* character of that act and the preceding and subsequent official acts implying recognition, the modes of which were the exchange of diplomatic representatives and the signing of a bilateral agreement.

UNITED ARAB REPUBLIC

Syria and Egypt united to form the United Arab Republic on February 22, 1958. This move was hailed as the first step toward Arab unity. Yet Yemen announced that it would become no more than an autonomous federal associate of the newly established United Arab Republic, and Iraq and Jordon formed the Arab Union as a countermove.

On February 2, 1958, the *New York Times* reported that the United States Government had on that day "reserved" its position "on the Union of Egypt and Syria until it had more information on whether the move would promote the welfare and stability of the Middle East." [332] This was twenty days prior to the official proclamation of the Union, negotiations concerning which had, however, been made public on February 1, 1958.[333] The Department of State took the position that "obviously there are a number of steps yet to be carried out before the Union is completed, and therefore it would be premature to comment definitely." [334] On February 11, 1958, Secretary of State Dulles made the following announcement at one of his news conferences:

> The United States recognizes the sentiment of the Arab people generally, particularly the Arab people in that area, to achieve a greater degree of unity, and we sympathize very much with that desire for increased Arab unity. I think that there are two conditions which need to be attached to the international changes there: the first is that they should be responsive to the desire of the people concerned there and, secondly, that they should be consistent with the peace

and welfare of the area as a whole and not in any sense designed to carry out aggressive designs against any of the neighboring countries.[335]

By February 25, three days after the official date of union, the United States was evidently satisfied that these conditions had been met. The United States Embassy in Cairo received a note from the Ministry of Foreign Affairs of the United Arab Republic on February 22, 1958, officially advising the United States Government of the establishment of the United Arab Republic and of the election of Gamal Abdel Nasser as its first President.[336] The United States, on February 25, then joined Portugal and Morocco in recognizing the United Arab Republic of Egypt and Syria. A Department of State press release stated that:

> The United States Government has been officially informed of the proclamation of the United Arab Republic following the plebiscite conducted in Egypt and Syria on February 21. The United States Government, having taken note of the assurances of the United Arab Republic that it intends to respect and observe its international obligations, including all international obligations of Egypt and Syria, respectively, existing at the time of the formation of the United Arab Republic, extended recognition to the Government of the United Arab Republic, with the expression of its good wishes.[337]

On the day preceding this express declaration of recognition, officials of the Department of State apparently still had reservations about the establishment of the United Arab Republic. Whiteman reports:

> When a suggestion was made that the United States might confine itself to "*de facto* recognition" of the United Arab Republic, the Department of State took the position that it believed that such a position, halfway between recognition and nonrecognition, would not result in whatever benefits might reside in either of the latter attitudes, and that, instead, by indicating doubt as to the legal qualifications of the U.A.R. for recognition, irritation and resentment might be caused, making it difficult for states extending "*de facto* recognition" to transact business with the government thus recognized. Further, the United States did not wish to cast doubt as to the *de jure* character of the U.A.R.[338]

In view of this statement and the caution with which the United States at first approached the federation of Syria and Egypt, the express statement of recognition issued on February 25 can validly be interpreted as *de jure* recognition, particularly because it makes reference to the fact that the United Arab Republic had given assurances that it would respect its international obligations. Reference to the plebiscite also indicates that the United States considered the new government as having legitimate political authority. Thus far, then, the mode of express declaration was employed. This was supplemented by the mode of exchanging ambassadors. Also on February 25, Raymond A. Hare, United States Ambassador to Egypt, called at the Foreign Ministry of the United Arab Republic to present his new letters of credence. Since President Nasser was not there at the time, he signed the visitor's book in the Presidential Palace, "as is customary on the presentation of credentials when the President is absent from the country." [339] Thus a full ambassador was accredited to the United Arab Republic almost immediately after it had come into existence. In addition, Ambassador Hare delivered a note to the authorities of the United Arab Republic on February 25, which read in part:

> The Government of the United States of America, having taken note of assurances of the United Arab Republic that it intends to respect and observe its international obligations, including all international obligations of Egypt and Syria, respectively, existing at the time of the formation of the United Arab Republic, is pleased to extend recognition to the Government of the United Arab Republic and to convey its good wishes on this occasion.[340]

Even though Syria seceded from the United Arab Republic on September 28, 1961, Egypt continues to refer to itself as the United Arab Republic.

YEMEN

In 1927, the Imam Yahya of Yemen for the first time proposed that the United States recognize his Kingdom and conclude a treaty concerning "friendship and business relations" with him. This proposal apparently caused the Department of State to instruct the American Consul at Aden that it approved of steps taken by the Consul to improve friendly relations with the Kingdom of Yemen, but that it was "not disposed" at that time "to proceed to the conclusion of formal treaty relations" with that country.[341] In addition, the Department stated that:

> Although this Government recognizes the renunciation of Turkish sovereignty in the detached Arab provinces of the former Ottoman Empire and has concluded or has under consideration agreements with respect to those portions thereof placed under French and

British mandate, it is not yet prepared to accord formal recognition in the manner suggested by the Imam of Yemen to the native states which have been established in the Arabian Peninsula since the World War. The unsettled political situation and the resulting uncertainty as to the permanency of the political entities so far may be mentioned as amongst the more obvious reasons which have led the Department to this position.[342]

At the invitation of the Imam of Yemen, Harlan B. Clark, American Consul at Aden, visited Yemen informally in March and April of 1945. At that time the Yemen Government for the second time requested recognition on the part of the United States and the conclusion of a treaty of friendship and commerce. Following this visit, Consul Clark argued that "there is no longer justification for the nonrecognition policy which the United States has followed with respect to the Yemen, and that on the contrary it may be highly to the disadvantage of our country to remain aloof from affairs in southern Arabia." He also urged that a United States mission be dispatched to conclude the requested treaty of friendship and commerce with Yemen.[343]

On February 12, 1948, the Department of State announced that the King of Yemen had invited the United States to send a special diplomatic mission for the purpose of discussing an agreement on commerce and friendship. It was also announced that the United States had considered the establishment of relations with Yemen for a number of years and that a mission was expected to leave soon.[344] Official recognition, by way of express declaration, was extended on March 4, 1946, when President Truman addressed the following letter to the King of Yemen:

> Mindful of the many centuries during which Your Majesty's ancestors have been Imams of the Yemen, and of the independence which Your Kingdom has enjoyed under Your Majesty's rule, I take pleasure in informing Your Majesty that the Government of the United States recognizes the absolute and complete independence of the Yemen and by this letter makes known its intent to accord you and Your Majesty's Government the privileges of such recognition and to endeavor to promote friendly relations between our two countries.[345]

Whiteman related the events that took place immediately following this act of express and formal recognition:

> On March 6, 1946, the Department of State announced the appointment of a Special Diplomatic Mission to the Kingdom of the

Yemen. To head the Special Diplomatic Mission, William A. Eddy was named "Chief of the Special Diplomatic Mission with the personal rank of Minister." The Department subsequently announced, on the occasion of its announcement of the intended visit to the United States of Prince Sain al-Islam Abdullah of Yemen, that "This Government and the Kingdom of Yemen established diplomatic relations on March 4, 1946," and in announcing, on May 14, 1946, the conclusion of certain of the work of the Special Diplomatic Mission, said: "The Government of the United States and the Kingdom of the Yemen concluded at San'a' on May 4, 1946, a provisional agreement covering diplomatic and consular representation, juridical protection, and commerce and navigation, following the recent recognition of the independence of the Yemen by this Government." [346]

The relations that had thus been established were interrupted in 1948, when the Imman of Yalya, the head of state in Yemen, was assassinated. Civil war ravaged the country until Crown Prince Ahmad was able to have himself elected successor to the throne. On February 14, 1950, a Department of State press release announced that the Yemeni Deputy Foreign Minister and Chief Delegate to the United Nations had called on the Department on December 22, 1949, and that he had given assurances that Yemen would respect its international obligations. In view of this situation, the Department announced that the United States had "renewed" recognition of Yemen. The press release stated that the United States had first recognized Yemen in April, 1946. However, this initial recognition must not have been considered conclusive, for in the same press release of February 14, 1950, the Department also stated that it was "completing recognition of Yemen." [347]

The types of entities recognized in this case are obviously a nation that had been in existence for some time and the government of that nation. In the first instance, the type of recognition was express and probably *de jure*. However, subsequently it does not appear to have been regarded as full recognition. While President Truman's letter of March 4, 1946, must certainly be said to have constituted full recognition at the time, the situation of unrest in revolutionary Yemen must have qualified this act of recognition sufficiently to cause the Department of State to announce that it was completing the recognition of Yemen in 1950. At any rate, the total procedure, beginning in 1946, and ending in 1950, certainly does constitute express and *de jure* recognition.

VI. Conclusions

Types, Modes, and Methods of Recognition

In almost every case of recognition of a new state during the period surveyed the type of recognition was effectively *de jure* if that term be understood to mean full, complete, unqualified, permanent recognition. But the qualifying words *"de jure"* were only actually used in connection with the recognition of Israel and Jordan.[348] There, it will be recalled, Israel was first accorded "full" recognition as a state, and its provisional government was recognized *de facto*. The glosses on that original recognition of the state of Israel read later by President Truman and by Ambassador Jessup emphasized, without using the words *"de jure,"* that Israel had indeed been recognized *de jure*. When Israel's government became permanent and was recognized *de jure*, Jordan's government was also recognized *de jure*. It is unclear whether at that time the *state* of Jordan was recognized *de jure* for the first time (whether it had previously been recognized *de facto*, perhaps as a matter of implied rather than express recognition). But in any event the only clear-cut use of the term *de jure* in this case was with respect to governments, not states. It can be argued, then, that in no case during this period was a newly recognized state expressly recognized *"de jure."*

For convenience, and in order to maintain continuity with the traditional language of international law and diplomacy, we have, therefore, characterized the great majority of the recognitions reported here as *"de jure,"* meaning full, complete, unqualified, and permanent. But there is reason to doubt whether *"de jure"* recognition of a state is a term of art, or a technical legal term. In close to sixty instances of recognition of a new state, recognition was not clearly characterized as *"de jure."* The two cases where the words *"de jure"* were possibly related to the state as well as to a particular government of that state—Israel (very questionable) and Jordan (ambiguous)—are so dubious as to incline us to say that the words *"de jure"* were not used since 1943 by the U.S. in recognizing a new state. Apparently there is no need to specify that recognition of a state is *de jure*. But the distinction between *de facto* and *de jure* recognition is still used in U.S. practice regarding recognition of new governments. A clarifying statement by the Department of State would be welcome. Of course, it is conceivable that there are political reasons for maintaining a certain degree of confusion on a subject that can sometimes have very real repercussions in international politics.

The statement in Whiteman's *Digest*, noted earlier, is not entirely satisfactory on this point. Whiteman, it may be recalled, gave this explanation:

> While the terms *"de facto* recognition" and *"de jure* recognition" are frequently employed, the expressions "recognition of a *de facto* government," situation, etc., and "recognition of a *de jure* government," etc., are preferable. The character of the object recognized may be recognized as *"de facto"* in existence or control. In prevailing practice, when the United States extends recognition, it is recognition *per se*, not *"de facto"* recognition. The United States may, however, should it so desire, recognize a *de facto* situation, government, state, etc.; that is to say, recognize that the situation, government, state, etc., in fact exists.[349]

It will be noted that she rejects the assumption made in this study and common to much traditional theory and practice that recognition of a state must be either *de facto* or *de jure*. (It was on the basis of this assumption that the authors concluded that a recognition which was not *de facto* and which seemed to be regular and permanent would have to be fitted into the alternative category of *de jure* recognition.) According to Miss Whiteman, recognition may also be *"per se,"* a characterization that the authors encounter for the first time.

It will be further noted that Miss Whiteman considers it "preferable" to attach the terms *de facto* and *de jure* to the entity recognized, rather than to the *type* of recognition accorded. However that may be the courts have been known to speculate over the possible differences *qua* legal consequences between *de facto* and *de jure* recognition.[350] A glance at the treatment of this subject by Professor Briggs, whose long-time concern with the *de facto–de jure* dichotomy is well known, leads one to suspect that even Miss Whiteman's suggestion as to what is "preferable" is still quite controverted.[351]

In any event, Whiteman does hold out the possibility that there could be recognition of a *"de facto"* state. As we have seen, with two possible exceptions, this has not occurred since 1943.

Virtually all of the recognitions were express. It is possible, but not established, that there was implied recognition of the Republic of Korea as a result of the making of a treaty prior to express recognition. The other cases where it appears possible that there was implied recognition for a time before express recognition occurred are all rather unclear. They involve the somewhat remote or unusual states of Yemen, Kuwait, and Nepal. Thus two traditionally controversial subjects—the distinction between *de facto* and *de jure* recognition, and the possibilities and difficulties of implied recognition—are of virtually no importance in U.S. recognition practice toward the new nations.

It is not necessary to comment further on the various methods of recognition except to make one point. Current U.S. practice generally utilizes several methods of recognition more or less simultaneously. This does contribute to the problem to be raised in the next section, namely, just *when* does recognition occur if there is a series of announcements that recognition will take place and that delegations to independence ceremonies will be sent, coupled with congratulatory messages dated before the day of independence? The very profusion of methods of recognition now being employed tends to make recognition a "process" rather than a single "act" or communication.

The Criteria for Recognition

Traditionally the basic prerequisite for recognition as a new state was possession of the physical attributes of statehood. This is no longer a self-evident proposition. A state was defined as a body politic in which a government ruled supreme within definite boundaries and maintained its independence in the society of nations. Most controversies over the theory and practice of recognition have arisen out of the introduction of subjective criteria requiring something more or different than the basic fact of actual control of an independent body politic. Usually these criteria resulted in nonrecognition of an entity that was clearly entitled to recognition if actual existence were the only or principal criterion. The recognition practice of the U.S. toward the new nations has, on the contrary, raised a quite different question. Its subjectivity has resulted in the accordance of recognition to entities that probably could not meet the traditional tests of statehood.

There may be a number of reasons for this. By and large, we have to deduce them from the facts we have rather than from official explanations. For one thing, the nature of the process whereby most of the new states studied herein came into existence removed one of the great safety valves of traditional practice, the fear of the consequences of premature recognition. Most of the transfers of sovereignty described herein were peaceful and orderly, at least by "independence day." In earlier times, new nations usually came into being as the result of a revolution or international war.[352] "Premature" recognition of a new nation was widely considered to be an illegal act of intervention. Some authorities said that the injured state had a right to "resent" such intervention, others went so far as to consider it a *casus belli*.[353] Broadly speaking, then, a state would incur a good deal of trouble and unpleasantness by recognizing a new state, and the reasons for granting recognition had to be rather compelling. Undoubtedly this led to slowness in coming to a decision on recognition, and this very slowness meant that there was more time for observation of the new state and reflection on its prospects.

We have seen that in the overwhelming majority of cases studied here, involving as they did a peaceful transfer of sovereignty, the United States did not take *any* time for observation and reflection. In the apt words of Denys Myers, U.S. recognition policy toward the new nations has been "instantaneous," at times even "anticipatory."[354] We have identified sixty instances of recognition of states since 1943.[355] In approximately forty-three of these cases, recognition was instantaneous, e.g., substantially concurrent with the official independence day.[356] We say "approximately" because, in view of the complexity of the recognition process, it is difficult and arbitrary to judge in many cases whether the recognition was anticipatory or instantaneous. It is possible to consider that in up to thirteen cases states were accorded anticipatory recognition prior to the date that they themselves hold to be the commencement of their independent existence.[357] Approximately eighteen states were informed in advance that they would be recognized.[358]

One solution to the problem of fixing the exact time of recognition would be to consider that apparent acts of recognition made prior to the date of independence claimed by the new state do not become completed or effective until the event to which they refer, the actual commencement of existence of the new state, takes place. This interpretation may be inferred from the following statement by Myers:

> In view of the several explicit or implicit forms which recognition may take, and considering that it is essentially a political act, which should be compatible with legal requirements, it is perhaps presumptuous and hazardous to give specific dates for each exercise of recognition. The need for a precise date of recognition of a new state is no more likely to be of practical value than the specific date of effectiveness of a treaty, which is now generally stated in the final

articles. The principle adopted here is that recognition dates from the direct or indirect act of the President in establishing relations with the highest authority in the new (or nascent) state; any such act that is inconclusive by itself becomes conclusive if followed by acts conclusive in themselves, which continuity would manifest continuing intention. For the sake of simplicity the date of a diplomatic commission has been used here, though it is only one step in accreditation, being preceded by *agrément* and confirmation by the Senate, and followed by taking the oath and presentation of credentials at the post. Recent recognitions have been accorded to entities advancing to independence by agreements which state when the transfer of sovereignty shall take place. Consequently, recognition has been cognitive of the new state and politically declaratory on the part of the United States.[359]

In any event, it is clear that in forty of fifty-nine cases, recognition was granted at once without any possibility of making an independent determination on whether the new nation did in fact possess the physical attributes of a sovereign state. Only in the cases of Lebanon, Syria, Jordan, Guinea, and possibly (the situation was unclear) Cambodia, Vietnam, and Laos, did the United States fail to accept the certification of a former ruler that its dependency qualified for statehood and full international personality on a specified independence day.[360]

Yet this uncritical U.S. acceptance of the new nations has come despite notorious doubts as to the capacity of these former colonial territories to produce viable states. The great majority of them are underdeveloped, politically, economically, and socially. They may have been "groomed" for self-government for varying periods and in the light of varying degrees of unpreparedness for self-rule, but it is fair to say that most of the new nations were launched with a high degree of apprehension over their chances of survival. We are not asserting that most, or even a substantial number, of the new nations were clearly *not* qualified for statehood. We are saying that there was and remains enough doubt regarding the real existence of the elements of an independent sovereign state to warrant caution and careful scrutiny prior to recognition, *if* traditional requirements for statehood are still considered controlling.

Clearly no such caution and careful scrutiny have marked U.S. recognition of the new nations. The United States has accepted the certification of the former ruler as conclusive. Naturally the United States would have possessed some information and some informed predictions from its own sources on the prospects of the new nations. But there are hardly any instances where, for any reason, the judgment of the former ruler was not accepted without question.

It may be said, of course, that the willingness of the former ruler to grant independence should engender a presumption of actual capacity for self-rule.[361] But this presumption is open to serious question. Most of the new nations came into existence peacefully, but as the result of enormous pressures on the colonial ruler. Independence normally did not come as the result of a revolutionary war that, however tragic, might serve to prove some capacity for organization and control on the part of the rebels. The nature of the pressures that have frequently led to independence has been different from those of coercion exercised by a rebel government. They have often been pressures that were strong enough to make continuance of the colonial relationship unbearable or unprofitable for the metropolitan power but that in themselves were not necessarily evidence of positive forces, within the indigenous community, sufficient to build a nation.

Internal pressures on colonial powers have usually been produced in great measure by the operations of European-trained elites, often in the absence of really informed support from the population of the territories. Benveniste and Moran observe:

> This new African elite was not prepared to accept a gradualist approach—they did not want to wait. Only in African-controlled independent states, they believed, could they realize their aspirations. President Nkrumah expressed their attitude when he said: "Seek ye first the political kingdom and everything else shall be added unto it." That nothing would hold them back in their pursuit of freedom can be seen also in this statement by President Sékou Touré of Guinea: "We would prefer poverty in freedom to riches in slavery." [362]

Calvocoressi writes:

> In our own day, however, the chief feature of all colonial partings has been haste, and consequently the preparation of colonies for independence has, with the striking exception of Malaya, everywhere borne the stamp not so much of experienced and wise European governors (though there were some such), but of strenuously militant nationalist movements, staking their pride upon a timetable and forming new states in the image of a revolutionary movement.[363]

When the populace supported "freedom," it was often quite unclear as to what freedom really would mean.[364] In these circumstances, it has often been quite possible to mobilize enough local pressure to oust a colonial power without at the same time producing a workable political base for an indigenous state.

Even these internal pressures, however, would probably have been insufficient to bring independence had they not operated in unison with a variety of external pressures, all building up a tidal wave of anticolonialism and independence. Various "Pan" movements, African, Arab, and others, as well as international Communist movements, have exercised a strong influence in the dependent areas and in international politics.[365] The U.N. has become a potent instrument of the underdeveloped peoples in their drive for equality.[366] Thus, on the world scene, the predominant trend has been to grant independence to every identifiable dependent territory. Needless to say, the antagonists in the Cold War must seek to identify themselves with this trend within the limits of their own policy goals and basic values. The practical and ideological costs of opposing it would be high. This basic fact would appear to explain more than any rationalization of traditional doctrine on recognition the policies followed by the U.S. toward the new nations. Thus, Vernon McKay finds a major change in policy toward the new nations as late as 1958. Prior to that time concern over the dangers of premature independence tended to prevail. Speaking on U.S. policy in the U.N. toward establishing a firm timetable for the independence of African states, he says:

> [I]t seems clear that the basic objective of the maneuver [whereby Deputy Representative Benjamin Gerig suggested the] establishment of target dates for the achievement of intermediate goals, not only in the field of economic, social and educational advancement, but for political advancement as well . . . was not to help African political advancement but to improve the U.S. image in the eyes of the anticolonials. This seems evident from the aforementioned policy declarations, which indicate that the Department was worried over the possibility that Africa was moving towards independence too fast for political and economic stability. . . .
> American officials were worried about the growing stereotype of the United States as a supporter of colonialism, and were looking for ways and means to change this image.[367]

To complete the picture, most of the colonial powers have expressed grave doubts of their own regarding the morality of colonialism, on the one hand, and the practical advantages of it, on the other. In these circumstances, the colonial powers gradually lost their ability and their desire to resist demands for immediate independence by backward colonial dependencies. Consequently, to return to the question of judging whether a new nation qualifies for statehood, the former ruler's grant of independence need *not* always create a presumption that the traditional prerequisites for statehood are in fact present. It is fairly evident that the decision to grant independence may be made not with confidence but with a mixture of relief at the relinquishing of a burden and apprehension as to what will happen to a polity the deficiencies of which are all too well known to the retiring colonial power.

The wisdom or justice of these policies is not our concern. What we are concerned with is an evaluation of their implications for the traditional criteria for recognition of states. The inescapable conclusion seems to be that the basic principle in the recognition of new states has changed. Formerly, nations that had demonstrated their capacity to exist as sovereign independent states were recognized, unless they failed to meet some other criteria. Today, demonstration of the capacity to exist independently is not usually required of new states. The simple certification of the existence of a new state through an orderly transfer of sovereignty from a metropolis state to a former dependency is taken, in most instances, without question, as satisfactory evidence that a new state, actually exercising sovereign powers, has come into existence and is eligible for recognition.

We may mention here that it is usual for the U.S. to support the admission of such new states to the U.N., again, with little or no pause to observe their progress.[368] However, this action does in a sense complement the act of recognition and underscore the unequivocal quality of the instantaneous recognitions that have been accorded most of the new nations.

What of other more subjective criteria for recognition? The record of recognition of states is largely void of the ideological prerequisites of other periods. Obviously the introduction of ideological considerations has been present in policies of nonrecognition of Communist governments of existing international persons such as China, various Communist satellites in Europe, and Cuba. There have also been instances of a return to Wilsonian requirements of constitutionality and democracy regarding recognition of new governments in non-Communist nations in Latin America. These are areas that deserve greater and more systematic study, but they are beyond the scope of this study and in many respects not immediately relevant to it. There are no examples of deliberate, outright nonrecognition of an existing new state because of objections to its ideology or form of government. (We mean here that there have been no nonrecognition policies of the kind once adopted toward the Soviets and now adopted toward the Red Chinese Government; or such as the U.S. holds with respect to the Soviet absorption of the Baltic states.)

However, there have been some cases of delay in recognizing new states, and they offer grounds for speculation as to whether the delay resulted primarily from a desire to ascertain whether the new states had the capacity to preserve an independent existence or whether other criteria were being applied. It is interesting that in the cases of the delayed recognition of Syria, Lebanon, and of the formation of the United Arab Republic, there is evidenced an interest in the new states' willingness and capacity to honor their obligations under international law.[369] These appear to be the only cases of recognition of states where that famous American criterion was in evidence. (It has, of course, played a continuing role with respect to recognition of new governments, notably in the case of Red China.)

In the case of the delayed recognition of Jordan, we have little on the public record to guide us. To a disinterested observer, Jordan appears not to be a particularly viable state, even today. It may well be that the careful policy toward Jordan that was followed up until the *de jure* recognition of the Israeli Government risked charges of playing favorites in the Middle East and precipitated the recognition of Jordan. But the caution displayed may have been based mainly on the traditional objective criteria that have been so widely ignored in recent times.

As we have seen, the case of the states emerging from French Indochina is somewhat ambiguous. However, given the notorious lack of indigenous political leadership and cohesion that had marked virtually all parts of Indochina, with the unfortunate exception of the followers of Ho Chi Minh, it seems quite possible that the cautious and somewhat ambiguous policies adopted were rooted in doubts as to the existence of the prerequisites for statehood.

The delayed recognition of Guinea, notwithstanding a perfectly orderly transfer of authority from France, seems to provide the clearest example in this body of practice of temporary nonrecognition on political and ideological grounds. There may well have been concern about Guinea's willingness to abide by her obligations under international law. Guinea began its existence with an attitude of defiance toward the West and with many indications of Marxist tendencies and sympathies in its internal and foreign policies. Moreover, the very bitter French reaction to Guinea's departure from the French Community may have inclined the U.S. to delay recognition out of concern for French sensibilities. Whereas all of Guinea's liberated neighbors were recognized instantly, Guinea was made to sweat out U.S. recognition. If there was an element of real doubt about the viability of the new state, proponents of objective recognition policies would not criticize this delay in recognition, but would have to point out that no such caution was displayed toward other new African states.[370]

We can say, then, that the recognition policies toward the new nations during this period were remarkably devoid of criteria concerning the acceptance of international law and of particular obligations, and of criteria concerning ideological or constitutional characteristics of the new regimes.

U. S. Recognition Policy Toward the New Nations: The Implications for the Institution of Recognition

Thus far we have largely limited our discussion to the point that recognition was given to most of the new nations before it was possible to ascertain whether they qualified for it in terms of real existence as sovereign states. Aside from the assertion that the evolution to independence was usually planned with precision—an assertion that we do not entirely accept—two rejoinders come to mind.[371] First, it can be noted that most of the new states that have been recognized have in fact survived.[372] Second, it can be pointed out that the fact that many of them are weak does not create a novel situation, since there have always been weak states in the international community.

Our rebuttal to these two points is as follows: (1) It is questionable whether many of the new states now "existing" are really independent sovereign states by traditional standards—and even their less-than-independent existences would in many cases cease were it not for massive foreign assistance.[373] (2) The traditional state system could tolerate and carry along *some* weak states, but the number and nominal importance of states so weak that the term statehood is of dubious relevance is so great that the whole international juridical order has been profoundly changed. One instrument for this change has been a greatly modified and diluted diplomatic-legal institution, recognition.

We have no desire to single out glaring examples for the embarrassment of former rulers, present would-be sovereigns, and acquiescing third parties, such as the U.S. Nor do we undertake here a

U.S. Recognition Policy Toward the New Nations

comprehensive critique of grants of independence since 1943. The cases mentioned below are believed, however, to support sufficiently the propositions asserted above, and it is believed that further study would produce additional support for them.

Africa offers the most disturbing examples of nonviable states. The core concept of nationalism, the societal substructure for the sovereign nation-state, was the existence of a "nation." However subjective that concept may be, there are limits to it. Many of the new African states are at one and the same time less-than-national and more-than-national in their orientation. They are often the products of purely artificial boundaries, drawn by colonial powers without reference to geographical considerations, tribal boundaries, resources, or any other element relevant to the establishment of a state. These states exist because they wanted independence and the colonial power was willing to give it to them, not because there is in fact any "nation" already in existence clamoring for self-determination. Perhaps because these states usually have no viable "national" base, they are prone to outbreaks of enthusiasm for supranational or international units. The only entities that were recognized by the U.S. that failed to survive have been federations.[374]

Consider Libya and Somalia. What forces determined that Libya would be one of the first new African states? The specter of Russian demands for trust territories in Africa, the desire of the British and Italians to vacate unproductive territories, and the urgings and recommendations of the Council of Foreign Ministers and the U.N. General Assembly produced the sovereign states of Libya and Somalia.[375] Of the creation of Libya, a sympathetic writer has said:

> On 24 December 1951 King Mohamad Idris Al Mahdi Al Senussi "joyfully" proclaimed "to the noble people of Libya that in fulfillment of their endeavours and of the United Nations resolution of 21 November 1949, our beloved country has, with the help of God, attained independence." Never has the United Nations undertaken a more difficult task than that of creating within two years a state out of three distinct provinces like "islands in an ocean of sand separated by several hundreds of miles of desert wastes" and inhabited by a people, ninety per cent of whom were illiterate and almost none of whom had any administrative experience or technical training. . . .
>
> It is possible that when Libya became an independent country in 1951, it was not yet ready to assume the economic and political burdens of self-government. It is the only country in the world today—

recently independent and after a colonial history—that has been launched into this new adventure without having first been tutored in the ways of being a nation.[376]

Twelve years after independence the amount of foreign aid required to sustain this country is conspicuously high, even in comparison to other new and underdeveloped countries.[377] In a similar vein, Castagno has written of Somalia:

> Given the heritage of the past and the legacies of the social system, the Assembly's resolution called for a revolution, not an evolution of Somali society. The population as a whole was politically immature and illiterate. The territory lacked economic resources, and tribalism constituted the basic element in Somali life. Could a viable, modern, and democratic state be created from this welter of difficulties within the span of ten years? Could modern education proceed fast enough to provide the Somalis with the concepts, knowledge and skill necessary to run a modern state? Could the economy be made sufficiently strong to sustain the costs of democracy and independence? It was left to the Administering Authority, with the aid and advice of the Advisory Council, to construct the details of the political, economic, and educational devices through which the transformation from a colony to an independent state could take place. But to the Somalis alone was willed the task of transcending in a decade the traditions of a millennium.[378]

Most of the former French dependencies are states of dubious viability. Pearcy remarks:

> We may look at the small states in Middle Africa—Dahomey, Gabon, Sierra Leone, or Togo—and see bleak futures if only the geographic realities are allowed to come into perspective. These countries in west Africa are basically strips of territory with ocean frontage, originally established by seafaring Europeans in search of routes to lands of fabulous riches. Individually each strip, or country, has a singularly small array of resources, and even the resources that have been developed are oriented primarily toward the former European metropole countries. Surface transportation in this part of Middle Africa conspicuously avoids crossing international boundaries.
> In light of their physical and economic inheritances, these new states have little choice other than to reorient their activities and their outlooks to a new locus. Because of small size, especially in a competitive world strongly influenced by great powers, any advance of status must in part at least depend upon membership in supranational organizations. Alliances capable of generating sustained support and cooperation may also be of infinite benefit. Aid from foreign

sources likewise may serve as a catalyst in providing a new state the means of extending its economic horizon.[379]

It is not surprising that most of these former French dependencies are not in fact "independent" of France in important matters relating to the exercise of sovereignty, nor that they are openly referred to as "client states." The foreign aid that they require to maintain their inadequate existence is formidable. The Economic Commission for Africa of UNESCO reports:

> On a *per capita* basis, African countries received about twice as much economic assistance as under-developed countries generally. . . . Among the African countries and territories listed, the countries and territories receiving a relatively large amount of assistance *per capita* included Libya ($35.6 [million]) and Algeria ($34.5 [million]). Countries in the intermediate range included the Congo (Leopoldville) ($5.6 [million]), Liberia ($6.7 [million]), Morocco and Tunisia ($9.9 [million]), Nigeria ($10.8 [million]), Somalia ($9.4 [million]) and the states of the former French Community, Cameroun and Togo ($9.4 [million]).[380]

Foreign aid represents approximately one-fifth of the combined foreign exchange receipts of the new African states.[381] But perhaps the most revealing indication of their lack of real independence is that the budgets for ordinary public expenditures of former French dependencies are subsidized by France in amounts ranging from 60 to 80 per cent of the total budget. The Economic Commission for Africa has observed:

> Further light on the relative significance of external resources in the economy of certain African countries is shed by information on their share in the financing of public expenditure. . . . This indicates that the contributions of France to meeting current expenditure in the overseas franc area increased substantially after 1956, the share of French assistance in the total being higher in former French Equatorial Africa (16 per cent in 1958) than in former French West Africa (12 per cent in 1958). In former French West Africa the share of public capital expenditure financed by France averaged 62 per cent for the years indicated; in former French Equatorial Africa the comparable figure was 80 per cent.[382]

In all these countries, qualified governmental personnel is lacking. It is questionable whether most of the basic functions of government could be carried on without foreign personnel, usually supplied by the former ruler. Indeed, outright intervention by the armed forces of former colonial powers has been necessary in Gabon, Kenya, Uganda, and Tanganyika. The need for foreign personnel in key government posts is particularly acute in the former French dependencies, but it is also true in great measure in former British dependencies.[383] Are these entities, these "client states," "states" and, if they are, what is happening to the meaning of the word "state"? Entities such as Kuwait and Yemen may perhaps be considered exceptional on a number of grounds, but in Africa the "exceptional" appears to be the normal.

The classic example of nominal statehood and actual chaos, of course, has been Congo-Leopoldville. Here there was a notorious lack of unity, of leadership, and of trained personnel. In addition, there was widespread foreign intervention, private as well as public. Independence meant license, atrocities, and division rather than solidarity and order. Experts on the underdeveloped world have invented the concept of "nation-building." In the case of the Congo, we have witnessed "nation-building" that was very largely initiated after independence. In order to build this nation, enormous aid and technical assistance has been required from individual states like Belgium and the U.S., as well as from the U.N. A U.N. force was required to establish control of the domain of the sovereign state of Congo. The cost and strain of this salvage operation has jeopardized the very existence of the U.N. Surely this has been a heavy price to pay for Belgium's jettisoning of the Congo. Coleman states:

> Indeed, in the former Belgian Congo, no serious efforts to develop an indigenous administrative and political capacity were made until the disastrous headlong rush to independence in the six months preceding the transfer of power in July, 1960. The simple fact is, of course, that none of the colonial powers intended to create modern self-governing democratic states in Africa. Western racialism and ethnocentricity perpetuated a widespread belief that the European "presence" in Africa was permanently necessary and desirable. When postwar African nationalism forced a change and imposed a timetable aimed at early independence, procedural and institutional innovations of a "democratic" character were launched on a "crash program" basis. Thus, although most new African states have possessed all of the paraphernalia and pretensions of democratic government at the time of independence, their leaders and peoples have had extremely limited experience with modern democratic institutions. Since survival of such institutions depends heavily upon acceptance and commitment by a people accustomed to their use and confident in their ultimate effectiveness in satisfying wants and at-

taining goals, the significance of the democratic component of the colonial legacy can be vastly exaggerated.[384]

Berg observes:

> The experience of the Congo, left at independence without a single African doctor, lawyer, engineer, or army officer, dramatically brought the African manpower problem to world attention. Many African countries are better endowed with highlevel manpower than was the Congo in 1960, but in all of them there exists a critical need to develop the skills and raise the level of education of their people.[385]

Calvocoressi speaks of the Congo, "where a new state, having been hustled into existence without the necessary civil apparatus, was found after ten days to have been deprived also of its ultimate source of authority, the army, which had disintegrated through bribery and become the basis for warlordism. Government was rendered ineffective or non-existent; civil war supervened; and, rightly or exaggeratedly, even world war seemed a possibility." [386]

These are only some of the more obvious examples of nominal states that were uncritically accepted into the world community but that do not, in all probability, meet the minimal requirements for statehood. The implications of this acceptance for international law are many and serious. As Crozier has put it:

> I happen to take an absolute view of independence. I consider a country to be independent when it runs its own army and civil service, pays its way, and controls its own foreign policy. By this token, a country must be strong enough to *have* a foreign policy in the first place; whether it can then apply it will depend on whether it is stronger than the other countries at whose expense the policy might be applied. It may be objected that this is arguing as though we still lived in a world of unrestrained power politics—a world without the United Nations or the nuclear balance of terror. That is a fair objection, but it happens to prove the point that "independence has lost its meaning." . . .
>
> If Russia and America enjoy only limited freedom of action, what are we to think of Niger or Tchad, Ceylon or Cambodia? It is, in fact, clear enough that most of the newly independent nations are too weak to have a foreign policy of their own, too poor to pay their own way, too meanly provided with doctors and lawyers, civil servants and technicians, to be regarded as independent in any but a nominal sense. Such States—Laos or the Congo, Mali or Jordan, to name random examples—seem to face one of two alternatives: either to abandon their pretensions to modern statehood, reverting to tradi-

tional ways of living; or to become more or less permanently dependent on the assistance of richer States. Can such nations really claim to be independent? [387]

Nor is the end in sight. Crozier describes Kenya, then close to independence, as "a country lacking national awareness, rent by tribal dissensions, oppressed by memories of Mau Mau's atavistic horror, with capital in full flight, heading for independence in destitution and insecurity, Kenya reflects the insoluble dilemma: to stay is to invite violence, to leave is to invite chaos. But Britain's colonial vocation is spent, and the only question is how soon the British will leave." [388] Britain was to return, of course, within less than two months—when its assistance was requested in the suppression of a mutiny in the Kenyan armed forces. Such examples are disturbing enough. What can we say of other prospective independent states, such as Rio Muni, Gambia, or Basutoland?

One obvious fact is that the political foundations of what we have been calling the "traditional" doctrine of recognition of new states have changed. Practice is changing accordingly. Much has been written recently about "system" and international law and relations. Thus a multipower, balance-of-power system may encourage legal institutions and rules that become unworkable in a bipolar system characterized by extreme conflict. In this context much has been said about the "third world," and the possibility that we may now have a tendency toward a three-bloc (or four-bloc, with the Peking-Moscow rift) system. But it is equally important to register the significance of the acceptance of large numbers of entities as sovereign states that do not really qualify for statehood.[389]

The sovereign "nation-state" has been the basic unit in both international politics and international law.[390] International law remained closely linked to political reality by assigning international rights and duties to real states possessing real power. To the extent that it followed objective criteria, recognition as an institution contributed to this process of linking real power to legal responsibility. We have seen that objective criteria followed the classic definition of a sovereign state.

Consider the galaxy of new entities possessing full international personality as the result of the action of the nations of the world through the recognition process.[391] It includes such dubious nations as Western Samoa, Nepal, Kuwait, Yemen, Libya, Somalia, Burundi, Rwanda, most of the former dependencies of French West and Equatorial Africa, and the Malagasy Republic. Not much more impressive are states such as Jordan and Trinidad and Tobago; somewhat firmer, but nonetheless still characterized by the prominent evidence of many of the problems described here are, for example, Vietnam, Cambodia, Korea, Algeria, Morocco, and Tunisia. By whatever system of classification, however, it takes quite a process of elimination to reach a solid core of obviously viable (even if underdeveloped) states such as India, Pakistan, Indonesia, Ceylon, the Philippines, Israel, Nigeria, and the like.

Paradoxically, at the same time that the new nations and those that recognize them are diluting the concept of statehood and stretching it downward to include entities that would never have been considered sovereign in the past, the older states are questioning the politico-economic-military viability of the traditional sovereign state and are seeking to evolve toward supranational or international organizations such as the EEC, NATO, OAS, and the like. In these circumstances, the basic unit of the sovereign state as it was until quite recently conceived is ceasing to be the "normal" unit of international politics. The consequences of this fact for international law will obviously be far-reaching. The old concept of sovereignty remains, enthusiastically embraced by all the Communist states and, certainly, by the new nations.[392] But that legal concept no longer corresponds to political reality, and this gap between law and facts cannot but be injurious to international law as a force in international politics.[393] The traditional formula for linking power and law had run thus: Real power creates legal sovereignty that engenders legal rights and duties; power creates legal responsibility. Whatever its faults, this system had the merit of linking material realities to legal rights and duties. The present trend toward instantaneous recognition brushes aside the very foundations for international responsibility, the concurrence of *actual* power with legal sovereign capacity.

We do not deny that in the past many entities that fell well below the general standard of actual power, civilization, and legal and moral responsibility were recognized as states. But there was never any question that these states were considered exceptions to the rule.

It is instructive to recall that the original attitude of the League of Nations toward applications for admission fairly bristled with demands for proof of statehood. Denys P. Myers recalls that "the first session of the Assembly tested applicants literally by the Covenant, using a questionnaire which warrants resurrection." The questions asked were:

1. Is the application for admission to the League of Nations in order?
2. Is your Government recognized *de jure* or *de facto*, and by which States?
3. Does your country possess a stable Government and settled frontiers? What are its size and population?
4. Is your country fully self-governing?
5. What has been the conduct of your country, including both acts and assurances, with regard to:
    (1) your international obligations;
    (2) the prescriptions of the League as to armaments? [394]

Today the "rule" is increasingly hard to find. In purely quantitative terms, the number of recognized states that would have difficulty in meeting the requirements for statehood is so great that the common denominator, the minimal definition of "sovereign state," has to be a very low one. A definition of "sovereign state" drawn empirically from contemporary recognition practice would, if the U.S. experience is typical, be so broad that it might be necessary to give up the undertaking, and, instead, try to discover what kinds of entities are clearly *not* states and cannot become states.

It may be granted that recognition as an institution of international law and diplomacy never performed perfectly (or perhaps even well) the function attributed to it by Lauterpacht, namely, the identification of the international persons who are at once subjects, makers, and enforcers of international law. But recognition *tended* to perform this function, no matter how imperfectly. Recognition practice, however affected by political or other biases, *tended* to serve as a means for identifying the real holders of power in the world so that the legal rights and duties that went with power could be assigned. We know that this important function had already been endangered by subjective policies of nonrecognition that tended to leave real powers outside of the pale of the law and of regular international intercourse. The tendency toward uncritical acceptance of the new nations would appear to add to the general trend toward the destruction of recognition as an institution for fact-finding and for assigning legal rights and duties.

It is impossible to say where this process that erodes the institution of recognition will end. Once one breaks loose from the objective criteria of the original Jeffersonian test of objective existence as an independent state, there is really no logical resting place. One can see that great political and ideological factors have brought recognition to its current condition. One can admit that there is nothing to be gained by trying to twist political facts to fit legal concepts and rules. Indeed, one of the purposes of this study has been to furnish data that may serve for realistic reappraisals of the theory and practice of recognition as an institution of international law and diplomacy. But all these admissions do not alter the fact that the trend toward uncritical, instantaneous recognition encourages a relativism and nominalism in international law and relations that may prove as harmful in the realm of international relations as in that of law. Our study, then, leaves us with disquieting doubts about the wisdom of ascribing to untried states of questionable viability legal rights and duties having their foundation in the assumption of an earlier period that they were linked to real power. In any event, clearly the treatment of recognition in future texts must be written with an awareness of the implications of instantaneous and anticipatory recognition for the future of international law.

Postscript

On April 23, 1964, the governments of Zanzibar and Tanganyika announced their intended merger into the United Republic of Tanganyika and Zanzibar, now known as Tanzania. When the merger bill had been approved by both Tanganyika's National Assembly and Zanzibar's Revolutionary Council, the instruments of ratification were exchanged and the new East African republic was established on April 26. Tanganyikan President Julius Nyerere was to be the new President while Abeid Karume of Zanzibar was to be Vice-President. The United States did not consider the formation of the union to substantially alter the status of relations between the entities. Diplomatic relations continued to be carried out through the American Embassy in Dar es Salaam. The American Embassy in Zanzibar was lowered to a Consulate-General at the request of the new government.

Appendix: NEWLY INDEPENDENT NATIONS

Name	Present Status	Former Status	Date of Independence or Coming into Existence	Date of U.N. Membership (Date of General Assembly Decision)	Date of U.S. Recognition	Date of Extinction
ALGERIA	Republic	French	July 3, 1962	October 8, 1962	July 3, 1962	
ARAB UNION	Extinct	Iraq and Jordan	May 19, 1958		May 19, 1958	August 1, 1958
BURMA	Republic	British	January 4, 1948*	April 19, 1948*	September 19, 1947*	
BURUNDI	Kingdom	Belgian Trusteeship	July 1, 1962	September 18, 1962	July 1, 1962 (June 28, 1962)	
CAMBODIA	Kingdom	French	November 8, 1949*	December 14, 1955*	February 7, 1950*	
CAMEROON	Republic	French Trusteeship	January 1, 1960*	September 20, 1960*	January 1, 1960* (December 29, 1959)	
CENTRAL AFRICAN REPUBLIC	Republic	French	August 13, 1960*	September 20, 1960*	August 13, 1960*	
CEYLON	Republic	British	February 4, 1948*	December 14, 1955*	April 8, 1948* (February 3, 1948)	
CHAD	Republic	French	August 11, 1960*	September 20, 1960*	August 11, 1960*	
CONGO (Leopoldville)	Republic	Belgian	June 30, 1960*	September 20, 1960*	June 30, 1960* (June 28, 1960)	
CONGO (Brazzaville)	Republic	French	August 15, 1960*	September 20, 1960*	August 15, 1960*	
CYPRUS	Republic	British	August 16, 1960*	September 20, 1960*	August 16, 1960†	
DAHOMEY	Republic	French	August 1, 1960*	September 20, 1960*	August 16, 1960* (July 29, 1960)	

PAKISTAN	Republic	British	August 15, 1947*	August 30, 1947* September 30, 1947||	August 15, 1947* (August 14, 1947)
PHILIPPINES	Republic	United States	July 4, 1946*	October 24, 1945* October 11, 1945‡§	July 4, 1946*
RWANDA	Republic	Belgian Trusteeship	July 1, 1962	September 18, 1962	July 1, 1962 (June 28, 1962)
SENEGAL	Republic	French	June 20, 1960* August 20, 1960‡	September 28, 1960*	June 20, 1960* September 24, 1960‡
SIERRA LEONE	Republic	British	April 27, 1961*	September 27, 1961	April 27, 1961* (April 26, 1961)
SOMALILAND	Extinct	British	June 26, 1960*		June 26, 1960	July 1, 1960
SOMALI REPUBLIC	Republic	Italian Trusteeship	July 1, 1960*	September 20, 1960*	July 1, 1960* (June 30, 1960)
SUDAN	Republic	Anglo-Egypt Condominium	January 1, 1956*	November 12, 1956*	January 2, 1956* January 1, 1956‡
SYRIA	Republic	French Mandate	January 1, 1944	October 19, 1945§	September 19, 1944 (September 7, 1944)
TANGANYIKA#	Republic	British Trusteeship	December 9, 1961	December 14, 1961	December 9, 1961	April 26, 1964
TOGO	Republic	French Trusteeship	April 27, 1960*	September 20, 1960*	April 27, 1960* (April 14, 1960)
TRINIDAD & TOBAGO	Republic	British	August 31, 1962	September 18, 1962	August 31, 1962 (August 29, 1962)
TUNISIA	Republic	French	March 20, 1956*	November 12, 1956*	March 22, 1956*
UGANDA	Republic	British Protectorate	October 9, 1962	October 25, 1962	October 9, 1962 (October 5, 1962)
UNITED ARAB REPUBLIC	Republic	Egypt and Syria	February 22, 1958	October 22, 1945§ (Egypt)	February 25, 1958
UPPER VOLTA	Republic	French	August 5, 1960*	September 20, 1960*	August 5, 1960* (July 29, 1960)

Appendix: Newly Independent Nations
(continued)

Name	Present Status	Former Status	Date of Independence or Coming into Existence	Date of U.N. Membership (Date of General Assembly Decision)	Date of U.S. Recognition	Date of Extinction
MALAGASY REPUBLIC	Republic	French	June 26, 1960*	September 20, 1960*	June 26, 1960 (June 24, 1960)	
MALAWI	Republic	British	July 6, 1964		July 6, 1964	
MALAYA	Extinct	British	August 31, 1957*	September 17, 1957*	August 31, 1957*	September 16, 1963. Absorbed by Federation of Malaysia
MALAYSIA	Federation	British and Federation Malaya	September 16, 1963		September 16, 1963	
MALI	Republic	French	June 20, 1960*	September 28, 1960*	September 24, 1960*	
MALI FEDERATION	Extinct	French	September 22, 1960‡			
			June 20, 1960		June 20, 1960	August 20, 1960
MAURITANIA	Islamic Republic	French	November 28, 1960*	October 27, 1961	November 28, 1960*	
MOROCCO	Kingdom	French	March 2, 1956*	November 12, 1956*	July 21, 1956*	
NEPAL	Kingdom		December 21, 1923*	December 14, 1955*	April 25, 1947*	
NIGER	Republic	French	August 3, 1960*	September 20, 1960*	August 5, 1960* (July 29, 1960)	
NIGERIA	Republic (Federation)	British	October 1, 1960*	October 7, 1960*	October 1, 1960* (September 24, 1960)	

GABON	Republic	French	August 17, 1960*	September 20, 1960*	August 11, 1960*
GHANA	Republic	British	March 6, 1957*	March 8, 1957*	March 6, 1957* (February 14, 1957)
GUINEA	Republic	French	October 2, 1958*	December 12, 1958*	November 1, 1958*
ICELAND	Republic	Danish	June 17, 1944	November 9, 1946	June 17, 1944 (June 14, 1944)
INDIA	Republic	British	August 15, 1947*	October 24, 1945* October 30, 1945‡§	December 18, 1942² (July 24, 1941)
INDONESIA	Republic	Netherlands	December 27, 1949* August 17, 1945‡	September 28, 1950	December 28, 1949*
ISRAEL	Republic	British Mandate	May 15, 1948* May 14, 1948‡	May 11, 1949	May 15, 1948* May 14, 1948‡
IVORY COAST	Republic	French	August 7, 1960*	September 20, 1960*	August 7, 1960* (July 29, 1960)
JAMAICA	Republic	British	August 6, 1962	September 18, 1962	August 6, 1962 (August 5, 1962)
JORDAN	Kingdom	British Mandate	June 17, 1946*	December 14, 1955*	February 28, 1949* January 31, 1949‡
KENYA	Republic	British Protectorate	December 12, 1963	December 16, 1963	December 12, 1963 (December 10, 1963)
KOREA	Republic	Japan-Occupied	August 15, 1948* December 12, 1948‡		August 24, 1948† September 11, 1948* January 1, 1949†
KUWAIT	Sheikdom	British Protectorate	June 19, 1961	May 13, 1963	unclear, completed September 22, 1961
LAOS	Kingdom	French	May 19, 1949*	December 14, 1955*	February 7, 1950*
LEBANON	Republic	French Mandate	Claimed by Lebanon: November 22, 1943	October 15, 1945§	September 19, 1944 (September 7, 1944)
LIBYA	Kingdom	British Trusteeship	December 14, 1951* December 24, 1951‡	December 14, 1955*	February 7, 1952² December 24, 1951‡

Appendix: NEWLY INDEPENDENT NATIONS
(continued)

Name	Present Status	Former Status	Date of Independence or Coming into Existence	Date of U.N. Membership (Date of General Assembly Decision)	Date of U.S. Recognition	Date of Extinction
VIETNAM	Republic	French	June 13, 1949* March 18, 1949‡		February 7, 1950*	
WESTERN SAMOA	Independent State	British Trusteeship	January 1, 1962		January 1, 1962	
YEMEN	Republic			September 30, 1947	April, 1946 (February 24, 1946)	
ZANZIBAR#	Republic	British Protectorate	December 9, 1963	December 16, 1963	December 9, 1963	April 26, 1964

* SOURCE: Denys P. Myers, "Contemporary Practice of the United States Relating to International Law," 55 *American Journal of International Law* 704 (1961).
† Dates believed by the authors of the present study to be correct, as distinct from dates listed by Myers. For details see individual case studies.
( ) Dates of U.S. recognition in parentheses refer to the initial acts of the U.S. Government forming part of an anticipatory process of recognition that was apparently intended to make recognition effective on the date of independence.
‡ Date of *express* U.S. recognition later than date of actual *implied* recognition.
§ Date of deposit of instrument of ratification (United Nations, *Status of Multilateral Conventions*).
|| *Status of Multilateral Conventions.*
Tanganyika and Zanzibar merged on April 26, 1964, to form the United Republic of Tanzania. See Postscript, p. 223.

4. THE NEW STATES AND THE UNITED NATIONS

BY J. E. S. FAWCETT

The two decades since 1940 form one of the great watersheds of history. Colonial systems, covering a third of the people of the earth, have broken up, with a consequent proliferation of independent states in Asia and Africa that are dedicated to political and social ideals novel in those continents. At the same time have occurred developments in nuclear power, electronics, the use of outer space, and biophysics, which for their speed, intensive interaction, and vast social implications have no parallel in the whole history of science and technology. Men have to try to ride this tempest of progress when half of them have too little to eat, having at their disposal institutions that belong largely to the eighteenth century, and methods of resolving international conflicts that belong to the Stone Age.

Here we shall look at a small but significant part of the picture: the United Nations and its agencies—the largest-scale institutions yet devised—and the effect upon them of the rapid emergence of many new states. But, to keep our discussion within bounds, we must further confine it to the effects of this emergence upon the distribution of forces within the U.N. itself.

The common characteristic of the U.N. and its agencies is that they have, in the words of Article 57 of the Charter, "wide international responsibilities" and are in effect world organizations. It is this characteristic that differentiates them from the many regional institutions.

Other characteristics of these world organizations bearing on our theme must briefly be described. The structure of an international organization in various ways resembles that of a national government, a limited company, and an association of clubs. These analogies become fanciful if pressed too far, but they can prove useful to our discussion.

The legislature in a national system of government corresponds in an international organization to the assembly or conference of the members, while the executive branch here consists of two elements: a directorate, in the form of an executive council or board, which is appointed by and from the members of the organization and which, like a national executive, is responsible for formulating general policy and for executing it; and a secretariat, headed by a director (or secretary general) having much the same position as the permanent staff of a government department.

Again, the directorate is not unlike the board of directors of a company, the director or secretary general sometimes sitting as chairman,[1] while the assembly or conference may be seen as the general meeting of shareholders. The ownership and management of the assets of an international organization also broadly follow the lines of a company. Finally, since many countries in the world form together various political and cultural groups, it is natural that when these countries come together in international organizations, they tend to form clubs: Some reasons will be given later for preferring this term to "blocs."

Member countries may be said to participate in the organs and work of an international organization in three ways: by right, in the assembly or conference; by election, in the directorate and the other organs of the organization; and, indirectly, by appointment of their nationals to posts in the secretariat.

Let us now begin to consider the new states we are to discuss. Admittedly, any categorization tends to be arbitrary and to exclude what it might be thought reasonable to include. Two criteria of what constitutes a "new nation" are adopted here and seem to be fairly comprehensive: The first is that the country has achieved the status of an independent state since 1945; the second, that the country was, upon its admission to the United Nations, a political newcomer upon the international scene.

Forty-seven countries satisfy the first criterion and all but two of them the second. The forty-seven countries are:

Africa: Algeria, Burundi, Cameroon, Central African Republic, Chad, Congo-Brazzaville, Congo-Leopoldville, Dahomey, Gabon, Ghana, Guinea, Ivory Coast, Kenya, Libya, Madagascar, Mali, Mauritania, Morocco, Niger, Nigeria, Rwanda, Senegal, Sierra Leone, Somali Republic, Sudan, Tanganyika, Togo, Tunisia, Uganda, Upper Volta, Zanzibar

The New States and the United Nations

Americas:	Jamaica	Trinidad and Tobago	
Asia:	Burma	India	Mongolia
	Cambodia	Indonesia	Pakistan
	Ceylon	Laos	Philippines
		Malaysia	
Europe:	Cyprus		
Middle East:	Israel	Jordan	Kuwait

All the countries listed above meet the first criterion in that they achieved full constitutional independence in or after 1945 and, except for India, Israel, Jordan, Libya, and Pakistan, after 1954. Furthermore, all except India and possibly Mongolia[2] satisfy the second criterion in that they entered for the first time upon the international political scene, as actors in their own right, upon attaining independence. As an original member both of the League of Nations and of the United Nations, India is properly excluded by the second criterion; and even though she did not attain full constitutional independence until 1947, it would be unrealistic to regard her as a new nation in the sense with which we are here concerned. However, India has been included in this categorization because, in her political and social aspirations, she has much in common with the new nations.

Some comment is also necessary upon Mongolia. It has evolved on similar lines to Tibet and its status is not less obscure. Both lie on the power frontier between the U.S.S.R., China, and India (as successor of Great Britain); both have long been hidden in the shadow of Chinese suzerainty, and, though remote from the community of nations, both have expressed a national individuality that vindicates their right to be called states. Just as Tibet may be said to have attained the status of independent state in 1913, only, it seems, to lose it again, so there is evidence that Mongolia was an independent state at least by 1945, if not before. By the Treaty of Kiakhta in 1915, concluded between representatives of Russia, China, and Outer Mongolia,[3] it was declared that Outer Mongolia was autonomous under the suzerainty of China; however, in 1924, the U.S.S.R. and China agreed formally to recognize that "Outer Mongolia was an integral part of the territory of China." Here there is a record of obscure and contradictory political descriptions of a territory similar to those we find in the earlier agreements between Great Britain, Russia, and China on the status of Tibet; indeed the terminology used in both cases is almost identical. But these descriptions were plainly designed less to state the constitutional facts of the relationship between Mongolia and Tibet on the one side and China on the other than to serve the transitory political interests of the large bordering countries. The Mongolian People's Republic was formed in 1926 and was recognized as an independent state by the U.S.S.R. in that year; but the northwestern province of Tannu Tura was incorporated, as an autonomous territory, in the U.S.S.R. China formally recognized the independence of the Mongolian People's Republic in 1945, but other states appear for the most part to have suspended judgment, though Mongolia was a candidate for admission to the United Nations from 1946 until 1961, when she was finally admitted. Her traditional remoteness and late membership in the U.N. seem to justify her inclusion here among the new states.

Excluding India, then, and also Korea and Vietnam, which are not U.N. members, we have forty-six countries, representing about 40 per cent of the membership in the U.N. Henceforth, for brevity, we will refer to them simply as "the new nations."

It would not be unfair to say of the new nations that they are for the most part small and inexperienced in government and that all are underdeveloped. Many of the new nations are small in population and existing resources, though not necessarily in territorial size. They are fragments of large colonial systems (twenty were formerly dependent territories of France and twenty-one of the United Kingdom), and there appear to be forces working to keep them small and numerous.

Professor Carrington has observed that:

> Since no limit was placed by the United Nations upon the admission of new members, since any political delegation from a small territory might claim national status, if only it had previously been under colonial rule, there was every inducement to balkanize the world into smaller fragments, and there was left no rational basis on which the metropolitan Power could make a stand. Not only the General Assembly of the United Nations but also Commonwealth membership was diluted by the admission of small states with no evident qualifications. With South Africa out, but with Cyprus and Sierra Leone in, what had the pattern of the Commonwealth become? [4]

Of the African countries in particular he had said, earlier in the address, "The fragmentation of *l'Afrique Noire d'expression française* into so many non-viable small states is quite deplorable and if they cannot soon combine into larger aggregations with a real economic substructure I see no better fate for them than the fate of ex-Spanish America in its first hundred years."

These severe judgments are quoted because they state forcefully the dangers of fragmentation, though their premises may at least in part be questioned. For the pattern of neither the U.N. nor the Commonwealth can be determined by the mere size in population of its members, as the example of New Zealand demonstrates; and it is not clear what "evident qualifications" there are for membership in the U.N. that all the small excolonial states lack: Qualifications as diverse as political good sense and ability to contribute to the maintenance of peace might be no better met by some old-established members. Further, it seems to be suggested that the exclusion of South Africa and the admission of Cyprus and Sierra Leone was an exchange in favor of small countries by which the pattern of the Commonwealth was altered for the worse; but South African national policies, for example in the field of nationality and Indian immigration, had worked for a long time against "the pattern of the Commonwealth," *apartheid* being the latest and worst of these policies; the exclusion of South Africa became necessary to preserve any Commonwealth pattern at all.

But the need for larger aggregations is plain, especially where the will to revive indigenous and ancient cultures and a mistrust of neighbors with different political habits and aspirations both serve to intensify local nationalism. Yet recent efforts to form political unions or federations have been strikingly unsuccessful: The Federation of Mali and Senegal has broken up, as did the United Arab Republic only partly to recover;[5] Jamaica has voted itself out of the British Caribbean Federation, which has been dissolved; Ghana and Guinea have made little progress in their projected union; the new federation of Malaysia is seriously threatened by hostile neighbors; and the Federation of Rhodesia and Nyasaland has been dissolved.

Inexperience in government is not to be equated with lack of political wisdom, though it can have some of the same consequences. However, the high intelligence of many of the leaders of the new nations cannot of itself make up for paucity of trained administrators and, until cadres can be built up, this must remain a weakness. Some new nations are better equipped in this respect than others.

The notion of underdevelopment has undergone a marked evolution. Countries outside the charmed circle of industrialization used to be regarded and described as uncivilized, primitive, and backward. But these descriptions came to be seen as mistaken, insofar as they suggested that conditions in these countries were immutable or were due simply to an unwillingness of their peoples to help themselves, as inappropriate of countries that had elaborate cultures when many of the industrialized countries were semibarbarous; and, in any case, as supercilious and self-complacent. As the vicious circle of ignorance, undernourishment, and underemployment of people and resources became more widely evident, the dynamic concept of "underdeveloped" came into use as a description of the poorer countries; and as development is seen to be a matter of degree they are sometimes called "less developed" or "developing."

An underdeveloped country has been well described thus:

> It is a country characterised by poverty, with beggars in the cities, and villagers eking out a bare subsistence. . . . It is a country lacking in factories of its own, usually with inadequate supplies of power and light. It usually has insufficient roads and railroads, insufficient government services, poor communications. It has few hospitals, and few institutions of higher learning. Most of its people cannot read or write. In spite of the generally prevailing poverty of the people, it may have isolated islands of wealth, with a few persons living in luxury. Its banking system is poor; small loans have to be obtained through moneylenders who are often little better than extortionists. Another striking characteristic of an underdeveloped country is that its exports to other countries usually consist almost entirely of raw materials, ores or fruits, or some staple product, with possibly a small admixture of luxury handicrafts. Often the extraction or cultivation of these raw material exports is in the hands of foreign companies.[6]

Other characteristics of such countries should perhaps be added. First, they will almost certainly have a relatively high birth rate, perhaps as much as double that of European or North American countries, and, because of disease and malnutrition, a high death rate, tending slowly to be diminished as these evils are attacked and eliminated. A consequence of great political and economic importance is that there is in the underdeveloped countries a markedly higher proportion of young people and a lower proportion of people over sixty than in the developed countries. Second, the dependence of many underdeveloped countries upon one or two raw material exports for the earning of the means to import the capital and consumer goods they so much need means that they are particularly vulnerable to changes in demand for, and prices of, these raw materials. With these characteristics in mind, it should be noted that the underdeveloped countries embrace the greater part of the people of the earth.

After this brief survey of some of the attributes of the new nations that seem likely to affect their participation in the U.N. system, we must examine that system itself in order to discern what effect the admission of the new nations has had upon the distribution of forces within it.

The structure of the U.N. was designed on two broad principles: hegemony and universality. The hegemony of the five permanent members of the Security Council is visible in the Charter at a number of points: in their power to intervene, through the Council, in disputes and situations of international concern and in their primary control of the use of force, both under Chapter VII and in the transitional period, contemplated in Article 106, before the implementation of Article 43; in the requirements that each accept the Charter as a condition of its entry into force, and that no amendment of the Charter be made effective until accepted by them. Since it is a characteristic of a great power that there is no part of the world in which it does not have an economic or political interest, it is not surprising that there have been few disputes or situations dealt with by the Security Council in which two or more permanent members have not been more or less directly involved; this suggests that the hegemonic solution of disputes and maintenance of peace is in its nature unworkable. Of the present state of the hegemony of the five permanent members, we shall say more later.

The principle of universality is manifest in the absence, stressed by Professor Carrington, of any limit upon the number of new members that may be admitted to the U.N. under Article 4; for the U.N. is designed to be a world organization. The terms of Article 73(b) of the Charter, envisage and indeed encourage the emergence of new states:

> Members of the United Nations which have or assume responsibilities for the administration of territories whose peoples have not yet attained a full measure of self-government . . . accept as a sacred trust the obligation . . . to develop self-government, to take due account of the political aspirations of the peoples, and to assist them in the progressive development of their free political institutions, according to the particular circumstances of each territory and its people and their varying stages of development.

The paragraph, in which the cautious hand of the colonial powers of 1945 can be seen, does not state its own logical conclusion, which is, of course, independence for the nonself-governing territories. Had the rapidity of the march to independence, which became a sprint after 1955, been foreseen at San Francisco, provision might well have been made for necessary changes in the structure and size of the principal organs of the U.N., to accommodate the influx of new states. Thus the exhaustive conditions of membership laid down in Article 4 do not impose any necessary limit upon the number of states which may be admitted.[7] Even the condition that the candidate state must be willing and able to perform its Charter obligations does not exclude even the smallest and weakest state. Its contribution to the U.N. budget will be fixed by the General Assembly with due regard to its capacity to pay. The ability to contribute to the maintenance of peace is only essential for election to the Security Council, or if the state should be called upon under Article 48 to assist the U.N. in an enforcement action. This is quite academic since, for reasons which will be discussed below, the Security Council is not likely to call upon the small and weak members. As far then as the Charter provides and practice since 1955 has indicated, the U.N. is committed to the inclusion of all independent countries in the world.[8]

Two other aspects of the structure of the U.N. must be noted: the division of powers between the principal organs, and the purpose and effect of Article 2(7). It is a peculiarity of the U.N. that, despite the superficial resemblances between its structure and that of a national government or a limited company, its principal organs are not related in a hierarchy as are the organs of a government or a company. The principal political organs of the U.N. are really coordinate agencies with distinct, though in part overlapping, functions. In short, the conflict between centralized and functional approaches to the distribution of power is unresolved in the U.N. Logically, the three Councils should be responsible and subordinate to the General Assembly, but the principle of hegemony forbade the subordination of the Security Council to the General Assembly, and only the Economic and Social Council and the Trusteeship Council, which have little political power, function "under the authority of the General Assembly." [9]

Article 2(7) is one of the most sensitive points in the Charter, and it would be idle to attempt any review here of the many problems to which it gives rise,[10] but in the context of a discussion of the place of the new nations in the U.N., a few remarks may be made on it. A general international organization like the League of Nations or the U.N., is constituted to develop and harmonize the political and economic relations among its member states and to prevent or soften collisions between them; it is not the intention of its founders that the organization should interfere, or even concern itself with the domestic policies and arrangements of its members. But there are forces working in the world against this neat constitutional principle; these are forces, both social and technological, that are, with an irresistible momentum, making for community and interdependence between peoples, and, though there is still a long way to go toward "one world," the line that Article 2(7) seeks to draw between what is international and what is domestic in a given policy or situation, becomes steadily harder to discern. There is no more prescient passage in the reports of the Permanent Court of International Justice than its finding that this distinction is a relative matter, depending upon the development of international relations; [11] and there will come a time when the U.N. and other international organizations will wither away, because the distinction will have disappeared.

Since the early days of the U.N., groupings of members have appeared in the General Assembly. These groupings have been dubbed "blocs," perhaps because the "Soviet bloc" was not only the first to identify itself but the most solid and the most rigorously managed. But the record of General Assembly practice suggests that these groupings should be more precisely described, and that there are really three kinds, coalitions, clubs, and blocs. These terms are designed to stress the fluidity of the groupings. Indeed, none of them is permanent, as the case of Yugoslavia has shown. Are these groupings inevitable? Yes, and even desirable, if they escape rigidity. "We ourselves [India] belong to various groups," said Krishna Menon,[12] "and I think that groups, in so far as they seek to offer to the Assembly the collective wisdom, are a constructive force. But if on the other hand blocs surround themselves with walls of isolation, then we shall divide the unity of this Assembly." But they have been criticized from countries that are not absorbed in any exclusive grouping: so Thor Thors of Iceland, with a very long experience in the U.N., deplored "the division and encirclement of delegations into blocs which vote together, act together, and jointly claim benefits, privileges and positions for their members.... We must avoid letting them develop to the extent that all decisions here in our Organisation are reached inside the blocs, but not by the nations individually." [13]

Yet groupings are inevitable because the General Assembly is composed in fact, not of those metaphysical abstractions, the member states, but of human beings, and some very political ones at that. The constellations of power, which are already well established in the world and which these people represent, compel them to come together in groups when they play their part in Assembly debates and decisions. Just as a parliament can rarely treat itself to the luxury of a "free vote," it would be a counsel of perfection to ask, as did Mr. Thors, that nations in the General Assembly should reach decisions individually. Groupings are even desirable, for, in the process of what Secretary of State Dean Rusk has called "parliamentary diplomacy," they assist in the process of diplomatic settlements, develop the sense of international community, and, like parliamentary parties, effect by collective action great savings in the time and effort involved in the execution of its tasks by the General Assembly, the latter alone being a modest but not negligible contribution.[14]

Coalitions are those usually temporary groupings that are formed to influence the Assembly in a particular direction or execute a particular policy: for example, India, Sweden, and Yugoslavia jointly moving in 1957 a resolution on "Peaceful and Neighbourly Relations between States"; the "neutral" countries in the recent work of the Disarmament Committee; and the sixteen member states that contributed forces to the U.N. operation in Korea and regularly consulted together on issues arising over Korea.[15] More enduring and more systematic are the Commonwealth, Latin American, and Afro-Asian groupings, and these may be fairly described as clubs.[16] They hold regular meetings of their delegations; they discuss all matters of common concern; they seek maximum agreement among themselves without forcing decisions to a vote; and, in the General Assembly itself, they take parallel but not necessarily uniform action. In other words, there is an understanding among them that they will keep in step, as far as possible, in formulating, debating, and voting on decisions in the U.N.; but just as the member of a club is free to hold and express divergent opinions on matters not essential to the purposes of the club, so individual members of a "club" in the U.N. may from time to time argue or vote on particular issues against the general line of the group. The Latin American countries have the oldest established, and, until the emergence of the Afro-Asian group, the largest of the General Assembly "clubs," and it is of interest to read the very frank Resolution in which they stated its purpose:

During the first session of the General Assembly in London, the Latin American States, acutely aware of their relative impotence individually, met together informally in an effort to capitalize on their joint voting. Initially their attention was directed to ensuring the election of as many Latin Americans as possible to key positions. . . . As time passed, the "Group" extended its activities to cover all issues of major concern. . . . The Latin Americans are proud of their "Group." . . . It provides an opportunity for discussion and clarification of important issues and for the adoption of reasoned positions whether or not a consensus is reached.[17]

The "Soviet bloc" differs from the "clubs" in that the countries composing it, the participants in the Warsaw Pact and Comecon, not only consult together on all major U.N. issues but also act together, both in speeches and votes, with a uniformity that renders the rare divergence remarkable. The Afro-Asian group, though more complex and looser than the Latin American group, has the character of a "club" within the U.N. It is still in evolution and, though it has shown increased cohesion in recent years, it may well disintegrate into smaller groups with different alignments as the tide of anticolonialism recedes with the general achievement of independence and as large geopolitical changes occur. The Afro-Asian group is not homogeneous either culturally, politically, or geographically, and its members have a number of cross-associations. The Middle Eastern countries form a highly individual group within the larger whole. The United Arab Republic, despite the defection of Syria, remains their natural leader, but is also associated in Africa with the Casablanca powers, composed of Morocco, Ghana, Mali, and Guinea, the new nations. Somewhat at odds with this association are the Monrovia powers, grouped around Liberia and Nigeria and embracing many former French colonies that are now independent.

The fact that a number of the new nations in the Afro-Asian group are members of the Commonwealth is another complicating factor. On the one hand, the increased membership in the U.N. of African and Asian countries will tend to intensify the division between the "inner circle" of the members of the Commonwealth and the "outer circle" of new members in the debates and decisions of the U.N.; but on the other hand, the objective of a multiracial Commonwealth, if it is held to, may yet overcome this division and raise the Commonwealth into an individual and powerful force within the U.N.

The Afro-Asian group appears then at present time, composed as it is in great part of the new nations, to lie somewhere between a coalition and a club, and its future is likely to be dissolution into smaller, better defined, and more cohesive groups.

The ways in which a body with three or more members may take a joint decision, that is, a decision to be binding upon all of them, can be gathered into three main classes: decision by a prescribed number of votes; decision by designated members; and decision by a combination of these methods. The prescription of the number of votes necessary for a decision will have two elements: the number of votes constituting the necessary majority (for example, 51 per cent or two-thirds or four-fifths either of the total votes held or of the votes held by those present and voting); and the allocation of votes to each member, which may be one vote, or more than one vote, under a system of weighted voting. The assent of designated members may also be prescribed as necessary for a decision: Thus all the members may be so designated, in which case there is, strictly speaking, no voting at all, but a rule of unanimity; or that of certain members only, in which case there is a system of weighting by persons. All these methods are represented, with various refinements, in the U.N. and other international organizations: Thus the League Council and the Council of the OEEC proceed by a rule of unanimity; the General Assembly proceeds by a rule of bare majority, with a requirement of a two-thirds majority in specified classes of decision, and with each member holding one vote; the International Monetary Fund operates with bare majorities and in certain cases qualified majorities, but with a system of weighted voting by which each member has 250 votes plus one vote for every $250,000 of its quota in the Fund;[18] and the Security Council cannot take other than procedural decisions save with the assent of seven members, including five designated members. It should be added that all elections in the General Assembly are conducted by secret ballot.[19]

A general comment may be appropriate here on the nature of majority rule.[20] While it marks usually a later stage in political evolution than the rule of unanimity, the justification for rule by the majority does not, it is suggested, rest upon some inherent right but upon two presuppositions: equality of representation and equality of commitment among the members of the community or body in which majority rule is exercised. Equality of representation means that the members have one vote each, or that, if a greater number of votes are allocated to some of the members, all have freely agreed to this in advance. Equality of commitment means

The New States and the United Nations

that a decision taken by the majority may justifiably be regarded as binding on all members only if the decision does not discriminate against members of the minority: Discrimination here means action decided upon by vote that is deliberately confined to the minority, though in its nature it can and should be extended to members of the majority.

After this long introduction, we may now be in a position to observe some of the effects of the admission of the new nations into the U.N. Let us examine the effect of the great increase in numbers of member states on the structure and working of the U.N., and the influence of the new nations on the direction and determination of U.N. policy.

We may start by recalling two speeches delivered by the British Foreign Secretary, Lord Home,[21] to a local branch and to the Council of the United Nations Association in the United Kingdom. In these speeches, he criticized some current U.N. policies, and by implication held some of the new nations to blame at least in part for the adoption of these policies. "A large number of countries," he said, "are putting their campaign for acceleration of independence for colonial territories before the main purpose of the Charter which is to provide peace and security." Not only were certain countries beginning to import "racialism and aggressive nationalism" into the U.N., but a double standard of judgment was being applied to "Russia's empire" and to the Commonwealth: "We are moving fast—perhaps faster than in prudence we ought—in the direction in which the new countries want to go. The United Nations members know that to be true, but they seldom condemn the Russians and constantly harass us."

Let us consider some recent U.N. resolutions in order to see how far these strictures upon the U.N. are justified. It must first be observed that the adoption of a resolution by the General Assembly or the Security Council is often a long and politically intricate process. A resolution may be voted upon paragraph by paragraph—even language in the preamble may receive a separate vote—before the resolution is voted upon as a whole; and caution must be exercised in drawing political inferences from a particular country's affirmative or negative vote or abstention. A country may abstain from voting upon an important paragraph and yet vote for the resolution as a whole: In such a case it is not easy to determine what its attitude is to the paragraph. A study of voting behavior in the General Assembly during its eleventh session in 1956–57 made by L. N. Reiselbach[22] reveals, with much refinement of analysis, some interesting patterns in voting. For the reasons already suggested, it may be that the refinement is at points taken further than the evidence will bear. However, by utilizing his analyses and applying his methods, we will try to discern general trends of action by the new nations in the United Nations. First, we will take a series of resolutions adopted at the 1961 session of the General Assembly upon the uses of nuclear devices and then we will turn to the issue of colonialism.

Resolution 1632–XVI, appealing to the U.S.S.R. to refrain from exploding a fifty-megaton bomb, was adopted by 87–11–1–4.[23] Resolution 1648–XVI urging continuation of the suspension of nuclear tests was adopted by 71–20–8–4. It is of interest to observe that among the countries voting against this resolution were Australia, Italy, Portugal, South Africa, and the three nuclear powers. Resolution 1649–XVI stressing the urgent need for a treaty to ban nuclear weapons was carried by 71–11–15–6. Resolution 1652–XVI called for the treatment of the continent of Africa as a denuclearized zone, in which no nuclear tests should be conducted and no nuclear weapons stored; this resolution had a tortuous passage and was carried by a strange combination of votes and abstentions, 55–0–44–4; the immediately following resolution 1653–XVI, calling for a flat prohibition of the use of nuclear weapons, as being contrary both to the United Nations Charter and to international law, and "a crime against mankind and civilisation" was carried 50–20–26–2. Finally, resolution 1665–XVI, urging the prevention of a wider dissemination of nuclear weapons (to other countries than those now in possession of them) was adopted unanimously. The first three resolutions were passed by heavy majorities of double or more the number of the new nations. A closer examination of the voting of the new nations shows the following: On the first three resolutions, the new nations were almost unanimous. All voted in favor of the appeal to the U.S.S.R. concerning the fifty-megaton bomb except Mongolia, which voted against; Mali, which abstained; and Dahomey, Morocco, and Somalia, which were absent; on the suspension of tests, all again voted in favor except Mongolia, and Dahomey, Gabon, Ivory Coast, and Niger, which were absent. On a treaty to ban the use of nuclear weapons, a similar pattern appeared but with more abstentions: Mongolia voted against, while Ghana, Guinea, Indonesia, Mali, and Morocco abstained; and the Central African Republic, Congo-Brazzaville, Ivory Coast, Somalia, and Upper Volta were absent. Thus the new nations were associated with a larger number of other countries in adopting these resolutions. Their votes cannot be regarded as necessarily more decisive. But resolutions 1652 and 1653 were more controversial.

The reasons for abstention on 1652-XVI were various and complex but what is of interest here is that, although it might have been expected that the resolution would generally have appealed to them, no less than nine new nations abstained: Cameroun, Chad, Congo-Brazzaville, Gabon, Israel, Madagascar, Mauritania, Niger, and Upper Volta. However, on 1653-XVI, recommending the prohibition of the use of nuclear weapons, only Malaya, of the new nations, abstained, the remainder voting in favor, except Laos, which was absent.

This record of voting on resolutions concerning the use and dissemination of nuclear weapons does not seem to convict the new nations as a group of special irresponsibility in the General Assembly. While the attitudes expressed in these resolutions may not be convenient to the nuclear powers, they are shared by many countries beside the new nations and were expressed in not immoderate language.

We may now turn to the issues of colonialism and independence, which Lord Home had particularly in mind in his speeches, and consider Rieselbach's study.[24] First, however, we must note the pattern of common voting in the eleventh session of the General Assembly as revealed in this study. Rieselbach's object is in part to identify those groups of countries that tend to vote together in the General Assembly, and the classes of issues that bring them together. For this purpose, a group is defined as a number of countries that vote in the same sense on at least 80 per cent of the occasions on which a vote is taken, on all issues or on a given set of issues. It follows that a group as so defined will correspond to a coalition, "club," or "bloc," according to the degree of voting cohesion that its members exhibit. The study has evolved indexes determining both the voting cohesion within a group and the cohesion, if any, between separate groups. Thus the indexes of cohesion revealed at the eleventh session of the General Assembly in 1956–57, unity representing a common vote on all issues, were: Soviet bloc, .859; Latin American group, .670; Western countries, .636; and Afro-Asian group, .420. The indexes of likeness between these separate groups were also revealing: that between the Western countries and the Latin American group was high, at .820, as was that between the Latin American and Afro-Asian groups, at .613; the index of voting likeness between Latin American countries and the Soviet bloc was .222, and between the Western countries and the Soviet bloc, .154.

In order to determine the pattern of voting revealed by the new nations, Rieselbach selected eight resolutions on or connected with colonial issues and arranged them in an order of subject matter, so that the earlier resolutions in the series might be roughly described as favorable to the colonial powers and the later resolutions as unfavorable, the resolutions moving progressively from favorable to unfavorable.[25] From this arrangement of the resolutions, a prediction might be made that a country voting affirmatively for the earlier resolutions would vote against the later, thus exhibiting sympathy with the colonial powers, and that a country feeling hostility to colonial powers would, if voting against the earlier resolutions, support the later.

Only eleven of the new nations were then members of the U.N., but the pattern of voting is not without interest here. Israel, by voting against resolutions 1–4 and 6, abstaining on 5, and voting for 7 and 8, might be described as taking a moderately "anticolonial" line; Pakistan took a more definite position in voting against the first three resolutions and for 4, 6, 7, and 8; Ceylon was very close to Pakistan in voting against resolutions 1 and 3 and for all the rest. The votes of Tunisia, which voted against the first resolution and for all the others, and of Burma, Indonesia, and Morocco, which all abstained on the first resolution and voted for all the rest, are harder to appreciate, and the votes of Libya and Jordan, which voted for all the resolutions, harder still, since all these countries appear to have voted against the pattern indicated by the resolutions.

Three resolutions on, or connected with, colonial issues adopted at the fifteenth, and three at the sixteenth, session of the General Assembly also deserve attention. 1597–XV concerned the treatment of people of Indian and Pakistani origin in South Africa, regretting the South African failure to reply to proposals made by the Indian and Pakistani governments. This resolution, adopted by 78–0–2, is of particular interest for the Australian explanation of its affirmative vote. Australia voted for the revolution on the grounds that, although it transgressed the limits imposed upon U.N. action by Article 2(7) of the Charter, an abstention might be misunderstood as being not an affirmation of the sense of Article 2(7), but a partial approval of, or at least an unwillingness to condemn the treatment of Indians and Pakistanis in South Africa. The resolution is also of interest because the U.K. took the opportunity of its adoption to say: "We think that it is essentially an aspect of apartheid which is no longer of purely domestic concern"; and to describe the resolution as "constructive and clear in its intention." Resolution 1578–XV dealt with race conflict in South Africa resulting from the execution of apartheid policies. The resolution condemns apartheid as a violation of the United Nations Charter. Paragraph 3 requested states to consider what separate or collective action they might take, in conformity with the Charter, to bring about an abandonment of these policies. This paragraph, voted upon separately, was adopted by 85–1–10, the U.S. and the new nations forming part of the majority, and European countries and Australia being among the abstainers. Paragraph 5, which was in effect a declaration that apartheid policies led to international friction and endangered peace and security, was adopted by 88–1–8, Australia having joined the majority. The whole resolution was passed by 95–1–0. (Portugal voted against it.) It was now Portugal's turn to be censured; and Resolution 1603–XV called on Portugal to consider the implementation in Angola of resolution 1514–XV, concerning independence for colonial peoples, and appointed a subcommittee (Bolivia, Dahomey, Malaya, Finland, and Sudan) "to receive further statements and documents, to conduct such enquiries as it may deem necessary, and to report to the Assembly. . . ." This resolution was carried by 73–2–9. Among those abstaining, the U.K. invoked Article 2(7).

Three similar resolutions were adopted by the General Assembly at its sixteenth session in 1961–62: 1654–XVI, which sought to implement 1514–XV by establishing the so-called "Special Committee of Seventeen"; 1663–XVI, which contained a new condemnation of apartheid in South Africa; and 1742–XVI, which deprecated the "repressive measures and armed action against the people of Angola" and called for the release of its political prisoners. What is remarkable about these resolutions is that they were adopted respectively by 97–0–4; 97–2–1 and 99–2–1, and so may be said to represent the judgment of the whole community of nations.

Again, while the language of some of these resolutions might from some points of view have been more measured, they were carried by very large, and in the case of those adopted at the sixteenth session, by overwhelming majorities. In particular, the Special Committee of Seventeen, which has given special offense to the United Kingdom by its intervention in the affairs of the Federation of Rhodesia and Nyasaland, was established by 97–0. It is difficult to see how the establishment of the Special Committee can be attributed simply to anticolonialist malice on the part of the new nations; however, its operations appear to raise questions of the control by majorities of the General Assembly procedure.

Turning to the Security Council, we find considered two resolutions concerning the seizure of Goa and Damao in December, 1961. Liberia, Ceylon, and the United Arab Republic presented a resolution that declared that "the enclaves claimed by Portugal in India constitute a threat to international peace and security and stand in the way of the unity of the Republic of India," moved that the charges of aggression by Portugal against India be rejected, and called upon Portugal "to terminate hostile action and cooperate with India in the liquidation of her colonial possessions in India." This resolution secured only four votes. A resolution tabled by the U.S., U.K., France, and Turkey, called for a cease-fire and withdrawal by India to the "positions prevailing before December 17, 1961," and urged India and Portugal to work for a permanent solution of their differences by peaceful means. This resolution received seven votes, but the Soviet Union, Ceylon, Liberia, and the United Arab Republic voted against, and it was therefore defeated. It seems not unfair to regard the votes of the minority as unabashed support for "aggressive nationalism."

A final observation may be made on the majorities by which Assembly resolutions are carried. All the new nations are underdeveloped by the criteria set out above. It follows that, while they are for the time being at least unable to contribute more than a little financially to the maintenance and operations of the U.N. and its agencies, they are among the greatest potential users and consumers of the aid and resources that the system is able to make available. The total contribution of the new nations to the U.N. budget is a bare 3 per cent of the total, while over 60 per cent of resources under the expanded Technical Assistance program were directed between 1950 and 1958 to Africa, Asia, and the Middle East. However, it is to be observed that within this percentage Africa received 9.5 per cent, a figure little higher than Europe, which in this period received 7.8 per cent. It is not surprising therefore that resolutions of the General Assembly aiming at economic and social development or betterment are passed unanimously or with negligible opposition.

It is possible now to draw certain inferences from the presence of the new nations in the U.N. First, the new nations play a strong part in the choice of issues that are made the subject of debate and resolutions. The overriding issues at the present time may be said to be: the uses of nuclear power; colonialism and self-determination of peoples; and economic aid and technical assistance to the underdeveloped countries.

Second, there has been through the 1950's a steady diminution in the collective influence in the United Nations of the five permanent members of the Security Council, a fact sharply underlined in U.S. Secretary of State Dean Rusk's January 8, 1964, proposals for structural changes. The virtual nonrepresentation of China, the disaffection of France, and the sharp conflict of objectives between the United States and the Soviet Union all served to undermine the principle of hegemony upon which the Charter was founded.[26] The Uniting for Peace Resolution, 1950, by which such power as the U.N. possesses passed into the hands of the General Assembly, was the logical consequence of this loss of influence. The redistribution of power has been intensified by the presence of the new nations. If we compare the position before 1955 with that now prevailing, we find that then, with 63 members, 42 represented a two-thirds majority. It was possible then for the United States and the Latin-American countries, with one or two others, to muster more than one-third of the votes and so block important resolutions. Now, with 113 members, no single "club" or "bloc" can alone muster the 38 votes necessary to prevent the adoption of a resolution. Furthermore, neutralism—deliberate nonalignment with the great powers on certain political issues—is more widespread among the new nations than among the old membership of the U.N., though the Belgrade Conference showed that the uncommitted countries have not yet succeeded in organizing themselves in a politically effective bloc either within or outside the U.N.[27] However, it may be said that by 1960, as a result of the admission of the new nations, and of policies of nonalignment, the great powers no longer dominated the General Assembly, though that is not of course to say that they have lost all influence or ability to manipulate the attitudes and votes of many smaller countries. Further, the principle of equality of commitment is no longer fully effective, since a majority of small countries is able to recommend policies from the effects of which they themselves escape or which they have not the capacity or means themselves to carry out.

It would be idle to speculate here on the effects of the two great geopolitical changes that have already marked the 1960's: the inexorable acceptance by the United States and the Soviet Union of a limitation upon the possibilities of conflict between them, and the new "cold war" between the Soviet Union and China. That the effects of these changes will last long and run deep is already obvious. One effect on the U.N. may at least be to upset the past slow crystalization of the "Afro-Asian bloc" into a defined political shape, and to set in motion a new process and polarities with China as one pole.

Various adjustments in the voting system have been suggested that might establish a better political balance in the General Assembly. Weighted voting has its supporters. It has been used with success in organizations having a technical or economic function. For example, in international commodity agreements, the relative economic interest of each country in the operation of the agreement is expressed in the number of votes it received, and at the same time equivalence in votes is established between importing and exporting countries. So under the International Wheat Agreement, 1,000 votes are allocated to the importing countries and the same number to the exporting countries. Within each group, votes are distributed in proportion to guaranteed purchases or guaranteed sales, as the case may be, for the current crop year. Similarly, the International Monetary Fund and the International Bank for Reconstruction and Development have a system of weighted voting based upon the quotas of members. These quotas are themselves determined by a number of economic and political factors. In the European Economic Community, there is a weighting of votes of the members over a comparatively narrow range of issues.

The difficulty of constructing a system of weighted voting for the U.N. General Assembly lies in the choice of the factors to be used in determining the allocation of votes. Population might be taken as the sole factor yielding a form of proportional representation; other factors that might be added are gross national product or level of literacy. But there is no factor or combination of factors that would not seem to work unfairly against certain countries, alter the distribution of forces unpredictably, or serve only, as Mr. Nicholas has pointed out,[28] to sanctify temporary majorities; and it is probable that the simple, though illogical, arrangement of one-state–one-vote is, for all its current disadvantages, the most acceptable. Other solutions of the problem might be to alter the majorities required; for example, a four-fifths majority would not be unreasonable for certain classes of resolution. Entrenchment of certain procedural provisions in the rules of the General Assembly might also help to prevent manipulation of the rules to enforce the passage of particular resolutions.

Third, we must notice the conflict between the principles of universality and of equal representation that has been brought about by the admission of the new nations. On the one hand, the U.N. now embraces nearly all the states in the world; on the other, its structure makes it impossible for them all to have adequate representation other than in the General Assembly. The facts that the number of members has been greatly increased and that many of the new nations are small and inexperienced in government affect their participation in the U.N. and its agencies in a number of ways. For example, it is impossible, without a rotation of membership that would reduce organizational effectiveness, for every country to serve a term in the principal organs of the U.N. except over a very long period of time indeed. At the beginning of 1962, the representation of new nations was very slight: Ghana in the Security Council; Jordan and Senegal among the eighteen members of the Economic and Social Council.[29]

It may be observed that under the convention of electing one Commonwealth member to the Security Council, in addition to the U.K., in rotation, it took about ten years to "rotate" five Commonwealth members thus: Australia, 1946–47; Canada, 1948–49; India, 1950–51; Pakistan, 1952–53; New Zealand, 1954–55; Australia, 1956–57. It will be seen that Ceylon and South Africa did not serve during this period, and the convention would have little value if a quarter of a century had to elapse before the last country in the list could have its term of service. It follows a fortiori that the problem of representation of the other new nations is even more acute, unprotected as they generally are by such conventions. Thus of the new nations, only Ceylon, Ghana, Pakistan, and Tunisia have served on the Security Council since 1946; but it must be borne in mind that few of the rest can make any notable "contribution . . . to the maintenance of international peace and security" as required by Article 23.

An examination of the subsidiary bodies of the U.N. reveals much the same picture, even if we select as having an especial interest those on which the new nations might be expected to serve. Thus, the following have been elected to political bodies:

Disarmament Committee (eighteen members): Burma, Nigeria
Advisory Committee on U.N. Emergency Force (seven members): Ceylon, Pakistan
Committee on Information from Non-Self-Governing Territories (sixteen members): Ceylon, Pakistan, Upper Volta

Commission on Permanent Sovereignty over Natural Resources (nine members): Philippines

Committee on Peaceful Uses of Outer Space (twenty-four members): Chad, Mongolia, Morocco, Sierra Leone

The position in bodies occupied with economic and social questions was the following in January, 1964:

Population Commission (eighteen members): Ghana, Ceylon, Tunisia

Social Commission (twenty-one members): Israel, Sudan, Malaysia, Gabon, Tunisia

Commission on Human Rights (twenty-one members): Philippines, Dahomey

Commission on the Status of Women (twenty-one members): Philippines, Ghana, Indonesia, Sierra Leone, Guinea

Commission on International Commodity Trade (twenty-one members): Malaysia, Ivory Coast, Madagascar, Mali

Technical Assistance Commission (thirty members): Algeria, Jordan, Senegal, Nigeria

Committee for Industrial Development (thirty members): Pakistan, Algeria, Philippines, Madagascar, Senegal, Tunisia, Central African Republic, Cameroun

Governing Council: U.N. Special Fund (eighteen members): Ghana, Indonesia, Senegal, Philippines, Tunisia

Executive Board: U.N. Children's Fund (thirty members): Tunisia, Israel, Nigeria, Pakistan, Senegal, Sudan, Philippines

Committee on Housing, Building and Planning (twenty-one members): Indonesia, Tanganyika, Israel, Madagascar, Nigeria.

While it would be a mistake to draw wide inferences from this list as to the representation of the new nations in U.N. bodies, a few remarks may be made. While in 1963 twenty-two new nations are represented in one body or another, seven are represented on not less than four: Nigeria, Ceylon, Pakistan, Ghana (including the Security Council), Indonesia, Philippines, and Senegal. The last two are in fact represented on five, surprisingly perhaps in the case of Senegal, which is a member of the Economic and Social Council. It will be noticed that four of these countries are members of the British Commonwealth and may perhaps be not unfairly described with Indonesia and the Philippines as among the new generation of rising middle powers.

However, representation in the councils and other bodies of

the United Nations may be less important than participation in the other organizations in the United Nations system, and here the new nations have a large place. In January, 1962, all were members of the Food and Agriculture Organization and the United Nations Educational, Scientific and Cultural Organization except Mongolia and Tanganyika, which had not yet joined any other agencies outside the United Nations itself; Mauritania was not a member of the World Health Organization, and Cambodia and Laos were not members of the International Labor Organization, but all the other new nations were. Beyond this there are certain functional organizations that the new nations have tended to avoid thus far. Less than half were members of the International Atomic Energy Agency or the group of financial institutions that includes the International Monetary Fund, the International Bank for Reconstruction and Development, the International Development Association, and the International Finance Corporation, or, as might be expected the International Maritime Consultive Organization. Nine new nations were also nonmembers of the International Civil Aviation Organization.

In general, it must be remembered that it is difficult for a small country to maintain the necessary number of representatives abroad to participate fully, even if it were elected, in the principal organs and subsidiary bodies[30] of the U.N., let alone its agencies. Walter Kotschnig recently observed that in 1962 not less than 400 international committees were holding sessions, and that to provide representation was a strain even on the U.S. Within the U.N., many small delegations have to cope with multifarious subjects, discussed in mountains of paper and on numerous committees. Finally, a small country itself short of trained men cannot easily spare them for service, even temporary, in the international secretariats, though there they could get invaluable experience. However, great efforts are being made, and not without success, to overcome this difficulty by training more diplomatic and technical personnel.

Enlargement of the membership of the principal organs and other bodies in the U.N. is an obvious device for dealing with the problem, but the efficacy of such a move is doubtful. It is common experience, both in governmental and international administration, that a committee changes its character and begins to lose efficiency when its number of members passes a certain optimum— possibly fifteen to eighteen. In the U.N. system, this difficulty manifests itself in nearly all the principal organs as at present organized. The publicity of their meetings and of the statements made at them already encourages their use as propaganda platforms; an increase in the number of their members could only intensify this and complete the destruction of such mutual confidence and cohesion as exists. This process might be reversed if sittings of, for example, the Security Council generally *in camera* were to be held. The question whether the International Court of Justice should be enlarged in face of the great increase in U.N. membership raises a number of problems; but it may be pointed out that the new nations have not in general shown any great interest in this body, at least as far as this interest might be evidenced by acceptance of the compulsory jurisdiction of the Court under Article 36(2) of its Statute.[31]

It would, it is believed, be wrong to conclude from these transitory difficulties that the U.N. is too big and that the world should turn back to regionalism. More and wider cooperation and mutual aid are needed, not less; this does not, of course, exclude regional cooperation and action. But it is only through the U.N. and its agencies, as world organizations, that the new nations can realize their full development and that the "one world" we all need is likely to be reached.

Notes

(*A key to the abbreviations used in the notes is on p. 315.*)

Chapter 1. "Independence and Problems of State Succession" by D. P. O'Connell

1. For contemporary literature on state succession, see D. P. O'Connell, "State Succession and the Effect upon Treaties of Entry into a Composite Relationship," 40 *B.Y.I.L.* (1963).

2. It was Hugo Grotius who introduced the Roman-law institution of *hereditas jacens* (succession upon death) into the law of nations. See his *De jure belli ac pacis*, ed. James Brown Scott, and trans. Francis W. Kelsey, with the collaboration of Arthur E. R. Boak, Henry A. Sanders, Jesse S. Reeves, and Herbert F. Wright (Oxford: The Clarendon Press, 1925), Book II, Chap. IX, paragraph XII. Samuel Pufendorf adopted this theory of state succession in his *De jure naturae et gentium*. See the 1688 edition (Oxford: The Clarendon Press, 1934), Book VIII, Chap. XII, paragraphs I–V, VII–IX. The universal-succession theory was also adopted by Emmerich de Vattel. See his *Le droit des gens ou principes de la loi naturelle* (London, 1758), Vol. II, Chap. XII, paragraph 191. Even though Max Huber no longer bases his arguments on the Roman-law principle of *hereditas jacens*, but on a combination of the sociological approach and a detailed survey of a considerable body of state practice, he also tends toward the principle of universal succession in his *Die Staaten-Succession* (Leipzig: Verlag Duncker & Humblot, 1898), particularly pp. 18–25.

3. For Arthur B. Keith's argument that a state seizes all its predecessor's rights and is bound by none of its obligations see his *Theory of State Succession with Special Reference to English and Colonial Law* (1907), cited in C. Wilfred Jenks, "State Succession in Respect of Lawmaking Treaties," 29 *B.Y.I.L.* 111–120 (1952). This negativist theory, which arose mainly under the influence "of the official pronouncements of the British Government, not from purely theoretical considerations" (Ernst H. Feilchenfeld, *Public Debts and State Succession* [New York: The Macmillan Co., 1931], p. 406), was also espoused by other English writers. (In this connection, see the *Robert E. Brown Claim*, in which case the British Government argued that "conquest and annexation is merely an act of appropriation by force; the title of the conqueror is founded on might; his title to the property of the former Government upon the fact of the physical control and his expressed intention to maintain it." *Answer of His Britannic Majesty's Government in the Robert E. Brown Claim*, p. 17.) Among the leading British writers tending toward the negativist position are William E. Hall, *A Treatise on International Law* (8th ed.; Oxford: The Clarendon Press, 1924), pp. 114–15; and L. Oppenheim, *International Law*, ed. Arnold D. McNair (4th ed.; London: Longmans Green & Co., 1928), I, 164–74. In H. Lauterpacht's 7th ed. of this work (1948), Oppenheim's originally negativistic position appears to have been substantially qualified. See also J. L. Brierly, *The Law of Nations* (5th ed.; New York: Oxford University Press, 1955), pp. 144 ff. John Westlake, *International Law*

253

(Cambridge: Cambridge University Press, 1910), Part I, pp. 59–85, does not commit himself to the negativist theory.

4. Among the American writers inclining toward the negativist position are Amos S. Hershey, *The Essentials of International Public Law and Organization* (Rev. ed.; New York: The Macmillan Co., 1927, pp. 216–28); and Charles G. Fenwick, *International Law* (New York: Appleton-Century-Crofts, 1948), pp. 151–52. Other American writers have evidenced a tendency toward the opposite view. See Kent, *Commentary on International Law*, Abdy's ed. (1878), p. 95, as cited in Jenks, *op. cit.*, p. 118; David Dudley Field, *Outlines of an International Code* (2d ed.; New York: Baker, Voorhis & Co., 1876), p. 12, Art. 24; Henry W. Halleck, *International Law*, ed. Sherston Baker (4th ed.; London: Kegan Paul, Trench, Trubner & Co., Ltd., 1908), I, 96–99; and Theodore D. Woolsey, *Introduction to the Study of International Law* (New York: Charles Scribner's Sons, 1898), pp. 38–39. Henry Wheaton, Charles Cheney Hyde, and Ellery C. Stowell take intermediate positions. See Wheaton, *Elements of International Law*, the literal reproduction of the edition of 1866 by Richard Henry Dana, Jr., ed., with notes by George Grafton Wilson (Oxford: The Clarendon Press, 1936), pp. 33 and 36 ff.; Hyde, *International Law, Chiefly as Interpreted and Applied by the United States* (2d rev. ed.; Boston: Little, Brown & Co., 1945), I, 358 ff., and II, 1539; and Stowell, *International Law, A Restatement of Principles in Conformity with Actual Practice* (New York: Henry Holt & Co., 1931), pp. 44–45.

5. See Herbert Arnold Wilkinson, *The American Doctrine of State Succession* (Baltimore: The Johns Hopkins Press, 1934), pp. 123 ff.

6. The outstanding representative of the Austinians is Keith. See his *Theory of State Succession*, p. 5. The Austinian dichotomy between law and morality prompts Hall to make the following statement: "No doubt the debt of a state from which another separates itself ought generally to be divided between the two proportionately to their respective resources as a matter of justice to the creditors, because it is seldom that the value of their security is not affected by a diminution of the state indebted to them; but the obligation is a moral, not a legal one. The fact remains that the general debt of a state is a personal obligation." Hall, *op. cit.*, p. 116, n. 1.

7. See Hall, *op. cit.*, pp. 20, 114.

8. In a communiqué, issued simultaneously on November 8, 1960, at London, Port-of-Spain, and Washington, the following statement was made: "There was acceptance by all parties of the basic principle that the West Indies, when independent, would have the right to form its own alliances and to conclude such agreements as it thought fit regarding military bases on its soil." "First-Stage London Talks held on West Indies," 43 *Dep't. of State Bulletin* 822 (1960). The fact that the West Indies Federation has been dissolved does not change the principle accepted by the United States and Britain in the above statement.

9. The United States rights with respect to the Guantanamo Naval Base derive from two arguments. The first is a lease agreement, signed by the President of the United States on February 23, 1903, and by the President of Cuba, on February 16, 1903. "This agreement set forth the boundaries of the area and granted the U.S. the right to do everything necessary to develop the area. While it recognized that Cuba retained ultimate sovereignty (meaning not defined) over the area, Cuba granted the U.S. complete jurisdiction and con-

trol during the period of U.S. use of the area." The second agreement was ratified on October 6, 1903, by both countries. In it provision was made for financial and other specific relations between the United States and Cuba with respect to the Naval Base. On June 9, 1934, the original Treaty of Relations between the two countries, ratified on May 22, 1903, was superceded by a new Treaty of Relations. Article III of this treaty provided that "so long as the United States of America shall not abandon the Naval Station of Guantanamo or the two governments shall not agree to a modification of its present limits, the station shall continue to have the territorial area that it now has with the limits it has on the date of the signature of the present treaty." On January 6, 1959, the Revolutionary Government of Fidel Castro advised the United States that "We are pleased to advise that the Revolutionary Government has complete control of the Republic . . . and that all international commitments and agreements in force will be fulfilled." See *United States Naval Base: Guantanamo Bay, Cuba*, mimeographed statement of August 10, 1962, prepared under the direction of the Director, Politico-Military Policy Division, Office of the Chief of Naval Operations, United States Department of Defense (3d ed.), pp. 1–2.

10. See H. L. A. Hart, "Definition and Theory in Jurisprudence," 70 *L.Q.R.* 37–60 (1954).

11. See Hans Aufricht, "State Succession under the Law and Practice of the International Monetary Fund," 11 *I.C.L.Q.* 158–60 (1962).

12. The Federation of Mali, established under French administration on April 4, 1959, is a case in point. On June 20, 1960, it became independent, and, on August 20, 1960, the Republic of Senegal seceded from it. Senegal adopted a new constitution on August 25, 1960, and the Republic of Mali was proclaimed on September 22, 1960. See U.S. Department of State, *Profiles of Newly Independent States*, Geographic Bulletin No. 1 (Washington, D.C.: Government Printing Office, 1963), pp. 16–17.

13. For example, see S. H. Guha Roy, "Is the Law of Responsibility of States for Injuries to Aliens a Part of Universal International Law?" 55 *A.J.I.L.* 863–91 (1961); and R. P. Anand, "Role of the 'New' Asian-African Countries in the Present International Legal Order," 56 *A.J.I.L.* 383–406 (1962). Of interest in this connection also is an address by Francis Deak, entitled "Observations on International Law in Underdeveloped Areas," *Proceedings of the American Society of International Law* at its Fifty-Sixth Annual Meeting (Washington, D.C.: American Society of International Law, 1962), pp. 54–63.

14. See the section on "Treaties in the Laws of State Succession" in the author's *The Law of State Succession*, pp. 14–74. With the exception of treaties of alliances and guarantees (*Die Staaten-Succession*, pp. 136–38), Huber argued for universal succession to treaties. It is his view that all other treaties, personal and dispositive, pass over in the case of a state formed by separation from another, pre-existing state. Even in case of conquest, treaties are held by him to pass over (*ibid.*, pp. 150–54). As for the great normative agreements of the civilized nations, the term succession is held to be inappropriate because the rights and obligations of the international legal community automatically bind a new state entering that community (*ibid.*, p. 154). See also Huber's *Die Soziologischen Grundlagen des Völkerrechts* (2d ed.; Berlin: Verlag Dr. Walther Rothschild, 1928), particularly pp. 40–60. Even though

Huber does not specifically discuss state succession here, his general theory of international law, particularly as expressed in the section referred to above, provides the groundwork upon which his theory of state succession was formulated. The negative school of thought with respect to succession to treaties is represented by Arrigo Cavaglieri and Keith. In his "Effets juridiques des changements de souveraineté territoriales," 15 R.D.I.L.C., 3d series, 219–48 (1934), (as cited in Jenks, op. cit., p. 114, n. 1), Cavaglieri argues that all acceptances of treaty obligations of the predecessor by a successor state are voluntary, on grounds of equity, convenience, or political interest. In this manner a new legal relationship is said by him to have been established—it may be identical in content with the old legal relationship, but it is said to be different in legal character. In his *Theory of State Succession*, Keith expresses the basic thesis that no treaties pass to a conqueror or cessionary state, but that the latter's treaties are extended over the territory conquered or ceded. P. 17.

15. See Albert J. Esgain, "Military Servitudes and the New Nations," this *Yearbook*, pp. 42–95, passim.
16. See Jenks, op. cit., pp. 104–44, especially p. 142.
17. See Aufricht, op. cit., pp. 155 ff.
18. See ibid., pp. 163–64.
19. United Nations, *Status of Multilateral Conventions* (ST/LEG/3).
20. By notification received on October 29, 1952, by the United Nations, France extended the application of the Road Traffic Convention to the French Protectorates of Morocco and Tunisia, to all French Overseas Territories, and to Togoland and the Cameroons under French Mandate. *Ibid.*, pp. 11–47 (September 30, 1956). On November 7, 1956, the Government of Morocco deposited with the Secretary General a declaration "stipulating that Morocco assumes the obligations arising out of the ratification by France in respect of Morocco of this Convention and that Morocco considers itself a Party to the Convention." *Ibid.*, pp. 11–47 (September 30, 1957). Tunisia's name does not, however, appear on the list of ratifications and accessions.
21. Jenks, op. cit., p. 142.
22. *Treaty Establishing the European Economic Community* (signed in Rome, March 25, 1957), Part IV, Arts. 131–36. See also the *Implementing Convention Relating to the Association with the Community of the Overseas Countries and Territories* (signed in Rome, March 25, 1957). The two documents are to be found in a volume entitled *Treaty Establishing the European Economic Community, and Connected Documents* (London: H.M. Stationery Office, 1957).
23. 6 *Bulletin of the European Economic Community* (Brussels) 21 (February, 1963). See also U.N. Doc. E/CN.14/207.
24. Robert B. Stewart, *Treaty Relations of the British Commonwealth of Nations* (New York: The Macmillan Co., 1939), p. 341.
25. These agreements are: Malaya, Cmnd. 345, U.N.T.S., CCLXXXVII, 234; Nigeria, Cmnd. 1212; Cyprus, Cmnd. 1252; Sierra Leone, Cmnd. 1464; Iraq, Cmnd. 3797; Transjordan, Cmnd. 6916; Burma, Cmnd. 7360. For references for Jamaica and Trinidad and Tobago, see O'Connell, op. cit.
26. See *Philippson v. Imperial Airways, Ltd.* [1939] A.C. 332.
27. See Lord McNair, *The Law of Treaties* (Oxford: The Clarendon Press, 1961), p. 511. Article 34 of the Harvard Research Draft, "Research in International Law on Treaties," Supplement to 29 A.J.I.L. (1953) states, however,

Notes

that "a treaty may be denounced by a party only when such denunciation is provided for in the treaty or consented to by all other parties."

28. See United Nations Secretariat, *Summary of the Practice of the Secretary-General as Depositary of Multilateral Agreements*, prepared by the Treaty Section of the Office of Legal Affairs, ST/LEG/7, August 7, 1959, pp. 50–51. See also A/CN.150 (1962).

29. "In the case of the Convention on the Privileges and Immunities of the United Nations, adopted by the General Assembly on 13 February, 1946, and the Convention on the Privileges and Immunities of the Specialized Agencies, adopted by the General Assembly on 21 November 1947, the Secretary-General decided as a matter of principle that, in view of their nature, these Conventions should be regarded as applying to the territories for the international relations of which the acceding States are responsible; this, indeed, is in accordance with the practice of the States parties to the Convention." *Ibid.*, p. 47. As for Morocco, it acceded on March 18, 1957, to the Convention of February 13, 1946, on the Privileges and Immunities of the United Nations. *Ibid.*, p. 58.

30. See *ibid.*, pp. 47 ff.

31. See United Nations, *Status of Multilateral Conventions* (ST/LEG/3), pp. 1–5.

32. Continuity of law was provided for in the following cases; also provision was sometimes made for the disposal of litigation: India 10 & 11 Geo. 6, c. 30; Burma, 11 & 12 Geo. 6, c. 3; Ghana, 5 & 6 Eliz. 2, c. 6; S.I., 1957, No. 277; 8 & 9 Eliz. 2, c. 41; Cyprus, 8 & 9 Eliz. 2, c. 52; S.I. 1960, Nos. 1368, 1369; Nigeria, 8 & 9 Eliz. 2, c. 55; S.I. 1960, No. 1652; Malaya, 5 & 6 Eliz. 2, c. 60; S.I. 1957, No. 1533; Somaliland, S.I. 1960, No. 1060; Sierra Leone, 10 & 11 Eliz. 2, c. 16; S.I. 1961, No. 741; Kuwait, 1961, No. 1001; Cameroons, *Clunet*, vol. 88 (1961), p. 1108; Central African Rep., Congo, Chad, *ibid.*, p. 1141; Gabon, *ibid.*, p. 1145; Ivory Coast, Dahomey, Niger, and Upper Volta, *ibid.*, p. 1149. For accord between France and Central African Rep., see *ibid.*, Vol. 88 (1961), p. 567. France and India, *Annuaire français*, 1956, p. 708.

33. *Tunis-Morocco Nationality Decrees*, Permanent Court of International Justice, 1923. Advisory Opinion, No. 4, Series B, No. 4.

34. The author of this study has dealt with Indian-British treaty relations in his *The Law of State Succession*, pp. 47–48.

35. United Nations Secretariat, *Summary of the Practice of the Secretary-General as Depositary of Multilateral Agreements*, pp. 57–58.

36. "The Government of the Federation of Malaya notified the Secretary-General on 31 August 1957 that the Federation of Malaya considered itself bound by the Convention of 13 February 1946 on the Privileges and Immunities of the United Nations as of 'Merdeka Day' (31 August 1957) as a result of the Diplomatic Privileges Order, 1949, which formed part of the existing law of the Federation in operation immediately before 'Merdeka Day' and which was continued in force after 'Merdeka Day.' " *Ibid.*, p. 58.

37. See *Sultan of Johore v. Abubakar Junku Aris Bendahar* [1952], A.C. 318.

38. See O'Connell, *op. cit.*, p. 103.

39. Int. L. Rep. (1956), pp. 81, 96, 106, 296, 299, 342, 659, 680, 801.

40. See O'Connell, *op. cit.*, pp. 116–19.

41. In *United States v. Perchman*, Supreme Court of the United States,

1833, 7 Pet. 51, 8 L. Ed. 604, Marshall, C.J. states that, with a change in sovereignty, "The people change their allegiance; their relations to their ancient sovereign is dissolved; but their relations to each other, and their rights to property, remain undisturbed."

42. See *Settlers of German Origin in Territory Ceded by Germany to Poland*, P.C.I.J., ser. B, no. 6, p. 6, and *Certain German Interests in Polish Upper Silesia*, P.C.I.J., ser. A, no. 7.

43. See O'Connell, *op. cit.*, p. 87

44. See *ibid.*, p. 201. See also Coleman Phillipson, *Termination of War and Treaties of Peace* (London: T. F. Unwin, 1961), p. 331; Keith, *op. cit.*, pp. 74–77; Georg Schwarzenberger, *International Law* (2d ed.; London: Stevens & Sons, 1949), I, 86; Cecil J. B. Hurst, "State Succession in Matters of Tort," 5 B.Y.I.L. 163–78 (1924); and Ernst Feilchenfeld, *Public Debts and State Succession* (New York: The Macmillan Co., 1931), pp. 689 ff.

45. *Robert E. Brown Claim*, American-British Pecuniary Claims Arbitration, Nielsen Rep. 187 (1923).

46. See p. 87, n. 43.

47. See O'Connell, *op. cit.*, pp. 212–13, n. 3.

48. *Kahlan v. Pakistan Federation* 2 K.B. 1003 [1951].

49. Diplomatic Immunities (Commonwealth Countries and Republic of Ireland) Act, 1952, 15 & 16 Geo. VI & I Eliz. II, c. 18.

50. G. P. Barton, "Foreign Armed Forces: Qualified Jurisdictional Immunity," 31 B.Y.I.L. 341 (1954).

51. See Sir Ivor Jennings, *The British Commonwealth of Nations* (London: Hutchinson University Library, 1958), pp. 155–56. See also D. P. O'Connell, "State Succession and Problems of Treaty Interpretation," 58 A.J.I.L. 41–61 (1964).

52. See R. Y. Jennings, "The Commonwealth and International Law," 30 B.Y.I.L. 335 (1953).

53. 11 & 12 Geo. VI, c. 56.

54. See Part I, Sec. III, Par. 1, of the British Nationality Act of 1948 (11 & 12 Geo. VI, c. 56) as quoted in Clive Parry, *British Nationality:* Including *Citizenship of the United Kingdom and Colonies and the Status of Aliens* (London: Stevens & Sons Ltd., 1951), p. 182. See also *ibid.*, pp. 81–87.

55. See *Bickness v. Brosnan* [1953] 2 Q.B. 77 and *Ullach v. Black* [1955] Crim. L.R. 380.

56. See Part I, Sec. III, Par. 2, of the British Nationality Act of 1948 (11 & 12 Geo. VI, c. 56) as quoted in Parry, *op. cit.*, p. 182.

57. Part II, Sec. XIII, Par. 1, of the British Nationality Act of 1948 as quoted in Parry, *op. cit.*, p. 188.

58. See *ibid.*, pp. 10–11, 94–97, 153–55.

59. See the *Nottebohm Case* (*Liechtenstein v. Guatemala*), I.C.J. Rep. 1955, p. 4.

60. *Ibid.*

Chapter 2. "Military Servitudes and the New Nations"
by Albert J. Esgain

1. See generally J. J. G. Syatauw, *Some Newly Established Asian States and the Development of International Law* (The Hague: Martinus Nijhoff, 1960);

and D. P. O'Connell, "Independence and Problems of State Succession," this *Yearbook*, pp. 7–41. See also the appendix to W. V. O'Brien and U. H. Goebel, "United States Recognition Policy Toward the New Nations," this *Yearbook*, p. 224.

2. "In direct violation of Security Council proceedings, the Soviet Union dispatched to the Congo hundreds of so-called technicians. . . . "Meanwhile, nearly two dozen Soviet transport aircraft and 100 Soviet trucks appeared in the Congo—not to participate in the U.N. program . . . but to promote strife and bloodshed. . . ." Statement of United States Representative James J. Wadsworth during the debate on the Congo in the fourth emergency special session of the U.N. General Assembly, September 17–20, 43 *Dep't. of State Bulletin* 585 (1960). The Soviet Union attempted in every conceivable way to "sabotage the U.N. operations in the Congo . . . hoping that the U.N. effort would fail so that it might move to take over an inexperienced Government." Address by Francis Wilcox, Assistant United States Secretary for International Organizational Affairs before the American Association for the U.N. at New York on September 18, 1960, *ibid.*, p. 510. "Despite United Nations resolutions to the contrary, the Soviet Union was pouring personnel, materials, and political agents into the Congo to establish what the Communists hoped would be a foothold in the heart of Africa. Secretary General Dag Hammarskjold challenged the Russians because . . . each Russian Ilyushin aircraft was bringing in political agents. . . ." Statement of Secretary of State Dean Rusk before the Subcommittee on African Affairs, Senate Foreign Relations Committee on January 18, 1962, 46 *Dep't. of State Bulletin* 217 (1962). The Belgians maintained and increased their troop strength in the Congo during the entire period of disorder there. After an on-the-spot investigation, the U.N. Conciliation Commission appointed by the U.N. Advisory Committee on the Congo to study the situation "deplored the continued presence in various parts of the Congo of large numbers of Belgian and other foreign military personnel . . . and mercenaries" and recommended that "immediate steps . . . be undertaken to remove forthwith all such personnel not under United Nations command from the territory of the Republic of the Congo." U.S. Department of State publication No. 7413, *U.S. Participation in the U.N.*, Report by the President to the Congress for the year 1961 (Washington, D.C.: Government Printing Office, 1962), pp. 56–61.

As of September 14, 1962, it was estimated that Russia had introduced as many as 4,000 military personnel in Cuba to train Cuban troops in the use and maintenance of military weapons that Russia had supplied to Cuba. (See the *New York Times*, September 14, 1962, Sec. C, p. 13, col. 2; and the transcript of President Kennedy's news conference in Washington on foreign and domestic matters on September 13, 1962, *ibid.*, p. 12.) Recent reports state that Moscow controls Cuba just as effectively as it does Bulgaria. A recent report observes that although Castro may not appear to have lost any of his authority it is only "a surface appearance." The Reds man many of the weapons with which they have provided Cuba, and "When Castro's presence is no longer necessary . . ." he will be discarded and Cuba will be "managed by men responsible to Moscow." (The *Washington Star*, September 16, 1962, Sec. A, p. 1, cols. 5, 6, and p. 8, col. 6.)

The Russia that urged Indonesia to invade West New Guinea has introduced into Indonesia, which had become a "virtual appendage of the Soviet bloc, even if an unwilling one," great numbers of technicians and military personnel to instruct and train the Indonesian armed forces in the use of the military equipment and armament, mostly aircraft and naval vessels, with which Russia had provided Indonesia. See the *New York Times*, January 14, 1962; April 2, 1962; May 2, 1962; May 8, 1962; June 4, 1962.

3. See, for example, Annex III (Accord of Cooperation on Matters of Defense) of the Accords between France and the Mali Federation of 1960, under which the Mali Federation "ceded" to France the strategic base of Cap-Vert (Dakar-Thies), the bases of St. Louis and Kati, and other air bases of Bamako, Gao, and Tessalit (Art. 1) and committed itself to respect the "existing servitude in favor of France" for the utilization of the bases (Art. 9) (*Journal officiel de la communauté*, August 15, 1960, No. 8, pp. 74–75). Under Annex III of the Accords between France and the Malagasy Republic of 1960, Malagasy grants to France the free use of the strategic base of Diego Suarez and commits itself to "respect the existing servitudes" for the utilization of the Diego Suarez base and other French military installations and to permit modifications in these "servitudes" in case of technical necessity. At Appendix 2, Annex III, it is specified that the zones placed under "defense servitudes" include Diego Suarez extending to the district of Anivorano–North and that other "servitudes" may be acquired for defense purposes (*ibid.*, pp. 87–88). The provisions of the Accords on Mutual Assistance and Facilities in Common Defense between France, the Republic of Chad, the Central African Republic, the Republic of the Congo, and the Republic of Gabon concluded in 1960 specify that France will continue to ensure the military missions assigned to it under existing rules and procedures (not specified) and that the contracting parties will assign to France the installations, barracks, buildings, airfields, and lands being used for defense purposes on the date of the signature of the agreement. Under the Quadrapartite Accords between France, the Central African Republic, the Republic of the Congo, and the Republic of Chad, the latter republics grant to France bases for the defense of the French Community. (*Journal officiel de la République française*, November, 1960, No. 60–277S, pp. 7826, 7840, 7860, 7882; and *Journal officiel de la communauté*, August 15, 1960, No. 8, pp. 108–15).

4. See F. A. Váli, *Servitudes of International Law* (2d ed.; New York: Frederick A. Praeger, 1958); D. P. O'Connell, *The Law of State Succession* (Cambridge: Cambridge University Press, 1956), pp. 51–59; Vladimir M. Shurshalov, *Osnovye Voroposy Teorii Mezhdunarodnogs Dogovora (Basic Questions of the Theory of International Treaties* (Moscow: Academy of Sciences of the U.S.S.R., 1959), Secs. 276–78.

5. *Infra*, pp. 72–82.

6. Váli, *op. cit.*, pp. 23–26, 48–49, 53, 309, 313–15, 319–30.

7. L. Oppenheim, *International Law, A Treatise*, ed. H. Lauterpacht (8th ed.; New York: Longmans, Green & Co., 1955) I, 536. Clauce Mercier, *Les Servitudes internationales* (Lausanne: F. Roth & Co., 1939), p. 27, defines an international servitude as "un droit réel d'usage déterminé sur un territoire étranger." Paul Pradier-Fodéré, *Traité de droit international public, européen et américain, suivant les progrès de la science et de la pratique contemporaire* (Paris: G. Pedone-Lauriel, 1885–1906), II, 397, defines an international servitude as a treaty restriction perpetually limiting the territorial sovereignty of states in favor of other states, as constituting a permanent real right.

8. See T. O. Thomas, *The Right of Passage over Indian Territory* (2d ed.; Leiden: A. W. Sythoff, 1959), p. 37, who points out that, in the Case Concerning Rights of Passage over Indian Territory (*International Court of Justice Reports*, 1957, p. 125), the Government of Portugal stated that its claim before the court was in no way based on the theory of international servitudes because the theory lacked coherence, and it was impossible for even the jurists to agree on the very *definition* of international servitudes, or on what constitutes their *characteristic features*, or on what makes it possible to distinguish them from other obligations to which a state may be subject in the exercise of its territorial jurisdiction, and, because an international servitude would imply a *dismemberment of territorial sovereignty*.

9. Váli, *op. cit.*, p. 42; Pasquale Fiore, *International Law Codified*, trans. E. Borchard (5th ed.; New York: Baker, Voorhis & Co., 1918), p. 435.

10. Hersch Lauterpacht, *Private Law Sources and Analogies of International Law* (London: Longmans, Green & Co., 1927), pp. 121-22, 124; A. D. McNair, *The Law of Treaties* (Oxford: The Clarendon Press, 1938), pp. 389, 444, 469, 538-39; D. P. O'Connell, *State Succession*, pp. 48-63, 276; Oppenheim, *op. cit.*, I, 541, 543; H. D. Reid, *International Servitudes in Law and Practice* (Chicago: University of Chicago Press, 1932), pp. xxii, 19-20, 25; Shurshalov, *op. cit.*, Secs. 276-78; Váli, *op. cit.*, pp. 25-29, 43-49, 69, 309; John Westlake, *International Law* (Cambridge: Cambridge University Press, 1904), pp. 60-61, 294-95; McNair, "So-Called State Servitudes, 6 B.Y.I.L. 126 (1925); O'Connell, "A Reconsideration of the Doctrine of International Servitudes," 30 *Canadian L.R.* 809-10, 812, 817-18 (1952); Baron Lage de Staël-Holstein, "La Doctrine des servitudes internationales et son application en Scandinavie," 3 R.D.I.L.C., 3ième série, 431, 458 (1922). O'Connell, *State Succession*, p. 809, lists authors who deny the existence of international servitudes. To this list may be added J. O. Soderhjelm, *Démilitarisation et neutralisation des îles d'Aland en 1856 et 1921* (Helsinki, 1928), p. 37; Mercier, *op. cit.*, pp. 107-15; Karl V. Fricker, *Gebiet und Gebietshoheit mit einem Anhang: vom Staatsgebiet* (Tübingen: H. Laupp, 1901), p. 74; Jean Perrinjaquet, *Des Cessions temporaires de territoires* (Paris: V. Giard et F. Brière, 1904), p. 223; Arrigo Cavaglieri, *La Dottrina della successione di stato a stato* (Pisa: Archivio Giuridico, 1910), p. 101; Franz von Liszt, *Das Völkerrecht systematisch dargestellt*, ed. Max Fleischman (12th ed.; Berlin: J. Springer, 1925), pp. 237-38; Theodor Niemeyer, *Völkerrecht* (Berlin: W. de Gruyter, 1923), p. 104; Erik Castrén, "Aspects récents de la succession d'états," 78 Hague, *Recueil*, 438-39, 448-51 (1951).

11. O'Connell, *State Succession*, states (p. 63) that the doctrine of "real rights is ... a potential instrument for compelling a State to acknowledge the contractual relations of its predecessor when justice demands it." See Lauterpacht, *Analogies*, p. 124; Oppenheim, *op. cit.*, I, 537; Reid, *op. cit.*, pp. xxi, 51, 203, 207-10; O'Connell, "A Reconsideration of the Doctrine of International Servitudes," *State Succession*, p. 810. But see P. B. Potter, "The Doctrine of Servitudes in International Law," 9 A.J.I.L. 628-30 (1915), who states that a right granted under certain conditions becomes odious in a situation where the same right would not be granted anew and where continuous performance itself renders the obligation obnoxious and burdensome. The inheritance of relationships of servitude by successive rulers—of obligations they have not contracted and from which they perhaps receive no benefit—

further aggravates the situation. He questions whether servitudes characterized by these traits of "reality and negativity," can survive in an age of equality and independence.

12. Jan de Louter, *Le Droit international public positif* (Oxford: Oxford University Press, 1920), I, 336-39; Arthur B. Keith, *The Theory of State Succession with Special Reference to English and Colonial Law* (London: Waterlow & Sons, 1907), p. 22; Mercier, *op. cit.*, pp. 117-18; Niemeyer, *op. cit.*, p. 104; Ernest Nys, *Le Droit international* (2d ed.; Brussels: M. Weissenbruch, 1912), II, 271; G. Crusen, "Les Servitudes internationales," 22 Hague, *Recueil*, 2ième série, 8, 31 (1928).

13. For purposes of this study, a personal right is one established by an agreement, either express or implied, that is available only against determinate states. It terminates, therefore, whenever the obligor or obligee ceases to exist. A "real" or absolute right is a right in land, established by an agreement, either express or implied, that is available against any state. It is a perpetual right that, being attached to the land itself, binds third states that acquire the land by purchase, descent, or otherwise.

14. See *supra*, note 12.

15. It is with respect to this particular category of international relationships that the term "servitude" is believed to have made its first appearance. Staël-Holstein, *op. cit.*, p. 459, cites Article 4 of the Treaty of Nöteborg of 1323 as an ancient precedent to a negative military servitude by which no fortifications were to be built on either side of the frontier in "Carélie." He cites (p. 436), however, a treaty concluded at Stettin in 1570 concerned with fishing rights and characterized as a "servitude" as the oldest in the history of international servitudes.

16. For a fairly complete list of writers who are partisans of the doctrine of international servitudes, see Crusen, *op. cit.*, p. 21. To this list should be added the names of Reid, *op. cit.*, Váli, *op. cit.*, and O'Connell, *State Succession*.

17. Those about which the signatories are, as of the time of signature, all fully independent and free to exercise an unrestrained will.

18. Those that are the result of duress or coercion—including treaties of peace imposing punitive terms upon a vanquished state.

19. Servitudes that permit actual interference with, or activity upon, the servient land, e.g., maintenance of a garrison.

20. Servitudes that permit no activity upon the servient land but that require the servient state to abstain from certain activity upon its land, e.g., not to erect fortifications.

21. Váli, *op. cit.*, p. 329.

22. Fernand de Visscher, "La Question des îles d'Aland," 2 *R.D.I.L.C.*, 3ième série, 257-59 (1921).

23. See Lauterpacht, *Analogies*, pp. 123-24.

24. See *supra*, note 16.

25. Reid, *op. cit.*, p. 25. As to the *North Atlantic Fisheries* case (*The Hague Court Reports*, ed. J. B. Scott, [New York: Oxford University Press, 1916], pp. 141-225), Reid states: "In spite of the ambiguity of the Hague award, the American fishery right remains intrinsically the most important of all existing international servitudes of the distributive type." P. 98. The tribunal in this case in fact rejected the doctrine of international servitudes *in casu*.

Notes

Reid, in effect, maintains that the whole doctrine of private-law servitudes may be applied to international relations *mutatis mutandis*.

26. Charles Calvo, *Le Droit international théorique et pratique* (5th ed.; Paris: A. Rousseau, 1896), Vol. III, Sec. 1583; Crusen, *op. cit.*, pp. 22, 55-64; Keith, *op. cit.*, pp. 23-24; W. F. Hall, *A Treatise on International Law*, ed. A. P. Higgins (Oxford: The Clarendon Press, 1924), p. 116; Oppenheim, *op. cit.*, I, 543, 938-42; Lauterpacht, *op. cit.*, pp. 167-75; A. D. McNair, "The Functions and Differing Legal Character of Treaties," *B.Y.I.L.*, 11-112 (1930); Potter, "The Doctrine of Servitudes in International Law," *op. cit.*, pp. 639-40; George G. Wilson, *Handbook of International Law* (2d ed.; St. Paul, Minn.: West Publishing Co., 1927), Sec. 87 (g); A. Rivier, *Principes du droit des gens* (Paris: A. Rousseau, 1896), I, p. 73; O'Connell, "Independence and Problems of State Succession," this Yearbook, p. 14; Wesley L. Gould, *An Introduction to International Law* (New York: Harper & Bros., 1957), pp. 339-45; Georg Schwarzenberger, *A Manual of International Law* (4th ed.; London: Stevens, 1960), pp. 158-59.

27. Reid, *op. cit.*, p. 25. Lauterpacht (*Analogies*, pp. 121-22) states: "It cannot be denied that there are international law relationships which present an analogy to praedial servitudes of the Roman law or to easements of the common law almost amounting to identity, namely, those relationships in which a part or the whole of the territory of one State is made to serve the *economic* needs of another. There exists in such cases not only a dominant tenement (*praedium dominans*) and a 'servient tenement' (*praedium serviens*) but also the possibility of most of the formal requirements of the private law servitudes being fulfilled," [italics added]. He continues: "It is submitted that ... relationships of this kind resemble closely servitudes in private law, and that it is convenient to classify them as such also in international law. Of course the classification as servitudes carries with it all the implications of a real right; [survives a change of sovereignty not only over the servient, but also over the dominant territory] the term itself would otherwise serve no useful purpose and would only encourage a laxity of language which international law has special reason to avoid. ..."

28. De Louter, *op. cit.*, p. 339, says: "Dans le droit international ... il n'y a absolument aucune place pour les droits réels ... les servitudes ne trouvent plus de place dans le droit international ... elles y ont introduit un élément de nuisable confusion et la théorie fera bien de suivre la pratique en renonçant à ce vestige de la minorité séculaire du droit international sous la tutelle gênante du droit romain. ..." Perrinjaquet, *op. cit.*, p. 223, inquiries: "Pourquoi transporter du droit de la propriété à celui de la souveraineté des mots et des idées uniquement applicables à la propriété et qui ne peuvent amener qu'obscurité, confusion et erreur?"

29. Váli, *op. cit.*
30. *Ibid.*, p. vii.
31. *Ibid.*, pp. 311-12, 315.
32. *Ibid.*, pp. 20, 49, 53.
33. *Ibid.*, pp. 23, 313-14.
34. *Ibid.*, pp. 319-20.
35. *Ibid.*, p. 320.
36. *Ibid.*, pp. 326-27.
37. *Ibid.*

38. Ibid., p. 323.
39. Ibid., p. 322.
40. Ibid., p. 324.
41. Ibid.
42. Crusen, op. cit., p. 9.
43. Mercier, op. cit., p. 19, states that "Il est évident que l'expression de servitude internationale doit se justifier, sinon par une similitude, du moins par une analogie avec la servitude du droit privé. Autrement dit, il faut que cette expression serve à désigner une catégorie de droit qui occupe, dans le droit des gens, une situation analogue à celle occuppée par les servitudes en droit privé." But see Váli, op. cit., pp. 60–61.
44. In primitive times, limitations on ownership or enjoyment of property were unknown. Restricted control—in the form, for example, of usufruct—that would appear to be necessary was the product of an evolution that lasted for centuries. The first concession necessitated by communal life was the recognition of contractual stipulations pursuant to which one was permitted to assume an obligation to do something for another. Relations of persons to things constituting rights and obligations *valent erga omnes*, however, were neither recognized nor protected until the classical period of Roman law. This was because the early Romans deemed "real" rights to be incompatible with the notions and economic functions of property and, as such, contrary to the interests of the state. Encumbered property was considered to be a source of potential dispute and friction.
45. W. W. Buckland, *A Manual of Roman Private Law* (2d ed.; Cambridge: Cambridge University Press, 1953), p. 153; R. Sohm, *Institutes of Roman Law*, trans. J. C. Ledlie (3d ed.; Oxford: The Clarendon Press, 1907), pp. 338–39; John H. Roby, *Roman Private Law* (Cambridge: Cambridge University Press, 1902), p. 484.
46. Buckland, *Manual*, pp. 153, 155; Sohm, op. cit., pp. 338–39; Roby, op. cit., p. 502.
47. W. W. Buckland, *Textbook on Roman Law* (2d ed.; Cambridge: Cambridge University Press, 1950), pp. 259, 261; Sohm, op. cit., pp. 338–39.
48. Buckland, *Manual*, pp. 153–54; Buckland, *Textbook on Roman Law*, pp. 259, 261; Sohm, op. cit., pp. 339, 342; Roby, op. cit., p. 500. As to *praedial* servitudes generally, see John B. Moyle, *Imperatoris Justiniani Institutiones* (5th ed.; Oxford: The Clarendon Press, 1912), pp. 212–21.
49. A *praedial* servitude had to relate to, and be for the benefit of, a dominant tenement only. Thus, one who had a right to draw water, *acquaehaustus*, could not sell it. (Buckland, *Manual*, p. 156; Roby, op. cit., p. 500.) Furthermore, such a servitude was indivisible. It attached to the *whole praedium* and could not be lost or acquired *pro parte* (Buckland, *Manual*, p. 156; Roby, op. cit., p. 502.)
50. Buckland, *Manual*, pp. 155, 157; Sohm, op. cit., p. 343; Roby, op. cit., p. 502.
51. Buckland, *Manual*, pp. 159–60; Sohm, op. cit., pp. 345–46.
52. The interdict forced the interferor to dispute the servitude by legal process. A "real" action, the *actio confessoria*, for the recovery of a servitude was also available, and an action called the *actio negatoria* was available to one who denied the existence of a servitude on his land. See Buckland, *Manual*, p. 161; Sohm, op. cit., pp. 346–48; and Roby, op. cit., pp. 503–4. The following

rules also applied to *praedial* servitudes: A person could not have a servitude over his own property (Buckland, *Manual*, p. 154); consistent with the advantages that were to be obtained, the rights that a servitude accorded had to be utilized so that they would interfere as little as possible with the exploitation of the servient land (the obligation of *civiliter uti*), and there could be no servitude that merely inconvenienced the servient holder and was of no real benefit to the dominant tenement. Since the servitude was an advantage to the tenement, rather than to the owner thereof personally, there could exist no servitude on matters such as picking flowers on the land, since such a right would be just as advantageous to any other person as it would be to the owner of the dominant tenement. Additionally, the *praedia* had to be close together, for otherwise the servitude could not be said to be of any advantage to the *praedium* as such.

53. Buckland, *Manual*, p. 110; Sohm, *op. cit.*, p. 339; Roby, *op. cit.*, p. 490.

54. The "real" servitude of Roman Law was incorporated with little or no change into the legal systems of most modern European states and adopted into the English common law under the terminology of "easements" or "covenants running with the land." See Reid, *op. cit.*, pp. 7–8. Crusen, *op. cit.*, p. 13, states that under German law a servient tenement may assume a positive obligation, *Reallast*, with respect to the dominant tenement, contrary to the rule of *servitus in faciendo consistere non potest* of Roman law, but that otherwise the German law of real servitudes corresponds to that of the Roman law in all fundamental respects. French law recognizes the *servitude d'utilité publique*, which is a burden upon particular land for the benefit of other land. This burden cannot be terminated by agreement or prescription. Generally, these apply to activities of public concern, such as military posts and communication facilities (see Reid, *op. cit.*, pp. 7–8).

55. Immanuel Clauss, *Die Lehre von den Staatsdienstbarkeiten* (Tübingen: H. Laupp, 1894), p. 37.

56. Ernest Nys, "Les Prétendues servitudes internationales," 13 *R.D.I.L.C.*, 2ième série, 318 (1911).

57. For example Württemberg, composed of several thousand enclaves, was obliged to obtain a right of passage for its citizens to go from one to another.

58. Crusen, *op. cit.*, p. 14. Baldus de Ubaldes (1323–1400) appears to have been the first to utilize the notion of servitude to characterize certain relationships of public law. He referred to these relationships as "quasi-servitudes" or having "a semblance of servitudes" (*quasi-servitudines sive ac similitudine servitudinum*). Zaius (1461–1535), the first to use the term German servitudes (*servitudines Germanorum*) in speaking of fishing and pasturing rights, said they were without doubt servitudes. See *ibid.*, p. 15.

59. The relations among the members of the German confederation during the eighteenth century were in some respects more analogous to international relations than to internal relations of an empire or confederation. German jurists dealt for all practical purposes with matters not substantially different from those of an international character, and it was only natural for them to apply the name and doctrine of "*servitus juris publici*" to corresponding international relationships.

60. Some authors, conscious of the lack of identity between strictly private servitudes and those pertaining to public bodies, referred to the latter as "splen-

dida servitus," "servitute innominatae," or as "nobiliorum servitutum species." See Crusen, *op. cit.*, p. 15. It is stated that Vitriarius was the first to resort to the technical term "servitus juris publici." See *Institutiones Juris Publici* (1686), and Clauss, *op. cit.*, p. 48.

61. See Elwert, *De Servitutibus sive Juribus in Aliorum Territorio Quaesitis* (1674), and Clauss, *op. cit.*, p. 51.

62. Only one contemporary writer, Joachim Erdtmann Schmidt, took strenuous objection to the reception of the principles of servitudes in public law. In a monograph published in 1764 under the title *"De servitutibus juris publici falso nomine sic appellatis,"* he stated that the juridical relations that had been recognized as servitudes created only personal obligations. Schmidt's contemporaries were not sufficiently advanced to comprehend his arguments, and it was not until a century later that his tenets were espoused and pressed. See Crusen, *op. cit.*, p. 17.

63. Christian Wolf, a German jurist, appears to have been the first to be concerned with international servitudes and to apply to them by analogy the principles of the private-law servitudes. His exposition (*Jus Gentium Naturale*, 1749) is a source from which jurists have drawn theories and principles concerning international servitudes. See Crusen, *op. cit.*, p. 19. The fundamental exposition of the doctrine, however, was to rest with later theorists such as Von Martens (*Primae linae iuris gentium europaeensis practici* [1785]) and subsequent "classical" authors of the nineteenth and twentieth centuries, such as Heffter, Klüber, Bluntschli, Vattel, Fiore, Pradier-Fodéré, Wheaton, Westlake, Rivier, Calvo, and Oppenheim.

64. An analogy presupposes a structural similarity between matters or activities that are parallel. See Reid (*op. cit.*, p. 24), who states: "Only if the term is ... restricted to a class of rights closely analogous to the *praedial* servitudes of Roman law can its use in international law be clearly justified."

65. See McNair, "So-Called State Servitudes," p. 126; Fricker *op. cit.*, pp. 9–12, 68–74; Nys, *op. cit.*, pp. 314–23, and R.D.I.L.C., 2ième série, 118–25 (1905); Váli, *op. cit.*, pp. 314–23; von Liszt, *op. cit.*, pp. 237–38; F. Despagnet, *Cours de droit international public*, ed. Charles de Boeck (4th ed.; Paris: L. Larose et L. Tenin, 1910), p. 245; Lauterpacht, *Analogies*, p. 105. De Visscher (*op. cit.*, p. 251) expresses the opinion that the conflict over the existence of servitudes is a quarrel over words that resolves itself into a question of ascertaining whether the analogies to servitudes of private law are sufficient to justify the use of the term in international law when it belongs to the language of private law. Niemeyer (*op. cit.*, p. 104) considers the doctrine of international servitudes innocuous only if it is realized that the sole point of resemblance to private-law servitudes is that they create a territorial restriction upon the sovereignty of a state, and if it is remembered that they usually do not create rights *in rem*.

66. Lauterpacht, *Analogies*, pp. 123–24.
67. Váli, *op. cit.*, pp. 53, 59–60.
68. *Ibid.*, p. 43.
69. *Ibid.*, p. 44.
70. *Ibid.*, p. 47.
71. *Ibid.*, p. 53.
72. *Ibid.*, pp. 48–49.
73. *Ibid.*, p. 319.

Notes 267

74. On this basis, international servitudes could not be recognized because of the nonexistence of the object, property wholly owned by the state, to which a servitude could attach. There are three theories on the legal nature of territorial sovereignty. The object theory considers territory as an object of a state's right. This permits the relation of the state to its territory to be considered as analogous to ownership in private law. The space theory that considers territory as an element of a state, but not as an object of its right, permits no analogy to private-law ownership, since the state then rules within, but not over, the territory. The competence theory considers territorial sovereignty as a sum of competencies allocated to persons of international law. See Lauterpacht, *Analogies*, pp. 92–96; Váli, *op. cit.*, pp. 6–15; Nys, *op. cit.*, p. 121; Fricker, *op. cit.*, pp. 68–74; von Liszt, *op. cit.*, pp. 237–38.

75. Váli, *op. cit.*, pp. 59–60; McNair, "So-Called State Servitudes," pp. 121–22. Although there is merit to the argument that no analogy between international servitudes and those of private law is possible because of a lack of *dominium* in states, it is not entirely accurate for states who own public lands and can dispose, encumber, or utilize them as can any other owner. In recent years, many treaties have been concluded that grant foreign forces many military privileges of a personal nature (e.g., the right to station a garrison, the use of forts) that have for their situs public lands of the grantor. In these instances, states would have not only competence within their territory, but *dominium*, as well, over certain portions of it.

76. McNair, *ibid.*, p. 122.

77. There is neither authority in international law, nor an enforcement agency to which resort may be had to prevent such acquisition. Under general international law, conquest is a legal act, a legitimate means of changing international rights—it is the consequence of the use of force permitted by international law. See Hersch Lauterpacht, *Recognition in International Law* (Cambridge: Cambridge University Press, 1948), on the question of nonrecognition of unlawfully acquired titles. See also S. L. Cohn, "Ex Injuria Jus Non Oritur: A Principle Misapplied," 3 *Santa Clara Lawyer* 23 (1963).

78. Germany's acquisition of Austria in 1938; Italy's acquisition of Ethiopia in 1936; and the absorption of Estonia, Latvia, and Lithuania by Russia in 1940. See Cohn, *ibid.*

79. Oppenheim, *op. cit.*, I, 891. He states (p. 892) that insofar as war is prohibited by the Charter of the United Nations and the General Treaty for the Renunciation of War, a state resorting to war contrary to its obligations under these instruments must be considered as having used force in a manner prohibited by law. "Accordingly, duress in such cases must, it is submitted, be regarded as vitiating the treaty."

80. See Lauterpacht, *Analogies*, pp. 95–96. The practice of states as to military servitudes is discussed on page 48 ff.

81. Restrictions upon the territorial supremacy of a state that are not attached to the land itself cannot be classed as servitudes. Thus, restrictions not to maintain military forces imposed by treaty are not servitudes, for they do not make the territory of the restricted state serve the interests of another. For the same reason, the neutralization of an entire state does not create a military servitude. See Potter, *op. cit.*, p. 628; Oppenheim, *op. cit.*, I, 538–39, 540, *n.* 2; Reid, *op. cit.*, pp. 22–24; E. von Ullmann, *Völkerrecht* (2d ed.; Tübingen: J. C. B. Mohr, 1908), Sec. 99; cf. Clauss, *op cit.*, p. 167. Crusen, *op. cit.*, states

(p. 23) that "capitulations" whereby Occidental powers acquired the right to exercise jurisdiction over their nationals in Turkey and the Orient are not international servitudes, because they conferred no "real" rights. Again, the concessions granted to European states by China in the latter part of the nineteenth and the first part of the twentieth centuries, as well as other lease arrangements between modern states, cannot be classed as servitudes, for they are limited in duration and thus could not establish "real" rights. See Mercier, *op. cit.*, p. 105; Reid, *op. cit.*, pp. 23–24, 110–11. But see Wilson, *op. cit.*, Sec. 57, pp. 149–51; Pradier-Fodéré, *op. cit.*, II, Sec. 1038. For an apparent self-contradiction to statements that state servitudes are perpetual and must be concerned with the territory itself, see Oppenheim, *op. cit.*, I, 536, 538, 540, *n.* 1, and 541, *n.* 1.

82. The states concerned must possess full sovereignty over the territories affected. See Reid, *op. cit.*, pp. 14–15; Clauss, *op. cit.*, p. 204. Rights granted by a state to foreign nationals and corporations are concessions, and cannot constitute, or be considered as, servitudes. See Oppenheim, *op. cit.*, I, 538. It is said that servitudes, other than military servitudes, may arise from prescription. See in this connection A. W. Heffter, *Das europäische Völkerrecht der Gegenwart auf den bisherigen Grundlagen*, ed. F. H. Geffcken (8th ed.; Berlin: H. W. Müller, 1888), p. 105; J. C. Bluntschli, *Droit international codifié*, trans. C. Lardy (5th ed.; Paris: Guillaumin et Cie., 1895), Sec. 354, p. 200. Some writers assert the existence of "natural" servitudes. It is generally agreed that such servitudes are properly to be considered as general restrictions upon territorial supremacy that accrue to all states alike, not from treaty but under the rules of international law itself. Oppenheim, (*op. cit.*, I, 54–55) is of the opinion that: "The reason for separating international servitudes from other legal relations is their territorial 'real' character. As general restrictions can never be 'real' in character as every State is bound to recognize them, there is neither ground for nor necessity for separating them from other restrictions of a general nature." Under the Roman law, a servitude could never be "natural"; it was always founded on a contract or prescription. See Hall, *op. cit.*, Sec. 42; Calvo, *op. cit.*, III, Sec. 1583; Oppenheim, *op. cit.* I, 536; Wilson, *op. cit.*, Sec. 68b; Váli, *op. cit.*, pp. 16–19, 54–55.

83. McNair, *The Law of Treaties*, pp. 309–18; Oppenheim, *op. cit.*, I, 925–26; P.C.I.J., Series A, No. 7, pp. 27–29.

84. Oppenheim, *op. cit.*, I, 926–27. The author (p. 927), referring to the Hay-Pauncefote Treaty between the United States and Great Britain of 1901, and the Hay-Bunau-Varilla Treaty between the United States and Panama concerning the Panama Canal, and the treaty between Argentina and Chile concerning the Straits of Magellan, states that the contracting parties may alter these treaties "provided the latter [third states] have not in the meantime acquired legal rights through the unanimous consent of all concerned."

85. McNair, "So-Called State Servitudes," pp. 122–23.

86. Ronald F. Roxburgh, *International Conventions and Third States* (New York: Longmans, Green & Co., 1917), pp. 51–60. Roxburgh confines his remarks to treaties falling within McNair's first classification. McNair ("So-Called State Servitudes," p. 123) believes the remark to be applicable as well to his second class. Roxburgh (*op. cit.*, p. 107), however, is of the opinion that a servitude cannot be established that vests the ownership of it in a state that is not a party to the treaty. In this connection, see *Off. J.* Special Supple-

ment No. 3, pp. 17–19 (October, 1920), concerning the fortification of the Aaland Islands. But see P.C.I.J., Series A/B, No. 46, p. 147, in the case of the *Free Zones of Upper Savoy and the District of Gex*.

87. Roxburgh, *op. cit.*, pp. 51–60, 80–82. But see Keith, *op. cit.*, pp. 20–25; Oppenheim (*op. cit.*, I, p. 927, n. 2) is of the opinion that treaties intended to establish an international regime or settlement "would seem to be a case of unanimous implied consent."

88. Note in this respect the unilateral denunciation on November 14, 1936, by Germany of Arts. 380–86 of the Treaty of Versailles, whereby the Kiel Canal and its approaches were to be maintained free and open to the commercial and war vessels of all nations at peace with Germany. Germany's action was not protested by the majority of the signatory powers.

89. Oppenheim, *op. cit.*, I, p. 927, n. 2.

90. This view was expressed by an international committee of jurists appointed by the Council of the League of Nations in 1920 to render an advisory opinion on the status of the Aaland Islands under a treaty purporting to accomplish a "territorial settlement." The committee in this case stated that "the existence of international servitudes in the true technical sense is not admitted." *Off. J.*, Special Supplement No. 3, p. 16.

Historically, a servitude could be used only in connection with, or for the benefit of, the dominant territory itself. The essence of the status created by lawmaking treaties "is neither the will of the parties nor the subservience of the one to the other but the higher norm of the solidarity of the international community" (O'Connell, *State Succession*, pp. 811–12). See in this respect de Visscher, "La Question des îles d'Aland," pp. 259–62; Mercier, *op. cit.*, pp. 73–79; Crusen, *op. cit.*, pp. 64, 69–70; von Liszt, *op. cit.*, p. 133; Lauterpacht, *Analogies*, p. 124. But see Mercier, *op. cit.*, pp. 107–9, who states that in order to say that international servitudes exist, a criterion must necessarily have been established that permits a differentiation between contractual obligations and international servitudes dealing with similar objects. The criterion must be such that a right from its inception could, because of its "real" character, be said to be one that is to subsist despite all changes in sovereignty. The criterion "express evidence of an international contract" proposed by the court in the North Atlantic fisheries case is inadequate for this purpose. To give rise to an absolute right a bilateral contract must be made along norms which, on the dictates of the legislator, produce such an effect, and under international law neither norms nor a legislator exists. See *supra*, note 91, and *The North Atlantic Fisheries Case* (Scott, *The Hague Court Reports*, pp. 141–225) in which the Permanent Court of Arbitration in 1910 asserted (p. 160) that the doctrine of servitudes was "but little suited to the principle of sovereignty which prevails in States under a system of constitutional government ... and to the present international relations of sovereign States" and that the doctrine of servitudes could be affirmed by it "*only on the express evidence of an international contract*" [italics added]. On the basis of this statement, Lauterpacht (*Analogies*, pp. 120–23) suggests that the construction of an obligation as a servitude should be resorted to when no doubt exists that the parties intended it to be a permanent right. This intent is to be inferred from (a) the express use of the term "servitude"; (b) words in the treaty which may reflect permanency, *e.g.*, remain unaffected by changes of sovereignty; (c) the character of the agreement, *e.g.*, number of signatories is such that the agreement is tantamount to international legislation creating universal law; (d) the fact that restrictions have been assumed repeatedly by successors so that its "real" character has been established by actual observance.

91. Oppenheim, *op. cit.*, I, 541–42; Lauterpacht, *Analogies*, p. 122; Victor Dalloz, *Répertoire pratique, méthodique et alphabétique de législation, de doctrine et de jurisprudence* (Paris: Bureau de la Jurisprudence, 1924), X, 788; Fiore, *op. cit.*, Sec. 1101, p. 435; Rivier, *Principes du droit des gens*, pp. 73, 215, 298; Reid, *op. cit.*, pp. 19–20; Henry Wheaton, *Elements of International Law*, ed. R. H. Dana, Jr. (8th ed.; Boston: Little, Brown & Co., 1866), Part III, Sec. 268, p. 340. Westlake (*op. cit.*, pp. 60–61) uses the word "transitory" to designate treaties intended to establish permanent relationships. Transitory conventions are perpetual in their nature, so that being once carried into effect, they subsist independently of any change in the sovereignty of the contracting parties. Such are treaties that are alleged to create a permanent servitude in favor of one nation within the territory of another. O'Connell, *State Succession*, pp. 807–8, uses the word "dispositive" to designate treaties intended to impress a permanent status upon a territory. See also O'Connell, *ibid.*, pp. 49–50.

92. Oppenheim, *op. cit.*, I, 541.
93. Lauterpacht, *Analogies*, p. 122.
94. O'Connell, *State Succession*, pp. 49–50.
95. Oppenheim, *op. cit.*, I, 543.
96. O'Connell, "Independence and Problems of State Succession," this *Yearbook*, pp. 13–15.
97. See K. Strupp, "Les Règles générales du droit de la paix," 47 Hague, *Recueil*, 447, 487 (1934).
98. 2 *Reports of International Arbitral Awards* 838 (1928).
99. McNair, "So-Called State Servitudes," p. 123.
100. Lauterpacht (*Analogies*, p. 125) considers that the problem of succession, as a problem of law, is identical in private and international law. In both cases, there is a substitution and continuation of rights and obligations, and the essential aspects of the problem are the same. See Rivier, *op. cit.*, I, 73, 215, 298; and C. W. Jenks, *op. cit.*, p. 142. But see Keith, *op. cit.*, pp. 20, 22. There is no customary rule of international law on the problem of succession. Although most treaties affirm the principle of succession, some deny it. Lauterpacht admits that the assumption of duties by successor states in the absence of treaty provisions on that point can be interpreted as an act of grace or political convenience rather than one of legal obligation. Lauterpacht, *Analogies*, pp. 127–28. See O'Connell, *State Succession*, pp. 808, 810–11; Westlake, *op. cit.*, pp. 60–61; and W. C. Jones, "State Succession in the Matter of Treaties," 24 *B.Y.I.L.* 375 (1947).
101. A. Cavaglieri, "Règles générales du droit de la paix," 26 Hague, *Recueil*, 376–86 (1929). Keith, *op. cit.*, p. 22; Crusen, *op. cit.*, p. 22 ff. But see Hall, *op. cit.*, p. 116; Rivier, *op. cit.*, pp. 73, 215, 299; S. Kiatibian, *Conséquences juridiques de la transformation des états sur les traités* (Paris: A. Giard et E. Brière, 1892), pp. 55 ff.; Lauterpacht, *Analogies*, p. 127; Oppenheim, *op. cit.*, I, 541–42.
102. Keith, *op. cit.*, p. 22. Keith (pp. 2–6) differentiates the various theories of succession as follows: (a) the universal theory, whereby one sovereign suc-

ceeds to the personality of another. He believes that this theory cannot be maintained in international law, for it has never been held that successor states are bound by treaties of alliance, etc., that are of a personal nature; (b) the theory that one sovereign succeeds not to the personality, but to the "jura" of another; (c) the theory that although one sovereign succeeds to the rights and obligations of another, he succeeds to them only in such a manner that its liabilities for the obligations of another are limited by the amount of assets derived from the former personality; (d) the theory of singular succession—succession is really a substitution of personalities, without any continuity. Here then is a succession to the rights, but not to the obligations, of a former personality. But see O'Connell, *State Succession*, pp. 6-7.

103. There exists no general rule of law that obliges an annexing state to assume the juridical consequences of acts of an extinguished state. Cavaglieri, *op. cit.*, p. 738. France did not acknowledge the obligations of Madagascar; the United States, those of Spain in Cuba and the Philippines; Germany, those of Austria; or Italy, those of Ethiopia. But see O'Connell, *State Succession*, p. 10.

104. See Fricker, *op. cit.*, pp. 68-74. Conquest and annexation is still permissible under international law. Neither the Kellogg-Briand Pact nor the Charter of the United Nations precludes a "nonaggressor" belligerent from annexing the territory of a vanquished aggressor.

105. As a practical matter, a proper interpretation of the convention that is alleged to have created such a servitude would in most instances preclude the descent of rights and obligations of dominant states.

106. Keith, *op. cit.*, p. 24. Cavaglieri, *op. cit.*, p. 375, states that in servitudes the personal character of the relationship is decisive. See C. C. Hyde, "The Termination of the Treaties of a State in Consequence of Its Absorption by Another—The Position of the United States," 26 A.J.I.L. 133-36 (1932).

107. De Visscher (*op. cit.*, pp. 251–59) appears to be the only exponent of international servitudes who specifically distinguishes servitudes of a military character from those of an economic character and denies the existence of the former.

108. *Infra*, pp. 72-82.
109. Mercier, *op. cit.*, p. 109; Fricker, *op. cit.*, pp. 68-74.
110. Scott, *op. cit.*, pp. 141–225; 1 *United States v. Great Britain in the Matter of the North Atlantic Coast Fisheries* (Washington, D.C.: Government Printing Office, 1913).
111. *Off. J.*, Special Supplement No. 3.
112. P.C.I.J., Series A, No. 1.
113. P.C.I.J., Series A, No. 22, and P.C.I.J., Series A/B, No. 46.
114. See Reid, *op. cit.*, p. 98.
115. VII Civil Division, April 21, 1914. (Reprinted in 8 A.J.I.L. 907-13 [1914].)
116. *Ibid.*, pp. 908-9.
117. *Ibid.* The court refers to Ullmann, *op. cit.*, p. 320 n., as its authority on this point. See *United States v. Winans*, 198 U.S. 371 (1905). See also *Luzerne v. Aargau*, Swiss Federal Court, R.O. 8, 55-57 (February 17, 1882); *St. Gall v. Thurgau*, Swiss Federal Court, R.O. 13, 408-10 (November 21, 1887); *Uri v. Schwyz*, Swiss Federal Court, R.O. 34, 274 n. (All reported by D. Schindler, "The Administration of Justice in the Swiss Federal Court in Intercantonal Disputes," 15 A.J.I.L. 149-89 [1921].) For other instances of

municipal pronouncement on servitudes, see Oppenheim, *op. cit.*, I, 940–41, n. 2.

118. McNair, "So-Called State Servitudes," pp. 122–23.

119. McNair (*The Law of Treaties*, pp. 538–39) maintains that: "There is a class of treaties which declares, creates or regulates rights usually of a kind regarded as permanent . . . which its owner cannot normally be deprived against his will . . . in the British view State rights of a proprietary kind, such as those created . . . by a treaty . . . of cessions, a boundary treaty . . . are not affected by the outbreak of war between the contracting parties." The theory in support of this view is believed by McNair (p. 542) to be "that the right once created acquires an existence independent of the treaty and independent, therefore, of the subsequent fate of the treaty." See *Sutton v. Sutton*, R. and M. 663 (Court of Chancery, 1830); J. B. Scott, *Cases on International Law* (2d ed.; St. Paul, Minn.: West Publishing Co., 1922), p. 468; Potter, *op. cit.*, p. 639; Oppenheim, *op. cit.*, II, 304–6.

120. McNair, *The Law of Treaties*, p. 547. Crusen (*op. cit.*, p. 49) states that: "Dans les conventions de cette nature, il sera permis de supposer comme volonté unanime des parties contractantes que l'état de guerre existant entre quelques-unes d'elles ne doit affecter ni l'existance ni le caractère universel d'un tel pacte . . . une guerre entre deux États signataires d'une telle convention n'aurait pour effet que de suspendre les droits et les obligations mutuelles de ces deux États pour la durée de la guerre."

121. Crusen, *ibid*. See Keith, *op. cit.*, pp. 22–24, for instances in the practice of states that support this view. Oppenheim, (*op. cit.*, I, 302–3) states that there is no unanimity and no uniform practice of states on this matter, the whole question remaining unsettled. Váli (*op. cit.*, p. 322) believes that rights in foreign territory are not generally annulled by a war between the parties, although neither the North American Fisheries arbitration nor the question of French fishing rights on the coast of Newfoundland offers a positive answer.

122. Crusen, *op. cit.*, p. 49. Oppenheim, *op. cit.*, II, 303–4. Spain in 1898, at the commencement of the Spanish-American War, and Turkey, at the commencement of its war with Italy in 1911, expressly declared that they considered all treaties between them and their adversaries annulled by the war.

123. T.I.A.S., No. 1648.
124. T.I.A.S., No. 1649.
125. T.I.A.S., No. 1650.
126. T.I.A.S., No. 1651.
127. T.I.A.S., No. 1652.
128. T.I.A.S., No. 2490.
129. T.I.A.S., No. 3298.
130. T.I.A.S., No. 3425. Documents relating to the Termination of the Occupation Regime in the Federal Republic of Germany, Germany No. 1 (1955), British Cmd. Papers 9368.

131. T.S. No. 725, effective October 6, 1925, as amended by T.S. No. 897 and T.I.A.S. No. 2972; 52 L.N.T.S. 133. M. E. Bathurst and J. L. Simpson, *Germany and the North Atlantic Community, A Legal Survey* (London: Stevens, 1956), pp. 108–9.

132. 5 U.S.T. & O.I.A. 1939; T.I.A.S. No. 3062; 253 U.N.T.S. 89. The Treaty of Friendship, Commerce and Navigation with Germany effective July

14, 1956, replaced the treaty of October 22, 1954. Sec. 7, *U.S.T. & O.I.A.* 1839; *T.I.A.S.* No. 3593; 273 *U.N.T.S.* 3.

133. Bathurst and Simpson, *op. cit.*, pp. 31–41. See also pp. 86, 88, 108–9, 117–18, 153, 188–89. Although war between a dominant and a servient state terminates political understandings such as military servitudes, the question is of little practical significance, since matters would be settled by the conventions that re-establish peace.

134. See N. Politis, *Neutrality and Peace*, trans. F. Macken (Washington, D.C.: Carnegie Endowment for International Peace, 1935); Quincy Wright, "The Present Status of Neutrality," 34 *A.J.I.L.* 391–415 (1940); H. Lauterpacht, "Neutrality and Collective Security," *Politica* 149 (1936).

135. Oppenheim, *International Law*, I, 643.

136. *Ibid.*, p. 647; H. Lauterpacht, "The Limits of the Operation of the Law of War," 30 *B.Y.I.L.* 237–39 (1953); J. F. Lalive, "International Organization and Neutrality," 24 *B.Y.I.L.* 74–85 (1947).

137. 46 Stat. 2343, *T.S.* No. 796, 94 *L.N.T.S.* 57. The treaty is binding upon more than sixty states, including all the Great Powers. Its duration is not expressly limited, and it is Oppenheim's opinion (*op. cit.*, I, 193–94) that it should be regarded as analogous to treaties of peace that, when concluded without an express time limit, cannot be unilaterally denounced or terminated by notice. He is further of the opinion, because of its object and the number of states bound by it, that this treaty must be considered as having the degree of permanency comparable to that applicable to rules of customary international law.

138. *Ibid.*, II, pp. 182–83, 191.

139. *Ibid.*, p. 643. While there is no right to discriminate against an aggressor in disregard of the traditional rules of neutrality under the Treaty, it is arguable that discrimination is permissible as a measure of reprisal. Since the outbreak of war will, as a rule, be due to a violation of the treaty by one of the belligerents, the guilty one, by breaching the treaty, has violated the rights of all the other signatories that, by way of reprisal, may choose, contrary to the traditional duties of a neutral, to subject the guilty party to discriminatory action (p. 644).

140. See C. J. Colombos, "The United Nations Charter," 1 *I.L.Q.* 28–39 (1947). No Great Power, it is believed, would vote itself an aggressor, or consent to measures against itself, or consent to take such action against states with which it has close connections.

141. Members that apply, upon call, the nonmilitary measures authorized by Article 41 (none of which is inherently belligerent) against other members could theoretically occupy a position of qualified neutrality. Although this position is characterized by measures of an unfriendly nature, the member affected by measures of this nature could not, because of them, lawfully take retaliatory action, for it is deemed by its acceptance of the Charter to have consented in advance to the application of such measures against it. (Lalive, "International Organization and Neutrality," p. 80; Oppenheim, *op. cit.*, II, 649.) He continues, however, that as a practical matter, "A weak neutral whose territory borders on that of a powerful belligerent will hardly be able to afford practical adherence to a principle which authorizes or enjoins him to discriminate against the aggressor and which exposes him to the danger of reprisals and invasion." (Lauterpacht, "The Limits of the Operation of the Law of War," p. 238.) It

is evident also that a state against which discriminatory action is being taken will, to the extent of its ability, oppose any departure from the principles of absolute impartiality required by the traditional conception of neutrality. Members that take the military measures specified in Article 42 become, of course, belligerents.

142. Oppenheim, *op. cit.*, II, 651–52.
143. *Ibid.*, p. 650.
144. Lalive, "International Organization and Neutrality," pp. 81–82.
145. *Ibid.*, p. 82.
146. Oppenheim, *op. cit.*, II, 652. Lalive ("International Organization and Neutrality," p. 85) suggests that a document like the Charter is more like a constitutional act of the community of states than like a simple treaty, although he states that there is no rule of international law to support this view.
147. The Charter makes no provisions for sanctions against members (other than their expulsion from the U.N. by the General Assembly upon the recommendation of the Security Council for persistent violation of the principles of the Charter [Article 6]) that do not comply with their duties under Article 2, paragraph 5, of the Charter, or that refuse to take the measures specified by the Security Council pursuant to Articles 41 and 42 of the Charter. Thus, the Security Council could not properly consider noncompliance as a threat to, or as a breach of, the peace, or as an act of aggression under Article 39 of the Charter. Other members, however, could subject a defecting member to discriminatory action as a measure of reprisal for having violated their rights under the Charter. In this respect, see Oppenheim, *op. cit.*, II, 644.
148. Lauterpacht, "The Limits of the Operation of the Law of War," p. 238.
149. See Váli (*op. cit.*, p. 324), who states: "At present no definite answer is deducible from the practice of States. Nevertheless, whether the answer be in the positive or in the negative . . . it can be one of three alternatives: first, that the grantor State is freed from its obligations as a neutral as far as they are contrary to its previous obligations of a territorial character; secondly, that the grantor State is freed from its obligations resulting from the right in foreign territory during the time of war as far as they are contradictory to the obligations of neutrality; or, thirdly, that the opponent of the grantee State is justified in undertaking military action against the troops or ammunition depots of the enemy even in the territory of the neutral State, without a breach of its obligations toward neutrals."
150. O'Connell, *State Succession*, pp. 49–50, 808, 811; Jones, "State Succession in the Matter of Treaties," p. 375.
151. Westlake, *op. cit.*, pp. 60–61.
152. Emmerich de Vattel, *Le Droit des gens ou les principes de la loi naturelle* (Washington, D.C.: Carnegie Endowment for International Peace, 1916), Vol. III, Book II, Chap. XII, par. 203.
153. Oppenheim, *op. cit.*, II, 653. The term violation of neutrality includes every act or omission contrary to the duty of either a neutral toward belligerents, or by the belligerents toward a neutral.
154. *Ibid.*, pp. 654, 698.
155. *Ibid.*, p. 675. See Arts. 4, 5, 10, 18, and 19 of Hague Convention (XIII) concerning the Rights and Duties of Neutral Powers in Naval War, 1907, and Arts. 2, 4, and 5 of Hague Convention (V) Respecting the Rights and Duties of Neutral Powers and Persons in Case of War on Land, *The Hague*

Notes

Conventions and Declarations of 1899 and 1907, ed. J. B. Scott (New York: Oxford University Press, 1915), pp. 133–34, 210–13.
156. Oppenheim, op. cit., II, 663–64, 702; Richard Kleen, Lois et usages de la neutralité (Paris: A. Chevalier-Marescq et Cie., 1900), Vol. I, Sec. 114. See Art. 3 Hague Convention (V), 1907, and Arts. 5 and 6, Hague Convention (XIII), 1907, in Scott, op. cit., pp. 133, 210.
157. Oppenheim, International Law, II, 675. Impartiality precludes any assistance or injury to one belligerent that would be detrimental to the other. This statement applies equally to transport or passage of aircraft, war material, provisions for troops, establishment of Prize Courts, prolonged stay of warships in territorial waters, or use of such waters for warlike activities.
158. Ibid., II, 686–87, 689–90, 698; Hall, op. cit., Sec. 215; Kleen, op. cit., I, Sec. 114; Calvo, op. cit., IV, Sec. 2594; Rivier, op. cit., II, 378; Ullmann, op. cit., Sec. 190; Hannis Taylor, A Treatise on International Law (Chicago: Callaghan & Co., 1901), Sec. 618. But see J. C. Bluntschli, Das moderne Völkerrecht der civilisirten Staaten (3d ed.; Nördlingen: C. H. Beck, 1878), Secs. 746, 759; J. L. Klüber, Europäisches Völkerrecht (2d ed.; Schaffhausen: Hurter, 1851), Sec. 281.
159. Hall, op. cit., p. 405; Oppenheim, op. cit., I, 897; Lauterpacht, Report on the Law of Treaties (United Nations Document A/CN, 4/63, March 24, 1953), pp. 195–97.
160. There can be little doubt that such servitudes are concluded solely with war in mind, for otherwise they would serve no purpose. No other reason could motivate their conclusion or be used to substantiate their existence.
161. The decision of the Permanent Court of International Justice in the case of the S.S. Wimbledon, August 17, 1923 (P.C.I.J., Series A, No. 1), is of no assistance in this matter, as it relates to obligations that arose out of a lawmaking treaty that permanently dedicated an artificial waterway to the use of the whole world.
162. McNair, The Law of Treaties, p. 113. See Lauterpacht, Report on the Law of Treaties, pp. 195–97.
163. Hall, op. cit., pp. 402–3. See Oppenheim, op. cit., I, 897, 946.
164. Oppenheim, op. cit., II, 718 ff.
165. Ibid., II, 663, 664–742.
166. Crusen, op. cit., pp. 49–50.
167. Clauss, op. cit., pp. 223–44; Westlake, op. cit., pp. 60–61; Rivier, op. cit., pp. 73, 215, 298; Kiatibian, op. cit., pp. 55 ff.; Reid, op. cit., p. 25.
168. Hall, op. cit., p. 407; Keith, op. cit., pp. 22–24; Pradier-Fodéré, op. cit., II, Sec. 845; Bluntschli, op. cit., Sec. 359; P. P. Fabre, Des Servitudes dans le droit international public (Paris: A. Rousseau, 1901), p. 30; Erich Kaufmann, Das Wesen des Völkerrechts und die clausula rebus sic stantibus (Tübingen: J. C. B. Mohr, 1911), p. 195; Crusen, op. cit., p. 60; O'Connell, "Independence and Problems of State Succession," this Yearbook, pp. 14, 21; Gould, op. cit., pp. 339–45; Schwarzenberger, op. cit., pp. 158–59; J. W. Garner and V. Jobst, "Unilateral Denunciation of Treaties," 29 A.J.I.L. 569–85 (1935).
169. Hall, op. cit., p. 407. McNair (The Law of Treaties, p. 232) defines an implied term of condition of treaties in this manner: "Circumstances arise in which it is necessary to imply a term or condition. That is to say, when it is clear that, if the parties when negotiating had averted to some contingency . . . they would have agreed to provide for it in a particular way, it is reasonable to

impute to them an intention to contract on the basis of such a provision and to imply it as a term or condition in the treaty."

170. Hall, *op. cit.*, pp. 415-16.

171. See Strupp (*op. cit.*, p. 487), who states that there is a presumption that a dispositive treaty survives until repudiated by the successor state, but denies that any obligation to respect dispositive rights and obligations can be inherited by a successor. Rivier (*op. cit.*, I, 73) is of the same opinion. Cavaglieri, *op. cit.*, pp. 375-76, states that the granting of a dispositive status is a concession of sovereignty motivated by a state's own interest and sustained by its own will, so that the regime loses its rationale once the interest and the will disappear. The dispositive treaty is essentially contractual, and the "personal character of the relationship is decisive." See Bluntschli, *op. cit.*, Sec. 359; Crusen, *op. cit.*, pp. 23, 56-60; Pradier-Fodéré, *op. cit.*, II, Sec. 845.

172. Rivier, *Principes du droit des gens*, I, 73. But see Westlake (*op. cit.*, p. 61), who believes that, for the doctrine to apply, it would have to be shown that the interests of third parties which the servitudes were intended to secure had ceased to exist in consequence of the change of sovereignty over the territory affected.

173. Oppenheim, *op. cit.*, I, 543. See also O'Connell, "Independence and Problems of State Succession," this *Yearbook*, pp. 12–14, 21.

174. Pierre Labrousse, *Des Servitudes en droit international public* (Bordeaux: Imprimerie commerciale et industrielle, 1911), p. 26.

175. Oppenheim, *op. cit.*, I, 543.

176. Kiatibian, *op. cit.*, p. 30.

177. Russia was rebuked, however, by a declaration adopted in a Protocol of January 17, 1871, signed by Austria, France, Germany, Great Britain, Italy, and Turkey, which provided: "It is an essential principle of the law of nations that no Power can liberate itself from the engagements of a treaty, nor modify the stipulations thereof, unless with the consent of the contracting parties, by means of an amicable arrangement." 61 B.F.S.P. 1198 (1870–71); Scott, *op. cit.*, p. 469.

178. Oppenheim, *op. cit.*, I, 943. See Georg von Martens, "Recueil des principaux traités des puissances et états de l'Europe," *Nouveau recueil général de traités, conventions et autres actes remarquables* ... (1843–1875), (Göttingen: Dietrich, 1843–75), XVIII, 278. In 14 *Nouveau recueil général*, 2ième série, 170 (1889).

179. Oppenheim, *op. cit.*, I, 943, 948. See *Off. J.* 312 (1936). Germany refused to submit the question of the compatibility of these treaties to any tribunal. The League of Nations found that Germany had breached international law by her unilateral repudiation of these obligations. *Off. J.* 340 (1936).

180. See *P.C.I.J.*, Series A/B, No. 46, p. 158.

181. T.I.A.S. No. 1819. See Schwarzenberger, *op. cit.*, pp. 158-59; "Editorial Comment: The Attorney General Invokes *rebus sic stantibus*," 36 A.J.I.L. 89–96 (1942).

182. 8 *Entscheidungen des Schweitzer Bundesgerichts* 57 (1882), cited by Schindler, *op. cit.*, pp. 164–65. See Oppenheim, *op. cit.*, I, 940 n.

183. *Ibid.*, I, 941–42; Crusen, *op. cit.*, pp. 60–61; Schwarzenberger, *op. cit.*, pp. 158–59. Oppenheim (*International Law*, I, 942) states that the refusal to submit the issue to judicial determination is prima facie evidence that the

doctrine has been invoked as an excuse for a breaking of the law of obligations, or that the beneficiary is determined to take advantage of a treaty that no longer has a legal reason for existence. The practice of states is inconclusive as to the liability for damages of a state that has legitimately renounced an obligation pursuant to the doctrine of *rebus sic stantibus*. Crusen (*op. cit.*, p. 61) believes that since the renunciating state has had resort to a right implied in all treaties, there would be no logical reason why it should be held to indemnify the other party. He states that in the annexation of Bosnia and Herzegovina by Austria-Hungary in 1908 Turkey did not obtain damages to which she believed herself entitled. But see Kaufmann, *op. cit.*, p. 195, and Crusen, *op. cit.*, p. 60.

184. Roxburgh, *op. cit.*, p. 20.
185. O'Connell, *State Succession*, pp. 32–33.
186. *Ibid.*, p. 43.
187. *Ibid.*, pp. 49–50, 56, 276.
188. Váli, *op. cit.*, pp. 199–252, 313–30.
189. French-American Agreement of December 22, 1950 (classified text not published), which authorized the United States to establish military bases in Morocco. According to French sources the agreement, a secret one, was concluded by France in conformity with her obligation to Morocco. *New York Times*, May 29, 1956, Sec. L, p. 4, col. 1; Váli, *op. cit.*, p. 246.
190. Agreement with Great Britain on Leased Naval and Air Bases, March 27, 1941, *Executive Agreement Series* 235 (effective March 27, 1941), and Exchange of Notes with Great Britain regarding the exchange of United States Destroyers for Naval and Air Facilities in British Transatlantic Territories, September 2, 1940, Annex 1, *Executive Agreement Series* 235.
191. Váli, *op. cit.*, p. 246.
192. *Ibid.*, pp. 246–47.
193. The text of this treaty is reprinted in 6 A.J.I.L. S. 207 (1912).
194. The Moroccans served notice that they did not recognize the U.S.-French agreement of December 22, 1950, and that they regarded it as an infringement on their sovereignty. *New York Times*, May 29, 1956, Sec. L, p. 4, col. 1; *New York Times*, June 12, 1956, Sec. L, p. 13, col. 1.
195. O'Connell, *State Succession*, p. 43; O'Connell, "Independence and Problems of State Succession," this *Yearbook*, p. 13. In the *United States Nationals in Morocco Case*, the International Court of Justice implied that the treaties that had been concluded by France during the protectorate to regulate Moroccan affairs would remain binding on Morocco upon the termination of the protectorate (*International Court of Justice Reports*, 1952, pp. 193–96, 217).
196. O'Connell, *State Succession*, pp. 51–63.
197. The Joint Declaration notes that the Treaty of Fez "no longer corresponds . . . to the necessities of modern life and can no longer govern Franco-Moroccan relations," specifies that the French Government "solemnly confirms the recognition of the independence of Morocco," and states that pending the application of new accords, the new relationships between France and Morocco will be founded on the text of an annexed protocol. The text of this Joint Declaration and the Protocol is reprinted in 34 *Dep't. of State Bulletin* 466–67 (1956) and in 51 A.J.I.L. 676–77 (1957).

198. 34 *Dep't. of State Bulletin* 466–67 (1956), and 51 A.J.I.L. 676–77 (1957).
199. Reprinted in 51 A.J.I.L. 679–81 (1957). See *New York Times*, May 29, 1956, Sec. L, p. 4, col. 1.
200. Letter from Ahmed Balafrej to Christian Pineau concerning the Franco-American agreement of December 22, 1950, on the American bases in Morocco, reprinted in 51 A.J.I.L. 682 (1957).
201. Letter from Christian Pineau to Ahmed Balafrej, *ibid.*, p. 683.
202. Text of a joint statement released at the close of discussions (November 25–28, 1957) between Mohammed V, King of Morocco, and U.S. Secretary of State John F. Dulles. 37 *Dep't. of State Bulletin* 956 (1957).
203. 41 *Dep't. of State Bulletin* 723 (1959).
204. 45 *Dep't. of State Bulletin* 973 (1961). The United States did not seek any financial settlement with the Moroccan Government even though it had built air bases there valued at $410 million (*New York Times*, May 28, 1956, Sec. L, p. 4, col. 2).
205. *New York Times*, October 1, 1961, Sec. L, p. 16, col. 1.
206. O'Connell, *State Succession*, pp. 7, 10.
207. *Executive Agreement Series* (E.A.S.) No. 235 (effective March 27, 1941).
208. *Ibid.*, Annex I.
209. Váli, *op. cit.*, pp. 230–36.
210. *Ibid.*, p. 236.
211. See O'Connell, *State Succession*, p. 15.
212. Oppenheim, *op. cit.*, I, 159.
213. See *U.S. Participation in the U.N.*, Report by the President to the Congress for the Year 1961, pp. 53–58.
214. See Barbados *Advocate* (editorial), November 2, 1960, on the subject of leased bases quoted in Dispatch No. 34 from the American Consulate, Barbados, to Department of State, November 8, 1960.
215. See O'Connell, "Independence and Problems of State Succession," this *Yearbook*, p. 18. By an Exchange of Letters between the United Kingdom and the Federation of Malaya relating to the inheritance of international rights and obligations by the Government of the Federation of Malaya signed September 12, 1957, the Federation of Malaya assumed "all obligations and responsibilities of the Government of the United Kingdom which arise from any valid instrument . . . insofar as such instrument may be held to have application to or in respect of the Federation of Malaya." (Cmd. 346.) In an Exchange of Letters between the Government of Ghana and the Government of the United Kingdom, November 25, 1957 (Cmd. 345), and between the Government of Sierra Leone, May 5, 1961 (Cmd. 1464), it is provided that "(1) all obligations and responsibilities of the Government of the United Kingdom which arise from any valid international instrument shall henceforth, insofar as such instrument may be held to have application to Ghana [Sierra Leone], be assumed by the Government of Ghana [Government of Sierra Leone]." By a note dated December 9, 1961, the Prime Minister of Tanganyika advised the Secretary General of the United Nations that "as regards bilateral treaties validly concluded by the United Kingdom on behalf of the Territory of Tanganyika, or validly applied or extended by the former to the territory of the latter, the Government of Tanganyika is willing to continue

to apply within its territory on a basis of reciprocity, the items of all such treaties for a period of 2 years from the date of its independence (*i.e.*, until December 8, 1963) unless abrogated or modified earlier by mutual consent. At the expiry of that period, the Government of Tanganyika will regard such of these treaties which could not by the application of the rules of customary international law be regarded as otherwise surviving, as having terminated."

216. Barbados *Advocate* (editorial), November 2, 1960.
217. *Ibid.*
218. 43 *Dep't. of State Bulletin* 822–23 (1960).
219. T.I.A.S., No. 4734.
220. *Ibid.* Also, *New York Times*, February 11, 1960, Sec. L, p. 4, col. 1.
221. See 43 *Dep't. of State Bulletin* 822–23 (1960). The second of these negotiations, held in Trinidad, consisted of two phases; during the first, discussions were held between representatives of the U.S. and Trinidad on matters that were of interest only to them. During the second phase, items of common interest were discussed with representatives from all the unit territories and with representatives of the West Indies Federation. The third stage, which resulted in the "Defense Areas" agreement, was signed by the Prime Minister of the Federal Government of the West Indies and the Chief Minister of Antigua, the Prime Minister of Barbados, the Premier of Jamaica, the Chief Minister of St. Lucia, and the Premier of Trinidad and Tobago, who were present on behalf of the Government of the Federation of the West Indies.
222. T.I.A.S., No. 4734, Art. XXIV.
223. *Ibid.* All other agreements between the United Kingdom and the United States concerning the grant of rights to the U.S. with respect to defense facilities in the Federation were, except as expressly provided in the agreement, to cease to have force or effect from February 10, 1961, insofar as they related to any territory of the Federation.
224. Jamaica, Trinidad, Barbados, Antigua, Dominica, Grenada, Monserrat, Saint-Christopher–Saint-Kitts–Nevis–Anguilla, Saint Lucia, and Saint Vincent.
225. *New York Times*, February 7, 1962, Sec. L, p. 4, col. 1; *New York Times*, February 2, 1962, Sec. L, p. 6, col. 3. Jamaica voted to secede in December, 1960, and Trinidad in January, 1961.
226. See The West Indies (Dissolution and Interim Commissioner) Order in Council, 1962, 10 and 11 Eliz. 2. C. 19. Statutory Instru. 1962 No. 1084. The West Indies Federation had been established by West Indies (Federation) Order in Council 1957, Statutory Instru. 1957/1364 (1957 I, 202).
227. Jamaica Independence Act, 1962. 10 and 11 Eliz. 2 C. 40. Jamaica (Constitution) Order in Council 1962, Statutory Instru. 1962 No. 1550. See the *Washington Star*, August 6, 1962, p. 1, cols. 6, 7.
228. Exchange of Letters between the Government of the United Kingdom of Great Britain and North Ireland and the Government of Jamaica Relating to the Inheritance of International Rights and Obligations by the Government of Jamaica. Cmd. 1918.
229. Trinidad and Tobago Independence Act, 1962.
230. Exchange of Letters between the Government of the United Kingdom of Great Britain and North Ireland and the Government of Trinidad and Tobago Relating to the Inheritance of International Rights and Obligations by the Government of Trinidad and Tobago. Cmd. 1919.
231. 3 *U.S.T. & O.I.A.* 4271; *T.I.A.S.* No. 2572; 173 *U.N.T.S.* No. 267.

232. Váli, *op. cit.*, p. 236. Charles Rousseau, *Droit international public* (Paris: A. Pedone, 1951), as cited in Váli, *op. cit.*, p. 236, *n.* 65.
233. Obtained by an agreement with the United Kingdom dated July 21, 1950. 1 *U.S.T. & O.I.A.* 545; *T.I.A.S.* No. 2099; 97 *U.N.T.S.* 193–225. See also Exchange of Notes effective March 2, 1953, in 4 *U.S.T. & O.I.A.* 429, *T.I.A.S.* No. 2789; 172 *U.N.T.S.* 257.
234. Obtained by an agreement with the Dominican Republic dated November 26, 1951, 133 *U.N.T.S.* 210–26. See also 133 *U.N.T.S.* 236–43 for the Exchange of Notes dated November 26, 1952, which extended the United States-Dominican Agreement of November 26, 1951, to the United Kingdom.
235. Obtained through an Exchange of Notes with the Federal Republic of Germany dated September 9, 1952. 151 *U.N.T.S.* 215–21.
236. Váli, *op. cit.*, pp. 200–210.
237. *Ibid.*, p. 205.
238. 1 *U.S.T. & O.I.A.* 545; *T.I.A.S.* No. 2099; 97 *U.N.T.S.* 193–225.
239. 133 *U.N.T.S.* 210–26, 236–43.
240. Váli, *op. cit.*, p. 205.
241. *Ibid.*, pp. 205–6.
242. *Ibid.*, pp. 208–52; 263–72.
243. *Ibid.*, p. 222; text published in 51 *A.J.I.L.* 672–73 (1957).
244. *Ibid.*
245. Reid, *op. cit.*, pp. 195–96; Váli, *op. cit.*, pp. 169–79; O'Connell, *State Succession*, pp. 55–56.
246. Edward Hertslet, *The Map of Europe by Treaty, 1814–1875* (London: Butterworth, 1875–91), I, 208–93.
247. *Ibid.*, p. 262; Mercier, *op. cit.*, pp. 81–83.
248. Article 92 of the Treaty of Vienna, June 9, 1815, provides that Sardinian troops were to withdraw "whenever . . . the neighboring Powers to Switzerland are in a state of open or impending hostilities"; that "no other armed troops of any other Power shall have the privilege of passing through or remaining in the said territories and provinces excepting those which the Swiss Confederation shall think proper to place there." See *ibid.*
249. Martens, XVI *Nouveau recueil général* (Partie II), pp. 539–40. Article 2 of this treaty provided: Il est également entendu que . . . le Roi de Sardaigne ne peut transférer les parties neutralisées de la Savoie qu'aux conditions auxquelles il les possède lui-même, et qu'il appartiendra à . . . l'Empéreur des Français de s'entendre, à ce sujet, tant avec les puissances représentées au Congrès de Vienne qu'avec la Confédération Helvétique, et de leur donner les guaranties qui résultent des stipulations rappelées dans le présent article." These provisions were never executed. During the Franco-Prussian War, 1870–71, and again during World War I, Switzerland reserved the right to occupy these provinces although she did not exercise the right. France, on the other hand, having little if anything to lose, acknowledged the communications without protesting their content. See Crusen, *op. cit.*, p. 66; Keith, *op. cit.*, p. 23.
250. Article VIII of the Treaty of May 20, 1815, between Austria, Great Britain, Russia, Prussia, France, and Sardinia, which was embodied in the Vienna Congress Treaty of June 9, 1815, as Article 92 thereof, and signed by Austria, France, Great Britain, Portugal, Prussia, Russia, and Sweden. Spain acceded to this treaty by an act dated June 7, 1817. (Hertslet, *op. cit.*, I,

Notes 281

155–58, 274.) See Reid, *op. cit.*, pp. 195–96; McNair, "So-Called State Servitudes," *op. cit.*, pp. 124–25. Mercier, *op. cit.*, p. 82, states that the right of passage through Valais can be discounted since the territory over which it was to be exercised was never the object of a change of sovereignty. It could also be maintained that the obligations of Sardinia were binding upon France on the basis that the treaty that imposed these restrictions was a "lawmaking" treaty that set up an international regime or status. See McNair's dissenting opinion in the decision of the Court of International Justice on the status of South West Africa in 1950 ("International Status of South West Africa," Advisory Opinion, *I.C.J. Rep.* 153–54 [1950]).

251. Reid, *op. cit.*, p. 194; Baron Lage de Staël-Holstein, "Autour de la conception juridique des servitudes internationales," 41 *R.D.I.L.C.* 17–18 (1934).

252. *Ibid.*

253. *T.I.A.S.* No. 2490; *United Kingdom, Treaties Series* No. 33 (1952) Cmd. 8601.

254. Mercier (*op. cit.*, p. 104) states that this instance is an example of doctrine contradictory to actual facts.

255. *U.S.T.S. & O.I.A.* H31; Malloy, *Treaties* I, pp. 1350 ff.

256. Reid, *op. cit.*, p. 190.

257. *Ibid.*

258. Tantamount to a leasehold retained by annual compensation for use.

259. Although the use, occupation, control, and defense of the Panama Canal Zone were granted to the United States in perpetuity in 1903 to the exclusion of the exercise of any sovereign rights by Panama, Panama retains in law the property in the territory. See Oppenheim, *op. cit.*, I, 458–59. Thus, although the United States is permitted to do whatever it likes within the Panama Canal zone, it cannot dispose of the territory by ceding it or any part of it to a third power without the consent of Panama. See Lester H. Woolsey, "The Sovereignty of the Panama Canal Zone," 20 *A.J.I.L.* 117–24 (1926).

260. Reid, *op. cit.*, p. 193.

261. Malloy, *Treaties* I, 358–59. By the Treaty of Havana, May 22, 1903, the United States guaranteed the independence of Cuba, and Cuba granted to the United States "the right to intervene for the preservation of Cuban independence, the maintenance of a government adequate for the protection of life, property and individual liberty."

262. The rights granted to France in 1648 by the Treaty of Münster to maintain a garrison in Philippeville (Philippsburg), a town belonging to the Bishop of Spire, and garrison rights such as those granted to Austria in Ferraro and Commechio by the Treaty of Vienna in 1815 have been cited as instances of positive military servitudes (see Crusen, *op. cit.*, p. 6; Reid, *op. cit.*, p. 194; and Robert Piedelièvre, *Précis de droit international public* [Paris: F. Pichon, 1894–95], I, 389). These rights, all now extinguished by merger or renunciation, were never subjected to any changes in sovereignty. Thus, the "real" character of the rights and obligations concerned has in no way been substantiated.

263. Staël-Holstein, "La Doctrine des servitudes internationales et son application en Scandinavie," pp. 453–54.

264. Martens, 31 *Nouveau recueil général*, 2ième serie, 572, 574 (1905).

265. See Mercier, *op. cit.*, pp. 79–81.

266. Hertslet, *op. cit.*, I, 346.
267. McNair, "So-Called State Servitudes," p. 65.
268. Keith (*op. cit.*, p. 23) states that the French Revolutionary Government in 1848 declared this provision no longer binding on France, and that it is by no means clear that there are any grounds for the theory that this alleged servitude still exists.
269. See Crusen, *op. cit.*, p. 65; Keith, *op. cit.*, p. 23; Mercier, *op. cit.*, p. 87. The binding effect, if any, of these obligations on Germany, can be attributed as well to the fact that the Treaty of Paris was a "lawmaking" treaty. See McNair, "So-Called State Servitudes," p. 124.
270. See *supra*, pp. 84–85.
271. *A Complete Collection of the Treaties and Conventions and Reciprocal Regulations at Present Subsisting between Great Britain and Foreign Powers* (1827–1913), ed. Edward Hertslet (London: Butterworth, 1827–95; and London: Her Majesty's Stationery Office, 1898-1925), XVII, 1133; Martens, 12 *Nouveau recueil général*, 2ième serie, 491–92 (1887).
272. Reid, *op. cit.*, p. 198 (citing J. Abribat, *Le Détroit de Magellan au point de vue international* [Paris: Chevalier-Marescq, 1902], p. 284). See Oppenheim, *op. cit.*, II, 245, who states that the neutralization of these Straits concerns the contracting parties only and has "no consequence for third States."
273. McNair would consider this treaty a "lawmaking" one.
274. Reid, *op. cit.*, pp. 189–99. See Declaration concerning Egypt and Morocco, April 8, 1904 (Hertslet, *op. cit.*, 402 [1907]).
275. 98 B. & F.S.P. 735 (1905).
276. Reid, *op. cit.*, p. 199; Staël-Holstein, "La Doctrine des servitudes internationales et son application en Scandinavie," p. 457.
277. T.I.A.S. 2490; United Kingdom, *Treaty Series*, No. 33 (1952), Cmd. 8601.
278. Reid, *op. cit.*, p. 199.
279. Article 42, Treaty of Peace Between the Allied and Associated Powers and Germany, 112 B.&F.S.P. 1–316 (1919); U.K. T.S. No. 4 (1919).
280. *Ibid.*, Art. 115.
281. *Ibid.*, Art. 195.
282. Reid, *op. cit.*, pp. 197–98. See also Oppenheim, *op. cit.*, I, 539, n. 3.
283. Art. 42 and 43 of the Treaty of Versailles. See U.K. T.S. Germany, No. 2 (1936), and Oppenheim, *op. cit.*, I, 943, 947, n. 4.
284. *Off. J.* 312 (1936). See Oppenheim, *op. cit.*, I, 948, n. 4.
285. *Off. J.* 340 (1936).
286. Oppenheim, *op. cit.*, I, 483.
287. Including Art. 115 (fortifications on Helegoland), Art. 180 (fortifications 50 kilometers to the east of the Rhine river), and Art. 195 (fortifications commanding the maritime routes between the North Sea and the Baltic).
288. T.I.A.S. No. 3425; *Documents Relating to the Termination of the Occupation Regime in the Federal Republic of Germany* (Germany), No. 1, 1955, Cmd. 9368. See T.I.A.S. No. 1964.
289. Staël-Holstein, "La Doctrine des servitudes internationales et son application en Scandinavie," pp. 456–57, Treaty between Finland and Russia dated October 4, 1920. See 113 B.&F.S.P. 977–1002 (1920).

Notes

290. T.I.A.S. No. 1648; 148 B.&F.S.P. 394 ff. (1947, Part II). U.K. T.S. No. 50 (1948). Cmd. 7481.
291. Art. 47 (1) (a). See also Art. 47 (4) (a) and 47 (5).
292. Art. 48 (1) (a). See also Art. 48 (4) (a) and 48 (5).
293. Art. 48 (6).
294. Art. 49.
295. Art. 50.
296. T.I.A.S. No. 1650; 148 B.&F.S.P. 313 ff. (1947, Part II). U.K. T.S. No. 52 (1948). Cmd. 7483.
297. Art. 12.
298. Oppenheim, *op. cit.*, I, 539, *n.* 3.
299. Cavaglieri, *op. cit.*, pp. 375–76.
300. See Mercier (*op. cit.*, p. 118), who states that since security is an illusion, let us have "souplesse" and autonomy of will and renounce the notion of servitudes and utilize the notion of obligations only. Under a contractual-obligation concept, when there is a change in sovereignty over the servient territory, it would be proper to presume, in all cases in which the utilization of servient territory corresponds to a permanent and fundamental need of dominant territory, that the new sovereign has assumed the burdens of his predecessor. In these special cases, the designation of servitude should not be applied, since that would only confuse matters and continue the belief that such relations have a "real" character.
301. Reid, *op. cit.*, pp. xxi–xxii, 209. Reid states (*ibid.*, p. 210) that ". . . a servitude does not and cannot limit or restrict the sovereignty of the servient state, but amounts at the most to a transfer of the right to exercise certain sovereign rights; so that no state need be deterred from employing so useful a concept by the fear that it may impair its sovereignty thereby." See O'Connell, *State Succession,* p. 63.
302. Reid, *op. cit.*, p. 39. See Lauterpacht, *Analogies,* p. 124.
303. Reid, *op. cit.*, p. 40.
304. *Ibid.*, p. 208.
305. Rivier, *op. cit.*, I, 297. Indeed this provides a means whereby a colonial power can, by what appears to be a grant of independence, appease public opinion in favor of self-determination, without materially lessening its actual control over certain colonial activities and resources.
306. Crusen, *op. cit.*, p. 23.
307. *Ibid.*, p. 71; Clauss (*op. cit.*, p. 177) states that military servitudes are of a particularly vexatious character.
308. Crusen, *op. cit.*, p. 73. Fabre, *op. cit.*, p. 130.
309. Nys, *op. cit.*, II, 123; Bluntschli, *op. cit.*, Sec. 359.
310. Théophile Funck-Brentano and Albert Sorel, *Précis du droit des gens* (Paris: E. Plon, 1877), p. 179. See Fabre, *op. cit.*, p. 131.
311. See Myres S. McDougal, "The Comparative Study of Law for Policy Purposes," 51 *Yale L.J.* 918 (1932).
312. Mercier, *op. cit.*, p. 117, states: "Ce qu'on reproche aux servitudes, c'est donc leur manque de souplesse, c'est la possibilité qu'elles ont de survivre aux raisons qui les avaient fait créer."
313. *Ibid.*, p. 118.

Chapter 3. "United States Recognition Policy Toward the New Nations"
by William V. O'Brien and Ulf H. Goebel

1. H. Lauterpacht, *Recognition in International Law* (Cambridge: Cambridge University Press, 1948); and Ti-Chiang Chen, *The International Law of Recognition*, ed. L. C. Green (London: Stevens & Sons Ltd., 1951).

2. Percy E. Corbett, *Law in Diplomacy* (Princeton, N.J.: Princeton University Press, 1959).

3. Among the English decisions frequently cited on this point are: *Mighell v. Sultan of Johore*, 1 Q.B. 149 [1894]; *The Gagara*, Probate 95 (1919); *Duff Development Co. v. Government of Kelantan* A.C. 797 (1924).

However, the responses of the executive to judicial inquiries on the status of a foreign country or government are not always clear, and courts have occasionally been obliged to interpret such responses to obtain an answer to their question. See *The Gagara*, Probate 95 [1919] and *Duff Development Co. v. Government of Kelantan*, A.C. 797 [1924]. Moreover, even the deference of the courts to the executive cannot prevent judges from dealing with the confused subject matter of *de facto* and *de jure* recognitions. In the first place, there is a recurring propensity to use the adjective "*de facto*" in two senses. Usually it means "recognized *de facto*," and the adjective has either legal or political significance (or both), depending on one's theory of recognition. But sometimes the adjective *de facto* means "actually in existence but not recognized." See, for example, *Salimoff v. Standard Oil Co. of New York*, 262 N.Y. 220 (1933); *Wulfsohn v. Russian Socialist Federated Republic* 234 N.Y. 372 (1923).

A second defect in the Anglo-American case law on recognition is its failure to decide whether there is any difference in terms of legal consequences between *de facto* and *de jure* recognition. *Oetjen v. Central Leather Co.*, 246 U.S. 297 (1918), a most influential case in Britain as well as in the U.S., asserts the rule of retroactivity with respect to acts of a foreign government done prior to its recognition *de jure*, but fails to indicate what, if any, difference there is between such a government and a government recognized *de facto*. *Luther v. Sagor*, 3 K.B. 532 [1921] raises the question, but does not answer it since the answer is not necessary to the decision.

As this study shows, diplomatic practice is quite eccentric regarding the use of *de facto* and *de jure* recognition. Quite often there is no express designation of either type. It is submitted that if one builds doctrine on this subject on the basis of statements in judicial decisions, rather than on actual diplomatic practice, the chances are that the doctrine will not correspond to reality. See Herbert W. Briggs, *The Law of Nations, Cases, Documents, and Notes* (2d ed.; New York: Appleton-Century-Crofts, Inc., 1952), pp. 127-29, 146-47, and cases and literature cited therein.

4. For the position that Austria's international personality survived its illegal, forcible annexation by Germany, see Krystyna Marek, *Identity and Continuity in Public International Law* (Geneva: Librairie E. Droz. 1954), pp. 365-66; the Austrian Supreme Court, *Jordan v. Austrian Republic and Tabner*, 41 *Annual Digest* (1947); and *Kleiths v. Republic of Austria*, 51 *Annual Digest* (1948).

The Geographer of the U.S. Department of State does not consider Austria a new nation. Rather, he holds that the "reestablishment of Austria" after the war constituted the revival of a "previously exist[ing]" state. G. Etzel Pearcy, "Forty Newly Independent States: Some Politicogeographic Observations," 45 *Dep't. of State Bulletin* 604, 606 (1961).

See Josef L. Kunz, "The State Treaty With Austria," 49 *A.J.I.L.* 535, 541 (1955), for an analysis of the implications of the Vienna Treaty of May 15, 1955, which "upheld" Austrian identity with the 1918 Republic, but also recognized the German annexation as a "fact." See also Sherman L. Cohn, "*Ex injuria jus non oritur:* A Principle Misapplied," 3 *Santa Clara Lawyer* 23 (1962); Robert E. Clute, *The International Legal Status of Austria 1938–1955* (The Hague: Nijhoff, 1962).

5. See the section entitled "Recognition of States," pp. 703–20, in Denys P. Myers, "Contemporary Practice of the United States Relating to International Law," 55 *A.J.I.L.* 697 (1961).

6. Lauterpacht, *op. cit.,* pp. 6–7.

7. Philip C. Jessup, *Modern Law of Nations* (New York: The Macmillan Co., 1948); U.N. Secretary General Trygve Lie, Memorandum of March 8, 1950, U.N. Doc. No. S/1466, reprinted in 4 *International Organization* 356–62 (1950); Lauterpacht, *op. cit.,* pp. 67–69; Chen, *op. cit.,* p. 222; Malbone W. Graham, "Some Thoughts on the Recognition of New Governments and Regimes," 44 *A.J.I.L.* 356 (1950).

8. Lauterpacht, *op. cit.,* pp. 2–3; Chen, *op. cit.,* p. 14.

9. Lauterpacht, *op. cit.,* pp. 2–3; Chen, *op. cit.,* pp. 14–15.

10. Lauterpacht, *op. cit.,* pp. 32–37.

11. See Charles Cheney Hyde, *International Law, Chiefly as Interpreted and Applied by the United States* (Boston: Little, Brown, 1947), I, 164–72; Green H. Hackworth, *Digest of International Law* (Washington, D.C.: Government Printing Office, 1940–44), I, 174–91; "United States Policy on Nonrecognition of Communist China," Department of State Memorandum to Missions Abroad, August 11, 1958, 39 *Dep't. of State Bulletin* 385 (1958).

An important statement of the position that recognition will not be accorded to a state whose government espouses politico-legal theories fundamentally incompatible with the foundations of international law is that of Secretary Colby regarding the U.S.S.R. He said:

It is not possible for the Government of the United States to recognize the present rulers of Russia as a government with which the relations common to friendly governments can be maintained. This conviction has nothing to do with any particular political or social structure which the Russian people themselves may see fit to embrace. It rests upon a wholly different set of facts. These facts, which none dispute, have convinced the Government of the United States, against its will, that the existing regime in Russia is based upon the negation of every principle of honor and good faith, and every usage and convention, underlying the whole structure of international law; the negation, in short, of every principle upon which it is possible to base harmonious and trustful relations, whether of nations or of individuals. . . . Indeed, upon numerous occasions the responsible spokesmen of this Power . . . have declared that it is their understanding that the very existence of Bolshevism in Russia, the maintenance of their own rule, depends, and must continue to depend, upon the occurrence of revolutions in all other great civilized nations, including the United States, which will overthrow and destroy their governments and set up Bolshevist rule in their stead. . . .

There cannot be any common ground upon which [the United States] can stand with a Power whose conceptions of international relations are so entirely alien to its own, so utterly repugnant to its moral sense. There can be no mutual confidence or trust, no respect even. . . . We cannot recognize, hold official relations with, or give friendly reception to the agents of a government which is determined and bound to conspire against our institutions. . . . —*Papers Relating to the Foreign Relations of the United States, 1920* (Washington, D.C.: Government Printing Office, 1931), III, 466–68.

12. As Secretary of State, Thomas Jefferson wrote on November 7, 1792, to Gouverneur Morris, American Minister in Paris: "It accords with our principles to acknowledge any Government to be rightful which is formed by the will of the nation, substantially declared." Quoted in John Bassett Moore, *A Digest of International Law* (Washington, D.C.: Government Printing Office, 1906), I, 120. It is interesting to note that the early American policy tended to disregard or deprecate the distinction between *de facto* and *de jure* recognition because it was thought to reflect the concept of monarchical legitimacy. See, for example, Moore, *op. cit.*, I, 137. For an excellent analysis of U.S. recognition practice up to World War I, see Julius Goebel, *The Recognition Policy of the United States* (New York: Columbia University Press, 1915).

13. See Jules Davids, *America and the World of Our Time* (2d ed.; New York: Random House, 1962), pp. 36–43, on Wilson's policies on the Huerta government in Mexico; on the practical considerations leading to the change of policy toward the Soviet Union under the Roosevelt administration in 1933, see *ibid.*, pp. 140–41.

On the theme that the American emphasis on international law and morality has been misguided and ingenuous, see generally George F. Kennan, *American Diplomacy, 1900–1950* (New York: Mentor Books, 1951), pp. 49–50, 53, 56. However, Kennan suggests that in some cases where a stand on principle is indicated, the U.S. has erred on the other side, by placing mundane interests first. This is his view of the evolution of U.S. recognition policy toward the Soviet Union. Kennan believes that the original Wilson-Colby position, to the effect that the Soviets by their own pronouncements of fundamental principles had made mutual faith, understanding, and intercourse impossible, was a sound basis for eliciting less harsh and dogmatic attitudes from the Soviets. It was increasingly subsumed, however, after Wilson's administration, under a concern for property rights, debts, and claims that was as selfish as it was legal or moral. Ultimately, Roosevelt was to recognize the Soviet Union without really confronting the Communists with the challenges implicit in the Wilson-Colby position and without obtaining adequate satisfaction on debts and claims. See George F. Kennan, *Russia and the West* (Boston: Little, Brown, 1960), pp. 205–7.

14. See Hyde, *op. cit.*, I, 374–75; Hackworth, *op. cit.*, I, 431–32.

15. Lauterpacht, *op. cit.*, pp. 6–7.

16. The Montevideo Inter-American Convention on Rights and Duties of States of 1933 takes the declaratory position. It states:

Art. 3. The political existence of the state is independent of recognition by other states. Even before recognition the state has the right to defend its integrity and independence, to provide for its conservation and prosperity,

Notes 287

and consequently to organize itself as it sees fit, to legislate upon its interests, administer its services, and to define the jurisdiction and competence of its courts. . . .

Art. 6. The recognition of a state merely signifies that the state which recognizes it accepts the personality of the other with all the rights and duties determined by international law. Recognition is unconditional and irrevocable.

The Charter of the Organization of American States of May 2, 1948, provides:

Art. 9. The political existence of the State is independent of recognition by other States. Even before being recognized, the State has the right to defend its integrity and independence, to provide for its preservation and prosperity, and consequently to organize itself as it sees fit, to legislate concerning its interests, to administer its services, and to determine the jurisdiction and competence of its courts. The exercise of these rights is limited only by the exercise of the rights of other States in accordance with international law.

Art. 10. Recognition implies that the State granting it accepts the personality of the new State, with all the rights and duties that international law prescribes for the two States—46 A.J.I.L. supp. p. 46 (1952).

That recognition is not solely a legal act carried out on behalf of the decentralized international community, but a mixture of legal, political, and even moral elements is frequently asserted. For rejections of the Lauterpacht theory, see, for example, Briggs, *op. cit.*, pp. 113–17, and authorities cited therein; J. L. Brierly, *The Law of Nations*, ed. Sir Humphrey Waldock (6th ed.; New York and London: Oxford University Press, 1963), pp. 137–40; Chen, *op. cit.*, pp. 3–17, and authorities cited therein; and Josef L. Kunz, "Critical Remarks on Lauterpacht's 'Recognition in International Law'," 44 A.J.I.L. 713 (1950).

17. See Permanent Court of Arbitration, 1928, The *Island of Palmas Case* (United States and the Netherlands); J. B. Scott, *Hague Court Reports*, 2d series, 83 (1932); and 2 U.N. Rep. Int. Arb. Awards, 829, for a classic exposition of this view of the international community.

18. See Whiteman, *Digest*, II, 2; Lauterpacht, *op. cit.*, pp. 26–30; Chen, *op. cit.*, pp. 54–62; Jean Charpentier, *La reconnaissance internationale et l'évolution du droit des gens* (Paris: Éditions Pedone, 1956), pp. 160–62; Hyde, *op. cit.*, I, 147–48; Paul Guggenheim, *Traité de droit international public* (Geneva: Librairie de l'Université, Georg & Cie., 1953), I, 190; Karl Strupp, Hans Jürgen Schochauer, *et al*, *Wörterbuch des Völkerrechts* (Berlin: Walter de Gruyter & Co., 1961–62), pp. 47–48; and Marcel Sibert, *Traité de droit international public* (Paris: Dalloz, 1951), I, 190.

19. It is true that this condition has been developed with a view to the question of recognizing governments rather than new states. But there is no reason to believe that the test would be less applicable to new states, and, as will be shown, it has indeed been applied to such new states as Lebanon, Syria, Egypt, and the United Arab Republic.

20. Lauterpacht, *op. cit.*, pp. 109–14; Chen, *op. cit.*, pp. 61–62; Charpentier, *op. cit.*, pp. 289–90.

21. Lauteracht, *op. cit.*, p. 109, n. 1.

22. See Timothy Taracouzio, *The Soviet Union and International Law* (New York: The Macmillan Co., 1935); Serge Krylov, "Les Notions Principales de droit international des gens," 70 Hague, *Recueil* I, 411–76 (1947);

Mintauts Chakste, "Soviet Concepts of the State, International Law and Sovereignty," 43 A.J.I.L. 21 (1949); George Guins, *Soviet Law and Soviet Society* (The Hague: Martinus Nijhoff, 1954); Hans Kelsen, *The Communist Theory of Law* (New York: Frederick A. Praeger, 1955); J. Y. Calvez, *Droit international et souveraineté en U.R.S.S.: L'évolution de l'idéologie juridique soviétique depuis la Révolution d'octobre* (Paris: A. Colin, 1953).

23. Chen asserts that "since no State can be outside the international society it has no choice not to submit to international law," and quotes Brierly as follows: "ils [these States] se sont placés automatiquement sous le droit international, sans qu'on leur demandât ou qu'ils donnassent leur consentement, et je ne vois pas pourquoi nous lirons dans leur premier act officiel une declaration d'intention sur un point qui selon toute probabilité était absolument absent de leurs délibérations."—Chen, *op. cit.*, p. 61, citing J. L. Brierly, "Le Fondement du caractère obligatoire du droit international," 23 Hague, *Recueil* 19 (1929).

However, one must view this attitude in the light of Kaplan and Katzenbach's observation that:

In point of fact, as might be expected, no major nation has ever really accepted the idea that lesser states had to consent to the rules of international law espoused by major nations in order to make them obligatory. Despite consent theories, the citizen must take municipal law as he finds it; so, too, the new state must take international law as it finds it. The less certain international law is, the less onerous is it for new states to accept existing norms of international law. And much international law doctrine is, to say the least, flexible.—Morton A. Kaplan and Nicholas deB. Katzenbach, *The Political Foundations of International Law* (New York: John Wiley, 1961), pp. 68–69. Note Professor O'Connell's treatment of this subject in "Independence and Problems of State Succession," this *Yearbook*, pp. 7–41.

24. See J. J. G. Syatauw, *Some Newly Established Asian States and the Development of International Law* (The Hague: Martinus Nijhoff, 1961), pp. 17–21; B. V. A. Röling, *International Law in an Expanded World* (Amsterdam: Djambatan, 1960); Wolfgang Friedmann, "The Changing Dimensions of International Law," 62 *Col. L.R.* 1146, 1148, 1150–53; Raymond Aron, *Paix et guerre entre les nations* (Paris: Calmann-lévy, 1962); Robert Bosc, S.J., "Natural Law and International Law in an Unstable International System," 4 *World Justice* (Louvain) 315 (1963); B. T. Halajczuk, "Peace, War and the Intermediate State in the System of International Law," 4 *World Justice* 331 (1963); Stanley Hoffmann, "International Systems and International Law," 14 *World Politics* 205 (1961).

Useful papers on the impact of non-Western cultures and legal systems on traditional international law are to be found in the *Proceedings of the American Society of International Law* of 1959 and 1960. See Harold D. Laswell, "Universality in Perspective"; Adda B. Bozeman, "Representative Systems of Public Order Today"; C. Wilfred Jenks, "The Challenge of Universality"; and Myres S. McDougal, "Perspectives for an International Law of Human Dignity," in *Proceedings*, 1959 (Washington, D.C., 1959), pp. 1, 10, 85, 107.

Among the interesting papers in *Proceedings*, 1960, are: D. P. O'Connell, "International Law and Boundary Disputes"; George M. Abi-Saab, "The Newly Independent States and the Scope of Domestic Jurisdiction"; and Bruce Marshall, "International Law and Politics in French Africa," pp. 77, 84, 91.

For a comprehensive and thoughtful study of the problems raised by the new nations, see R. P. Anand, "Role of the 'New' Asian-African Countries in the Present International Legal Order," 56 A.J.I.L. 383 (1962).

25. Hackworth, *Digest*, I, 167. See also Alfred Verdross, *Völkerrecht* (Vienna: Springer Verlag, 1959), p. 186.

26. Another case in which a clear distinction was made between the recognition of the new state and that of its government was the U.S. recognition of Israel.

27. For general discussion of the recognition of states or nations, see: Hackworth, *Digest*, I, 195–222; *International Law, A Treatise by L. Oppenheim*, ed. H. Lauterpacht (New York: Longmans, Green & Co., 1952), I, 120–46; Chen, *op. cit.*, pp. 13–93; Lauterpacht, *Recognition*, pp. 1–86. For specific examples of "completely independent" states and of independent or autonomous states associated in some way with the former metropole, see *infra*, pp. 145, 148.

28. Thus the recognition of Yemen was not completed until February 14, 1950. See 22 *Dep't. of State Bulletin* 326 (1960). Nepal was not recognized by the U.S. until 1947, when an agreement of Commerce and Friendship was signed with that nation, which came in closer contact with the outside world after India's independence. 25 *Dept. of State Bulletin* 443 (1951).

29. See *infra*, p. 159, for a discussion of the case of implied U.S. recognition of dependent India.

30. A White House press release of July 1, 1960, stated that the President had sent a message to Dr. Kwame Nkrumah, President of the Republic of Ghana, on the occasion of the accession of Ghana to the status of a republic and the inauguration of Dr. Nkrumah as the first President. 43 *Dep't. of State Bulletin* 147 (1960).

31. For a discussion of U.S. recognition of the Federation of Mali, Mali and Senegal, the Somali Republic, and Burma, see *infra*, pp. 141–42, 145–47, 195–97, respectively.

32. On January 20, 1946, the *Dep't. of State Bulletin* announced that the Allied Council in Austria had recommended the recognition of the elected Austrian Government, that the President had approved such recognition, and that the U.S. member of the Allied Council was instructed to notify the newly established Austrian Government of this decision. The Department of State also announced, however, that this recognition of the Austrian Government would "in no way" interfere with the supreme authority of the Allied Council which would continue its work of denazification and reconstruction. 14 *Dep't. of State Bulletin* 81 (1946). Not until the Austrian State Treaty came into force on July 26, 1955, did an independent Austrian State begin to exist. T.I.A.S. 3298, U.S. Department of State, *American Foreign Policy 1950–1955*, I, 643–75.

33. On December 23, 1945, the Department of State announced that the Yugoslav elections on November 11, 1945, had not been held in accordance with the Yalta agreements, that the Yugoslav Ambassador in Washington had announced certain constitutional changes in the Yugoslav governmental structure, and that the United States took note of these changes and recognized the new Yugoslav regime. 13 *Dep't. of State Bulletin* 1020–21 (1945). It was also announced, however, that the United States Government "desires that it be understood that the establishment of diplomatic relations with the present

regime in Yugoslavia should not be interpreted as implying approval of the policies of the regime, its methods of assuming control . . .," etc. See Whiteman, *Digest*, II, 80–81.

34. According to a Department of State press release of December 6, 1955, the Austrian Government requested the recognition of its neutrality on the part of the United States in a note submitted to the United States Government on November 14, 1955. Similar requests were made to all countries with which Austria had diplomatic relations. On December 6, 1955, in answer to this request, Secretary of State John Foster Dulles delivered a note to the Austrian ambassador, informing the Austrian Federal Government that the United States herewith recognized the neutrality of Austria as defined in the Federal Constitutional Law approved by the Austrian Parliament on October 26, 1955. 33 *Dep't. of State Bulletin* 1011 (1955). France, Great Britain, and Russia submitted identical, but separate, notes on the same day.

35. Lauterpacht, *International Law*, I, 140. See also Lauterpacht. *Recognition in International Law* (1947), 370–71, 405–6, as quoted in Whiteman, *Digest*, II, 48–49.

36. Lauterpacht, *International Law*, I, 340–41; and Chen, *op. cit.*, pp. 270–73, 282–83, 289–91. Hyde displays considerable doubt about the *de facto-de jure* distinction in the recognition of new states. See Hyde, *op. cit.*, I, 193–95. Interestingly, neither Moore nor Hackworth raises the question of distinguishing *de facto* from *de jure* recognition of new states.

37. Whiteman, *Digest*, II, 3.

38. See *infra*, pp. 147–51, for a discussion of U.S. recognition of Cambodia, Vietnam, and Laos.

39. See *infra*, pp. 179–80, for a discussion of U.S. recognition of Sudan. Express conditional recognition was extended to the Austrian Government while Austria was still under Allied occupation.

40. In the case of the recognition of Yemen, the U.S. expressly referred to renewal and completion of recognition. Recognition through the resumption of normal diplomatic relations has occurred, for example, in the following case of the recognition of a new government. On June 7, 1951, the Department of State announced that the American chargé d'affaires at Bolivia had been instructed to resume diplomatic relations with the Bolivian Government then in power. 24 *Dep't. of State Bulletin* 979 (1951). For the supplementation of recognition of a provisional or interim government by a formal announcement, see the study below of U.S. recognition of Israel.

41. See Chen, *op. cit.*, pp. 189 ff.

42. If the recognition of the new government or nation is specifically mentioned, as in the Treaty of General Relations between the United States of America and the Republic of the Philippines (ratified August 16, 1946), then it is certainly express. Article I of this treaty provides that "The United States of America . . . does hereby recognize the independence of the Republic of the Philippines as a separate and self-governing nation . . . and . . . acknowledges the authority and control over the same by the government instituted by the people thereof." T.I.A.S. 1568; 61 *U.S. Statutes at Large* 1174.

43. Chen, *op. cit.*, pp. 194–95. For an example of a bilateral treaty implying recognition, see the Korean case study below. The Turkish international-law scholar Metin Tamkoc deals with the question whether the U.S., which

at the time had not expressly recognized the Republic of Turkey, accorded implied recognition by signing two treaties with Turkey in 1923. Although Hackworth has said that these acts constituted recognition, even though the treaties were not ratified by the United States (Hackworth, *Digest*, I, 312), Tamkoc holds that there was no recognition until two exchanges of notes between Turkey and the U.S. in 1926. See Metin Tamkoc, "The Question of the Recognition of the Republic of Turkey by the United States," 1 *Turkish Yearbook of International Relations* 92, 116–20 (1960). See also Whiteman, *Digest*, II, 52, where she quotes a memorandum she had written to the Legal Adviser of the Department of State on March 25, 1959:

It is possible for bilateral treaties or agreements entered into not to constitute recognition. Thus, during the years 1919 and 1920 a number of bilateral treaties or agreements providing for the repatriation of prisoners of war and nationals were entered into with the Soviet Government, without being regarded as resulting in recognition. Thus, the British, French, Danish, Belgian Governments concluded such agreements at a time when those Governments did not recognize the Soviet Union, and without the agreements being considered as constituting recognition. There are other examples.

The conclusion of a bilateral treaty normally, however, does constitute recognition. I have no doubt that the conclusion of bilateral treaties, particularly comprehensive treaties, more or less permanent in character, or treaties dealing with highly political matters—as distinguished from treaties or agreements dealing with administrative matters, certain business transactions or a very limited or local subject matter not tinged with such political complexion, as for example the exchange of prisoners of war or nations, exit permits, and the like,—are properly to be regarded and doubtless would be regarded as recognition of a state or government competent to enter into such a treaty.

44. As is indicated by a reading of the section on U.S. practice, in most cases of recognition, the exchange of diplomatic representatives is supplementary. Of interest here is Chen's discussion of the Indian case. As the reader will probably discover, the authors of this study contend that India was probably recognized as a dependent entity long before its formal recognition as an independent Dominion within the British Commonwealth of Nations. Chen has the following to say: "Perhaps the view that the exchange of diplomatic representatives is an absolute indication of recognition does not entirely apply in the case of India. India entered into international relations with other powers after the signing of the Versailles Treaty. For many years, foreign countries have exchanged resident representatives with her, styled as 'commissioners,' who were diplomats in everything but name. Before the transfer of power on August 15, 1947, several States had exchanged regular diplomatic representatives with her. Did India become an independent State at the time of the accrediting of the commissioners or the ambassadors? Probably the case of India is unique, and must be regarded as an exception to the general rule." Chen, *op. cit.*, p. 197.

45. See Chen, *op. cit.*, p. 222. For a discussion of the collectivization of the process of recognition, see Lauterpacht, *Recognition*, pp. 67–69. By way of example of collective recognition in substance, on November 4, 1945, the Department of State announced that "Before making its decision to recognize

the new Government of Venezuela, the Government of the United States of America exchanged views and consulted with the governments of the other American Republics." 13 *Dep't. of State Bulletin* 734 (1945).

46. Wright, for example, argues that "general recognition" of statehood or of any other international status can be accomplished "when the important states which are in an important degree affected by the status in question, have expressly recognized the status, or, in case conditions exist clearly defined by international law as requisite for the status, can be presumed to have acquiesced by refraining from an explicit declaration of non-recognition." General recognition is distinguished from the particular recognition granted by a state or by a number of states in a case of collective recognition. Wright argues that an international organization recognizes by admitting a state, and that such admission requires the members to deal with the new state *within the organization*. Such admission, he says, does not "in principle oblige them to deal with the state or government elsewhere or to exchange diplomatic officers." Quincy Wright, "Some Thoughts About Recognition," 44 A.J.I.L. 548–59 (1950).

Chen contends: "Admission to the United Nations would be a positive proof of the possession of the quality of statehood, though it does not mean that other members are obliged to enter into relations with it to the full extent." Chen, *op. cit.*, p. 215. See *infra*, the case of Kuwait's admission to UNESCO, although not a U.N. member, pp. 165–67.

47. See Chen, *op. cit.*, p. 204. For a firm denial that recognition would result from East Germany's adhesion and a restatement of the U.S. position that recognition is a matter of intent, and that intent must be clearly shown for recognition to occur, see the testimony of Secretary of State Dean Rusk before the United States Senate Committee on Foreign Relations. The record of his testimony also includes relevant parts of the President's Press Conference of August 1, 1963, a Department of State briefing of August 2, 1963, and an Opinion of the Legal Adviser of August 12, 1963. U.S. Congress, Committee on Foreign Relations, U.S. Senate, 88th Congress, 1st Session, *Hearings: Nuclear Test Ban Treaty*, August 12, 13, 14, 15, 19, 20, 21, 22, 23, 26, and 27, 1963 (Washington, D.C.: Government Printing Office, 1963), pp. 14–18.

It has been contended that the admission of representatives of East Germany to the Geneva Conference of Foreign Ministers beginning May 11, 1959, resulted in "partial" recognition. See Jean Edward Smith, *The Defense of Berlin* (Baltimore: The Johns Hopkins Press, 1963), pp. 203, 206.

48. See Chen, *op. cit.*, pp. 198–200. See also Whiteman's interesting discussion of the difficulties encountered by the U.S. in attempting to retain consular representation in Italian-occupied Ethiopia without recognizing the Italian conquest. *Digest*, II, 62.

49. Express announcements of recognition can be found throughout the section of this article that deals with case studies. Hackworth discusses the method of officially receiving the continuing foreign representative of a nation in which a change of government or constitution has taken place. Hackworth, *Digest*, I, 168. For the Presidential reception of the envoy of an unrecognized state or one being recognized, see *infra*, p. 159. A good example of recognition through the acknowledgment of a letter received from the foreign government recognized is the American recognition of Guinea's independence. See also Whiteman, *Digest*, II, 51 ff.

50. For an example of a congratulatory message from the Secretary of State to the ambassador of a newly independent nation already resident in Washington, see the case study on Burma. As for the Secretary's reply to a note received from the ambassador of an already recognized nation that a change of government had taken place, in press release No. 299, dated May 17, 1957, the Department of State announced that the Colombian Embassy had been informed, in reply to notes received from the Colombian Ambassador, that the military junta in power in Colombia at that time was recognized as the Provisional Government of Colombia. 36 *Dep't. of State Bulletin* 901 (1957). For an example of a formal supplemental announcement of recognition, see the case study on Israel. See also Hackworth, *Digest*, I, 168.

51. Whiteman, *Digest*, II, 60.

52. See Hackworth, *Digest*, I, 167. On January 7, 1959, the Department of State announced that the United States Embassy at Havana had informed the Foreign Minister of Cuba that the United States Government had recognized the new Government of Cuba. The note was delivered personally by Ambassador Earl E. T. Smith to the new Foreign Minister. 40 *Dep't. of State Bulletin* 128 (1959). An example of employing this type of methodology toward a new state is the recognition of Sudanese independence. But the American representative was a liaison officer, not a diplomatic representative in the strict sense of the word.

53. Thus, the recognition of the state of Tunisia by the U.S. was expressed in a message from the American consul general in Tunis to the Bey of Tunis, on March 22, 1956. Myers, *op. cit.*, p. 716.

54. The unique employment of a liaison officer occurred in the Sudanese case.

55. On January 21, 1949, the Department of State announced that the United States Ambassador at San Salvador had formally replied to a note received from the new Salvadorean Foreign Minister. This was referred to as an act of resuming relations with the provisional government then in power. 20 *Dep't. of State Bulletin* 150 (1949). On March 6, 1948, the American Ambassador at Bangkok accorded recognition to the new Siamese Government through an exchange of letters with the minister of foreign affairs of the new government. 18 *Dep't. of State Bulletin* 360 (1948).

56. This is a common method that has become part of a pattern established in the procedure of recognizing new nations since about 1957. See, for example, the discussion below of the American recognition of Togo's independence.

57. See the section below on U.S. recognition of Dahomey, Niger, Upper Volta, and Ivory Coast, members of the Conseil de l'Entente.

58. On December 28, 1949, the U.S. commissioned its representative at the Round Table Conference as ambassador to Indonesia.

59. This occurred in the Sudanese case.

60. For example, on July 20, 1956, President Eisenhower named Secretary of State John Foster Dulles as his personal representative to head a delegation to the inauguration of President-elect of Peru, Dr. Manuel Prado Ugarteche. 35 *Dep't. of State Bulletin* 187 (1956). Another example is to be found in the procedure of U.S. recognition of Ghana's independence. From March 3 through 10, 1957, a U.S. delegation, headed by Vice-President Nixon and including members of Congress, participated in the ceremonies celebrating the independence of Ghana. Myers, *op. cit.*, p. 719.

61. Whiteman, *Digest*, II, 60.

62. Subsequent to, simultaneous with, or antecedent to formal recognition, the U.S. Government has usually sent or accredited a diplomatic representative of some kind to the newly established nation or government in question. In most such cases, formal recognition had already been extended by the time the diplomat arrived at the foreign capital. However, his arrival, if nothing else, served to confirm or enhance the act of recognition. Numerous examples of this are to be found in the case studies in the following section.

63. See Hackworth, *Digest*, I, 168. For examples of such messages, see the account of U.S. recognition of the Union of Burma and of the change of Ghana from Dominion status to Republic status. The reader will find that similar messages have been employed in many of the cases analyzed in this study. See also Whiteman, *Digest*, II, 60–61.

64. Much of the information concerning the political circumstances surrounding the emergence to full independence of most states discussed in this and succeeding case studies, data on the former status of these states, the relevant dates of changes in political status—such as the attainment of autonomy, association with other states, or accession to full independence—and facts about international relations subsequent to independence has been taken from Whiteman's *Digest* and from the following Department of State publication: Bureau of Intelligence and Research, Office of Research in Economics and Science, U.S. Department of State, *Profiles of Newly Independent States*, Geographic Bulletin No. 1 (Washington, D.C.: Government Printing Office, 1963). This is an excellent source of information. It contains a list of most newly independent states since 1943 and chronologically considers each state, giving the important facts concerning former status, independence, and present status. Although this source will not be cited in each instance where it has been used, much of the historical data used in the various case studies has been taken from it. The information that was not found here has been taken from the State Department's "Newly Independent Nations Series." To date, fact sheets discussing briefly the history, government, economy, and foreign relations of the individual country have been published on the following new nations: *Africa:* Libya, Sudan, Morocco, Tunisia, Ghana, Guinea, Togo, Malagasy Republic, Ivory Coast, Chad, Congo-Brazzaville, Gabon, Nigeria, Mauritania, Tanganyika; *Near East and South Asia:* Jordan, Pakistan, India, Israel, Cyprus; *Far East:* Burma, Korea, Vietnam, Philippines, Indonesia, Laos, Cambodia, Malaya; *Western Hemisphere:* Jamaica. Office of Media Services, Bureau of Public Affairs, U.S. Department of State, *The Newly Independent Nations* (Washington, D.C.: Government Printing Office, 1962).

65. "Ambassador Hare (Cairo) to the Secretary of State, telegram, September 19, 1958, MS. Department of State, file 751S.02/9-1958; the Department of State, circular telegram, September 19, 1958, *ibid.*; Ambassador Yost (Rabat) to the Secretary of State, telegram, September 19, 1958, *ibid.*, file 751S.00/9-1958; Ambassador Jones (Tunis) to the Secretary of State, telegram, September 19, 1958, *ibid.* file 751S.02/9-1958; the Department of State, circular telegram, September 20, 1958, *ibid.* /9-2058." Whiteman, *Digest*, II, 74–75.

66. "The American Ambassador at Paris (Gavin) to the Secretary of State (Rusk), telegram, July 3, 1962, MS. Department of State, file 751S.00/7-362." Whiteman, *Digest*, II, 133.

Notes 295

67. 47 *Dep't. of State Bulletin* 135 (1962).
68. "Secretary Rusk's News Conference of July 12, 1962," Department of State Press Release No. 456, dated July 13, 1962, p. 6. Whiteman also regards President Kennedy's congratulatory message as constitutive of recognition. Whiteman, *Digest*, II, 134.
69. 47 *Dep't. of State Bulletin* 560 (1962).
70. *Ibid.*, p. 945.
71. U.S. Department of State, *The Newly Independent Nations: Cyprus*, p. 2.
72. For details, see Whiteman, *Digest*, II, 149–50.
73. "Secretary of State Herter, memorandum for the President, 'Independence Day Message from You to the President of Cyprus,' August 9, 1960, MS. Department of State, file 780A.02/8-960." Whiteman, *Digest*, II, 150.
74. *Public Papers of the Presidents of the United States, Dwight D. Eisenhower 1960–61* (1961), p. 633.
75. Department of State press release No. 464, dated August 16, 1960, as reproduced in 43 *Dep't of State Bulletin* 388 (1960).
76. 43 *Dep't. of State Bulletin* 461 (1960).
77. 21 *Dep't. of State Bulletin* 448 (1949).
78. *Ibid.* See also Myers, *op. cit.*, pp. 713–14.
79. Whiteman, *Digest*, II, 165.
80. 21 *Dep't. of State Bulletin* 753 (1949).
81. Whiteman, *Digest*, II, 167.
82. 22 *Dep't. of State Bulletin* 55 (1950).
83. U.S. Department of State, *The Newly Independent Nations: Indonesia*, p. 1.
84. On May 14, 1948, an agent of the Provisional Council of the State of Israel notified the President of the United States that "the state of Israel has been proclaimed as an independent republic within frontiers approved by the General Assembly of the United Nations in its resolution of November 29, 1947, and that a provisional government has been charged to assume the rights and duties of government." Myers quite correctly points out that "The armistices left half again as much territory in Israel's control as was stipulated in the Plan of Partition." Myers, *op. cit.*, p. 710. For the U.N. General Assembly Resolution, see Resolution 181 (III), U.N. General Assembly, Official Records, Doc. A/519, as cited in Myers.
85. "The Department considers, however, that it would be premature to take any decision at the present time with respect to the question of its recognition of Trans-Jordan as an independent state." Myers, *op. cit.*, p. 709. Quoted from 14 *Dep't. of State Bulletin* 765 (1946). On October 21, 1945, the Department of State further stated that "The substance of this Government's position has been that this Government would not support a final decision which in its opinion would affect the basic situation in Palestine without full consultation with both Jews and Arabs." 13 *Dep't. of State Bulletin* 623 (1945).
86. Whiteman, *Digest*, II, 172.
87. 18 *Dep't. of State Bulletin* 673 (1948).
88. Myers, *op. cit.*, p. 710.
89. Professor Jessup stated: "So far as recognition of the States is concerned . . . the recognition accorded by the United States Government to the State

of Israel was immediate and full recognition. There was no qualification. It was not conditional; it was not de facto recognition; it was full recognition of the State. So far as the Provisional Government of Israel is concerned, the United States did extend de facto recognition to that Provisional Government of Israel." U.N. Security Council, 3d Year, Department of State Official Records, No. 130, p. 12, as cited in Myers, *op. cit.*, p. 711.

90. See Whiteman, *Digest*, II, 169; 19 *Dep't. of State Bulletin* 582 (1948).
91. 20 *Dep't. of State Bulletin* 205 (1949).
92. Myers, *op. cit.*, p. 711. Announcement that the United States and Israel had agreed on the exchange of diplomatic missions was made on June 2, 1948.
93. See Whiteman, *Digest*, II, 139–40 and 213.
94. 47 *Dep't. of State Bulletin* 159–65 (1962).
95. Haut Commissariat de la République Française au Cameroun, Direction des Relations Extérieures, *Cameroun, 1946 from Trusteeship to Independence 1960*, pp. 9–13. Although Whiteman consistently employs the spelling "Cameroon," an important distinction appears to have been made in the official messages that were exchanged. The entire Trusteeship territory, under both British and French administration, may be correctly referred to as the "Cameroons." However, the part of the territory that became the State of Cameroun under French administration in 1957 and became independent on January 1, 1960, consistently referred to itself as "Cameroun," and was referred to as such in the United States messages. The spelling was officially changed after the Southern Cameroons, the part of the territory formerly administered by Britain, joined with the Republic of Cameroun on October 1, 1961, forming the Federal Republic of Cameroon.
96. See Whiteman, *Digest*, II, 142–43.
97. "The American Consul General at Yaoundé (More) to the Secretary of State, airgram No. G-18, Nov. 29, 1959, MS. Department of State, file 651.51U/11-2959; and same to same, telegram, December 29, 1959, *ibid./12-2859*." Whiteman, *Digest*, II, 143.
98. "Secretary of State Herter, memorandum for the President (Eisenhower), Dec. 30, 1959, MS. Department of State, file 851U.424/12-3059." Whiteman, *Digest*, II, 144.
99. "Secretary of State Herter to the American Consulate General, Yaoundé, telegram, December 31, 1959, MS. Department of State, file 851U.424/12-3159." Whiteman, *Digest*, II, 144.
100. "Official U.S. Delegates to the Cameroun Independence Ceremonies and the Inauguration of President William V. S. Tubman of Liberia," Department of State press release No. 882, dated December 29, 1959.
101. "The American Consulate General, Yaoundé, to the Secretary of State, telegram, Jan. 6, 1960, MS. Department of State, file 870C. 424/1-660." Whiteman, *Digest*, II, 144.
102. See the New York *Times*, January 2, 1961, p. 1.
103. 42 *Dep't. of State Bulletin* 174 (1960). It was stated here (Department of State press release No. 1, dated January 5, 1960) that "Cameroun obtained its independence as a result of a resolution of the United Nations resumed 13th General Assembly passed on March 13, 1959 [U.N. Doc. A/RES/1349 (XIII)], declaring that the trusteeship agreement would cease to be in force on January 1."
104. In the press release referred to in note 103 it was also announced that

"Bollard More has been named Chargé d'Affaires." Thus, the supplementary mode of exchanging diplomatic representatives was added to that of express declaration.

105. U.N. Doc. A/RES/425, as cited in 36 *Dep't. of State Bulletin* 106–9 (1957).

106. Treaty File, MS. Department of State, as cited in Whiteman, *Digest*, II, 153.

107. Department of State press release No. 113, dated March 5, 1957 (Announcement of U.S. Recognition), as reproduced in 36 *Dep't. of State Bulletin* 489–90. Also reproduced in *ibid.* is a message from President Eisenhower to the Government and People of Ghana (White House press release, dated March 6, 1957).

108. *Ibid.*, 950.

109. Henry Cabot Lodge, United States Representative to the United Nations General Assembly, made the following statement: "The United States will vote here in the General Assembly for the admission of Ghana to the United Nations as we did in the Security Council. ..." *Ibid.*, 490.

110. The congratulatory messages, as quoted by Whiteman, were as follows: "S. Res. 111, 85th Congress, extending cordial greetings to the Legislative Assembly of Ghana, adopted March 5, 1957, 103 Cong. Rec., pt. 3, pp. 3105, 3107; H. Res. 185, 85th Congress, extending cordial greetings to the Legislative Assembly of Ghana, adopted March 6, 1957, *ibid.*, pp. 3182–3183; and H. Res. 18, House of Representatives, State of Michigan, adopted March 5, 1957, extending to the people of Ghana sincere congratulations, Journal of the House, No. 30, p. 411; *ibid.*, No. 32, p. 431." Whiteman, *Digest*, II, 153.

111. 43 *Dep't. of State Bulletin* 147 (1960).

112. 13 *Dep't. of State Bulletin* 435 (1945).

113. 17 *Dep't. of State Bulletin* 618–20 (1947); see Whiteman, *Digest*, II, 173–75.

114. "For the texts of the resolutions of November 14, 1947, see U.N. Res. 112 (II) (A) and (B); 'The U.S. and the U.N.,' report by the President to Congress for the year 1947, pp. 157–159." Whiteman, *Digest*, II, 175.

115. Myers, *op. cit.*, p. 708.

116. "Political Adviser Joseph E. Jacobs (CG USAFIK), Seoul, to the Secretary of State, telegram, Aug. 9, 1948, MS. Department of State, file 501.BB KOREA/8-948." Whiteman, *Digest*, II, 175–76.

117. 19 *Dep't. of State Bulletin* 242 (1948).

118. Whiteman, *Digest*, II, 177.

119. *Ibid.*

120. "Secretary of State Marshall to the American Representative, Seoul, Korea, telegram, Aug. 26, 1948, MS. Department of State, file 895.01/8-1348." Whiteman, *Digest*, II, 177–78.

121. T.I.A.S. 1918. 62 *U.S. Statutes at Large* 3817–23. This agreement entered into force on August 24, 1948.

122. T.I.A.S. 1851. 62 *U.S. Statutes at Large* 3422–46. At the time he signed this agreement, the United States ambassador was still unconfirmed. The treaty entered into force on September 20, 1948.

123. Myers, *op. cit.*, p. 708. This treaty was based on Congressional legislation that, on June 28, 1948, authorized aid to the Republic of Korea.

124. General Assembly Resolution 195 (III), December 12, 1948, as cited

in *ibid.*, pp. 707–8. See also 20 *Dep't. of State Bulletin* 59–60 (1949).

125. 22 *Dep't. of State Bulletin* 434 (1949).

126. Myers, *op. cit.*, p. 709. Myers also states that, "by the accepted standard that recognition of a new state consists of international action, explicit or implicit, which creates rights and obligations between the parties that are legally enforceable, recognition of the Republic of Korea by the United States antedated January 1, 1949." *Ibid.*, p. 708. See also Tamkoc, "The Question of the Recognition of the Republic of Turkey by the United States," p. 21, *n.* 49.

127. Myers, *op. cit.*, p. 713; Whiteman, *Digest*, II, 198–99.

128. 25 *Dep't. of State Bulletin* 1057 (1951).

129. "The Chargé d'Affaires ad interim of the United States (Andrew G. Lynch) to the Foreign Minister of Libya (Mahmoud Bey Muntasser) note No. 1, Dec. 24, 1951, MS. Department of State, despatch No. 100, Jan. 8, 1952, file 773.02/1-852, encl. 3." Whiteman, *Digest*, II, 200.

130. 25 *Dep't. of State Bulletin* 1957 (1951).

131. Department of State press release No. 357, dated June 27, 1960, as reproduced in 43 *Dep't. of State Bulletin* 87 (1960).

132. Department of State press release No. 373, dated June 30, 1960, as reproduced in *ibid.*, p. 162.

133. Department of State press release No. 371, dated June 30, 1960, as reproduced in *ibid.*, p. 118.

134. *Ibid.*, pp. 149–53.

135. Whiteman, *Digest*, II, 227.

136. Department of State press release No. 866, dated December 9, 1961, as reproduced in 45 *Dep't. of State Bulletin* 1072 (1961).

137. 46 *Dep't. of State Bulletin* 37 (1962).

138. MS. Department of State, file 711.11-KE/12-961, as cited in Whiteman, *Digest*, II, 226.

139. U.S.–U.N. press release No. 3889, as reproduced in 46 *Dep't. of State Bulletin* 37 (1962).

140. See Whiteman, *Digest*, II, 227.

141. *Ibid.*, p. 228.

142. Department of State press release No. 193, dated April 14, 1960. "Other delegates with the rank of Special Ambassador" were James K. Penfield, Deputy Assistant Secretary of State for African Affairs, and Arthur J. Weaver of Nebraska. It was also announced that two "public members" of the United States delegation had been appointed. They were George H. Becker, Jr., Deputy Assistant Secretary of Commerce for International Affairs, and Dr. Frank M. Snowden, Jr., Dean, College of Liberal Arts, Howard University.

143. Department of State press release No. 219, dated April 27, 1960, as reproduced in 42 *Dep't. of State Bulletin* 806 (1960). In this connection, it is interesting to note a change in the nature of the Togolese governmental system recognized by the United States on June 6, 1963. Department of State press release No. 305 of June 6, 1963, reads as follows:

> The Government of the United States received a request for recognition from the Provisional Government of the Republic of Togo. In this request the Provisional Government stated that its first goal was to 're-establish legality' rapidly by organizing general elections. On May 5, the Togolese people adopted a new constitution, chose deputies representing all political parties to the National Assembly, and elected a new president and vice-president.

The Togolese Government has also stated that it is prepared to respect its international obligations.

Believing that these declarations and events provide a basis for democratic rule in Togo and expressing the hope that all the elements in Togo will cooperate toward that end, the United States has decided to recognize the Government of the Republic of Togo. The United States has instructed its representatives in Togo to confirm this decision in writing to the Ministry of Foreign Affairs of the Republic of Togo.

144. Whiteman, *Digest*, II, 228.
145. *Profiles of Newly Independent States*, p. 18. See also Whiteman, *Digest*, II, 239.
146. E. J. Thrasher, Officer in Charge of Australian and New Zealand Affairs, U.S. Department of State.
147. Department of External Affairs, Wellington, New Zealand, "Independence Celebrations in Western Samoa: 1–5 January, 1962," 12 *External Affairs Review* 3 (1962).
148. As reproduced in Whiteman, *Digest*, II, 239.
149. *Ibid.*, 138–39.
150. 16 *Dep't. of State Bulletin* 258 (1947).
151. 16 *Dep't. of State Bulletin* 1314 (1947).
152. 17 *Dep't. of State Bulletin* 101 (1947).
153. 17 *Dep't. of State Bulletin* 648–49 (1947), as quoted in Whiteman, *Digest*, II, 137.
154. 17 *Dep't. of State Bulletin* 648 (1947), as quoted in Myers, *op. cit.*, p. 713.
155. 18 *Dep't. of State Bulletin* 61 (1948). See also Myers, *op. cit.*, p. 713.
156. Myers, *op. cit.*, pp. 714–15. Myers' date for the French-Laotian Agreement (May 19, 1949) is incorrect. See Whiteman, *Digest*, II, 184. See, in general, *ibid.*, pp. 140–42, 184–88, and 234–38.
157. 22 *Dep't. of State Bulletin* 244 (1950); 2 *American Foreign Policy, 1950–1955: Basic Documents* (1957) 2363–64.
158. Whiteman, *Digest*, II, 235.
159. 22 *Dep't. of State Bulletin* 291 (1950); 2 *American Foreign Policy, 1950–1955: Basic Documents* (1957) 2364; Whiteman, *Digest*, II, 140.
160. Myers, *op. cit.*, p. 714.
161. 22 *Dep't. of State Bulletin* 291 (1950).
162. "In June last year, this Government expressed its gratification at the signing of the Franco-Vietnamese agreements of March 8, which provided the basis for the evolution of Vietnamese independence within the French Union. These agreements, together with similar accords between France and the Kingdoms of Laos and Cambodia have now been ratified by the French National Assembly and signed by the President of the French Republic. This ratification has established the independence of Vietnam, Laos, and Cambodia as associated states within the French Union." *Ibid.*
163. See Myers, *op. cit.*, p. 175.
164. Department of State press release No. 394, dated July 21, 1954.
165. 31 *Dep't. of State Bulletin* 162–64 (1954).
166. 29 *Dep't. of State Bulletin* 114–24 (1953); Whiteman *Digest*, II, 186–87; for the 1955 elevation of diplomatic missions to embassy status, see 33 *Dep't. of State Bulletin* 299–300 (1955).

167. Whiteman, *Digest*, II, 188.
168. 43 *Dep't. of State Bulletin* 350 (1960).
169. Department of State press release No. 596, dated October 13, 1960, as reproduced in *ibid.*, 702.
170. "The American Chargé d'Affaires at Brazzaville to the Department of State, telegram, Aug. 15, 1960, MS. Department of State, file 770P.02/8-1560; *Public Papers of the Presidents of the United States, Dwight D. Eisenhower 1960–61* (1961), pp. 630–61." Whiteman, *Digest*, II, 145.
171. "The American Consul at Brazzaville to the Department of State, telegram, Aug. 12, 1960, MS. Department of State, file 770M.02/8-1160, *Public Papers of the Presidents of the United States, Dwight D. Eisenhower 1960–61* (1961), p. 629." Whiteman, *Digest*, II, 147. See also the *New York Times*, August 12, 1960, p. 4.
172. *Public Papers of the Presidents of the United States, Dwight D. Eisenhower 1960–61* (1961), p. 631, as cited in Whiteman, *Digest*, II, 149. Relevant telegrams, also cited in *ibid.*, are as follows: "The American Chargé d'Affaires at Brazzaville to the Department of State, telegram, Aug. 15, 1960, MS. Department of State, file 770R.02/8-1560; the American Chargé d'Affaires at Brazzaville to the Department of State, telegram, Sept. 2, 1960, MS. Department of State, file 123 Lukens, Alan W." See also the *New York Times*, August 16, 1960, pp. 1 and 2.
173. "The American Chargé d'Affaires at Brazzaville to the Department of State, telegram, Aug. 17, 1960, MS. Department of State, file 770S.02/8-1760. For the message of President Eisenhower to President M'Ba on the occasion of the independence of the Republic of Gabon, August 17, 1960, see *Public Papers of the Presidents of the United States, Dwight D. Eisenhower 1960–61* (1961), p. 644." Whiteman, *Digest*, II, 152.
174. See Whiteman, *Digest*, II, 146.
175. 18 *Dep't. of State Bulletin* 316 (1948).
176. See Whiteman, *Digest*, II, 147.
177. Department of State press release No. 370, dated June 28, 1960, as reproduced in 43 *Dep't. of State Bulletin* 118 (1960). See also Myers, *op. cit.*, p. 706.
178. White House press release, dated June 30, 1960, as reproduced in 43 *Dep't. of State Bulletin* 162 (1960). Also printed in *Public Papers of the Presidents of the United States, Dwight D. Eisenhower 1960–61* (1961), p. 544.
179. Whiteman, *Digest*, II, 147.
180. *New York Times*, July 3, 1960, p. 21.
181. 43 *Dep't. of State Bulletin* 262 (1960).
182. See Myers, *op. cit.*, p. 719. See also Department of State press release No. 423, dated July 29, 1960, as reproduced in 43 *Dep't. of State Bulletin* 262 (1960).
183. *Ibid.*, p. 702, where Department of State press release No. 596, dated October 13, 1960, is reproduced.
184. *Public Papers of the Presidents of the United States, Dwight D. Eisenhower 1960–61* (1961), p. 608.
185. *Ibid.*, p. 612.
186. *Ibid.*, pp. 610–11.
187. Department of State press release No. 853, dated December 6, 1961.
188. Myers, *op. cit.*, p. 718.
189. "Prime Minister of Guinea (Sékou Touré) to President Eisenhower,

Notes

Oct. 2 and 13, 1958, MS. Department of State, files 770B.02/10-258, *ibid.*/10-1358." Whiteman, *Digest*, II, 155.

190. As reproduced in *ibid.* and in White House press release, dated November 2, 1958, 39 *Dep't. of State Bulletin* 966 (1958).

191. "The American Consul General at Dakar (Dumont) to the Department of State, file 770B.02/10-858." Whiteman, *Digest*, II, 155.

192. "The American Consul General at Dakar to the Department of State, telegram, Oct. 13, 1958, MS. Department of State, file 770B.02/10-1358." Whiteman, *Digest*, II, 155.

193. "The American Consul General at Dakar to the Department of State, despatch No. 99, Oct. 24, 1958, MS. Department of State, file 770B.02/10-2458, encl. (French text)." Whiteman, *Digest*, II, 155.

194. 39 *Dep't. of State Bulletin* 966 (1958).

195. Myers, *op. cit.*, p. 718. According to Whiteman, the date of the establishment of the American Embassy in Conarky was February 13, 1959. Whiteman, *Digest*, II, 156. See 40 *Dep't. of State Bulletin* 390 (1959).

196. Myers, *op. cit.*, p. 712.

197. Whiteman, *Digest*, II, 164.

198. D. P. O'Connell states that Pakistan, upon separation from India and establishment as a newly independent Dominion, claimed to have inherited the same international rights and duties as the new Dominion of India. This claim was based on the contention that the personality of British India had been divided and that both new Dominions were successors to the rights and duties of British India. Thus Pakistan claimed automatic membership in the United Nations. However, the British Government held that Pakistan was a new international person and the United Nations Secretariat held that, as a rule, territory which breaks off from a member state of the United Nations will not automatically have membership in the United Nations. The Legal Committee of the United Nations also held that a territory breaking off from a member state cannot automatically claim membership in the organization and must make a new application for membership. D. P. O'Connell, *State Succession*, pp. 41–43 and 65–66. See also the following documents cited in *ibid.*, p. 66: U.N. Doc. S/496, August 18, 1947; U.N. Doc. A/C6/156, October 2, 1947; U.N. Doc. A/C1/212, October 11, 1947; U.N. Press Release, P.M. 473, August 12, 1947.

199. 17 *Dep't. of State Bulletin* 396 (1947). On the emergence of India and Pakistan, see Russell H. Fifield, "New States in the Indian Realm," 46 A.J.I.L. 450–63 (1952).

200. Myers, *op. cit.*, p. 712.

201. 17 *Dep't. of State Bulletin* 296 (1947). The telegram from President Truman to Lord Mountbatten, Governor General of the Dominion of India, read as follows: "We welcome India's new and enhanced status in the world community of sovereign independent nations." The telegram from President Truman to the new Governor General of the new Dominion of Pakistan, Mohammed Ali Jinnah, began as follows: "On this conspicuous day which marks the emergence among the family of nations of the new Dominion of Pakistan. . . ." Because of transmission difficulties, the substance of President Truman's message to the Governor General of Pakistan was delivered by letter on August 14, 1947, according to Whiteman. The full text was received and communicated to the Governor General later. Whiteman, *Digest*, II, 211.

202. Myers, *op. cit.*, p. 712.

203. *Ibid.*, p. 711. The following remark in one of Myers' footnotes is interesting: "Diplomatic representation between the United States and India was reciprocally complete months before independence on August 15, 1947. The Agent General of India in the British Embassy at Washington, an official dating from July, 1941, was made a chargé d'affaires in November, 1946, and was accredited as ambassador in February, 1947, six months in advance of independence. The United States followed with appointment of a chargé d'affaires *vice* the commissioner, in December, 1946, and of an ambassador in April, 1947." *Ibid.*, p. 712.

204. According to Myers, India was recognized by the U.S. on December 18, 1942, the date of the accreditation of a senior foreign service officer with the rank of ambassador to India. Myers, *op. cit.*, p. 704.

205. 215 *F.* 2d 547, 551–52 (2d Cir. 1954); Whiteman, *Digest*, II, 163–65.
206. Whiteman, *Digest*, II, 164.
207. *Ibid.*, 162.
208. Whiteman, *Digest*, II, 170; the *New York Times*, August 5, 1962, sec. 11, p. 2.
209. *New York Times*, August 5, 1962, p. 1.
210. *Ibid.*, August 6, 1962, p. 1.
211. 47 *Dep't. of State Bulletin* 751 (1962).
212. White House press release, dated December 10, 1963; 50 *Dep't. of State Bulletin* 18 (1964).
213. Department of State press release No. 79, dated February 24, 1964.
214. 50 *Dep't. of State Bulletin* 18 (1964).
215. Pearcy, "Forty Newly Independent States: Some Politicogeographic Observations," p. 607.
216. *Ibid.*
217. *Ibid.*, p. 606.
218. 44 *Dep't. of State Bulletin* 244 (1961).
219. T.I.A.S. 1580, cited in *ibid.*
220. Pearcy, "Forty Newly Independent States: Some Politicogeographic Observations," p. 606.
221. See *Profiles of Newly Independent States*.
222. Department of State press release No. 654, dated September 22, 1961, as reproduced in 45 *Dep't. of State Bulletin* 588 (1961).
223. Whiteman, *Digest*, II, 183–84.
224. *Ibid.*, 200–201.
225. Department of State press release No. 352, dated June 24, 1960, as reproduced in 43 *Dep't. of State Bulletin* 73–74 (1960).
226. White House press release, dated June 26, 1960, as reproduced in *ibid.*, p. 87.
227. *New York Times*, July 6, 1964, p. 1.
228. White House press release, dated June 26, 1964.
229. Department of State press release No. 314, dated July 3, 1964.
230. *New York Times*, July 6, 1964, p. 2.
231. See Whiteman, *Digest*, II, 201.
232. Department of State press release No. 432, dated July 24, 1957, as reproduced in 37 *Dep't. of State Bulletin* 298 (1957).
233. Department of State press release No. 451, dated August 7, 1957.
234. Whiteman, *Digest*, II, 201.

235. 37 *Dep't. of State Bulletin* 474 (1957).
236. Whiteman, *Digest*, II, 204.
237. *New York Times*, December 6, 1960, p. 13.
238. As reproduced in Whiteman, *Digest*, II, 204.
239. *Ibid.*
240. *New York Times*, December 13, 1960, p. 17.
241. United States Delegation press release No. 3599, dated December 4, 1960, as reproduced in 43 *Dep't. of State Bulletin* 976–77 (1960).
242. 45 *Dep't. of State Bulletin* 169 (1961).
243. Myers, *op. cit.*, pp. 715–16.
244. *Ibid.*, p. 715. See also Whiteman, *Digest*, II, 204–5.
245. Department of State press release No. 117, dated March 7, 1956, and No. 118, dated March 8, 1956, respectively, as reproduced in 34 *Dep't. of State Bulletin* 466 (1956).
246. *Ibid.* The note to King Mohammed V was answered by the Prime Minister of Morocco with a note of gratitude, delivered to Diplomatic Agent Holmes on March 14, 1956. Whiteman, *Digest*, II, 205.
247. Department of State press release No. 186, dated April 19, 1956, as reproduced in *Dep't. of State Bulletin* 667 (1956). See also Whiteman, *Digest*, II, 206.
248. Myers, *op. cit.*, p. 716.
249. 35 *Dep't. of State Bulletin* 44 (1956).
250. 43 *Dep't. of State Bulletin* 590 (1960).
251. Department of State press release No. 573, dated September 30, 1960, as reproduced in *ibid.*, p. 630.
252. *Ibid.*, pp. 643–44. *Public Papers of the Presidents of the United States, Dwight D. Eisenhower 1960–61* (1961), p. 741.
253. Department of State press release No. 572, dated September 30, 1960, as reproduced in *ibid.*
254. Whiteman, *Digest*, II, 209.
255. 48 *U.S. Statutes at Large* 456, as cited in Myers, *op. cit.*, p. 707. See also Whiteman, *Digest*, II, 211–13.
256. 15 *Dep't. of State Bulletin* 66–69 (1946).
257. Myers, *op. cit.*, p. 707. For the treaty, see U.S. T.I.A.S. 1958.
258. Whiteman, *Digest*, II, 214–15.
259. *Ibid.*, p. 215.
260. 44 *Dep't. of State Bulletin* 733–34 (1961).
261. Department of State press release No. 264, dated April 27, 1961, as reproduced in *ibid.*
262. 45 *Dep't. of State Bulletin* 238 (1961).
263. Department of State press release No. 1, dated January 2, 1956, as reproduced in 34 *Dep't. of State Bulletin* 85 (1956).
264. Department of State press release No. 2, dated January 2, 1956, as reproduced in *ibid.*
265. *Ibid.* See also Myers, *op. cit.*, p. 715.
266. Department of State press release No. 87, dated February 17, 1956, as reproduced in 34 *Dep't. of State Bulletin* 356 (1956).
267. Department of State press release No. 100, dated February 14, 1962, as reproduced in 46 *Dep't. of State Bulletin* 438 (1962).
268. Department of State press release No. 529, dated August 29, 1962.

269. Whiteman, *Digest*, II, 229.
270. U.S.–U.N. press release No. 4037, as reproduced in 47 *Dep't. of State Bulletin* 503 (1962).
271. Department of State press release No. 648, dated October 29, 1962.
272. Myers, *op. cit.*, p. 717.
273. *Ibid.*
274. Department of State press release No. 154, dated March 22, 1956, as reproduced in 34 *Dep't. of State Bulletin* 552–53 (1956).
275. *Ibid.*
276. 35 *Dep't. of State Bulletin* 214 (1956).
277. Department of State press release No. 438, dated July 30, 1957.
278. 47 *Dep't. of State Bulletin* 641 (1962).
279. Department of State press release No. 608, dated October 8, 1962, as reproduced in *ibid.*, p. 670.
280. *Ibid.* The following statement was also made in this press release: "The United States has maintained a consular office in Kampala since May 1957. An information center was established there in August of the same year. A technical assistance program, primarily in agricultural development and technical training, was initiated in 1954 under the United States–United Kingdom Technical Cooperation Agreement of 1951 [*T.I.A.S.* 2281]. A mission of the Agency for International Development was established in Uganda in July 1962." See also Whiteman, *Digest*, II, 230.
281. U.S.–U.N. press release No. 4065, reproduced in 47 *Dep't. of State Bulletin* 705 (1962).
282. *Ibid.*, 771.
283. 50 *Dep't. of State Bulletin* 17–18 (1964).
284. Department of State press release No. 80, dated February 23, 1964.
285. "The American Embassy, Baghdad, to the Department of State, despatch No. 1132, June 2, 1958, encl. 1, MS. Department of State, file 786.02/6–258; the American Embassy, Amman, to the Department of State, telegram, May 20, 1958, *ibid.*, file 786.00/5–2058." Whiteman, *Digest*, II, 135.
286. "The American Embassy, Baghdad, to the Department of State, despatch No. 1132, June 2, 1958, encls. 2, 3, and 4, MS. Department of State, file 786.02/6–258." Whiteman, *Digest*, II, 135.
287. *Ibid.*
288. 48 *Dep't. of State Bulletin* 992 (1958).
289. "The American Embassy, Karachi, to the Department of State, despatch No. 150, Aug. 15, 1958, MS. Department of State, file 786C. 00/8–1558." Whiteman, *Digest*, II, 136.
290. Whiteman, *Digest*, II, 156.
291. *Ibid.*, 156–57. See also George Stambuk, *American Military Forces Abroad: Their Impact on the Western State System* (Columbus, Ohio: Ohio State University Press, 1963).
292. Whiteman, *Digest*, II, 157.
293. *Ibid.*, 160.
294. *Ibid.*, 159.
295. "The Icelandic Prime Minister (Jonasson) to Secretary of State Hull, telegram, April 15, 1940, MS. Department of State, file 701.59A11/1, 1940, *For. Rel.*, vol. II, pp. 675–76; Secretary Hull to the Icelandic Prime Minister (Jonasson), telegram, April 16, 1940, *ibid.*" Whiteman, *Digest*, II, 157.

Notes

296. U.S. EAS 232, as cited in Whiteman, *Digest*, II, 159.
297. *Ibid.*, 158.
298. *Ibid.*, 159.
299. 5 *Dep't. of State Bulletin* 315 (1941).
300. *Ibid.*, p. 409–10.
301. 10 *Dep't. of State Bulletin* 281 (1944).
302. Department of State press release, dated June 17, 1944, as reproduced in *ibid.*, pp. 557–58.
303. *Ibid.*
304. 11 *Dep't. of State Bulletin* 126 (1944).
305. See Whiteman, *Digest*, II, 188 ff. and 218 ff.
306. *Ibid.*, 191 and 220.
307. 5 *Dep't. of State Bulletin* 440 (1941).
308. "Paul Alling, Division of Near Eastern Affairs, 'Recognition of Syria and the Lebanon,' memorandum, May 11, 1942, MS. Department of State, file 890D.01/604." Whiteman, *Digest*, II, 191–92.
309. "Under Secretary of State Welles to President Roosevelt, letter dated Sept. 1, 1942, MS. Department of State, file 890D.01/641." Whiteman, *Digest*, II, 193–94.
310. 7 *Dep't. of State Bulletin* 828 (1942).
311. 11 *Dep't. of State Bulletin* 313–14 (1944).
312. *Ibid.*, p. 314.
313. *Ibid.*
314. White House and Department of State press releases of September 20 and September 19, 1944, respectively, as reproduced in *ibid.*, p. 313.
315. *Ibid.*, p. 332.
316. Read to news correspondents on September 14, 1963, as reproduced in 49 *Dep't. of State Bulletin* 542 (1963).
317. Transcript of the press briefing of Monday, September 16, 1963.
318. *Ibid.*
319. Whiteman, *Digest*, II, 202.
320. *Ibid.*, 202–3.
321. Department of State press release No. 338, dated June 20, 1960, reproduced in 43 *Dep't. of State Bulletin* 73–74 (1960).
322. Whiteman, *Digest*, II, 203.
323. *Ibid.*, 214.
324. 43 *Dep't. of State Bulletin* 806 (1960).
325. Whiteman, *Digest*, II, 214.
326. Myers, *op. cit.*, p. 705, *n.* 5.
327. Whiteman, *Digest*, II, 206–7.
328. 16 *Dep't. of State Bulletin* 598 (1947).
329. *Ibid.*, p. 949.
330. T.I.A.S. 1585; 61 U.S. Stat. 2566–72.
331. 25 *Dep't. of State Bulletin* 443 (1951).
332. *New York Times*, February 2, 1958, p. 12.
333. Whiteman, *Digest*, II, 230.
334. *New York Times*, February 2, 1958, p. 12.
335. 38 *Dep't. of State Bulletin* 332 (1958).
336. Whiteman, *Digest*, II, 231.
337. Department of State press release No. 87, dated February 25, 1958; 38 *Dep't. of State Bulletin* 418 (1958).

338. Whiteman, *Digest*, II, 4.
339. *New York Times*, February 26, 1958, p. 5. He was confirmed on March 10, 1958. 38 *Dep't. of State Bulletin* 586 (1958).
340. Whiteman, *Digest*, II, 232.
341. *Ibid.*, 240.
342. As reproduced in *ibid*.
343. *Ibid.*
344. 14 *Dep't. of State Bulletin* 297 (1946).
345. As reproduced in Whiteman, *Digest*, II, 241.
346. *Ibid.*, 241-42. See 14 *Dep't. of State Bulletin* 446 (1946); 17 *Dep't. of State Bulletin* 101 (1947); 14 *Dep't. of State Bulletin* 917 (1946).
347. 22 *Dep't. of State Bulletin* 326 (1950).
348. See above, p. 127. For Myers' explanation of this usage, see Myers, *op. cit.*, p. 717, and below, p. 210, *n.* 361.
349. Whiteman, *Digest*, II, 3.
350. See *Oetjen v. Central Leather Co.* 246 U.S. 297 (1918); *Luther v. Sagor* [1921] 3 K.B. 532; *Haile Selassie v. Cable and Wireless, Ltd.* (no. 2), [1939] Ch. 182. For a discussion of this question during the period under study see *Muraka et al v. Bachrack Bros. Inc.* 215 F. 2d. 547 (2d Cir. 1954) and discussion thereof *supra*, p. 161, and in Whiteman, *Digest*, II, 162-65.
351. Herbert W. Briggs (ed.), *The Law of Nations* (2d ed; New York: Appleton-Century-Crofts, Inc., 1952), pp. 127-32.
352. See, for example, the states recognized by the United States in the nineteenth century in Moore, *Digest*, I, 74-119.
353. Lauterpacht states:

Premature recognition is a tortious act against the lawful government; it is a breach of international law. If States could proceed in this matter regardless of what is now a well-established legal principle, the result might be that in case of a civil war in a foreign country or, for that matter, even before actual hostilities have taken place there on a large scale, there would be nothing to prevent any State so minded from withdrawing recognition from the established government and transferring it to the rebellious party, with all the far-reaching consequences of the change thus affected in the legal position. The result, in international law, would be to reduce the established government to the status of a rebellious group and to raise the newly recognized authority to the position of the legitimate government to which support and encouragement may lawfully be given. Such abuse of the power of recognition is vividly illustrated by the recognition by Germany and Italy of the Spanish insurgents in the early stages of the Spanish Civil War in 1936, two and a half years before the termination of the civil war, at a time when the issue of the struggle was altogether uncertain. Lauterpacht, *Recognition*, p. 95.

Chen says that "premature recognition, though resorted to by States on numerous occasions, has received the almost unanimous condemnation of international lawyers." Chen, *op. cit.*, pp. 50-51. See also his comments, pp. 85-86, 106, 343, 358, 416.

Moore held that "Premature recognition constitutes an act of intervention, committed in favor of insurgents or of a conqueror." Moore, *Digest*, I, 73.

Hyde approaches the subject by noting first that "the propriety of recognition, according to American theory, depends upon a fact, namely, the success of the revolutionary force, and that regardless of the illegitimacy thereof in the eyes of the parent State. Thus recognition based upon careful regard for such a fact is deemed to be consistent with the maintenance of friendly relations between the recognizing State and the parent State, and as not reasonably provocative of war." Hyde, *op. cit.*, I, 153. He then goes on to say:

The according of recognition to a country still in the throes of warfare against the parent State partakes of a different character. Such action constitutes participation in the conflict. It makes the cause of independence a common one between the aspirant for it and the outside State. Participation must be regarded as intervention, and therefore essentially antagonistic to that State.

Thus the propriety of recognition as such depends in each case upon its unlikeness to participation in the conflict. When the struggle is over and independence won, recognition bears no resemblance to such conduct. On principle, the test should always be whether the contest is practically at an end. As there may be great difficulty in ascertaining with precision when such a moment has arrived, *the wisdom of allowing an interval to elapse between the termination of the struggle and the according of recognition is apparent.* The deliberation of States in this regard is, however, due to a sense of expediency rather than to one of duty. As soon as a revolting colony has in fact gained its independence and attained the qualifications for statehood, the according of recognition is not at any time thereafter to be deemed premature. [italics added]

354. Recognition by the U.S. of the states that have become independent since the U.N. came into being is characterized by instantaneous, sometimes even anticipatory, response to the fact of independence. Since 1945, no attainment of independence and eligibility for recognition has been sudden. All but eight of the states listed in the table above came into independence under the influence of the Charter. Six of them were graduated mandate or trust territories, and in 1946 the others were subjects of reports on their economic, social, and educational conditions under the Declaration regarding Non-Self-Governing Territories (Chapter XI) of the Charter. As a consequence, their evolution was well known, their advance under international observation, and the target dates of their independence scheduled far ahead. In an international atmosphere conducive to independence, granting independence became almost an industry of the metropoles, and recognition of the result politically automatic. The various ways in which the U.S. has accorded recognition of the new states are summarized. (Myers, *op. cit.*, pp. 706-7.)

355. See the appendix, p. 224.

356. Cyprus, Indonesia, Israel, Cameroon, Ghana, Libya, Somaliland, Somali Republic, Tanganyika, Togo, Western Samoa, Burma, Central African Republic, Chad, Congo-Brazzaville, Gabon, Ceylon, Congo-Leopoldville, Dahomey, Niger, Upper Volta, Ivory Coast, India, Kenya, Pakistan, Jamaica, Malagasy Republic, Malawi, Malaya, Mauritania, Morocco, Nigeria, Philippines, Sierra Leone, Sudan, Trinidad and Tobago, Tunisia, Uganda, Iceland, Malaysia, Mali Federation, Mali, Zanzibar.

We have not included Senegal as a state receiving instantaneous recognition since it claims independence as of August 20, 1960, in contrast to its former partner, Mali, which claims September 22, 1960, as independence day. The U.S. recognized both on September 24, 1960, close enough to Mali's claim for our purposes, but a little too removed from Senegal's to warrant including the latter with this category. It is not believed that this apparent delay was particularly significant, and it would obviously have been awkward to recognize one before the other.

357. Burundi, Rwanda, Ghana, Togo, Burma, Dahomey, Niger, Upper Volta, Ivory Coast, India, Malagasy Republic, Malaya, Uganda.

358. Jamaica, Malagasy Republic, Nigeria, Philippines, Sierra Leone, Trinidad and Tobago, West Indies Federation, Uganda, Burundi, Rwanda, Cameroon, Ghana, Somali Republic, Togo, Burma, Ceylon, Congo–Leopoldville, Kenya.

359. Myers, *op. cit.*, pp. 705–6.

360. Sir Ralph Hone, a high British official who has been concerned with constitutional and other legal preparations for the independence of British dependencies, holds to the traditional view of recognition when he states: "I need not elaborate this point further, except to stress that the emergent territory must secure for itself a constitutional basis which will ensure its recognition internationally as a sovereign state, freed of the erstwhile elements of tutelage. Let it be said that the mere declaration by the metropolitan State that independence has been granted is not of itself sufficient." Sir Ralph Hone, "International Legal Problems of Emergent Territories," *Report of International Law Conference*, July 2–3, 1960 (London: The David Davies Institute of International Studies, 1960), pp. 14, 16.

361. It may be recalled that Myers has stated:
A general pattern of preparing for independence has evolved since 1945 that virtually inhibits anything but acceleration of the attainment of political autonomy. A certain precision has grown up in the advancement of territories toward independence that makes recognition of the new state only a cordial cognitive act. The Mandates which became trust territories have been carefully developed until the Trusteeship Council has recommended independence and the General Assembly has fixed its date well ahead, with the certainty that admission to membership in the United Nations will follow. Most of the other new states emerge from dependency on France or the United Kingdom, both of which have been exercising a policy of preparing entities for independence, optionally retaining membership in the French Community or the British Commonwealth and with immediate membership in the United Nations. Obviously recognizing such a state is convenient and simply cognitive.—(Myers, *op. cit.*, p. 703.)

While there is much truth in Mr. Myers' statement, we are a bit disturbed by the expression "a certain precision." In some cases this has been so, in others "a tidal wave of irresistible pressure" could be substituted in the same sentence.

362. Guy Benveniste and William E. Moran, Jr., *Handbook of African Economic Development* (New York: Frederick A. Praeger, 1962), p. 20.

363. Peter Calvocoressi, *World Order and New States* (New York: Frederick A. Praeger, 1962), p. 37.

364. The rapid evolution of former French territories through autonomy to independence suggests that not even a large measure of autonomy, assistance, and trade protection is enough to withstand these demands. Africans are not satisfied with the semblance of independence. They want the reality. So all-embracing is their belief in the automatic improvements independence

confers, that sometimes the actuality proves to be a great disappointment. This feeling can hardly be more drastically demonstrated than in the Congo, where the soldiers mutinied because independence had not brought more Congolese officers, better conditions, and more status immediately. The exaggerated picture of the changes freedom will produce is not limited to any one country. The basic theme of all independence movements in Africa is Africanization—the promotion of Africans, ready or not, to positions of control. Where this has been understood and a real effort made to accelerate the movement before independence, the transition has taken place fairly easily, but throughout Africa, it will pose difficult problems for some time.— (Benveniste and Moran, *op. cit.*, p. 21.)

365. See Vernon McKay, "Changing External Pressures," in Walter Goldschmidt (ed.), *The United States and Africa* (rev. ed.; New York: Frederick A. Praeger, 1963), pp. 75–112; Rupert Emerson, "Pan-Africanism," in Norman J. Padelford and Rupert Emerson (eds.), *Africa and World Order* (New York: Frederick A. Praeger, 1963), pp. 7–22.

366. Herbert J. Spiro, *Politics in Africa* (Englewood Cliffs, N.J.: Prentice-Hall, 1962), pp. 12–23; McKay, *op. cit.*, pp. 75–80.

367. Vernon McKay, *Africa in World Politics* (New York: Harper & Row, 1963), pp. 337, 338. See Spiro, *Politics in Africa*, pp. 24–42; Victor C. Ferkiss, "U.S. Foreign Policy Toward Southern Africa," in John A. Davis and James K. Baker (eds.), *Southern Africa in Transition* (New York: Frederick A. Praeger, forthcoming); and Rupert Emerson, "The Character of American Interests in Africa," in Goldschmidt, *op. cit.*, pp. 27, 34–35.

368. Note, for example, U.S. support for Jordan, p. 127; Ghana, p. 133; Libya, p. 140; Somalia, p. 141; Tanganyika, p. 143; Malagasy Republic, p. 168; Mauritania, p. 172; and Uganda, p. 183.

369. It is ironic that the issue of willingness and capacity to observe international obligations raised within the U.S. Government at the time the intention to recognize the Congo was being formulated was apparently never raised with the Congolese authorities themselves.

370. See L. Gray Cowan, "Guinea," in Gwendolen M. Carter (ed.), *African One-Party States* (Ithaca, N.Y.: Cornell University Press, 1962), pp. 149–236, particularly 187–88 on the Marxist component in the political theory of the Parti Démocratique de Guinée, and 230–35 on the comparatively non-Western and pro-Communist tendencies of Guinea's "positive" neutralism.

371. See Myers, *op. cit.*, p. 703.

372. Federations have provided the only fatalities among the newly recognized states. The Mali Federation failed, the United Arab Republic has not enjoyed a continuous existence, and the West Indian Federation perished before birth.

373. "On the definition of the independent sovereign state, refer to the Austro-German Customs Union Case, 1931. *P.C.I.J.*, Ser. A/B, No. 41, 2 Hudson, *World Court Reports* 711 (1935). Article 1 of the Montevideo Convention on Rights and Duties of States of December 26, 1933, is frequently quoted in this regard. (T.S., No. 881, 6 Hudson, *International Legislation* 1932–34 620.) In his individual opinion, M. Anzilotti says:

The conception of independence, regarded as the normal characteristic of States as subjects of international law, cannot be better defined than by comparing it with the exceptional and, to some extent, abnormal class of States known as "dependent States." These are States subject to the authority of one or more States. The idea of dependence therefore necessarily implies a relation between a superior State (suzerain, protector, etc.) and an inferior or subject State (vassal, *protégé*, etc.); the relation between the State which can legally impose its will and the State which is legally compelled to submit to that will. Where there is no such relation of superiority and subordination, it is impossible to speak of dependence within the meaning of international law.

It follows that the legal conception of independence has nothing to do with a State's subordination to international law or with the numerous and constantly increasing state of *de facto* dependence which characterizes the relation of one country to other countries.

It also follows that the restrictions upon a State's liberty, whether arising out of ordinary international law or contractual engagements, do not as such in the least affect its independence. As long as these restrictions do not place the State under the legal authority of another State, the former remains an independent State however extensive and burdensome those obligations may be.—2 Hudson, *World Court Reports* 726 (1935).

By this standard the weaker new nations whose independence we question are "independent" in the sense that they are not under the *legal* authority of another state. We are here questioning their material independence.

374. See James S. Coleman, "The Politics of Sub-Saharan Africa," in Gabriel A. Almond and James S. Coleman (eds.), *The Politics of Developing Areas* (Princeton, N.J.: Princeton University Press, 1960), pp. 247–368.

375. See Benjamin Rivlin, *The United Nations and the Italian Colonies* (New York: Carnegie Endowment for International Peace, 1950).

376. Agnese Nelms Lockwood, "Libya—Building a Desert Economy," 512 *International Conciliation* 312 (1957).

377. African countries receive about twice as much economic assistance as underdeveloped countries generally. Libya received the most assistance per capita of any African country in the period covered by the report of the Economic Commission for Africa, Fourth Session, Provisional Agenda Item 12 (a), United Nations Economic and Social Council, *International Economic Assistance to Africa*, 1960. E/Cw.14/152. December 28, 1961, p. 8 [hereinafter cited U.N. Economic Commission for Africa, 1960 *Report*].

378. A. A. Castagno, Jr., "Somalia," 522 *International Conciliation* 347 (1959).

379. Pearcy, "Forty Newly Independent States: Some Politicogeographic Observations," pp. 604, 610. See Emerson, "The Character of American Interests in Africa," in Goldschmidt, *op. cit.*, p. 23. Although the prospects of former British dependencies seem to be generally better than the French, they too in many instances lack the elements of a cohesive national society. See James S. Coleman, "The Character and Viability of African Political Systems," in Goldschmidt, *op. cit.*, pp. 48–49. Sierra Leone was, of course, a British dependency.

380. U.N. Economic Commission for Africa, 1960 *Report*, p. 8; Economic Commission for Africa, Fifth Session, Leopoldville, February-March, 1963, Provisional agenda item 11, United Nations Economic and Social Council, *International Economic Assistance to Africa*, 1961 E/CN/.14/209, p. 10. February 19, 1963 [hereinafter cited U.N. Economic Commission for Africa, 1961 *Report*].

Notes

381. U.N. Economic Commission for Africa, 1960 *Report*, p. 11.
382. *Ibid.*, pp. 12–13. See U.N. Economic Commission for Africa, 1961 *Report*, p. 17, for further indications of this situation. See the comments of Elliot J. Berg, "The Character and Prospects of African Economies," in Goldschmidt, *op. cit.*, pp. 139, 145; and Andrew M. Karmarck, "The African Economy and International Trade," in Goldschmidt, *op. cit.*, pp. 175, 177.
383. "Even in those few countries that nominally do not receive budgetary support, France pays for services that in other countries would come under the budget—this includes in most cases air, meteorological, and defense services, as well as a substantial part of the cost of the salaries of French personnel working for the countries. . . . The British Government also stands ready to help finance the extra cost of British civil servants kept on after independence and is, in addition, actively engaged in providing and helping finance personnel requested by the newly independent countries." Goldschmidt, *op. cit.*, pp. 175, 177. France intervened in Gabon on February 22, 1964, to restore order. Britain intervened in Kenya, Tanganyika, and Uganda to restore order on January 24–25, 1964.
384. Coleman, "The Character and Viability of African Political Systems," in Goldschmidt, *op. cit.*, p. 46.
385. Berg, "The Character and Prospects of African Economies," in Goldschmidt, *op. cit.*, pp. 130–31.
386. Calvocoressi, *op. cit.*, p. 13. For an excellent factual summary and analysis see Stanley Hoffman, "In Search of a Threat: The U.N. in the Congo Labyrinth," in Padelford and Emerson, *op. cit.*, pp. 63–93.
387. Brian Crozier, *The Morning After* (New York: Oxford University Press, 1963), pp. 16–17.
388. *Ibid.*, p. 285.
389. See Hoffman, "International Systems and International Law," pp. 208–12; Kaplan and Katzenbach, *Political Foundations*.
390. Calvocoressi rightly observes that:
Modern politics are based on the idea of society as nation, and a nation has been defined as a "materially and morally integrated society, with a stable and enduring authority at the centre, with fixed frontiers, and with a relative moral and spiritual and cultured unity shared by those who consciously belong to the state and accept its laws:" (M. Mauss in *La Nation*. "L'Année sociologique (1953–54)," Paris, 1957, p. 17) integration, not agglomeration. Disintegrated nations are a source of instability in international society.— Calvocoressi, *op. cit.*, p. 39.
391. If it is controversial whether an unrecognized but actually viable state possesses international personality (it is believed that it does), it is generally conceded that the existing international persons of the international community have the power to endow other entities with international personality, either that full personality which a state possesses or something less than that. See *Reparations for Injuries in the Service of the United Nations*, International Court of Justice, Advisory Opinion of April 11, 1949, *I.C.J. Rep.*, 1949, p. 174.
392. See Rupert Emerson, *From Empire to Nation: The Rise to Self-Assertion of Asian and African Peoples* (Cambridge: Harvard University Press, 1960).
393. The following analysis from a leading work on the new nations is worthy of note:

The traditional premises of international relations were a product of the European nation-state system within which differences in culture and technology were not great. The concept of a community of nations implied the tacit acceptance of a set of standards and principles of action, such as nonintervention in the domestic affairs of other societies in the community, conduct of diplomacy according to certain formal rules, and use of alliances against common dangers. The concept of national sovereignty presumed that governments were able without qualification to commit their people to whatever international obligations they saw fit to make.

The entrance of new and underdeveloped countries as actors upon the international scene has brought many of these principles into question. Can relations among societies continue to be limited primarily to the formal relations among governments? Can the presumption of unconcern about internal developments in other nations be maintained when a primary international activity must be the transferring of talents and skills, including those of administration and policy making? And when there is a gross difference in levels of technology, can the obligations of alliances be shared equally?

Such questions make clear the need to create a new system of international affairs which can provide an acceptable basis for relationships among societies at radically different stages of development. International policy must be shaped to meet that need. These relationships must be grounded in a shared interest in furthering a process of modernization which will enable the transitional societies to develop their own versions of responsible government and to play a cooperative role in a new world order. To the extent that such an overlap of interest and vision can be established between the modern societies and those now in the process of transition, it must be translated into joint programs for action. In short, both parties must acknowledge that the relationship transcends that of conventional international behavior and may involve activities within other societies which formerly would have been precluded.—Max F. Millikan and Donald L. M. Blackmer (eds.), *The Emerging Nations: Their Growth and United States Policy* (Boston: Little, Brown, 1961), pp. 132–33.

394. Denys P. Myers, "How To Graduate States," 125 *World Affairs* 235–36 (1956).

Chapter 4. "The New States and the United Nations"
by J. E. S. Fawcett

1. As in the International Monetary Fund and the International Bank for Reconstruction and Development.
2. Morocco and Tunisia might also be regarded as partial exceptions.
3. Inner Mongolia has always been regarded territorially as part of China.
4. C. E. Carrington, "Decolonization—The Last Phase," 38 *International Affairs* 29 (1962).
5. The federal link between the United Arab Republic, by which title Egypt continues to be called, and Yemen, has led to sharp intervention by Egypt in the civil war.
6. Paul G. Hoffman, *One Hundred Countries and One and a Quarter Billion People* (Washington, D.C.: Albert D. and Mary Lasker Foundation, 1960).

7. See advisory opinion of the International Court of Justice, "Admission of a State to Membership in the United Nations," 57 *I.C.J. Rep.* (1948).
8. By a sensible convention, Liechtenstein, Monaco, San Marino, and Andorra are not regarded as potential U.N. members. Liechtenstein is, however, a party to the statute of the International Court of Justice and has appeared as plaintiff before it.
9. Articles 60 and 85(2) of the Charter.
10. It occupies over 150 pages in the *Repertory of United Nations Practice* up to 1958.
11. "Nationality Decrees in Tunis and Morocco," *P.C.I.J.* Series B4, 23–24 (1923).
12. U.N. General Assembly, October 6, 1959, A/PV823, p. 58.
13. U.N. General Assembly, October 5, 1959, A/PV820, p. 36.
14. See Sydney D. Bailey, *The General Assembly of the United Nations* (London: Stevens, 1960), Chap. 2. See also H. G. Nicholas, *The United Nations as a Political Institution* (London: Oxford University Press, 1959).
15. Bailey, *op. cit.*, p. 29.
16. Compare in the economic field the "Hague Club," a term in actual use.
17. 12 *Dep't. of State Bulletin* 450 (1945), cited by Bailey, in *op. cit.*, p. 33.
18. E.g., the United Kingdom with a quota of $1.95 billion has 8,058 votes; a member with a quota of $250 million would have 1,250 votes. For the role of voting in the Fund, see J. E. S. Fawcett, "The Place of Law in an International Organisation," 36 *B.Y.I.L.* 321 (1960).
19. Rule 94 of the Rules of Procedure.
20. For a short but penetrating historical discussion, see D. V. Cowen, *The Foundations of Freedom* (London: Oxford University Press, 1961).
21. See the London *Times*, December 29, 1961, and July 14, 1962.
22. L. N. Rieselbach, "Quantitative Techniques for Studying Voting Behaviour in the General Assembly," 14 *International Organisation* 291 (1960).
23. The figures represent in order from left to right: votes in favor; votes against; abstentions; absentees. It should be noted that Algeria, Burundi, Jamaica, Kuwait, Rwanda, Trinidad and Tobago, Uganda, and Zanzibar did not become members until September, 1962.
24. Rieselbach, *op. cit.*
25. 1. Approval "with satisfaction" of the achievements of the French trust administration of Togoland;
2. Decision that the requirement to transmit information on nonself-governing territories under Article 73e of the Charter be subject to a two-thirds majority of the General Assembly;
3. Decision to establish an *ad hoc* committee to check information under Article 73e;
4. Call for maintenance of *status quo* in West Irian pending negotiations between Indonesia and the Netherlands;
5. Call upon administering powers to estimate time and limits for grant of independence to trust territories;
6. Adoption of the West Irian dispute on to the agenda;
7. Concern with, and recommendation on, race conflict in South Africa;
8. Recommendations on treatment of Indians in South Africa.
26. This idea is well expressed in *Le Monde Diplomatique* (May, 1962), p.

4: "Le règlement des problèmes internationaux importants ne peut pas être le monopole des grandes puissances étant donné que ces problèmes touchent directement les intérêts fondamentaux de tous les pays qu'ils soient grands ou petits, engagés ou non engagés, et quelle que soit leur situation géographique."

27. Nevertheless, the Conference must not be written off as a failure. It may have consequences that are important in the long run for the U.N., for it tended to strengthen the U.N. as the exclusive instrument of peaceful change. This movement appeared in the united votes of the new nations and the other Belgrade Conference countries at the sixteenth session, and especially in the part they played in bringing about agreement in the nomination of U Thant as acting Secretary General. In short, a determination to make all possible use of the U.N. was an indirect outcome of the Belgrade Conference. But it also underlined the fact that, while the new nations are not yet consolidated and may yet indeed separate into more than one bloc, they form a coalition against great power groupings; what binds them together in this coalition is nonalignment, the refusal to join the great power groupings or to engage in the controversies that divide them. The Belgrade Conference and the sixteenth session of the General Assembly also reveal certain countries as emerging leaders of the coalition: Cambodia, India, Indonesia, United Arab Republic, and Yugoslavia.

28. Nicholas, *op. cit.*, p. 119.

29. Ghana until December 31, 1963; Jordan until December 31, 1963; Senegal until December 31, 1964.

30. At the beginning of 1960, of the fifteen new nations then members only two, Ceylon and Pakistan, were represented on more than one standing committee of the United Nations, and six were represented on none.

31. Pakistan has accepted the "optional clause" without reservations of intra-Commonwealth disputes. Cameroon and Cambodia have both invoked the jurisdiction of the Court.

Abbreviations Used in the Notes

A.C.	Appeal Cases, Great Britain
A.J.I.L.	American Journal of International Law
Annual Digest	Annual Digest and Reports of Public International Law Cases
B. & F.S.P.	British and Foreign State Papers
B.Y.I.L.	British Yearbook of International Law
Ch.	Chancery Division, Great Britain, High Court of Justice
Crim. L.R.	Criminal Law Review
Dep't. of State Bulletin	Department of State Bulletin
F.R. 2d	Federal Reporter, second series
Hackworth, Digest	Green Haywood Hackworth, Digest of International Law
Hague, Recueil	Recueil des Cours de l'Académie de Droit International de La Haye
I.C.J. Rep.	International Court of Justice Reports
I.C.L.Q.	International and Comparative Law Quarterly
Int. L. Rep.	International Law Reports
K.B.	King's Bench Division, Great Britain, High Court of Justice
L.N.T.S.	League of Nations Treaty Series
L.Q.R.	Law Quarterly Review
Malloy, Treaties	William M. Malloy, ed., Treaties, Conventions, International Acts, Protocols, and Agreements between the United States of America and Other Powers, 1776–1909
Martens, Nouveau recueil général	Georg Von Martens, Nouveau recueil général de traités, conventions et autres actes remarquables (1843–1875)
Moore, Digest	John Bassett Moore, A Digest of International Law
N.Y.	Court of Appeals of New York
Off. J.	Official Journal of the League of Nations

P.C.I.J.	Publications of the Permanent Court of International Justice
Probate	Probate, Divorce, and Admiralty Division, Great Britain, High Court of Justice
Q.B.	Queen's Bench Division, Great Britain, High Court of Justice
R.D.I.L.C.	*Revue de droit international et de législation comparée*
Stat.	U.S. Statutes at Large
T.I.A.S.	U.S. Treaties and Other International Acts Series
T.S.	Treaty Series
U.N. Doc.	United Nations Documents
U.N. Rep. Int. Arb. Awards	United Nations Reports of International Arbitral Awards
U.S.	U.S. Supreme Court Reports
U.S.T. & O.I.A.	United States Treaties and Other International Agreements
Whiteman, *Digest*	Marjorie M. Whiteman, A *Digest of International Law* (2 vols. to date)

NOTES ON THE CONTRIBUTORS

WILLIAM V. O'BRIEN, Chairman of the Institute of World Polity, is Associate Professor of Government at Georgetown University, where he teaches international law in the School of Foreign Service and in the Graduate School. He was educated at Georgetown University (B.S.F.S., M.S.F.S., Ph.D.) and at the Sorbonne, where he was a Fulbright Fellow. Professor O'Brien has edited, with Walter H. E. Jaeger, a casebook in international law and has contributed to scholarly journals and symposia in the United States and Europe.

D. P. O'CONNELL, a New Zealander by birth, was educated at the University of New Zealand and at Cambridge University, where he obtained his Ph.D. under the direction of the late Judge Hersch Lauterpacht. His monograph *The Law of State Succession* (Cambridge University Press, 1956) was the fifth volume in the Cambridge Series on International and Comparative Law. This work, the leading monograph on the subject, is now in its second edition. In addition to numerous articles in learned journals all over the world, Professor O'Connell has written a major treatise on international law that will appear shortly. He has been Professor of International Law and Jurisprudence at the University of Adelaide, Australia, since 1961, and is *rapporteur* of the Committee on State Succession of the International Law Association.

ALBERT J. ESGAIN was educated in political science and law at Ohio State University, Duke University, Cambridge University, the Hague Academy of International Law, and George Washington University. He has had wide experience, first as an officer and now as a civilian legal specialist, with the United States Army in Europe and in the Pentagon. Presently, he is senior civilian lawyer in the Opinions Branch, International Relations Division, Office of the Judge Advocate General, Department of the Army. He contributes to legal journals and serves as a consultant to private organizations on questions of international and comparative law.

ULF H. GOEBEL is completing his Ph.D. in political theory and international relations at Georgetown University. He has been a research assistant in the Institute of World Polity since 1960.

J. E. S. FAWCETT was educated at Oxford University. He became a Fellow of All Souls College, Oxford, in 1939. From 1945 to 1950, he was Assistant Legal Adviser to the United Kingdom Foreign Office; from 1955 to 1960, he was General Counsel of the International Monetary Fund. He was re-elected Fellow of All Souls College in 1960, and was elected Associate Member of the Institute of International Law in 1961. His publications include *The Inter-se Doctrine of Commonwealth Relations* (London: Institute of Commonwealth

Studies, 1958) and "Intervention in International Law," Hague *Recueil des Cours* (1961). He edited the *International and Comparative Law Quarterly* from 1952 to 1955, has contributed frequently to learned journals, and appeared as counsel before the International Court of Justice in the Nottebohm Case.

INDEX

Aaland Island, 59
Acheson, Dean, 124, 140, 148, 162, 177
Act of State (English doctrine), 30, 32-33
Africa, 7, 11, 12, 31
Ahamdou, Ahidjo, 130, 131
Ahmad, Crown Prince, 204
Algeria, 20, 119-21
Arab League, 11
Arab Union, 184-86
Argentina, 89-90
Ashenheim, Neville Noel, 163
Asia, 7, 12
Attwood, William, 165
Australia, 17-18, 23, 34, 37
Austria, 62, 100, 109, 110

Bahamas, the, 82-84
Bahia Honda, 87
Balewa, Sir Abubakar Tafawa, 176
Balkans, the, 7, 8
Bao Dai, 148
Beach, Arthur E., 179-80
Belgium, 11, 17, 22, 88, 154
Ben Bella, Ahmed, 121
Benveniste, Guy, 210
Bermuda, 76-82
Bjornsson, Sveinn, 189-90
Bowles, Chester, 142
British Guiana, 76-82
Bulgaria, 62, 92-93
Burma, 145-47
Burundi, 128-29
Bustamante, Sir Alex, 163

Calvocoressi, Peter, 210, 219
Cambodia, 147-51, 209
Cameroon, 129-32, 175
Canada, 18, 81
Carolines, Islands of the, 85-86
Carrington, C. E., 232, 235
Castagno, A. A., Jr., 216

Castro, Fidel, 10
Central African Republic, 151-53
Ceylon, 153-54
Chablais province, 84-85, 89
Chad, 24, 151-53
Chang, Dr. John M., 138
Chen Ti-Chang, 99, 112
Chile, 89-90
China, 103, 118, 213, 231-32
Clark, Harlan B., 203
Clarke, Ellis Emmanuel Innocent, 181
Clement, Dr. Rufus E., 168-70
Cochran, H. Merle, 124-25
Cole, Felix, 153
Congo-Brazzaville, 151-53
Congo-Leopoldville, 154
Corbett, Percy, 99
Crozier, Brian, 219
Cuba, 8, 10, 27, 86-87, 212
Cyprus, 121-23

Dacko, David, 152
Daddah, Mokhtar, 171-73
Dahomey, 24, 155-56
Dean, John Gunther, 197
Deming, Olcott H., 183
Denmark, 186
Diap, Ousmane Soce, 197
Dicri, Prime Minister, 156
Dominican Republic, 82
Douglas-Home, Sir Alec, 241
Dreyfus, Louis G., Jr., 189
Duggan, William, 142
Dulles, John Foster, 170-71, 200-201
Dumont, Donald, 129, 196
Dutch East Indies, 33

Egypt, 11, 16, 84, 201-2
Eisenhower, Dwight, 122, 131, 133, 150, 152, 154, 155, 157-59, 170, 171-73, 175-76, 179, 196
Elizabeth II, 178

319

Elizalde, Joaquin M., 177
European Economic Community, 17, 248

Faucigny province, 84–85, 89
Finland, 59, 62, 92
Flake, Wilson C., 133
France, 8, 13–14, 17, 23, 24, 59, 69–70, 72–76, 89, 108, 120, 213
Franco-Soviet Pact (1935), 70, 91
Frazer, Wilkins, 123
Funck-Brentano, Théophile, 95

Gabon, 151–53
German public law, servitude of, 49–50
Germany, 14, 59, 60, 62–63, 83, 85, 88, 89, 91–92, 114
Ghana, 35, 38, 40, 132–34
Gilstrap, Samuel Patrick, 168
Goldberg, Arthur, 156
Government contracts, succession to, 26–32
Grady, Henry F., 153
Great Britain, 7, 8, 11, 18–19, 23, 24, 32, 43, 59, 72, 76–84, 108, 121–22, 125–26; Commonwealth problems of, 34–40, 108–9
Greece, 7, 8, 62, 121–22
Guantanamo, 87
Guinea, 156–59, 209

Hackworth, Green H., 108
Hall, W. F., 68
Hare, Raymond A., 202
Hastie, William, 180
Heath, Donald, 149
Heck, L. Douglas, 123
Herter, Christian, 130–31, 141, 170–71, 175
Ho Chi Minh, 213
Hodge, General, 135, 137
Hoff, Philip H., 183
Hogland, 92
Holmes, Julius, 174
Home, Lord. See Douglas-Home, Sir Alec
Houphouet-Boigny, Félix, 156
Huber, Max, 56
Hüningen, City of, 89
Hughes, Morris N., 181

Hull, Cordell, 189
Hungary, 62

Iceland, 186–90
Idris I, 139, 140
India, 24, 33, 108, 124, 159–62, 231, 238
Indonesia, 109–10, 113, 123–25
International Court of Justice, 24, 30, 36, 58, 237, 252
Iraq, 184–85
Ireland, 34, 37–40
Israel, 11, 15, 20, 112, 125–28, 205
Italy, 7, 62, 92
Ivory Coast, 155–56

Jacobs, John Roland, 168
Jamaica, 80–81, 162
Japan, 62, 86, 90
Java, 123
Jenks, C. Wilfred, 15, 17
Jessup, Philip, 126, 127
Johnson, Lyndon B., 163, 164, 168, 183
Johnson, U. Alexis, 195
Jones, G. Lewis, 182
Jordan, 125–28, 184–85, 205, 209

Kaiser, Philip M., 173
Karume, Abeid Amani, 184
Kasavubu, Joseph, 154
Katanga, 10–11, 31
Kayibanda, Grégoire, 129
Keita, Modibo, 196
Keith, Arthur B., 57
Kelfa-Caulker, Richard E., 178
Kennedy, John F., 120, 121, 129, 142, 145, 156, 163, 178, 180, 182–83
Kenya, 16, 164–65
Kenyatta, Jomo, 164
Khemisti, Mohammed, 121
Korea, 117, 134–39, 238
Kuwait, 165–67, 207

Labrousse, Pierre, 69
Lamm, Donald W., 133
Laos, 147–51, 209
Lauterpacht, Hans, 50, 55, 99, 101, 103–4, 106
League of Nations, 58, 91, 128
Leased Bases Agreement, 76–82

Index

Lebanon, 190–94, 209
Legal system, succession to, 32–34
Leonhart, William, Jr., 184
Libya, 139–41, 215–16
Lodge, Henry Cabot, 130–31
Long, Oren E., 144–45
Lovett, Robert A., 147
Lukens, Alan W., 152
Lynch, Andrew G., 140, 141

McClintock, Robert, 150
McKay, Vernon, 211
MacKnight, Jesse M., 144
McNair, Lord, 21, 56, 60, 67
Madagascar, 167–68
Madura, 123
Maga, Hubert, 155–56
Mak, Dayton, 166
Makarios, Archbishop, 122
Malagasy, 20, 167–68
Malawi, 168–70
Malaya, 24, 25, 170–71
Malaysia, 194–95
Mali, 195–97, 233
Manbey, David J. S., 129
Marshall, George C., 134–35, 137, 146
Marshall, Thurgood, 178
Mauritania, 171–73
M'Ba, Léon, 152
Mecklenburg-Schwerin, City of, 87–88
Mexico, 8
Military: and coaling stations in the Pacific islands, 85–86; and leased naval and air bases, 10, 76–82; and missile proving ground in the Bahamas, 82–84; and servitudes, 42–97; and U.S. rights in Morocco, 72–76
Military Bases Agreement, 72–76
Mohammed V, 174
Mongolia, 231–32
Moore, Sir Henry, 153
Moran, William E., Jr., 210
Morocco, 16, 22, 24, 25, 43, 72–76, 173–75, 201
Mueller, Fred H., 141
Murphy, Robert D., 154
Mwambutsa IV, 129
Mya, Thakin, 146

Myers, Denys P., 101, 126, 138–39, 157, 160, 161, 208–9, 221–22

Nasser, Gamal Abdel, 201
Nehru, Pandit, 162
Nepal, 198–200, 207
Netherlands, 60, 113, 124
Neutrality, law of, 65–68
Newfoundland, 59, 76–82
New Zealand, 17–18, 23, 34, 37, 38, 39
Niger, 155–56
Nigeria, 175–76
Nkrumah, Kwame, 133
Norway, 90
Nyasaland, 168, 233
Nyerere, Julius, 142, 223

Obote, A. Milton, 182, 183
O'Connell, D. P., 55, 56
Olds, Herbert V., 129
Olympio, Sylvanus, 144
Oppenheim, L., 55, 56, 66, 69

Pakistan, 159–62
Palaos, Islands of the, 85–86
Palestine, 11
Palmer, Joseph, II, 175
Panama, 38, 86
Pantellaria, 92
Pearcy, G. Etzel, 165, 166, 216, 217
Pelogian Island, 92
Permanent Court of International Justice, 24, 30, 36, 58, 237, 252
Petchenga, 92
Philippines, the, 8, 27, 176–77
Phouma, Souvanna, 151
Pianosa, 92
Poland, 22
Porter, William J., 121
Portugal, 201
Powell, Adam C., 163
Prussia, 13, 89

Rahman, Tunku Abdul, 170–71
Recognition: criteria for, 207–14; function of, 101–8; implications for the institution of, 214–23; methods of, 114–18, 205–7; modes of, 112–14, 205–7; objects of, 108–10; policies of the U.S., 98–117; practices of the U.S. (1943–64), 118–205;

Recognition (*Con't.*):
  theories of, 101–8; types of, 110–12, 205–7; United Nations policies and, 113, 118, 123–24, 126–27
Reid, H. D., 45
Reiner, Herbert, 178
Reiselbach, L. N., 241, 243, 244
Rhee, Syngman, 135–37
Rhodesia, 233
Richards, James P., 170
Rivier, A., 69
Rockefeller, Nelson, 176
Rogers, William P., 144
Roland, Donald R., 155
Roman law, servitude of, 48–49
Romania, 62
Roosevelt, Franklin D., 142, 159, 187–89, 194
Roxburgh, Ronald F., 54
Rusk, Dean, 120–21, 238, 247
Rwanda, 128–29

Sakhalin, 90
Sardinia, 84–85, 92
Satterthwaite, Joseph C., 199
Sears, Mason, 131
Senegal, 195–97, 233
Servitude: of the German public law, 49–50; international, 43–48, 50–71, 93–95; law of neutrality and, 65–68; military, 42–97; private law, 48–50; of the Roman law, 48–49
Sheik of Kuwait, 165
Sierra Leone, 177–78
Slim, Mongi, 182
Smith, Benjamin A., II, 183
Smith, Walter B., 150
Somali, 141–42, 215–16
Sorel, Albert, 95
Soudan, 195
Southern Rhodesia, 23, 37
Spain, 27, 85
Staël-Holstein, Baron Lage de, 92
Stevenson, Adlai E., 142–43, 165, 181, 183
Stimson, Henry, 103
Straits of Magellan, 89–90
Succession: to delictual claims, 31–32; to governmental contracts, 26–32; to the legal system, 32–34; state, problems of, 7–41; to treaties, 13–26
Sudan, 179–80
Sukarno, Achmed, 123, 125
Sumatra, 123
Sweden, 87–88, 90, 238
Switzerland, 59, 70, 84–85
Syria, 11, 16, 190–94, 201–2, 209

Tanganyika, 19, 20, 142–43, 223
Tanzania, 143, 184, 223, 228
Thaike, Sao Shwe, 147
Thor, Vilhjalmer, 189
Thors, Thor, 189, 237
Timberlake, Clarence H., 154
Tobago, 81, 180–81
Togo, 143–44
Touré, Sékou, 157–59
Transvaal, 32
Treaties: problem of, in the British Commonwealth, 35–36; succession to, 13–26
Treaty of Dorpat (1920), 92
Treaty of Portsmouth (1905), 90
Treaty of Stockholm (1905), 90
Treaty of Versailles (1919), 59, 70, 84, 89, 91–92
Trinidad, 81, 180–81
Truman, Harry S., 125, 126–28, 134, 137, 138, 140, 147, 153, 160, 161, 176–77, 199–200, 203
Tsiranana, Philibert, 168
Tunisia, 16, 24, 25, 181–82
Turkey, 62, 84, 121–22

Udall, Stewart L., 164
Uganda, 19, 20, 182–83
Union of Soviet Socialist Republics, 69, 90, 106–7, 213, 231–32, 242
United Arab Republic, 11, 16, 200–202, 233, 239
United Nations, 11, 16, 17, 19, 21–22, 35, 58, 86, 101, 118; Charter of, 64–65, 67, 68, 103, 113, 235–36; independence under auspices of, 128–45; the new states and, 229–52; recognition policies and, 113, 118, 123–24, 126–27; subsidiary bodies of, 249–50
United States, 8, 10, 23, 27, 59, 70,

72; Cuba and, 86–87; leased naval and air bases of, 76–82; military rights in Morocco, 72–76; missile proving ground in the Bahamas, 82–84; Panama and, 86; recognition practice (1943–64), 118–205
Upper Volta, 155–56
Urundi, 128–29

Váli, F. A., 46–47, 50–51, 71, 72, 83–84
Vattel, Emmerich de, 66
Vietnam, 147–51, 209
Villard, Henry S., 171–73, 196–97

Wadsworth, George, 193, 194
War: between a dominant and a third state, 63–68; between servient and dominant states, 61–63
Warsaw Convention on Air Carriage, 18, 20, 22, 35
Watson, James E., 163
Welles, Sumner, 192–93
West Indies, 10, 43, 72, 76–82, 180
Western Samoa, 144–45
Whiteman, Marjorie, 111, 115, 117, 119–20, 132–33, 143, 148, 151, 167, 170, 171–72, 197, 198, 201, 203–4, 206
Williams, Eric, 180
Williams, G. Mennen, 168
Wright, Thomas K., 197

Yahya, Imam, 202–4
Yemen, 202–4, 207
Youlou, Fulbert, 152
Yugoslavia, 237, 238

Zanzibar, 19, 20, 183–84, 223